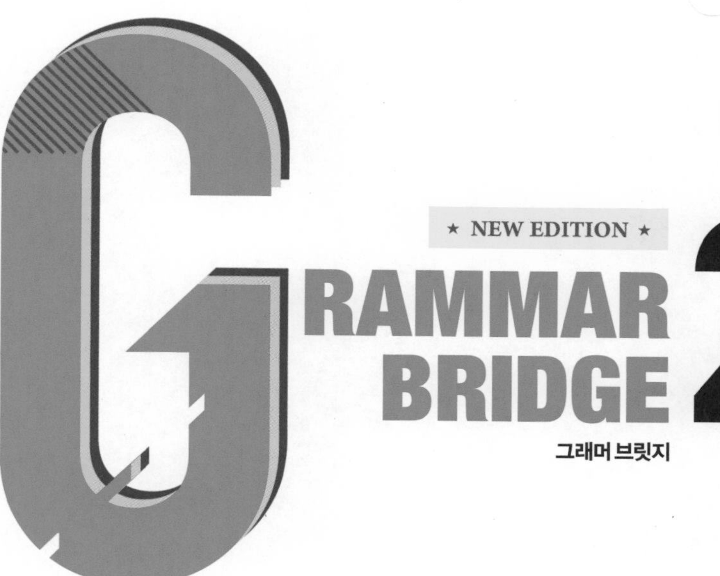
★ NEW EDITION ★
GRAMMAR
BRIDGE 2
그래머 브릿지

Grammar Bridge NEW EDITION 2

지은이 넥서스영어교육연구소, 김경태
펴낸이 임상진
펴낸곳 (주)넥서스

출판신고 1992년 4월 3일 제311-2002-2호 3-1
10880 경기도 파주시 지목로 5
Tel (02)330-5500 Fax (02)330-5555

ISBN 979-11-6683-358-8 54740
979-11-6683-360-1 54740 (SET)

가격은 뒤표지에 있습니다.
잘못 만들어진 책은 구입처에서 바꾸어 드립니다.

www.nexusbook.com

그래머 브릿지

GRAMMAR BRIDGE

넥서스영어교육연구소 · 김경태 지음

Level
2

The bridge that takes
your English to the next level

NEXUS Edu

영어하면 떠오르는 말이 무엇입니까?
시험, 성적, 내신일지도 모릅니다.

하지만, 영어 하면 떠오르는 말은 시험, 성적, 내신이 아니어야 합니다. 영어는 우리말과 같은 하나의 언어입니다. 영어는 어렵고 암기해야 할 것이 많은 학습의 대상이 아니라, 자연스럽게 습득하고 이해해야 하는 언어입니다. 영어과 교육과정의 학습 목표가 의사소통에 필요한 언어 형식의 학습인 것을 보아서도 알 수 있듯이 우리는 영어를 의사소통을 위한 도구로 활용할 수 있어야 합니다.

영어의 가장 기본이 되는 것은 단어입니다. 단어가 모여서 문장이 됩니다. 하지만, 단어를 아무렇게나 나열한다고 해서 문장이 되는 것은 아닙니다. 제대로 된 문장을 만들려면 문법을 알아야 합니다. 하지만, 문법을 무조건 암기하는 것은 효과적인 학습법이 아닙니다.

우리는 학교에서 국어를 배웁니다. 영어도 배웁니다. 국어와 영어는 학습적인 측면에서 차이가 없는 것처럼 보일지도 모르지만, 언어 사용적 측면에서는 현격한 차이가 납니다. 우리는 영어보다 국어를 훨씬 많이 사용합니다. 전문가들은 영어를 모국어처럼 사용하고자 한다면 약 4배 더 많이 사용하고 접해야 한다고 말합니다.

더욱 강화된 **GRAMMAR BRIDGE** NEW EDITION!
유형별 보너스 문제와 워크북을 추가하여
영문법 체화 학습의 길을 더욱더 견고히 다졌습니다.

우리가 국어를 많이 사용해서 자연스럽게 그 쓰임을 익히듯이, 영문법 또한 그 쓰임을 자연스럽게 익힐 수 있는 방법이 있다면 적극적으로 활용해야 할 것입니다. 학습자들이 영어를 어려운 외국어로 보지 않고, 자연스럽게 이해하고 체득할 수 있도록 도와드리고자 고민하였습니다. 가능한 한 간단하게 한 번에 한 가지씩 문법 요소를 설명하려 했습니다. 쉽고 간단한 문법 요소에서 시작해서 높은 수준의 문법 요소로 학습이 진행되는 계단식 학습 방식을 고려하였습니다.

기본보다 더 다양하고 많은 문제를 제공할 수 있도록 NEW EDITION 개정을 통해 실제 시험과 유사한 서술형 문제와 수능 대비형 문제를 수록하여 학습 자극을 유도하도록 했습니다. 또한 워크북을 새롭게 추가하여 철저하게 단원 학습을 마무리할 수 있도록 했습니다. 보다 더 강화되고 풍부해진 문제와 간단하고 이해하기 쉬운 설명, 단계적 연습 문제를 통해 영문법을 쉽고 체계적으로 익힐 수 있기를 기대합니다.

이 책의 구성과 특징

Grammar Point

학교 내신 시험에 꼭 나오는 문법 사항을 수록하였습니다. 여러 가지 문법 요소를 나열한 것이 아니라 한 번에 한 가지 문법 요소를 설명하여 이해가 쉽게 했습니다. 헷갈리기 쉬운 부분에 Tips를 달아 다시 한번 개념 정의를 돕도록 구성하였습니다.

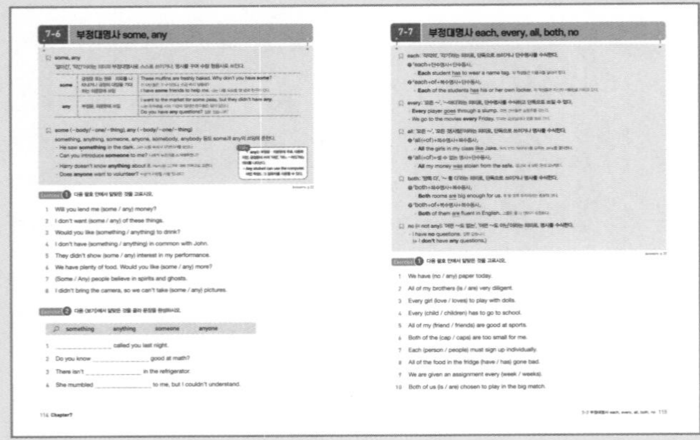

Exercise

문제를 푸는 동안 저절로 문법을 습득할 수 있도록 풍부한 연습문제를 수록하였습니다. 문법 개념을 이해하고 문제를 푸는 학습뿐만 아니라, 문제를 풀면서 스스로 문법 개념을 체계화할 수 있도록 구성하였습니다.

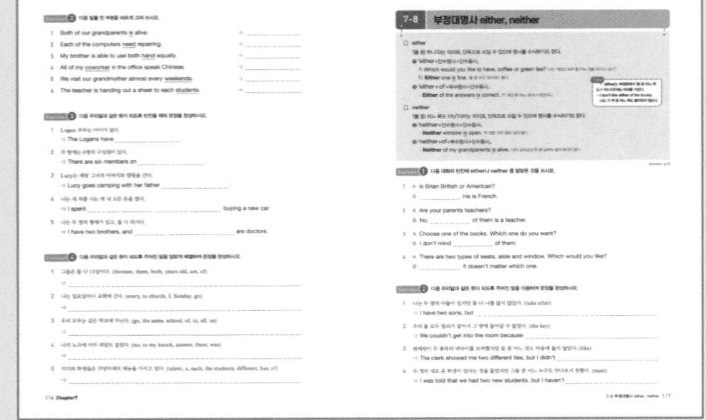

Review Test

실제 내신 기출 문제를 분석하여 수록하였습니다. 객관식, 단답식 유형뿐만 아니라, 점점 증가하는 서술형 문제에도 대비할 수 있도록 다양하고 많은 문제를 수록하였습니다.

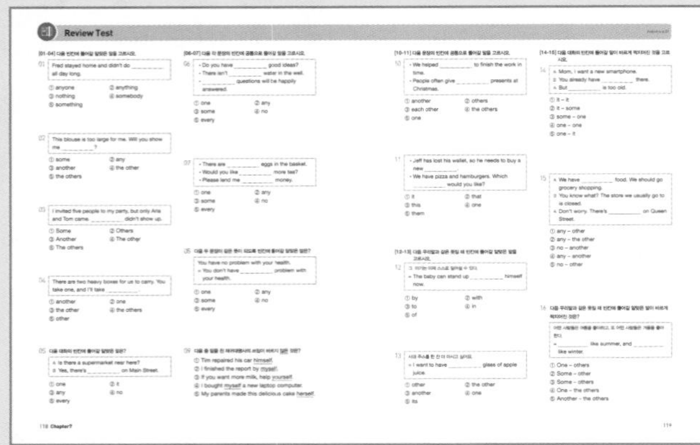

보너스 유형별 문제

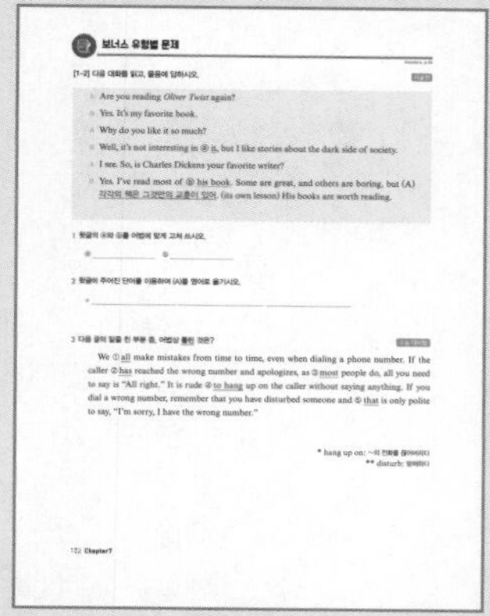

각 Chapter를 완벽하게 마무리 지을 수 있도록 실제 시험과 같은 서술형 문제를 수록하여 내신을 대비할 수 있습니다. 또한 고난도의 수능 대비형 문제를 풀어보며 자신의 실력을 점검해 볼 수 있고 그에 따른 학습 동기 부여의 효과를 기대할 수 있습니다.

Workbook

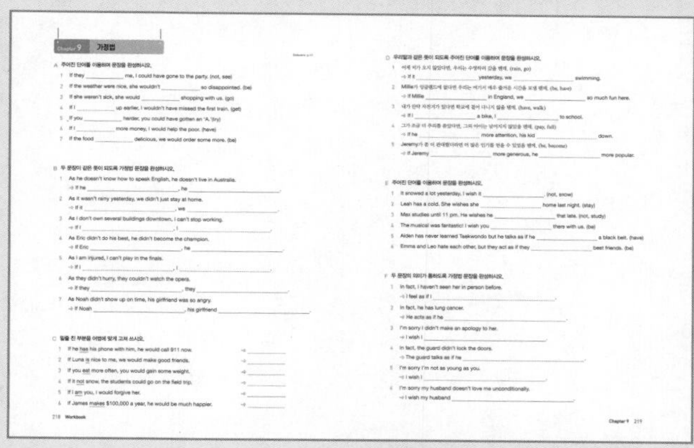

Chapter별로 다양한 유형의 단답형/서술형 연습문제를 수록하여 학습한 내용을 종합적으로 점검할 수 있도록 Workbook을 새롭게 추가하였습니다.

부가자료 무료 제공(www.nexusbook.com)

모바일 단어장 & VOCA TEST

어휘 리스트 & 어휘 테스트

문장 배열 영작

통문장 영작

기타 활용 자료

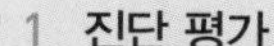

1 진단 평가
2 문법 용어 정리
3 불규칙 동사 변화표
4 형용사와 부사의 비교급 리스트

이 책의 차례

» Chapter 1

시제

1-1 현재시제 012
1-2 동사의 변화 013
1-3 과거시제 015
1-4 진행시제 016
1-5 현재완료 017
1-6 현재완료의 용법 018
1-7 현재완료: 주의해야 할 표현 019
Review Test 020
보너스 유형별 문제 024

» Chapter 2

조동사

2-1 조동사 026
2-2 can 028
2-3 may 030
2-4 will / be going to 031
2-5 would 032
2-6 must / have to 033
2-7 should / had better 035
2-8 used to / would 037
Review Test 038
보너스 유형별 문제 042

» Chapter 3

수동태

3-1 수동태 044
3-2 수동태의 시제 046
3-3 조동사가 쓰인 수동태 047
3-4 수동태의 부정문 048
3-5 수동태의 의문문 049
3-6 by이외의 전치사를 쓰는 수동태 050
3-7 동사구의 수동태 051
3-8 4형식의 수동태 052
3-9 5형식의 수동태 053
Review Test 054
보너스 유형별 문제 058

» Chapter 4

부정사

4-1 to부정사의 명사적 쓰임 : 주어 역할 060
4-2 to부정사의 명사적 쓰임 : 보어 역할 062
4-3 to부정사의 명사적 쓰임 : 목적어 역할 063
4-4 의문사 + to부정사 064
4-5 to부정사의 형용사적 쓰임 065
4-6 to부정사의 부사적 쓰임 067
4-7 to부정사의 부정 069
4-8 to부정사의 의미상 주어 070
4-9 to부정사의 관용 표현 071
4-10 원형부정사 I 072
4-11 원형부정사 II 073
Review Test 074
보너스 유형별 문제 078

» Chapter 5

동명사

5-1 동명사의 역할 I 080
5-2 동명사의 역할 II 081
5-3 동명사와 to부정사 I 083
5-4 동명사와 to부정사 II 084
5-5 동명사의 관용 표현 086
Review Test 088
보너스 유형별 문제 092

» Chapter 6

분사

6-1 분사 094
6-2 명사를 수식하는 분사 095
6-3 동사의 활용에 쓰이는 분사 097
6-4 감정을 나타내는 분사 098
6-5 현재분사와 동명사 100
6-6 분사구문 101
Review Test 102
보너스 유형별 문제 106

» Chapter 7

대명사

7-1 재귀대명사 108
7-2 재귀대명사의 관용 표현 109
7-3 가주어 it 110
7-4 부정대명사 one, another, other 111
7-5 부정대명사 표현 113
7-6 부정대명사 some, any 114
7-7 부정대명사 each, every, all, both, no 115
7-8 부정대명사 either, neither 117
Review Test 118
보너스 유형별 문제 122

» Chapter 8

형용사/ 부사/ 비교

8-1 형용사의 용법 124
8-2 주의해야 할 형용사 126
8-3 형용사의 어순 127
8-4 주의해야 할 부사 I 128
8-5 주의해야 할 부사 II 130
8-6 주의해야 할 부사 III 131
8-7 원급 비교 132
8-8 비교급 134
8-9 최상급 136
Review Test 138
보너스 유형별 문제 142

» Chapter 9

가정법

9-1 가정법 과거 144
9-2 가정법 과거와 단순 조건문 146
9-3 가정법 과거완료 147
9-4 I wish 가정법 148
9-5 as if 가정법 149
Review Test 150
보너스 유형별 문제 154

» Chapter 10

관계사

10-1 관계대명사와 선행사 156
10-2 주격 관계대명사 157
10-3 목적격 관계대명사 159
10-4 소유격 관계대명사 161
10-5 관계부사 162
Review Test 164
보너스 유형별 문제 168

» Chapter 11

전치사와 접속사

11-1 시간을 나타내는 전치사 170
11-2 장소 · 방향을 나타내는 전치사 171
11-3 기타 전치사 172
11-4 명사절을 이끄는 접속사 174
11-5 간접의문문 176
11-6 시간을 나타내는 접속사 178
11-7 이유 · 양보를 나타내는 접속사 180
11-8 조건을 나타내는 접속사 181
11-9 상관접속사 183
11-10 선택의문문 184
Review Test 186
보너스 유형별 문제 190

» Workbook

Workbook 194

Chapter
1

시제

1-1 현재시제
1-2 동사의 변화
1-3 과거시제
1-4 진행시제
1-5 현재완료
1-6 현재완료의 용법
1-7 현재완료: 주의해야 할 표현
Review Test
보너스 유형별 문제

1-1 현재시제

현재시제

❶ 현재의 사실이나 상태를 나타낸다.

- I **have** two brothers and one sister. 나는 두 명의 오빠와 한 명의 언니가 있다.
- Jason **works** at a company as an accountant. Jason은 한 회사에서 회계사로 일한다.

❷ 반복적인 행동이나 습관을 나타낸다.

- My parents usually **go** to bed at ten. 우리 부모님은 주로 10시에 주무신다.
- The old man **takes** his dog everywhere. 그 노인은 그의 개를 어디든지 데리고 다닌다.

❸ 변하지 않는 진리나 일반적인 사실을 나타낸다.

- The Earth **revolves** around the Sun. 지구는 태양의 주위를 공전한다.
- There **are** more than eight billion people in the world. 전 세계의 인구는 80억 명이 넘는다.

❹ 시간표 등에 의해 확정된 미래의 일을 나타낸다.

- The meeting **starts** at noon. 회의는 정오에 시작됩니다.
- The ship **leaves** for the next port tomorrow. 그 배는 내일 다음 항구로 떠난다.

Answers: p.02

Exercise 1 다음 괄호 안에서 알맞은 것을 고르시오.

1 Turn off your phone. The movie (starts / started) in a few minutes.

2 Winter vacation (began / begins) next month.

3 My family (goes / went) to church every Sunday. So we can't go camping on the weekend.

4 The blue shirt you are wearing (looks / looked) great on you.

5 There (are / will be) more than 50 trillion cells in the human body.

Exercise 2 다음 우리말과 같은 뜻이 되도록 주어진 말을 이용하여 문장을 완성하시오.

1 너의 의견은 완벽한 것 같다. (sound)

⇒ Your idea ________________ perfect.

2 기차는 30분 내에 도착해요. (arrive)

⇒ The train ________________ in half an hour.

3 멜버른으로 가는 비행기는 오전 아홉 시에 출발한다. (depart)

⇒ The flight to Melbourne ________________ at 9 a.m.

4 평균적으로 여자가 남자보다 더 오래 산다. (live)

⇒ Women ________________ longer than men on average.

5 나는 이틀에 한 번 헬스클럽에서 운동한다. (work out)

⇒ I ________________ at the gym every other day.

1-2 동사의 변화

규칙 변화 동사

동사	과거형/과거분사형	예
대부분의 동사	+ed	paint**ed**, talk**ed**, start**ed**, visit**ed** …
-e로 끝나는 동사	+d	like**d**, hope**d**, move**d**, invite**d** …
「자음+y」로 끝나는 동사	y를 i로 고치고+ed	stud**ied**, repl**ied**, tr**ied**, worr**ied** …
「모음+y」로 끝나는 동사	+ed	play**ed**, enjoy**ed** …
「단모음+단자음」으로 끝나는 동사	자음 한 번 더 쓰고+ed	stop**ped**, pop**ped**, occur**red** …

불규칙 변화 동사

원 형	과거형	과거분사형	원 형	과거형	과거분사형
A-A-A					
cost	cost	cost	cut	cut	cut
hit	hit	hit	hurt	hurt	hurt
let	let	let	put	put	put
A-B-B					
bring	brought	brought	build	built	built
buy	bought	bought	catch	caught	caught
feel	felt	felt	fight	fought	fought
find	found	found	get	got	got(ten)
hear	heard	heard	hold	held	held
keep	kept	kept	leave	left	left
lend	lent	lent	lose	lost	lost
mean	meant	meant	meet	met	met
pay	paid	paid	read	read[red]	read[red]
say	said	said	sell	sold	sold
send	sent	sent	sleep	slept	slept
spend	spent	spent	stand	stood	stood
teach	taught	taught	tell	told	told
think	thought	thought	understand	understood	understood
A-B-C					
begin	began	begun	bite	bit	bitten
blow	blew	blown	break	broke	broken
choose	chose	chosen	draw	drew	drawn
drive	drove	driven	fall	fell	fallen
fly	flew	flown	forget	forgot	forgotten
grow	grew	grown	hide	hid	hidden
ring	rang	rung	rise	rose	risen
speak	spoke	spoken	steal	stole	stolen
swim	swam	swum	throw	threw	thrown
wake	woke	woken	write	wrote	written

Answers: p.02

Exercise 1 다음 동사의 과거형과 과거분사형을 쓰시오.

1	die	______	______	2	fight	______	______
3	catch	______	______	4	reply	______	______
5	stop	______	______	6	worry	______	______
7	find	______	______	8	lend	______	______
9	tell	______	______	10	hop	______	______
11	hurry	______	______	12	wash	______	______
13	pay	______	______	14	hope	______	______
15	teach	______	______	16	break	______	______
17	arrive	______	______	18	marry	______	______
19	keep	______	______	20	read	______	______
21	meet	______	______	22	hurt	______	______
23	dance	______	______	24	ring	______	______
25	let	______	______	26	steal	______	______
27	bite	______	______	28	pass	______	______
29	hear	______	______	30	decide	______	______
31	study	______	______	32	feel	______	______
33	sing	______	______	34	choose	______	______
35	carry	______	______	36	throw	______	______
37	hit	______	______	38	apply	______	______
39	prepare	______	______	40	rise	______	______

Exercise 2 다음 주어진 동사를 이용하여 문장을 완성하시오.

1 Jackie ______________ the ball, and Fred caught it. (throw)

2 Mom ______________ the big cake into eight pieces. (cut)

3 We ______________ our best and achieved our goal. (try)

4 The rabbit ______________ into the hole and disappeared. (hop)

5 I ______________ a magazine on the subway this morning. (read)

6 Sam ______________ for photos and then walked confidently down the red carpet. (stand)

1-3 과거시제

과거시제

❶ 과거에 이미 끝난 동작이나 상태, 습관을 나타낸다.

- I **got** up early this morning. 나는 오늘 아침 일찍 일어났다.
- My mother **was** a successful businesswoman. 내 어머니는 성공한 사업가였다.
- Daniel **played** baseball for his school team when he was in high school.
  Daniel은 고교 시절 학교 팀에서 야구를 했다.

❷ 과거에 있었던 역사적 사실을 나타낸다.

- Vincent van Gogh **painted** *Starry Night*. 빈센트 반 고흐가 '별이 빛나는 밤'을 그렸다.
- Neil Armstrong **set** foot on the Moon on July 21, 1969.
  닐 암스트롱이 1969년 7월 21일 달에 발을 디뎠다.

❸ 특정한 과거 시점을 나타내는 부사(구)와 함께 쓰인다.

yesterday, at that time, then, last ~, ~ ago, in+과거년도 ...

- I **ran** into my old friend Bob yesterday. 나는 어제 옛 친구인 Bob을 우연히 만났다.
- Julie **entered** Yale University last year. Julie는 작년에 예일대에 입학했다.
- My family **visited** the Grand Canyon a couple of months ago.
  우리 가족은 두어 달 전에 그랜드캐니언을 방문했다.

Answers: p.02

Exercise 1 다음 괄호 안에서 알맞은 것을 고르시오.

1 I (buy / bought) this camera online last week.

2 Eddie often (goes / went) fishing on weekends these days.

3 The Sun (rises / rose) in the east and sets in the west.

4 Thomas Edison (invents / invented) the light bulb in 1879.

5 Mr. Jackson (leaves / left) for New Zealand a few days ago.

6 I often (play / played) tennis with my dad when I was young.

7 Frank (drops / dropped) by my office on his way to work this morning.

8 I usually go to school on foot, but I (take / took) the subway yesterday.

Exercise 2 다음 주어진 동사를 이용하여 문장을 완성하시오.

1 The Korean War ____________________ in 1950. (break out)

2 I ____________________ this skirt when I was in high school. (buy)

3 We ____________________ scuba diving in Cairns last summer. (go)

4 I ____________________ my key yesterday, and I'm still looking for it. (lose)

5 The men ____________________ hands after they made an agreement. (shake)

6 Grace ____________________ an argument with her mom this morning. (have)

1-4 진행시제

현재진행

「am/are/is + -ing」의 형태로, 현재 진행 중인 일이나 최근 일정 기간 지속되는 일을 나타낸다.

- Jessica **is reading** a book in the living room.
  Jessica는 거실에서 책을 읽고 있다.
- They **are watching** a baseball game on TV.
  그들은 텔레비전으로 야구를 보고 있다.

> **TIPs** 이미 확정된 일정이나 계획은 현재진행 시제로 가까운 미래를 나타낼 수 있다.
> - Chase and Jasmine **are getting married** next month.
>   Chase와 Jasmine은 다음 달에 결혼해.

과거진행

「was/were + -ing」의 형태로, 과거의 한 시점에서 진행 중인 동작이나 일을 나타낸다.

- Jeremy **was taking** a shower when his mom arrived home.
  엄마가 집에 도착했을 때 Jeremy는 샤워를 하고 있었다.
- While you **were having** dinner, she finished her homework.
  당신이 저녁 먹는 동안 그녀는 숙제를 끝냈다.

진행형으로 쓰지 않는 동사

일반적으로 소유, 감정, 지각 등을 나타내는 상태동사는 일반적으로 진행형으로 쓰지 않는다.

like(좋아하다), **want**(원하다), **know**(알다), **feel**(느끼다), **smell**(냄새가 나다), **sound**(~처럼 들리다), **have**(가지다), **belong**(~에 속하다), **resemble**(닮다) ...

- We **like** Korean food. 우리는 한국음식을 좋아합니다.
- Roger **resembles** his father. Roger는 그의 아버지를 닮았다.

> **TIPs** 소유, 감정, 지각 등을 나타내는 상태동사도 동작을 나타내는 경우 진행형으로 쓸 수 있다.
> - I'm **having** a great time at summer camp.
>   나는 여름 캠프에서 즐거운 시간을 보내고 있다.

Answers: p.02

Exercise 1 다음 괄호 안에서 알맞은 것을 고르시오.

1 I (feel / am feeling) tired when I get back from work.

2 The flowers in the garden (smell / are smelling) sweet.

3 Mr. Cohen (has / is having) three puppies and two kittens.

4 They (have / are having) a wonderful time in Hawaii now.

5 What (are / were) you doing when I called you a few hours ago?

Exercise 2 다음 주어진 동사를 이용하여 질문에 알맞은 대답을 쓰시오.

1 A What is your sister doing in the kitchen?
  B She ________________ the dishes. (do)

2 A What were you doing when you broke your leg?
  B I ________________ down the ladder. (come)

3 A Is Henry doing his assignment now?
  B No, he isn't. He ________________ a comic book. (read)

4 A Did you go somewhere last night? I came by your house, but you weren't there.
  B I stayed at home. Probably, I ________________ when you visited. (sleep)

1-5 현재완료

현재완료

과거의 한 시점에서 일어난 동작이나 상태가 현재까지 영향을 미칠 때 사용한다.

- Kelly **lost** her favorite necklace. (과거) Kelly는 자신이 아끼는 목걸이를 잃어버렸다.
  (Kelly가 과거에 목걸이를 잃어버렸고 현재 찾았는지 못 찾았는지는 알 수 없음)
- Kelly **has lost** her favorite necklace. (현재완료) Kelly는 자신이 아끼는 목걸이를 잃어버렸다.
  (Kelly가 과거에 목걸이를 잃어버렸고 아직도 찾지 못했음)

현재완료의 형태

❶ 긍정문: 「have/has + 과거분사」
- I **have done** my homework. 나는 숙제를 끝냈다.
- Mr. Hubert **has lived** in this neighborhood for 15 years. Hubert 씨는 15년 동안 이 동네에 살고 있다.

❷ 부정문: 「have/has + not / never + 과거분사」
- The teacher **hasn't decided** what to do next. 선생님은 다음에 무엇을 할지 결정하지 못했다.
- **I've never forgotten** your kindness. 나는 너의 친절을 잊은 적이 없다.

❸ 의문문: 「Have/Has + 주어 + 과거분사 ~?」
- **Have** you **been** to Las Vegas? 너는 라스베이거스에 가본 적 있니?
- **Has** it **stopped** snowing yet? 이제 눈이 그쳤니?

Exercise 1 다음 주어진 단어를 이용하여 문장을 완성하시오. Answers: p.02

1 I have ____________ the story before. (hear)
2 Ted has ____________ Japanese for a year. (study)
3 They have already ____________ each other. (meet)
4 I have ____________ to Europe several times. (be)
5 Have you ____________ Susan recently? (see)
6 I'm starving. I haven't ____________ since this morning. (eat)

Exercise 2 다음 우리말과 같은 뜻이 되도록 주어진 말을 이용하여 문장을 완성하시오.

1 너는 캥거루를 본 적이 있니? (see)
⇨ __________ you ever __________ a kangaroo?

2 Donaldson 씨는 새로운 사업을 시작하러 중국에 가 있다. (go)
⇨ Mr. Donaldson __________ __________ to China to start a new business.

3 내 여동생은 어젯밤부터 감기로 앓아누워 있다. (be)
⇨ My little sister __________ __________ in bed with a cold since last night.

4 Jennifer는 지난주에 싸운 후로 나에게 말을 걸지 않는다. (speak)
⇨ Jennifer __________ __________ __________ to me since our fight last week.

1-6 현재완료의 용법

현재완료의 용법

❶ **완료**: 과거에 시작한 일이 현재에 완료된 것을 나타낸다.

- Dad **has** already **arrived** at the airport. 아빠는 이미 공항에 도착했다.
- I **have** just **finished** writing an essay on Shakespeare's *Hamlet*.
  나는 방금 셰익스피어의 햄릿에 대한 에세이를 끝냈다.

❷ **경험**: 과거에서 현재까지의 경험을 나타낸다.

- I **have seen** him before. 나는 전에 그를 본 적이 있다.
- Vanessa **has been** to more than ten countries so far.
  Vanessa는 지금까지 열 개가 넘는 나라를 가 보았다.

❸ **계속**: 과거에 시작한 일이 현재까지 계속되는 것을 나타낸다.

- The Robinsons **have been** married for ten years.
  Robinson 부부는 결혼한 지 10년이 되었다.
- I **have lived** in Los Angeles since last year.
  나는 지난해 이래로 로스앤젤레스에 살고 있다.

❹ **결과**: 과거에 일어난 일이 현재까지 영향을 미치고 있음을 나타낸다.

- Jeffrey **has lost** his glasses. Jeffrey는 안경을 잃어버렸다.
- They **have gone** back to their homeland. 그들은 고국으로 돌아갔다.

Answers: p.02

Exercise 1 다음 두 문장이 같은 뜻이 되도록 주어진 단어를 이용하여 문장을 완성하시오.

1 The man told me his name, but I can't remember it.
⇨ I __________ __________ the man's name. (forget)

2 I started composing a poem this morning, and I'm still on it.
⇨ I __________ __________ __________ composing a poem yet. (finish)

3 My parents went to Australia to visit a relative, so they are not home now.
⇨ My parents __________ __________ to Australia. (go)

4 Bill moved to the countryside last month and he is still living there.
⇨ Bill __________ __________ in the countryside since last month. (live)

5 Steve visited Hong Kong five years ago, and he went there again last year.
⇨ Steve __________ __________ to Hong Kong twice. (be)

Exercise 2 다음 빈칸에 been 또는 gone을 쓰시오.

1 Where is my daughter? Has she __________ out?

2 This place looks familiar. I guess I've __________ here before.

3 I'm so excited to go overseas. I've never __________ to another country.

4 Mr. Green is not in the office now. He has __________ to Bali on vacation.

1-7 현재완료: 주의해야 할 표현

현재완료와 함께 쓰이는 표현

완료	**just, already, yet**
경험	**ever, never, before, once, twice, ~ times**
계속	**for, since**

· Jack **has** already **made** his decision. Jack은 이미 결정을 내렸다.
· **Have** you ever **seen** a giraffe? 너는 기린을 본 적이 있니?
· I **have played** tennis since I was ten. 나는 열 살 때부터 테니스를 쳤다.

TIPs
for vs. since
· **for**+기간을 나타내는 말: ~ 동안
for three days, **for** two months
· **since**+시작 시점을 나타내는 말: ~ 이래로
since last year, **since** yesterday

현재완료와 함께 쓰이지 못하는 표현

현재완료는 yesterday, last month, three years ago 등과 같이 특정한 과거의 시점을 나타내는 부사(구)와 함께 쓸 수 없다.

· Ruth **visited** me two days ago. Ruth는 이틀 전에 나를 찾아왔다.
· Ruth has visited me two days ago. (×)
· When **did** your father **go** to Malaysia? 네 아버지는 언제 말레이시아로 갔니?
· When has your father gone to Malaysia? (×)

Answers: p.03

Exercise 1 다음 괄호 안에서 알맞은 것을 고르시오.

1 Have you (ever / yet) seen the movie '*The Little Mermaid*'?
2 When (did you meet / have you met) your fiancé?
3 I (saw / have seen) her standing at the bus stop yesterday.
4 Mindy (played / has played) the viola since she was seven.
5 I (didn't receive / haven't received) any answers to my questions yet.
6 My kids (didn't go / have never been) to a theme park before. This is their first time.

Exercise 2 다음 주어진 말을 이용하여 대화를 완성하시오.

1 A I'm looking for Mrs. Jones. Have you seen her?
B No. I ________________ her since yesterday. (not, see)

2 A How is the weather in London today?
B Well, it started raining this morning and ________________ yet. (not, stop)

3 A You look tired. What's wrong?
B I have trouble sleeping lately. I ________________ well in three days. (not, sleep)

4 A Have you been to the new restaurant on Fifth Avenue?
B Yes, I have. My wife and I ________________ there a couple of days ago. (have dinner)

Review Test

[01-02] 다음 중 동사의 과거형과 과거분사형이 바르지 않은 것을 고르시오.

01 ① like – liked – liked
② play – plaied – plaied
③ wash – washed – washed
④ study – studied – studied
⑤ stop – stopped – stopped

02 ① let – let – let
② win – win – win
③ fly – flew – flown
④ swim – swam – swum
⑤ catch – caught – caught

[03-07] 다음 빈칸에 들어갈 알맞은 말을 고르시오.

03 I haven't completed the project ___________.

① for ② ever
③ already ④ yet
⑤ since

04 Amanda ___________ absent from school yesterday.

① is ② was
③ have been ④ has been
⑤ will be

05 Rebecca has stayed in Italy ___________.

① for three years ② last year
③ three years ago ④ in 2022
⑤ on Monday

06 I have ___________ my leg. It's hurting me.

① break ② broke
③ broken ④ breaking
⑤ been broken

07 I ___________ the navy coat for you.

① chosen
② had chose
③ have just chose
④ have already choose
⑤ have already chosen

[08-09] 다음 두 문장을 한 문장으로 바꾼 것으로 알맞은 것을 고르시오.

08 My husband isn't home now. He went out for a walk.
⇒ ______________________________

① My husband goes out for a walk.
② My husband will go out for a walk.
③ My husband has gone out for a walk.
④ My husband was going out for a walk.
⑤ My husband is going to go out for a walk.

09 Peter started learning Taekwondo five years ago. He still learns it.
⇒ ______________________________

① Peter learned Taekwondo for five years.
② Peter learned Taekwondo five years ago.
③ Peter has learned Taekwondo for five years.
④ Peter was learning Taekwondo for five years.
⑤ Peter is going to learn Taekwondo for five years.

[10-12] 다음 대화의 빈칸에 들어갈 알맞은 말을 고르시오.

10

A What were you doing when she knocked on the door?

B ____________________

① I listen to music with my earphones on.
② I'll listen to music with my earphones on.
③ I listened to music with my earphones on.
④ I'm listening to music with my earphones on.
⑤ I was listening to music with my earphones on.

11

A What did you do yesterday?

B ____________________

① I played soccer with my friends.
② I will play soccer with my friends.
③ I've played soccer with my friends.
④ I'm playing soccer with my friends.
⑤ I'm going to play soccer with my friends.

12

A ____________________

B No, I have never met him before.

① Do you meet Mr. Brown?
② Did you meet Mr. Brown?
③ Are you meeting Mr. Brown?
④ Were you meeting Mr. Brown?
⑤ Have you ever met Mr. Brown before?

13 다음 중 어법상 바른 것은?

① I have gone to San Francisco.
② Did you ever seen a ghost?
③ I have ridden a horse last year.
④ They have just finished their dinner.
⑤ He has bought a new computer yesterday.

[14-15] 다음 밑줄 친 부분의 쓰임이 다른 하나를 고르시오.

14 ① I have met him once.
② Miyuki has gone back to Japan.
③ I have never been so embarrassed.
④ Have you ever seen any celebrities in person?
⑤ Have you eaten at the new Italian restaurant?

15 ① I've just had a big lunch.
② How long have you lived in Seoul?
③ They haven't taken a shower for days.
④ I have known Serena for about ten years.
⑤ Carol and James have been married since 2020.

[16-17] 다음 빈칸에 들어갈 말이 바르게 짝지어진 것을 고르시오.

16

My uncle __________ a car accident last Saturday. He __________ in the hospital since then.

① had – was
② has had – was
③ has had – is
④ had had – was
⑤ had – has been

17

I have never __________ to Brazil. This __________ my first trip to South America.

① been – is
② gone – is
③ been – was
④ been – has been
⑤ gone – has been

[18-20] 다음 중 어법상 어색한 것을 고르시오.

18 ① I haven't returned the books yet.
② My father lost his cell phone yesterday.
③ We have already seen the film at home.
④ Last week, my uncle has driven a new car.
⑤ She didn't win the contest three years ago.

19 ① It sounds familiar to me.
② Jennifer resembles her mother.
③ This land belongs to my uncle.
④ They are liking each other very much.
⑤ I'm having a great time here in Las Vegas.

20 ① I'm leaving for Osaka tomorrow.
② The thieves stole the painting in 1999.
③ When have you woken up this morning?
④ I was taking a bath when you called me.
⑤ Steven has never flown across the Atlantic.

21 다음 대화 중 자연스러운 것은?

① A What are you doing?
B I learn to play the drums after school.
② A How was the concert last night?
B It has been very exciting.
③ A What did you do last night?
B I just stayed at home and watched TV.
④ A Did you have fun at the beach?
B Yes. It has been sunny all day.
⑤ A When is your brother leaving for Scotland?
B He has been there once.

[22-23] 다음 우리말을 영어로 바르게 옮긴 것을 고르시오.

22 Eric은 5개월 동안 체중이 20파운드 늘었다.

① Eric gains 20 pounds in five months.
② Eric gains 20 pounds five months.
③ Eric gained 20 pounds five months ago.
④ Eric has gained 20 pounds in five months.
⑤ Eric was gaining 20 pounds five months ago.

23 비서는 정오에 돌아올 것이다.

① The secretary came back at noon.
② The secretary is coming back at noon.
③ The secretary has come back at noon.
④ The secretary was coming back at noon.
⑤ The secretary has been coming back at noon.

[24-25] 다음 문장의 밑줄 친 부분과 쓰임이 같은 것을 고르시오.

24 I have never been to Tokyo.

① I have already done my report.
② I have just arrived at the station.
③ I have met the movie star before.
④ How long have you been in this city?
⑤ Jill and I have known each other since high school.

25 Sandra has lost her purse.

① I have read the book twice.
② The kids have gone to the library.
③ He has worked as a teacher for 10 years.
④ Jessica has never swum in the river.
⑤ I have loved George since I was eighteen.

26 다음 대화 중 자연스럽지 않은 것은?

① A Where is your book?
  B I left it at home.
② A Have you sent the letter to him?
  B No, not yet.
③ A How long have you known Jake?
  B For over three years.
④ A Why are you coughing so much?
  B I've caught a cold last week.
⑤ A My girlfriend has gone to her hometown.
  B Do you miss her?

[27-29] 다음 〈보기〉에서 빈칸에 알맞은 말을 골라 쓰시오.

보기	yet	for	since

27 Scott has studied Spanish ________ three years.

28 My aunt has lived in London ________ last year.

29 Jeremy quit his job a few months ago and hasn't found another job ________.

30 다음 대화의 빈칸에 공통으로 들어갈 말을 쓰시오.

A Have you ever ________ to Singapore?
B Of course. I have ________ there several times because my parents live there.

[31-32] 다음 문장을 주어진 지시대로 고쳐 쓰시오.

31 Sam has found a new place to live. (의문문으로)

⇒ ____________________

32 I have heard the song before. (부정문으로)

⇒ ____________________

[33-34] 다음 주어진 글을 읽고, 빈칸에 알맞은 말을 쓰시오.

33 Kevin lost his pet snake yesterday. He doesn't know where she is.

⇒ Kevin ________ ________ his pet snake.

34 Alice moved out of her parents' house six months ago. She now lives on her own.

⇒ Alice ________ ________ on her own for six months.

[35-36] 다음 우리말과 같은 뜻이 되도록 빈칸에 알맞은 말을 쓰시오.

35 그는 열두 살 때부터 축구 선수가 되기를 원해왔다.

⇒ He ________ ________ to be a soccer player since the age of twelve.

36 너는 네 미래에 대해서 생각해 본 적 있니?

⇒ ________ you ________ about your future?

보너스 유형별 문제

Answers: p.04

[1-3] 다음 두 문장을 한 문장으로 연결하시오. 서술형

조건 1. 현재완료 시제로 쓸 것
2. 주어진 단어를 이용할 것

1

Oscar started to play soccer 5 years ago. He still plays soccer now. (play)

→ Oscar ________________ soccer for 5 years.

2

I left my driver's license at home. I don't have it now. (leave)

→ I ______________________ at home.

3

Cora was sick last week. She is still sick now. (be)

→ Cora _______________ since last week.

4 다음 글의 밑줄 친 부분 중, 어법상 틀린 것은? 수능 대비형

Thank you very much for the invitation to your gallery's grand-opening. Last night I ① have heard from my assistant, Kate, that you are inviting all the people who have helped you in the process. Your deep appreciation was shown through the kind words in your letter. But unfortunately I ② won't be able to make it that day. As much as I'd love to be there and give you my support, I have an important conference ③ to attend. The keynote speaker of the conference is an old friend of ④ mine. I will tell you more about it ⑤ when I get back.

* invitation: 초대
** make it: 참석하다
*** keynote speaker: 기조연설자

Chapter
2

조동사

2-1 조동사
2-2 can
2-3 may
2-4 will / be going to
2-5 would
2-6 must / have to
2-7 should / had better
2-8 used to / would
Review Test
보너스 유형별 문제

2-1 조동사

조동사

문장에서 본동사를 도와주는 동사로 가능, 추측, 의무, 요청, 허가, 제안 등의 의미를 나타낸다.

❶ 조동사는 주어의 인칭, 수에 관계없이 항상 동사원형과 쓰인다.

- He **can play** the guitar. (o) 그는 기타를 연주할 수 있다.
- He **can plays** the guitar. (×) / He **can played** the guitar. (×)

❷ 조동사는 주어의 인칭, 수에 관계없이 항상 형태가 일정하다.

- He ~~**cans**~~ play the guitar. (×) / He ~~**canned**~~ play the guitar. (×)

❸ 조동사(can, will, must, may)는 중복해서 사용할 수 없기 때문에 다른 표현을 이용한다.

- You **will must** go to bed early tonight. (×)
  ⇒ You **will have to** go to bed early tonight. (o)
  너는 오늘 밤 일찍 자야 할 것이다.
- She **will can** do the work. (×)
  ⇒ She **will be able to** do the work. (o)
  그녀는 그 일을 할 수 있을 것이다.

조동사의 부정문: 「주어+조동사+not+동사원형 ~」

- You **will not have** any troubles. 너는 아무 문제도 없을 것이다.
- We **should not be** so negative. 우리는 이렇게 부정적이어서는 안 된다.

조동사의 의문문: 「조동사+주어+동사원형 ~?」

- **Shall we take** a walk? 우리 좀 걸을까요?
- **Can you sing** a song for me? 나에게 노래 한 곡 불러줄 수 있나요?

> **TIPs**
> **조동사의 종류**
> - 일반동사의 부정문, 의문문을 만드는 **do**
> - 시제를 나타내는 **be(진행)**, **have(완료)**
> - 동사의 의미를 보충하는 **will, may, can, must, should** 등

> **TIPs**
> 조동사는 주어의 인칭과 수에 관계없이 형태가 일정하고 동사원형과 함께 쓰이지만, **be, do, have**는 예외이다.

> **TIPs**
> **조동사+not의 축약형**
> will not → **won't**
> would not → **wouldn't**
> can not → **cannot/can't**
> could not → **couldn't**
> should not → **shouldn't**

Answers: p.05

Exercise 1 다음 괄호 안에서 알맞은 것을 고르시오.

1. No one (can / cans) keep a secret.
2. He will (do / does) anything for you.
3. Eva might (look / looks) for a new job.
4. We must (are / be) honest all the time.
5. It might (snow / snows) this afternoon.
6. Daniel will (can / be able to) join our club.
7. Ryan will (must / have to) change his plan.
8. I could (smell / smelled) something burning.
9. She could not (answer / to answer) the question.
10. Mickey will (not go / go not) to school tomorrow.
11. You might (should / have to) pay for extra services.
12. You may (go / going) out when you finish your homework.

Exercise 2 다음 문장에서 어법상 어색한 부분을 찾아 바르게 고치시오.

1 I cannot spoke Chinese. ⇒ ______________

2 My cat can jumps really high. ⇒ ______________

3 Ashley not may come here today. ⇒ ______________

4 She will has to complete the work by noon. ⇒ ______________

5 Everyone musts obey the rules of the road. ⇒ ______________

Exercise 3 다음 문장을 부정문으로 바꿔 쓰시오.

1 She may be in her office.

⇒ ______________________________

2 We must tell Jake the truth.

⇒ ______________________________

3 I can see the stars from the window.

⇒ ______________________________

4 You should be proud of yourself.

⇒ ______________________________

5 Emma will tell you what happened.

⇒ ______________________________

Exercise 4 다음 문장을 의문문으로 바꿔 쓰시오.

1 Aaron can drive a car.

⇒ ______________________________

2 Jennifer will be happy to see you.

⇒ ______________________________

3 You can dive in deep seas.

⇒ ______________________________

4 You would like to come to my party.

⇒ ______________________________

5 You can call me before you come to my office.

⇒ ______________________________

2-2 can

can

❶ 능력 · 가능성: '~할 수 있다' (= be able to)

· Sue **can** speak five languages. Sue는 5개 국어를 말할 수 있다.
= Sue **is able to** speak five languages.

· He **couldn't** do his homework by himself. 그는 스스로 숙제를 할 수 없었다.
= He **wasn't able to** do his homework by himself.

· They **will be able to** arrive here tomorrow.
그들은 내일 이곳에 도착할 수 있을 것이다.

❷ 허가: '~ 해도 좋다' (= may)

· **Can** I ask you a favor? 내가 부탁 하나 해도 될까?
= **May** I ask you a favor?

· You **can** borrow my book if you want to. 원하면 내 책을 빌려도 돼.
= You **may** borrow my book if you want to.

❸ 요청: '~해 주시겠어요?'

· **Can** you hand me the bag? 그 가방을 건네주시겠어요?

· **Could** you turn the light off? 불 좀 꺼주시겠어요?

❹ 추측: '~일 수도 있다'(can, could), '~일 리가 없다'(can't)

· He **could** be tired. 그가 피곤할 수도 있다. (현재 · 미래의 불확실한 추측)

· It **can't** be true. 그것은 사실일 리가 없다. (부정적 추측)

TIPs 능력 · 가능성을 나타내는 **can**의 과거형은 **could** 또는 「**was/were able to+동사원형**」으로, 미래형은 「**will+be able to+동사원형**」으로 나타낸다.

TIPs 요청이나 허가의 의미를 나타낼 때 **can** 대신 **could**를 쓰면 더욱 정중한 표현이 된다.
• **Could** you lend me a dollar?
1달러만 빌려주시겠습니까?

Answers: p.05

Exercise 1 다음 두 문장이 같은 뜻이 되도록 빈칸에 알맞은 말을 쓰시오.

1 Can I turn on the TV?
⇨ ______________ I turn on the TV?

2 We are able to fix the problem.
⇨ We ______________ fix the problem.

3 Carol was able to ride the motorcycle.
⇨ Carol ______________ ride the motorcycle.

4 He can't attend the meeting today.
⇨ He ______________ attend the meeting today.

5 You may visit the island at any time.
⇨ You ______________ visit the island at any time.

6 My grandfather could play the drums.
⇨ My grandfather ______________ play the drums.

7 My sister can play both the violin and the cello.
⇨ My sister ______________ play both the violin and the cello.

Exercise 2 다음 문장의 빈칸에 can 또는 be able to를 쓰시오. (단, 둘 다 가능할 때는 can을 쓸 것)

1 How ______________ this happen to me?

2 Will we ______________ meet the deadline?

3 I ______________ have a day off tomorrow.

4 Lisa will ______________ come to my party this Friday.

5 Ron is a genius. He ______________ solve very difficult math problems.

Exercise 3 다음 밑줄 친 조동사의 의미를 〈보기〉에서 골라 쓰시오.

능력	허가	요청	추측

1 Can I turn up the volume? ⇒ __________

2 Could you pass me the salt? ⇒ __________

3 I can't believe it. He can't be a thief. ⇒ __________

4 Excuse me, can you lend me a hand? ⇒ __________

5 You can call me anytime if you need help. ⇒ __________

6 He says that he can jump twice his height. Can it be possible? ⇒ __________

Exercise 4 다음 우리말과 같은 뜻이 되도록 주어진 단어를 이용하여 문장을 완성하시오.

1 저를 위해 문 좀 열어주시겠습니까? (open)

⇒ __________ you __________ the door for me?

2 나는 그가 무엇을 말하는지 이해할 수 없었다. (understand)

⇒ I __________ __________ what he was saying.

3 객실 키를 안내 데스크에 맡겨놓으셔도 됩니다. (leave)

⇒ You __________ __________ your room key at the front desk.

4 우리는 그 터널을 빠져나올 수 있었다. (escape)

⇒ We __________ __________ __________ __________ from the tunnel.

5 Charles는 아주 어려 보인다. 그는 대학생일 리가 없다. (be)

⇒ Charles looks so young. He __________ __________ a college student.

6 비행기는 정각에 이륙할 수 있을 것이다. (take off)

⇒ The plane __________ __________ __________ __________ __________ __________ on time.

2-3 may

may

❶ 불확실한 추측: '~일지도 모른다'

- Tommy **may** not come. Tommy는 오지 않을지도 모른다.
- He **may** be late for school today. 그는 오늘 학교에 늦을지도 모른다.
- Henry **may** not know the truth. Henry는 진실을 모를지도 모른다.

❷ 허가: '~해도 좋다' (= can)

- You **may** go now. 당신은 이제 가도 됩니다.
- **May** I use your computer? 제가 당신의 컴퓨터를 써도 될까요?
- **May** I drive your car? 제가 당신의 차를 운전해도 될까요?
  - Of course you **may**[can]. 물론 해도 되죠.
  - I'm sorry, but you **may not**[can't]. 미안하지만 안 돼요.
  - No, you **must not**. 아니오, 안 됩니다.

TIPs
might는 **may**보다 더 불확실한 추측을 나타낸다.
- He **might** be able to help us.
  그가 우리를 도와줄 수 있을지도 모른다.

Answers: p.05

Exercise 1 다음 밑줄 친 조동사가 추측과 허가 중 어떤 의미인지 쓰시오.

1 May I see your passport? ⇨ ________
2 Take an umbrella with you. It may rain today. ⇨ ________
3 You may use my computer if yours is not working. ⇨ ________
4 She may be tired from work and want to take a rest. ⇨ ________
5 You may open your eyes now and begin writing the answers. ⇨ ________
6 Why don't you call him first? He may not know your number. ⇨ ________

Exercise 2 다음 우리말과 같은 뜻이 되도록 may와 주어진 말을 이용하여 문장을 완성하시오.

1 주목해 주시겠어요? (have your attention)
⇨ ________________________________, please?

2 그는 그것에 아직 준비되지 않았을지도 모른다. (ready)
⇨ He ________________________________ for it.

3 편지를 뜯어서 읽어보셔도 됩니다. (open, the letter)
⇨ You ________________________________ and read it.

4 Jonas 씨에게 가서 이야기해 봐. 그가 너를 도와줄지도 몰라. (help, you)
⇨ Go talk to Mr. Jonas. He ________________________________.

5 Jessica가 곧 모국으로 돌아갈지도 몰라. (go back)
⇨ Jessica ________________________________ to her homeland soon.

2-4 will / be going to

will

❶ 미래의 일 · 의지 · 계획: '~할[일] 것이다'

· We **will** do our best to beat them. 우리는 그들을 이기기 위해 최선을 다할 것이다.

· **Will** the meeting take place next week? 회의가 다음 주에 열릴 건가요?

❷ 요청: '~해 주시겠어요?'

· **Will** you help me? 나를 도와주겠니?

· **Will** you do me a favor? 부탁 하나 해도 될까요?

> **TIPs** 요청을 할 때 **would**는 **will**보다 더 정중한 표현을 나타낸다.
> • **Would** you bring me a glass of water? 물 한 잔 갖다 주실 수 있나요?

be going to

❶ 가까운 미래의 예측: '~일 것이다'

· Look at the clouds. It**'s going to** rain. 구름을 보아라. 비가 내릴 것이다.

· The game **is not going** to be canceled. 경기는 취소되지 않을 것이다.

❷ 계획: '~할 것이다'

· **I'm going to** look for a new house. 나는 새 집을 찾을 것이다.

· What **are** you **going to** do about this? 이 일은 어떻게 처리할 것이니?

> **TIPs** **shall**은 보통 질문에 많이 쓰이며, 대개 **I**와 **we** 이외의 주어와는 쓰지 않는다.
> • **Shall I ~?** : 상대방의 의향을 묻는 표현
> **Shall I** close the window? 제가 창문을 닫을까요?
> • **Shall we ~?** : 제안 · 권유하는 표현
> **Shall we** take a break for a while? 잠깐 쉴까요?

Answers: p.05

Exercise 1 다음 문장을 주어진 지시대로 바꿔 쓰시오.

1 You are going to buy the book online. (의문문으로)
⇨ ______________________

2 The exam is going to be easy for you. (부정문으로)
⇨ ______________________

3 It will take a long time to find a perfect house. (부정문으로)
⇨ ______________________

4 You will invite all your classmates to the party. (의문문으로)
⇨ ______________________

Exercise 2 다음 우리말과 같은 뜻이 되도록 주어진 말을 알맞게 배열하여 문장을 완성하시오.

1 목이 마르다. 물 좀 갖다 주겠니? (some, you, give, will, water, me)
⇨ I'm thirsty. ______________________?

2 지하철에 많은 사람들이 있을 것이다. (will, be, there, people, a lot of)
⇨ ______________________ on the subway.

3 그녀는 방과 후에 수학 시험공부를 할 것이다. (going, study, to, is, the math test, for)
⇨ She ______________________ after school.

4 Jade는 송년회에서 바이올린을 연주할 것이다. (is, going, the violin, play, to)
⇨ Jade ______________________ at the year-end party.

2-5 would

- would like+명사: '~을 원한다' (= want+명사)
  - I **would like** some milk. 저는 우유를 좀 원해요.
    = I **want** some milk.
  - I just made a chocolate cake. **Would** you **like** some?
    제가 막 초콜릿 케이크를 만들었어요. 좀 드실래요?

- would like to+동사원형: '~을 하고 싶다' (= want to+동사원형)
  - I **would like to** stay here. 나는 여기 머물고 싶다.
    = I **want to** stay here.
  - What **would** you **like to** have for dessert? 디저트는 뭐로 드시겠어요?

- would rather+동사원형: '차라리 ~하는 게 더 낫다'
  - It's too cold. We **would rather** stay inside.
    너무 춥다. 우리는 차라리 안에 있는 게 낫겠다.
  - I **would rather** keep away from the dangerous area.
    나는 그 위험한 지역에 가까이 가지 않는 게 낫겠다.

TIPs
「인칭대명사+would」의 축약형
I would → **I'd**
you would → **you'd**
(s)he would → **(s)he'd**
we would → **we'd**
they would → **they'd**
it would → **it'd**

TIPs
would rather의 부정은 「**would rather not**」으로 나타낸다.

TIPs
would rather A than B는 'B하느니 차라리 A하겠다'는 의미를 나타낸다.
- I **would rather** be hungry **than** eat the questionable food.
  그 미심쩍은 음식을 먹느니 배고픈 게 낫겠다.

Answers: p.05

Exercise 1 다음 밑줄 친 부분을 바르게 고쳐 쓰시오.

1 I would rather to stay at home. ⇨ ____________
2 Would you like to some cookies? ⇨ ____________
3 I'd not rather care about it anymore. ⇨ ____________
4 Would you like go to the movies with me? ⇨ ____________
5 We would rather watch TV to do nothing. ⇨ ____________

Exercise 2 다음 우리말과 같은 뜻이 되도록 주어진 말을 알맞게 배열하여 문장을 완성하시오.

1 나는 차라리 빨간 셔츠를 사겠다. (buy, rather, I'd)
⇨ ____________________ the red shirt.

2 나는 새로운 언어를 배우고 싶다. (learn, would, I, like, to)
⇨ ____________________ a new language.

3 당신은 우리의 다과회에 오시겠습니까? (you, like, to, come, would)
⇨ ____________________ to our tea party?

4 우리는 당신의 지원에 감사드리고 싶어요. (you, would, we, to, like, thank)
⇨ ____________________ for your support.

5 저는 참치 샌드위치와 오렌지주스를 원해요. (like, a tuna sandwich, I'd)
⇨ ____________________ and orange juice.

6 나는 집에 일을 가져가느니 추가 근무를 하겠다. (rather, extra hours, work, I'd, than)
⇨ ____________________ bring work home.

2-6 must / have to

must

❶ 의무: '~ 해야 한다' (= have to)

· You **must** wear seat belts. 너는 안전벨트를 매야 한다.
  = You **have to** wear seat belts.

· We **had to** finish the report by Monday. 우리는 월요일까지 보고서를 끝내야 했다.

❷ 강한 추측: '~임에 틀림없다' (↔ can't)

· He **must** be angry at you. 그는 분명 너에게 화났을 것이다.

· He **can't** be angry at you. 그는 너에게 화났을 리가 없다.

> **TIPs** **must**(의무)는 과거시제와 미래시제를 표현할 수 없으므로 **had to**로 과거시제, **will have to**로 미래시제를 나타낸다.

have to

'~해야 한다'라는 뜻으로 의무를 나타내며 must와 바꿔 쓸 수 있다.

· Mike **has to** do the work by himself. Mike는 그 일을 스스로 해야 한다.

· Do I **have to** wear a tie? 내가 넥타이를 매야 할까?

· I **had to** stay up late to finish my report. 나는 보고서를 끝내기 위해 늦게까지 깨어 있어야 했다.

must not vs. don't have to

❶ must not(금지): '~해서는 안 된다'

· We **must not** jaywalk. 우리는 무단횡단을 하면 안 된다.

· You **must not** tell anyone about it.
  너는 그것에 대해 누구에게도 말해선 안 된다.

❷ don't have to(불필요): '~할 필요 없다'

· You **don't have to** buy it. 너는 그것을 살 필요 없다.

· He **doesn't have to** go to work today. 그는 오늘 일하러 갈 필요 없다.

> **TIPs** **have to**의 부정형 **don't have to**는 '~할 필요가 없다'라는 의미로, **don't need to** 또는 **need not**으로 바꿔 쓸 수 있다.
> • You **don't have to** bring your lunch. 너는 점심을 가져올 필요 없다.
>   = You **don't need to** bring your lunch.
>   = You **need not** bring your lunch.

Answers: p.06

Exercise 1 다음 괄호 안에서 알맞은 것을 고르시오.

1 You (must / have) to do it by yourself.

2 They (must / have) follow the directions.

3 Does he (must / have / has) to leave now?

4 You don't need (to go / go) to the gym today.

5 You will (have to / must) stay up late at night.

6 Do I (must / have) to get up early tomorrow?

7 Tommy (must / has / had) to finish it by yesterday.

8 Did I (must / have / had) to buy something for her?

9 You (don't have to / do have to not) worry about it.

10 Jessica (must / has to) be exhausted from the journey.

11 Harry (must / have / has) take his dog for a walk every day.

12 Catherine (musted / had to) be in the hospital for three months.

Exercise 2 다음 우리말과 같은 뜻이 되도록 주어진 말을 이용하여 문장을 완성하시오.

1 너는 내게 거짓말을 하면 안 된다. (lie, to)
⇨ You ______________________.

2 너는 실수를 했다. 너는 문제를 고쳐야 한다. (correct the problem)
⇨ You made a mistake. You ______________________.

3 벌써 9시다. 나는 가야겠다. (go)
⇨ It's already nine. I ______________________ now.

4 나는 그에게 시험결과를 알려야 했다. (tell)
⇨ I ______________________ about the test results.

5 Paul은 그의 책을 가져오지 않아도 된다. 내가 두 권을 갖고 있다. (bring)
⇨ Paul ______________________ his book. I have two.

6 제가 내일까지 이 책들을 반납해야 하나요? (return)
⇨ ______________________ these books by tomorrow?

7 Willy는 오늘 일찍 집을 나섰다. 그는 늦을 리가 없다. (late)
⇨ Willy left home early today. He ______________________.

8 그들은 자매임이 분명해. 눈이 똑 닮았다. (be, sisters)
⇨ They ______________________. They have the same eyes.

Exercise 3 다음 문장을 주어진 지시대로 바꿔 쓰시오.

1 He has to go to the hospital. (부정문으로)
⇨ ______________________

2 Jacob had to pay for the damage. (의문문으로)
⇨ ______________________

3 Juliet must tell her mom the truth. (미래시제로)
⇨ ______________________

4 She must treat them very carefully. (과거시제로)
⇨ ______________________

5 Gary has to wear a suit and tie to work. (의문문으로)
⇨ ______________________

6 You must open the box when you're alone. (부정문으로)
⇨ ______________________

2-7 should / had better

should

❶ 권유 · 충고: '~해야겠다', '~하는 게 좋겠다'

- You don't look well. You **should** see a doctor. 너는 아파 보인다. 의사의 진찰을 받아야겠다.
- You **should** focus more on studying now. 너는 지금 공부에 더 집중해야겠다.

❷ 의무 · 당연: '~해야 한다' (= ought to)

- Everyone **should** have the textbook. 모두 교과서를 지참해야 한다.
  = Everyone **ought to** have the textbook.
- He **should** be wearing a seat belt. 그는 안전벨트를 매고 있어야 한다.
- We **should** not climb over the fence.
  우리는 울타리를 넘지 말아야 한다.

> **TIPs** 「**ought to**+동사원형」은 '~해야 한다'라는 의미로, 의무나 충고를 나타내며 부정형은 「**ought not to**+동사원형」이다.

> **TIPs** '~해야 한다'는 의미의 **should**는 **must**보다 약한 의미의 의무나 당연을 나타낸다.

had better

'~하는 게 낫다'라는 의미로, 충고나 경고를 나타내 따르지 않으면 위험이나 문제가 있을 수 있는 경우에 쓴다. 부정형은 「had better not+동사원형」이다.

- **I'd better** wear a thick coat. 나는 두꺼운 코트를 입어야겠다.
- You **had better** tell her everything. 너는 그녀에게 모든 것을 말하는 게 낫다.
- You**'d better not** go into the deep water. 너는 깊은 물에 들어가지 않는 게 낫겠다.

> **TIPs** **had better**는 축약형인 「주어**'d better**」의 형태로 자주 쓰인다.

Answers: p.06

Exercise 1 다음 괄호 안에서 알맞은 것을 고르시오.

1 You are shivering. You (would like to / should) cover yourself.

2 It's too dark outside. You (had better / had better not) go out.

3 Here comes a truck. You (had better / don't have to) watch out.

4 Look at your dirty hands. You (should / don't have to) wash them first.

5 You are too close to the TV. You (ought to / shouldn't) sit farther away from the screen.

Exercise 2 다음 문장에서 어법상 어색한 부분을 찾아 바르게 고치시오.

1 We should go not into the room. ⇨ ______________

2 We ought to finding a new house. ⇨ ______________

3 You'd not better climb the tree. ⇨ ______________

4 Joe would better go alone this time. ⇨ ______________

5 Students ought respect their teachers. ⇨ ______________

6 We ought to not waste so much water. ⇨ ______________

7 You'd better to finish your homework before dinner. ⇨ ______________

8 You should always remembers to feed the dog before leaving. ⇨ ______________

Exercise 3 다음 우리말과 같은 뜻이 되도록 should와 주어진 단어를 이용하여 문장을 완성하시오.

1 그들은 지금 학교에 있어야 한다. (at school, be)

⇨ They ______________________ now.

2 나는 우리가 그들을 위해 무언가를 해야 한다고 생각한다. (do, something)

⇨ I think we ______________________ for them.

3 너는 피곤해 보인다. 오늘은 일찍 자는 게 좋겠다. (early, go to bed)

⇨ You look tired. You ______________________ today.

4 너는 기침을 많이 한다. 약을 좀 먹어야겠다. (take, medicine, some)

⇨ You are coughing too much. You ______________________.

Exercise 4 다음 우리말과 같은 뜻이 되도록 had better와 주어진 단어를 이용하여 문장을 완성하시오.

1 너는 새치기하지 않는 게 좋을 것이다. (cut)

⇨ You ______________________ in line.

2 그는 학교에 걸어가지 않는 것이 나을 것이다. (walk)

⇨ He ______________________ to school.

3 너는 그녀를 파티에 초대하지 않는 게 좋을 것이다. (invite)

⇨ You ______________________ to the party.

4 그녀는 지금 바로 그에게 전화하는 게 좋을 것이다. (call)

⇨ She ______________________ him right away.

5 너는 또 늦었구나. 내일은 제시간에 오는 게 좋을 거다. (on time, be)

⇨ You're late again. You ______________________ tomorrow.

Exercise 5 다음 우리말과 같은 뜻이 되도록 주어진 말을 알맞게 배열하여 문장을 완성하시오.

1 너는 그렇게 많이 먹으면 안 돼. (too, eat, much, you, shouldn't)

⇨ ______________________

2 너는 그 버튼을 누르면 안 된다. (press, ought, you, not, to, the button)

⇨ ______________________

3 우리는 이번 기회를 놓쳐서는 안 된다. (to, not, ought, lose, this, we, chance)

⇨ ______________________

4 네가 그 청바지를 사는 게 좋을 것 같아. (buy, you, I, should, think, those, jeans)

⇨ ______________________

2-8 used to / would

- **used to**: (더 이상 그렇지 않은) 과거의 반복적인 행동이나 습관 · 상태를 나타낸다.

  ❶ 과거의 반복적인 행동이나 습관: '~하곤 했다'
  - Cathy and I **used to** hang out together. Cathy와 나는 같이 어울리곤 했었다.
  - I **used to** walk to work, but now I take the bus. 나는 걸어서 출근하곤 했지만, 지금은 버스를 타고 다닌다.

  ❷ 과거의 상태: '~이 있었다'
  - There **used to** be a big theater downtown. 시내에는 큰 영화관이 있었다.
  - I **used to** have a car. 나는 차를 갖고 있었다.

- **would**: 과거의 반복적인 행동이나 습관을 나타낸다.
  - My dad and I **would** go fishing when I was young. 어릴 때 아빠와 나는 낚시를 가곤 했다.
  - After dinner, Taylor **would** read the newspaper. 저녁을 먹은 후 Taylor는 신문을 읽곤 했다.

TIPs
would는 **used to**와 달리 과거의 상태를 나타내지 못한다.
- There **used to** be a big tree near here. 이 근처에 큰 나무가 있었다.
- There ~~would~~ be a big tree near here. (×)

Exercise 1 다음 〈보기〉에서 알맞은 단어를 골라 used to와 함께 문장을 완성하시오.

Answers: p.06

eat	be	smoke	live	have

1 I ____________________ long curly hair.

2 There ____________________ a big tower in my neighborhood.

3 I hardly eat candy, but I ____________________ lots of it when I was young.

4 They ____________________ in a big city, but now they live in a small village.

5 Henry stopped smoking a few years ago. He ____________________ a pack a day.

Exercise 2 다음 우리말과 같은 뜻이 되도록 주어진 말을 이용하여 문장을 완성하시오.

1 나는 패스트푸드를 많이 먹곤 했지만 지금은 아니다. (a lot of, fast food)
⇒ I ____, but now I don't.

2 나는 동물원에서 일했었지만 2년 전에 그만뒀다. (the zoo)
⇒ I ____, but I quit two years ago.

3 그는 뚱뚱했었지만 지금은 빨대처럼 말랐다. (fat)
⇒ He ____, but now he's thin as a straw.

4 아버지는 대학 다니실 때 하키를 하곤 하셨다. (hockey)
⇒ My father ____ when he was in college.

5 우리 학교에는 큰 강당이 있었지만 지금은 식당이 되었다. (big, auditorium)
⇒ There ____ in my school, but now it is a cafeteria.

Review Test

[01-04] 다음 빈칸에 들어갈 알맞은 말을 고르시오.

01

You ____________ be quiet in the library.

① can ② may
③ must ④ would
⑤ might

02

He always lies to us. So his words ____________ be true.

① can't ② may
③ must ④ should
⑤ had better

03

____________ we go fishing this weekend? I know a good place.

① Should ② Shall
③ Must ④ Might
⑤ May

04

You had better ____________ at home. It's very cold outside.

① stay ② staying
③ to stay ④ stayed
⑤ to staying

[05-07] 다음 대화의 빈칸에 들어갈 알맞은 말을 고르시오.

05

A I'm cold. ____________ I close the window?
B Sure.

① Need ② Would
③ Can ④ Do
⑤ Might

06

A I am nervous. I have an important test tomorrow.
B Come on. You've done your best. You ____________ worry about it.

① don't have to ② need
③ must ④ can
⑤ may

07

A Where's the remote control? I want to change the channel.
B I don't know. It ____________ be under the couch.

① need ② shall
③ may ④ had better
⑤ ought to

[08-09] 다음 빈칸에 공통으로 들어갈 말을 고르시오.

08

You ____________ to work late yesterday. So you ____________ better go home early and take some rest.

① have ② should
③ had ④ may
⑤ could

09

When you go to the movies, you ____________ turn off your cell phone. Also, you ____________ not kick the seat in front of you.

① may ② will
③ can ④ should
⑤ have to

10 다음 빈칸에 들어갈 말로 알맞지 않은 것은?

You ________ not park here. It's for people with disabilities.

① must ② should
③ had better ④ can
⑤ might

11 다음 질문에 대한 응답으로 알맞지 않은 것은?

A May I borrow the book?
B ____________

① Of course.
② Yes, you may.
③ I'm afraid not.
④ No, you must.
⑤ I'm sorry. You may not.

[12-13] 다음 밑줄 친 부분과 바꿔 쓸 수 있는 것을 고르시오.

12 You don't have to take an umbrella. It will be sunny today.

① must ② need not
③ must not ④ should not
⑤ had better

13 I used to go camping with my father when I was young.

① must ② need
③ would ④ should
⑤ had better

[14-16] 다음 우리말을 영어로 바르게 옮긴 것을 고르시오.

14 나는 텔레비전을 보느니 차라리 책을 읽겠다.

① I ought to read a book than watch TV.
② I'd like to read a book than watch TV.
③ I'd rather read a book than watch TV.
④ I'd better read a book than watch TV.
⑤ I have to read a book than watch TV.

15 너는 그것에 대해 미안해할 필요가 없다.

① You must not feel sorry about it.
② You should not feel sorry about it.
③ You'd rather not feel sorry about it.
④ You'd better not feel sorry about it.
⑤ You don't have to feel sorry about it.

16 James는 스파이일 리가 없다.

① James can be a spy.
② James must be a spy.
③ James has to be a spy.
④ James can't be a spy.
⑤ James is not a spy.

17 다음 문장의 밑줄 친 부분과 쓰임이 같은 것은?

Can you give me a hand?

① I believe I can fly.
② Can you swim fast?
③ Can you open the door?
④ You can visit me if you want to.
⑤ He can go to Canada next year.

[18-19] 다음 문장의 밑줄 친 부분과 쓰임이 다른 것을 고르시오.

18 You must come back before 10 p.m.

① I must study tonight.
② We must save energy.
③ He must be upset with me.
④ All students must wear uniforms.
⑤ He must see a dentist tomorrow.

19 You may ask another question.

① May I come in?
② It may rain tomorrow.
③ You may take one of them.
④ May I use your cell phone?
⑤ You may go out with your friends.

[20-21] 다음 중 어법상 바른 문장을 고르시오.

20 ① I should go to bed early today.
② He may can go fishing tomorrow.
③ You'd better to stay at home today.
④ Can you played the computer game?
⑤ He is going to visits his uncle tomorrow.

21 ① We had not better go to the party tonight.
② I am going to buy a new pencil case.
③ I use to go to the beach with my friends.
④ The baseball player is able run fast.
⑤ He may not likes her.

[22-23] 다음 중 어법상 어색한 문장을 고르시오.

22 ① Can you go faster?
② May I turn off the radio?
③ We had to wait for a long time.
④ Will you can come by my office?
⑤ You will be able to see him there.

23 ① I wasn't able to get out of bed.
② When I was five, I could not swim.
③ I could smell something delicious.
④ You ought to not spit on the floor.
⑤ If you study hard, you can pass the exam.

24 다음 대화 중 어색한 것은?

① A Would you like to have some coffee?
B I'd love to.
② A Can you meet them every week?
B Of course, I can.
③ A You must not park here.
B Why not?
④ A Can I smoke here?
B I'm afraid not.
⑤ A May I sit here?
B No, thanks.

[25-26] 다음 문장과 의미가 같은 문장을 고르시오.

25 Do you want me to turn off the stove?

① Shall I turn off the stove?
② Shall we turn off the stove?
③ Can you turn off the stove?
④ Would you turn off the stove?
⑤ Will you turn off the stove?

26 You don't have to care what people think of you.

① You must not care what people think of you.
② You'd better care what people think of you.
③ You ought to care what people think of you.
④ You need not care what people think of you.
⑤ You should not care what people think of you.

[27-29] 다음 우리말과 같은 뜻이 되도록 〈보기〉에서 알맞은 말을 골라 문장을 완성하시오.

보기	had better	would rather	used to

27 나의 집 옆에는 큰 나무가 있었다.

⇒ There ______________ be a big tree by my house.

28 너는 다시는 그곳에 가지 않는 것이 좋겠다.

⇒ You ______________ not go there again.

29 나는 일찍 일어나느니 아침을 거르겠다.

⇒ I ______________ skip breakfast than get up early.

[30-32] 다음 문장과 같은 뜻이 되도록 빈칸에 알맞은 말을 쓰시오.

30 You need not hurry.

⇒ You ______________ hurry.

31 I wore glasses when I was young, but now I don't.

⇒ I ______________ wear glasses when I was young.

32 Dorothy would like to study biology in college.

⇒ Dorothy ______________ biology in college.

[33-35] 다음 주어진 말을 알맞게 배열하여 문장을 완성하시오.

33 You don't look well. You ______________ ________ today. (better, leave, had, early)

34 You sprained your ankle. You ______________ ________ for a while. (not, ought, to, walk)

35 A I'm going camping this Sunday.
B ______________ (I, you, can, join)

[36-37] 다음 문장을 주어진 지시대로 바꿔 쓰시오.

36 Fred can go home for the holidays. (미래시제로)

⇒ ______________

37 We must get up early to catch the flight. (과거시제로)

⇒ ______________

[38-39] 다음 우리말을 주어진 말을 이용하여 영작하시오.

38 내가 그를 파티에 초대해도 될까요? (invite)

⇒ ______________

39 너는 그녀에게 사과할 필요 없다. (apologize, to)

⇒ ______________

보너스 유형별 문제

Answers: p.08

[1-2] 밑줄 친 우리말과 같은 뜻이 되도록 주어진 단어를 이용하여 대화를 완성하시오. 서술형

조건 1. 조동사를 이용할 것

A 1 저녁으로 무엇을 먹고 싶니?
B Could you make spaghetti for me?
A Of course. Did you have fun at school?
B Yes, I did. I played basketball with my classmates after school.
A 2 그럼, 너 틀림없이 배가 많이 고프겠구나. But you'd better finish your homework before dinner.
B Okay, Mom.

1 What ________ ________ ________ ________ ________ ________ ________? (have, for dinner)

2 Then, ________ ________ ________ ________ ________. (be, very, hungry)

3 다음 글의 밑줄 친 부분 중, 어법상 틀린 것은? 수능 대비형

It was an ordinary day at the office for Frank. After working hard, he had a fun Friday dinner with friends ① until quite late. When he got to his apartment, he ② noticed smoke coming out from downstairs where an old couple lived. He couldn't believe it at first and didn't know what to do. He thought about calling 911 and then he realized it ③ would take a while for the rescuers to arrive. There was no time to wait for them. He knew that he ④ has to do something immediately, so he broke down the door and ran through the smoke-filled house to wake the couple. They were already unconscious ⑤ so Frank pulled them out of the house one by one. The young hero was quite modest about his actions and said simply, "I'm just glad they are alright."

* unconscious: 의식을 잃은
** modest: 겸손한

Chapter 3

수동태

3-1 수동태
3-2 수동태의 시제
3-3 조동사가 쓰인 수동태
3-4 수동태의 부정문
3-5 수동태의 의문문
3-6 by이외의 전치사를 쓰는 수동태
3-7 동사구의 수동태
3-8 4형식의 수동태
3-9 5형식의 수동태
Review Test
보너스 유형별 문제

3-1 수동태

능동태와 수동태

능동태	주어가 동작이나 행위의 주체로서 화제의 초점이 된다. J. K. Rowling wrote *Harry Potter*. J. K. Rowling이 Harry Potter를 썼다.
수동태	주어가 동작이나 행위를 당하거나 영향을 받는 대상이 되어 화제의 초점이 된다. *Harry Potter* was written by J. K. Rowling. Harry Potter는 J. K. Rowling에 의해 쓰였다.

수동태의 형태: 「be동사+과거분사(+by+행위자)」

주어
동사
목적어
능동태
My father
built
this house. 우리 아버지가 이 집을 지었다.
수동태
This house
was built
by my father. 이 집은 우리 아버지에 의해 지어졌다.
주어
be동사+과거분사
by+행위자

❶ 능동태의 목적어 → 수동태의 주어
- I cleaned **the bathroom**.
- **The bathroom** was cleaned by me.

❷ 능동태의 동사 → 「be동사+과거분사」
- I **cleaned** the bathroom.
- The bathroom **was cleaned** by me.

❸ 능동태의 주어 → 「by+행위자(목적격)」
- **I** cleaned the bathroom.
- The bathroom was cleaned **by me**.

TIPs 주어의 인칭과 수, 문장의 시제에 유의하여 수동태의 be동사를 결정한다.
- My parents love me.
  → I **am loved** by my parents.
  나는 부모님께 사랑받는다.
- A famous actress wore this dress.
  → This dress **was worn** by a famous actress.
  이 드레스는 유명한 여배우가 입었다.

Answers: p.08

Exercise 1 다음 괄호 안에서 알맞은 것을 고르시오.

1 My grandfather (bore / was born) during the Korean War.
2 The boy was (bit / bitten) by a dog.
3 The picture was drawn (by / with) Mark.
4 A bee (stung / was stung) me on the nose.
5 Smartphones (used / are used) in many ways.
6 Fresh milk (delivers / is delivered) every morning.
7 A buffet-style dinner is prepared (by /with) our chef.
8 Kate is loved (with / by) everybody around her.
9 Some of the items (buy / are bought) from an online store.
10 My sister and I (brought / were brought) up by our grandparents.

Exercise 2 다음 문장을 수동태로 바꿀 때 빈칸에 알맞은 말을 쓰시오.

1 Dad did the dishes.
⇒ The dishes ________ ________ by Dad.

2 An old man stopped the car.
⇒ The car ________ ________ by an old man.

3 She delivered the note.
⇒ The note was delivered ________ ________.

4 A hurricane destroyed the town.
⇒ The town ________ ________ by a hurricane.

5 My uncle made these chairs.
⇒ These chairs ________ ________ by my uncle.

6 All the students respect Mr. Green.
⇒ Mr. Green ________ ________ by all the students.

7 A ten-year-old boy composed the song.
⇒ The song ________ ________ ________ a ten-year-old boy.

Exercise 3 다음 우리말과 같은 뜻이 되도록 주어진 말을 이용하여 문장을 완성하시오.

1 그 쿠키들은 누나에 의해 만들어졌다. (make)
⇒ Those cookies ____________________ my sister.

2 영어는 많은 나라에서 사용된다. (speak)
⇒ English ____________________ in many countries.

3 그 영화배우는 어린 소녀들에게 사랑받고 있다. (love)
⇒ The movie star ____________________ young girls.

4 그 아름다운 조각은 이탈리아에서 만들어졌다. (make)
⇒ The beautiful sculpture ____________________ in Italy.

5 그 유능한 선수는 감독에게 신임을 받고 있다. (trust)
⇒ The talented player ____________________ the coach.

6 그 신비로운 성은 산으로 둘러싸여 있다. (surround)
⇒ The mysterious castle ____________________ mountains.

7 그 사고는 운전자의 부주의로 일어났다. (cause)
⇒ The accident ____________________ the carelessness of the driver.

3-2 수동태의 시제

수동태의 시제

수동태 현재 「am/are/is+과거분사」	His cartoons **are loved** by people all around the world. 그의 만화는 전 세계 사람들에게 사랑받고 있다.
수동태 과거 「was/were+과거분사」	The island **was discovered** in 1821. 그 섬은 1821년에 발견되었다.
수동태 미래 「will+be+과거분사」	You **will be remembered** for a long time. 너는 오랫동안 기억될 것이다.
수동태 진행 「be동사+being+과거분사」	My car **is being repaired** at a shop. 내 차는 정비소에서 수리되고 있다.
수동태 완료 「have/has+been+과거분사」	The room **has been cleaned** by someone. 그 방은 누군가에 의해 청소되었다.

TIPs 수동태에서 행위의 주체를 말하지 않아도 알 수 있거나 나타낼 필요가 없는 경우에는 「by+행위자」를 생략한다.

Answers: p.08

Exercise 1 다음 문장을 수동태로 바꿀 때 빈칸에 알맞은 말을 쓰시오.

1 Bell invented the telephone in 1876.
⇨ The telephone ________ ________ by Bell in 1876.

2 My brother will water the plants this afternoon.
⇨ The plants ________ ________ ________ by my brother this afternoon.

3 Billions of people all around the world use the Internet.
⇨ The Internet ________ ________ by billions of people all around the world.

4 The kind neighbor has helped us since we moved in.
⇨ We ________ ________ ________ by the kind neighbor since we moved in.

Exercise 2 다음 우리말과 같은 뜻이 되도록 주어진 말을 이용하여 문장을 완성하시오.

1 내 컴퓨터는 아버지에 의해 사용되고 있다. (use)
⇨ My computer ______________________________ my father.

2 내일 비가 오면 견학 일정은 변경될 것이다. (reschedule)
⇨ The field trip ______________________________ if it rains tomorrow.

3 그 건물은 유명한 건축가에 의해 개조되었다. (remodel)
⇨ The building has ______________________________ a famous architect.

4 이 멋진 사진들은 나의 남동생에 의해 찍혔다. (take)
⇨ These amazing pictures ______________________________ my little brother.

3-3 조동사가 쓰인 수동태

조동사가 쓰인 수동태

「조동사+be+과거분사(+by+행위자)」의 어순으로 쓰인다.

- A cart can carry these heavy boxes.
  ⇒ These heavy boxes **can be carried** by a cart. 이 무거운 상자들은 수레로 운반될 수 있다.
- We will discuss the issue next week.
  ⇒ The issue **will be discussed** next week. 그 문제는 다음 시간에 논의될 것이다.
- You must send this letter by tomorrow.
  ⇒ This letter **must be sent** by tomorrow. 이 편지는 내일까지 보내져야 한다.
- We should preserve nature.
  ⇒ Nature **should be preserved.** 자연은 보존되어야 한다.

Answers: p.08

Exercise 1 다음 문장을 수동태로 바꿀 때 빈칸에 알맞은 말을 쓰시오.

1 You must finish it in time.
⇒ It ________ ________ ________ in time.

2 We can solve the problem.
⇒ The problem ________ ________ ________ by us.

3 We should paint those fences yellow.
⇒ Those fences ________ ________ ________ yellow by us.

4 Young people will love that song.
⇒ That song ________ ________ ________ by young people.

Exercise 2 다음 우리말과 같은 뜻이 되도록 주어진 말을 이용하여 문장을 완성하시오.

1 그의 식사는 미리 준비되어야 한다. (should, prepare)
⇒ His meal ____________________ in advance.

2 너의 편지는 잘못된 주소로 보내질 수도 있다. (might, send)
⇒ Your letter ____________________ to the wrong address.

3 진심이라면 네 사과가 받아들여질 것이다. (will, accept)
⇒ If you really mean it, your apology ____________________.

4 네가 망원경을 쓴다면 더 많은 별들이 보일 것이다. (can, see)
⇒ More stars ____________________ if you use a telescope.

5 전기 요금은 이번 달 말까지 지불되어야 한다. (must, pay)
⇒ The electricity bill ____________________ by the end of the month.

3-4 수동태의 부정문

수동태의 부정문

❶ 현재 · 과거시제: 「be동사+not+과거분사」
- This book **is not[isn't] read** by the young. 이 책은 젊은 사람들에게는 읽히지 않는다.
- I **was not[wasn't] invited** to their wedding. 나는 그들의 결혼식에 초대받지 않았다.

❷ 진행시제: 「be동사+not+being+과거분사」
- The children **are not[aren't] being taken** care of. 그 아이들은 보살핌을 받고 있지 않다.

❸ 미래시제: 「will+not+be+과거분사」
- The concert **will not[won't] be canceled** even if it rains.
연주회는 비가 와도 취소되지 않을 것이다.

❹ 완료시제: 「have/has+not+been+과거분사」
- My car **has not[hasn't] been washed** in a long time. 내 차는 오랫동안 세차되지 않았다.

❺ 조동사가 쓰인 수동태: 「조동사+not+be+과거분사」
- The stain **cannot[can't] be removed.** 그 얼룩은 지워질 수 없다.

Answers: p.09

Exercise 1 다음 우리말과 같은 뜻이 되도록 주어진 말을 알맞게 배열하여 문장을 완성하시오.

1 저희 가게에서는 담배를 팔지 않습니다. (sold, is, tobacco, not)

⇨ ______________________ in our store.

2 네 자전거는 아직 수리되지 않았다. (fixed, yet, hasn't, been)

⇨ Your bicycle ______________________.

3 내가 집에 왔을 때 그 문은 잠겨 있지 않았다. (was, locked, not, the door)

⇨ When I arrived home, ______________________.

4 주소에 우편번호를 적지 않으면 당신의 편지는 배달되지 않을 것이다. (be, your letter, delivered, won't)

⇨ ______________________ if you don't include the postal code on the address.

Exercise 2 다음 문장을 부정문으로 바꿔 쓰시오.

1 The bridge was built in 2001.

⇨ ______________________

2 The trash can has been emptied.

⇨ ______________________

3 The door can be closed automatically.

⇨ ______________________

4 My sons are being taught by Ms. Parker.

⇨ ______________________

3-5 수동태의 의문문

수동태의 의문문

❶ 현재 · 과거시제: 「Be동사+주어+과거분사 ~?」

- **Is** your bag **packed**? 네 가방은 꾸려져 있니?
- **Were** you really **hit** by a car? 너 진짜 차에 치인 거 맞니?

❷ 진행시제: 「Be동사+주어+being+과거분사 ~?」

- **Is** your cell phone **being used**? 네 휴대전화는 사용 중이니?

❸ 미래시제: 「Will+주어+be+과거분사 ~?」

- **Will** the work **be completed** by Monday? 그 작업이 월요일까지 완료될까?

❹ 완료시제: 「Have/Has+주어+been+과거분사 ~?」

- **Have** you **been stung** by a bee? 너는 벌에 쏘여 본 적 있니?

❺ 조동사가 쓰인 수동태: 「조동사+주어+be+과거분사 ~?」

- **Can** the book **be checked** out? 그 책은 대출이 가능한가요?

Answers: p.09

Exercise 1 다음 우리말과 같은 뜻이 되도록 주어진 말을 이용하여 문장을 완성하시오.

1 너는 어디에서 태어났니? (bear)

⇨ Where ________ ________ ________?

2 저 건물은 언제 완공되나요? (complete)

⇨ When ________ that building ________ ________?

3 '맥베스'가 셰익스피어에 의해 쓰였니? (write)

⇨ ________ *Macbeth* ________ ________ Shakespeare?

4 비용이 카드로 지불될 수 있을까요? (pay)

⇨ ________ the charge ________ ________ by credit card?

Exercise 2 다음 문장을 의문문으로 바꿔 쓰시오.

1 The window was broken by Bill.

⇨ ________________________________

2 The event will be held on Saturday.

⇨ ________________________________

3 The camera was invented in the 19th century.

⇨ ________________________________

4 You have been robbed twice in the last three months.

⇨ ________________________________

3-6 by 이외의 전치사를 쓰는 수동태

by 이외의 전치사를 쓰는 수동태

수동태의 행위자는 「by+행위자」로 나타내는 것이 일반적이지만, with, at, to 등의 전치사가 쓰이는 경우도 있다.

be covered **with** ~로 덮여 있다	be disappointed **with** ~에 실망하다
be excited **about** ~에 흥분해 있다	be filled **with** ~로 가득 차 있다
be interested **in** ~에 관심이 있다	be known **to** ~에게 알려지다
be made **of/from** ~로 만들어지다	be pleased **with** ~에 기뻐하다
be related **to** ~와 관련이 있다	be satisfied **with** ~에 만족해하다
be surprised **at/by** ~에 놀라다	be tired **of** ~에 싫증 나다

· The town **is covered with** snow. 마을이 눈으로 덮여 있다.
· I **was disappointed with** his performance. 나는 그의 공연에 실망했다.
· I **am** so **interested in** fashion. 나는 패션에 관심이 많다.
· This cake **is made from** rice. 이 케이크는 쌀로 만들어졌다.

TIPs
'사람'에게 실망할 때는 전치사 in을 쓴다.
• I am so disappointed **in** you.
나는 네게 매우 실망했어.

Answers: p.09

Exercise 1 다음 문장의 빈칸에 알맞은 전치사를 쓰시오.

1 I am tired __________ being alone.
2 My boss is satisfied __________ my work.
3 The bottles are filled __________ fresh milk.
4 We were surprised __________ his decision.
5 The movie star is known __________ everybody in the world.
6 My mom was so pleased __________ the news that I got a scholarship.

Exercise 2 다음 우리말과 같은 뜻이 되도록 〈보기〉의 단어를 이용하여 문장을 완성하시오.

excite	cover	surprise	satisfy

1 Tommy는 그의 새 직업에 만족한다.
⇒ Tommy ____________________ his new job.

2 다락방은 먼지로 뒤덮여 있다.
⇒ The attic ____________________ dust and dirt.

3 그 소년들과 소녀들은 여행 때문에 들떠 있다.
⇒ The boys and girls ____________________ the trip.

4 나는 그녀가 아직도 살아 있다는 사실에 놀랐다.
⇒ I ____________________ the fact she was still alive.

3-7 동사구의 수동태

「동사+전치사」가 동사의 역할을 하는 동사구는 하나의 동사로 취급하여 수동태 문장을 만든다.

bring up ~을 기르다	call off ~을 취소하다	laugh at ~을 비웃다
look after ~을 돌보다	look down on ~을 얕보다	look up to ~을 존경하다
make use of ~을 이용하다	put off ~을 연기하다	run over ~을 치다
take care of ~을 돌보다	turn on ~을 켜다	turn off ~을 끄다

- We **put off** the plan. 우리는 그 계획을 연기했다.
  ⇒ The plan **was put off by** us. 그 계획은 우리에 의해 연기되었다.
- All his classmates **laughed at** him. 그의 반 친구들 모두 그를 비웃었다.
  ⇒ He **was laughed at by** all his classmates. 그는 반 친구들 모두에게 비웃음을 샀다.

Answers: p.09

Exercise 1 다음 문장을 수동태로 바꿔 쓰시오.

1 Jenny takes good care of my baby.
⇒ My baby ______________________ Jenny.

2 They have to finish the project by Friday.
⇒ The project ______________________ by Friday.

3 Someone took away my watch last night.
⇒ My watch ______________________ someone last night.

4 We make use of the Internet to sell our homemade cakes.
⇒ The Internet ______________________ to sell our homemade cakes.

5 My grandparents brought up my mother and five other siblings.
⇒ My mother and five other siblings ______________________ by my grandparents.

Exercise 2 다음 우리말과 같은 뜻이 되도록 〈보기〉의 단어를 이용하여 문장을 완성하시오.

put off　turn on　look up to　take care of

1 그는 주변 사람들로부터 존경받는다.
⇒ He ______________________ people around him.

2 그 가여운 아이들은 어느 착한 아주머니에 의해 돌봐졌다.
⇒ The poor kids ______________________ a nice lady.

3 텔레비전은 남동생에 의해 켜졌다.
⇒ The TV ______________________ my younger brother.

4 나의 비행이 궂은 날씨 탓에 연기되었다.
⇒ My flight ______________________ because of bad weather.

3-8 4형식의 수동태

4형식의 수동태

4형식(주어+동사+간접목적어+직접목적어)은 두 개의 목적어(간접목적어, 직접목적어)가 있고, 둘 다 수동태의 주어로 쓸 수 있다. 단, 직접목적어를 주어로 하여 수동태 문장을 만들 때는 간접목적어 앞에 전치사(to, for, of)를 쓴다.

· The Queen gave Snow White(간접목적어) a poisoned apple(직접목적어). 왕비는 백설공주에게 독이 든 사과를 주었다.

⇒ **Snow White** was given a poisoned apple by the Queen. (주어: 간접목적어)

⇒ **A poisoned apple** was given **to** Snow White by the Queen. (주어: 직접목적어)

간접목적어에 쓰이는 전치사

give, bring, show, send, lend, tell, teach ...	**to**
buy, make, get, cook ...	**for**
ask, inquire ...	**of**

· Jake lent me his car this morning. Jake는 오늘 아침 나에게 그의 차를 빌려주었다.

⇒ Jake's car was lent **to me** this morning.

· The interviewer asked me an interesting question. 면접관이 나에게 재미있는 질문을 했다.

⇒ An interesting question was asked **of me** by the interviewer.

· My fan made me a sweater. 팬이 나에게 스웨터를 만들어 주었다.

⇒ A sweater was made **for me** by my fan.

TIPs

buy, make, cook 등의 동사가 쓰인 문장의 수동태는 주로 직접목적어를 주어로 쓴다.

• Dad bought me a cute hairpin.
아빠가 나에게 예쁜 머리핀을 사주셨다.
→ **A cute hairpin** was bought for me by Dad. (o)
→ I was bought a cute hairpin by Dad. (x)

Answers: p.09

Exercise 1 다음 문장을 수동태로 바꿔 쓰시오.

1 Someone told me an interesting story.

⇒ I ______________________ by someone.

2 They served us hot tea with some snacks.

⇒ Hot tea with some snacks ______________________.

3 Her husband bought her the earrings.

⇒ The earrings ______________________ by her husband.

4 Gwen sent me these beautiful flowers.

⇒ These beautiful flowers ______________________ by Gwen.

5 One of my students wrote me this letter.

⇒ This letter ______________________ by one of my students.

6 My mom made us these cookies this morning.

⇒ These cookies ______________________ by my mom this morning.

3-9 5형식의 수동태

5형식의 수동태

5형식(주어+동사+목적어+목적격보어)은 목적어를 주어로 하여 수동태를 만든다. 이때 목적격보어는 그대로 뒤에 위치한다. 단, 목적격보어가 동사원형인 경우에는 앞에 to를 붙인다.

- They named their baby Emma. 그들은 아기의 이름을 Emma라고 지었다.
  ⇨ **Their baby** was named Emma (by them).
- His songs make me happy. 그의 노래는 나를 기쁘게 한다.
  ⇨ **I** am made happy by his songs.
- We saw a boy running after a car.
  우리는 한 남자아이가 차를 쫓아가는 것을 보았다.
  ⇨ **A boy** was seen running after a car (by us).
- My mother made me clean the bathroom.
  어머니가 나에게 욕실 청소를 시켰다.
  ⇨ **I** was made **to clean** the bathroom by my mother.

TIPs
5형식의 목적격보어를 주어로 하여 수동태를 만들 수 없다.
- Everyone calls him "Mr. Perfect."
  모두가 그를 '완벽한 남자'라고 부른다.
  → ~~Mr. Perfect~~ is called him by everyone. (x)

Answers: p.09

Exercise 1 다음 우리말과 같은 뜻이 되도록 주어진 말을 이용하여 문장을 완성하시오.

1 그는 우리에게 작은 거인이라 불린다. (call, Little Giant)
⇨ He ______________________ by us.

2 그 가수는 이 노래로 유명해지게 되었다. (make, famous)
⇨ The singer ______________________ by this song.

3 내가 다섯 살 때 어머니는 내게 피아노 강습을 받게 했다. (make, take piano lessons)
⇨ I ______________________ by my mom when I was five.

4 지난달에 우리는 중요한 프로젝트 때문에 계속 바빴다. (keep, busy)
⇨ We ______________________ by an important project last month.

Exercise 2 다음 문장을 수동태로 바꿔 쓰시오.

1 We saw Laura dancing with Jack at the party.
⇨ ______________________

2 Ms. Miller told us to keep on trying.
⇨ ______________________

3 I made my little brother run an errand.
⇨ ______________________

4 We elected Mr. Hanson chairman of the board.
⇨ ______________________

Review Test

[01-05] 다음 빈칸에 들어갈 알맞은 말을 고르시오.

01 The ring __________ my fiancée.

① bought for ② was bought for
③ was bought to ④ was given for
⑤ will give to

02 The old man __________ by his only son.

① looks after ② looked after
③ is looked after ④ is looking after
⑤ has looked after

03 What a poor dog! The dog __________ by a car yesterday.

① hit ② hits
③ is hit ④ was hit
⑤ will be hit

04 My car suddenly stopped while I was driving. It must __________ right now.

① check ② checked
③ be checked ④ is checked
⑤ be checking

05 Mom and Dad are pleased __________ my achievement.

① in ② on
③ to ④ with
⑤ around

[06-07] 다음 빈칸에 들어갈 말이 바르게 짝지어진 것을 고르시오.

06
• He was disappointed __________ the test results.
• The boy is looked down on __________ some mean kids.

① of – on ② with – by
③ to – for ④ at – with
⑤ for – in

07
• The arena is filled __________ loud cheers.
• My daughter is very interested __________ modern art.

① with – in ② to – of
③ in – for ④ for – in
⑤ with – of

[08-09] 다음 대화의 빈칸에 들어갈 알맞은 말을 고르시오.

08
A Mom, where's my favorite cap?
B It __________ in the washing machine.

① washes ② washed
③ is being washed ④ has washed
⑤ was washing

09
A Your painting is great. Did you paint it by yourself?
B Not really. I __________ by my sister.

① help ② helped
③ am helping ④ was helped
⑤ will be helped

[10-11] 다음 우리말을 영어로 바르게 옮긴 것을 고르시오.

10 그 스위트룸은 지금 청소되고 있습니까?

① Is the suite clean now?
② Is the suite cleaned now?
③ Has the suite been clean now?
④ Is the suite being cleaned now?
⑤ Has the suite been cleaned now?

11 콘택트렌즈는 체코의 한 화학자에 의해 발명되었다.

① Contact lenses invented a Czech chemist.
② Contact lenses invent by a Czech chemist.
③ A Czech chemist invented by contact lenses.
④ A Czech chemist was invented contact lenses.
⑤ Contact lenses were invented by a Czech chemist.

[12-13] 다음 중 어법상 어색한 것을 고르시오.

12 ① The rules must obey by everyone.
② The picture was painted by Picasso.
③ Many questions will be asked of you.
④ This song is sung by a Chinese singer.
⑤ This cozy sofa has been used for more than ten years.

13 ① The tickets are all sold out.
② The roof is covered with leaves.
③ My house should be painted again.
④ My works will be exhibited in the museum.
⑤ Does the building designed by Chris Norman?

[14-15] 다음 대화의 빈칸에 들어갈 알맞은 말을 고르시오.

14
A Your shirt looks great!
B Thanks. It ________________ fine cotton.

① makes of
② made from
③ is made of
④ is made for
⑤ is making from

15
A Let's go through the tunnel.
B We can't. The tunnel ________________ the heavy rain last month.

① destroyed by
② is destroyed of
③ was destroyed by
④ has been destroyed for
⑤ had been destroyed of

16 다음 중 문장 전환이 바르지 않은 것은?

① Did Brian sell the car?
⇒ Was the car sold to Brian?
② The landlord has to pay the bill.
⇒ The bill has to be paid by the landlord.
③ We should finish the work by tomorrow.
⇒ The work should be finished by tomorrow.
④ We can spend the money on anything.
⇒ The money can be spent on anything.
⑤ The young boy delivers newspapers.
⇒ Newspapers are delivered by the young boy.

[17-18] 다음 문장을 수동태로 바꿀 때 빈칸에 들어갈 말을 고르시오.

17

> They called off the trip to Italy.
> ⇒ The trip to Italy ______________.

① called off by them
② is called off by them
③ is called by them off
④ was called off by them
⑤ was called by them off

18

> I saw Betty talking to the principal today.
> ⇒ Betty ______________ today.

① saw talking to the principal
② is seen to talk to the principal
③ was seen talking to the principal
④ was seen to talk to the principal
⑤ was seen to talking to the principal

[19-22] 다음 문장을 수동태로 바르게 바꿔 쓴 것을 고르시오.

19

> Did Sue erase the scribble?

① Was the scribble erased Sue?
② Was the scribble erased by Sue?
③ Was Sue erased by the scribble?
④ Did the scribble be erased by Sue?
⑤ Did the scribble be erasing by Sue?

20

> James made me wait all day long.

① I made James waiting all day long.
② I was made wait all day long by James.
③ James made to wait all day long by me.
④ I was made to wait all day long by James.
⑤ I was made waiting all day long by James.

21

> Norah gave me the letter.

① I was given the letter to Norah.
② I was given the letter of Norah.
③ The letter is given to me by Norah.
④ The letter was given to me by Norah.
⑤ The letter was given for me by Norah.

22

> We will move the furniture into the hall.

① The furniture will moved into the hall by us.
② The furniture will be moved into the hall by us.
③ The furniture will be moving into the hall by us.
④ The furniture is being moved into the hall by us.
⑤ The furniture is going to move into the hall by us.

[23-24] 다음 빈칸에 공통으로 들어갈 말을 고르시오.

23

> • Downtown is always crowded ______________ people and traffic.
> • The closet is filled ______________ old books.

① to　② with
③ of　④ at
⑤ in

24

> • I was surprised ______________ the size of the ship.
> • Jason was laughed ______________ by his co-workers for wearing a ridiculous hat.

① to　② with
③ of　④ at
⑤ in

[25-27] 다음 우리말과 같은 뜻이 되도록 주어진 단어를 이용하여 문장을 완성하시오.

25 캐나다에서는 영어와 불어가 모두 사용된다. (speak)

⇨ Both English and French ________ ________ in Canada.

26 별들은 밤에 길을 찾는 데 사용될 수 있다. (use)

⇨ The stars can ________ ________ to navigate at night.

27 이 방은 파티가 시작되기 전에 장식되어야 한다. (decorate)

⇨ The room has to ________ ________ before the party starts.

[28-30] 다음 문장을 수동태로 바꿀 때 빈칸에 알맞은 말을 쓰시오.

28 The waitress brought Fred a wrong dish.

⇨ A wrong dish ________ ________ ________ Fred by the waitress.

29 My father bought me a smartphone.

⇨ A smartphone ________ ________ ________ me by my father.

30 I gave him two tickets to the concert.

⇨ Two tickets to the concert ________ ________ ________ him by me.

[31-32] 다음 중 어법상 어색한 부분을 바르게 고쳐 쓰시오.

31 A lot of questions were asked for him during the interview.

⇨ ________________

32 These bottles are filled in freshly squeezed orange juice.

⇨ ________________

[33-34] 다음 우리말과 같은 뜻이 되도록 주어진 말을 알맞게 배열하여 문장을 완성하시오.

33 그 컴퓨터는 현재 수리되고 있는 중이다.

⇨ ________________

(repaired, the computer, being, is)

34 우리 부모님은 내 성적에 만족하셨다.

⇨ ________________

(my parents, satisfied, were, my grades, with)

[35-36] 다음 문장을 수동태 문장으로 바꿔 쓰시오.

35 Dad made me mow the lawn.

⇨ ________________

36 The earthquake damaged some buildings in the city.

⇨ ________________

보너스 유형별 문제

Answers: p.11

[1-3] 다음 교칙을 읽고, 의미가 통하도록 주어진 단어를 이용하여 문장을 완성하시오. 서술형

조건 1. 수동태를 사용할 것

School Rules

· Do not run in the hallways.

· Be respectful at all times.

· Help each other.

· Play safely.

1 · Share your equipment with others.

2 · Follow teachers' directions.

3 · Do not use smartphones in class.

1 Your equipment ______________________________. (should)

2 Teachers' directions ______________________________ by students. (must)

3 Smartphones ______________________________ in class. (shouldn't)

4 다음 글의 밑줄 친 부분 중, 어법상 틀린 것은? 수능 대비형

This is a wonderful single family home in a nice area of Sycamore complete ① with 4 bedrooms, 3 baths, hardwood floors, and a fireplace in the main living room. The kitchen was ② update 1 year ago and features a new oven, range, and dishwasher. It's ③ located on a quiet street with newer homes. The location is ④ close to schools, shops, and transportation. No open house is scheduled but a private showing can ⑤ be requested.

* locate: 두다, 설치하다
** open house: 주택 공개 (행사)
*** request: 요청[요구]하다

Chapter 4

부정사

4-1 to부정사의 명사적 쓰임 : 주어 역할
4-2 to부정사의 명사적 쓰임 : 보어 역할
4-3 to부정사의 명사적 쓰임 : 목적어 역할
4-4 의문사+to부정사
4-5 to부정사의 형용사적 쓰임
4-6 to부정사의 부사적 쓰임
4-7 to부정사의 부정
4-8 to부정사의 의미상 주어
4-9 to부정사의 관용 표현
4-10 원형부정사 I
4-11 원형부정사 II
Review Test
보너스 유형별 문제

4-1 to부정사의 명사적 쓰임: 주어 역할

to부정사: 「to+동사원형」의 형태로 문장에서 명사, 형용사, 부사의 역할을 한다.

to부정사의 명사적 쓰임

문장에서 주어, 보어, 목적어의 역할을 하며 '~하는 것', '~하기'로 해석한다.

주어 역할

- **To be** a good dancer is difficult. 좋은 댄서가 되는 것은 어렵다.
- **To learn** another foreign language is my plan for this year.
  또 다른 외국어를 배우는 것이 나의 올해 계획이다.

> **TIPs** to부정사가 주어로 쓰이는 경우에는 to부정사를 단수 취급해 단수동사가 온다.
> - To watch horror movies is not easy for me.
>   공포영화를 보는 것은 내게 쉽지 않다.

가주어와 진주어

to부정사가 이끄는 구가 주어로 오는 경우, to부정사 주어를 문장 뒤로 보내고 그 자리에 it을 쓴다.
이때 it은 의미가 없는 주어로 '가주어'라고 하며, 뒤로 보내진 to부정사구가 실질적인 주어로 '진주어'라고 한다.

- **To make** a good friend is not easy. 좋은 친구를 사귀는 것은 쉽지 않다.
  ⇒ **It**(가주어) is not easy **to make** a good friend(진주어).
- **To run** in the hallway can be dangerous. 복도에서 뛰는 것은 위험할 수 있다.
  ⇒ **It**(가주어) can be dangerous **to run** in the hallway(진주어).
- **To say** no to ice cream is hard. 아이스크림을 거부하는 것은 어렵다.
  ⇒ **It**(가주어) is hard **to say** no to ice cream(진주어).

Answers: p.11

Exercise 1 다음 문장에서 to부정사를 찾아 밑줄을 치시오.

1 To see is to believe.

2 I hope to see you soon.

3 Thanks to you, I now have less work to do.

4 Do you want me to get you something to eat?

5 I'm so happy to hear that you are going to a good college.

6 I decided to take a break and went to Boston to see my brother.

Exercise 2 다음 괄호 안에서 알맞은 것을 고르시오.

1 To travel to other countries (is / are) a lot of fun.

2 It is dangerous (swim / to swim) in the deep sea.

3 It is difficult (understand / to understand) his speech.

4 (To become / To becomes) a good scientist is his dream.

5 (That / It) was exciting to watch the fireworks over the river.

Exercise 3 다음 〈보기〉와 같이 문장을 바꿔 쓰시오.

> To play the piano is always fun.
> ⇒ It is always fun to play the piano.

1 To watch TV too much is not good.
⇒ ______________________________

2 To keep your promises is important.
⇒ ______________________________

3 To learn new languages is interesting.
⇒ ______________________________

4 To wash fruits and vegetables is necessary.
⇒ ______________________________

5 To bully weak people is not good behavior.
⇒ ______________________________

6 To take a risk and try something new is not easy.
⇒ ______________________________

7 To use visual aids in your presentation is very helpful.
⇒ ______________________________

Exercise 4 다음 우리말과 같은 뜻이 되도록 주어진 말을 이용하여 문장을 완성하시오.

1 새로운 어떤 것을 발명하는 것은 쉽지 않다. (invent, new, something)
⇒ ______________________________ is not easy.

2 정시에 그곳에 도착하는 것은 불가능하다. (impossible, there, arrive)
⇒ It is ______________________________ on time.

3 일주일 안에 그 일을 끝마치기는 어렵다. (finish, the work, difficult)
⇒ It is ______________________________ in a week.

4 해안을 따라 운전하는 것은 항상 즐겁다. (pleasant, drive)
⇒ It is always ______________________________ along the seaside.

5 적이 누군지 아는 것이 승리를 위한 첫걸음이다. (know, enemy, your)
⇒ ______________________________ is the first step to achieving victory.

4-2 to부정사의 명사적 쓰임: 보어 역할

보어 역할

❶ 주격보어 : 「주어+동사+주격보어」 어순의 문장에서 주어를 보충 설명한다.

- His dream is **to win** a Nobel Prize. 그의 꿈은 노벨상을 타는 것이다.
- Anna's birthday wish is **to get** good grades in all subjects.
  Anna의 생일 소원은 모든 과목에서 좋은 성적을 받는 것이다.

❷ 목적격보어 : 「주어+동사+목적어+목적격보어」 어순의 문장에서 목적어를 보충 설명한다.

- I want you **to deliver** this note to Mr. Jackman.
  나는 네가 이 메모를 Jackman 씨에게 전달해주길 원한다.
- Mom asked me **to do** the dishes before she left.
  엄마가 나가시기 전에 나에게 설거지를 해달라고 하셨어요.

TIPs
to부정사를 목적격보어로 쓰는 동사
want, tell, need, ask, order, allow, expect, would like …

Answers: p.11

Exercise 1 다음 〈보기〉의 단어를 이용하여 문장을 완성하시오.

water visit get lose share

1 My plan is ______________ ten pounds this month.
2 I told you ______________ the food with your brother.
3 My birthday wish this year is ______________ a puppy.
4 Mom wants me ______________ the plants in our garden.
5 Jeremy's plan for this weekend is ______________ his grandmother.

Exercise 2 다음 우리말과 같은 뜻이 되도록 주어진 말을 알맞게 배열하여 문장을 완성하시오.

1 그의 일은 편지와 소포를 구분하는 것이다. (letters, to, and, parcels, sort out)
⇨ His job is ______________________________.

2 당신은 제가 라디오를 끄기를 원하시나요? (turn off, me, to, want)
⇨ Do you ______________________________ the radio?

3 나는 네가 내 친구 Emily를 만났으면 한다. (meet, would like, you, to)
⇨ I ______________________________ my friend, Emily.

4 나는 아들에게 고양이를 씻기라고 부탁했다. (my son, asked, the cat, bathe, to)
⇨ I ______________________________.

5 Michael은 나에게 자신의 아이들을 돌봐달라고 부탁했다. (me, to, asked, take care of)
⇨ Michael ______________________________ his children.

6 Peterson 선생님은 내가 화장실에 가는 것을 허락하지 않으셨다. (to, to me, the bathroom, allow, go)
⇨ Mr. Peterson didn't ______________________________.

4-3 to부정사의 명사적 쓰임: 목적어 역할

목적어 역할

- I really want **to go** to Paris. 나는 정말 파리에 가기를 원한다.
- Sam decided **to tell** his father the truth. Sam은 아버지에게 사실을 말하기로 결심했다.
- My sister and I agreed **to share** the room. 여동생과 나는 방을 나눠 쓰기로 동의했다.

to부정사를 목적어로 취하는 동사

want	would like	need	choose	hope	plan
decide	learn	expect	agree	refuse	promise …

TIPs 동사에 따라 to부정사만을 목적어로 취하거나, 혹은 동명사만을 목적어로 취하는 경우가 있으니 유의한다.

Answers: p.12

Exercise 1 다음 〈보기〉의 단어를 이용하여 문장을 완성하시오.

move　　have　　think through　　speak　　look

1 I would like ____________ something to eat.
2 She decided ____________ to another city for college.
3 Both my sister and I want to learn ____________ Spanish.
4 Everyone needs ____________ at the bright side of things.
5 We need ____________ all the options and make our decision.

Exercise 2 다음 우리말과 같은 뜻이 되도록 주어진 말을 이용하여 문장을 완성하시오.

1 그는 자신의 새 사업으로 성공하길 바란다. (succeed, hope)
⇒ He ____________ in his new business.

2 우리는 Gemma의 파티에 가려고 계획하고 있다. (plan, go)
⇒ We are ____________ to Gemma's party.

3 그는 Klein 씨를 만나서 도움을 구할 필요가 있다. (meet, need)
⇒ He ____________ Mr. Klein and ask him for help.

4 위원회는 정기회의를 취소하기로 합의했다. (agree, cancel)
⇒ The board ____________ the regular meeting.

5 나는 그녀와 친구가 되어 그녀에 대해서 더 많이 알고 싶다. (be friends, want)
⇒ I ____________ with her and know more about her.

6 그들은 커서 어려움을 극복하는 것을 배울 것이다. (learn, overcome)
⇒ They will ____________ difficulties when they grow up.

7 우리는 먼저 스페인으로 가서 사흘을 지내기로 결정했다. (decide, go)
⇒ We ____________ to Spain first and stay there for three days.

4-4 의문사+to부정사

의문사+to부정사

문장에서 명사처럼 쓰여 주어, 보어, 목적어 역할을 한다.

how+to부정사 어떻게 ~하는지	Can you tell me **how to get** to City Hall? 시청에 어떻게 가는지 말씀해 주실 수 있나요?
what+to부정사 무엇을 ~할지	I don't know **what to do** for her. 나는 그녀를 위해 무엇을 해야 할지 모르겠다.
where+to부정사 어디를 ~할지	Please let us know **where to go**. 우리가 어디로 갈지 알려주세요.
when+to부정사 언제 ~할지	I'm not sure **when to feed** the puppies. 나는 그 강아지들에게 언제 먹이를 줘야 할지 잘 모르겠다.
who(m)+to부정사 누구를 ~할지	They've decided **who to hire**. 그들은 누구를 고용할지 결정했다.
which+to부정사 어느 것을 ~할지	I'm still considering **which to choose** between the two. 나는 아직도 그 둘 중 어느 것을 선택할지 생각 중이다.

TIPs 「why+to부정사」는 쓰지 않는다.

Answers: p.12

Exercise 1 다음 우리말과 같은 뜻이 되도록 주어진 말을 이용하여 문장을 완성하시오.

1 나는 아직도 누구를 뽑아야 할지 잘 모르겠다. (vote for)
⇒ I still don't know ______________________.

2 언제 들려야 하는지 저에게 알려주세요. (stop by)
⇒ Please let me know ______________________.

3 나는 그녀에게 무슨 말을 해야 할지 몰랐다. (say)
⇒ I had no idea ______________________ to her.

4 우리는 어디에서 묵을지 아직 정하지 못했다. (stay)
⇒ We haven't decided ______________________ yet.

5 이 기계를 어떻게 켜는지 나에게 말해줄 수 있니? (turn on)
⇒ Can you tell me ______________________ this machine?

Exercise 2 다음 〈보기〉에서 알맞은 단어를 골라 의문사를 이용하여 문장을 완성하시오.

do	speak	play	bake	wear

1 Mom taught me ______________________ a cake.

2 Please let me know ______________________ next.

3 We are learning ______________________ Japanese.

4 Could you show me ______________________ the guitar?

5 I'm not sure ______________________ for this Halloween.

4-5 to부정사의 형용사적 쓰임

to부정사의 형용사적 쓰임

'~하는', '~할'이라는 의미로, 앞에 있는 명사를 수식하는 형용사 역할을 한다.

❶ 「명사+to부정사」

- I have many things **to do.** 나는 해야 할 많은 일이 있다.
- Can you get me something **to drink**? 내게 마실 것을 가져다줄 수 있니?
- Susan bought a beautiful dress **to wear** to the party.
  Susan은 파티에서 입을 아름다운 드레스를 샀다.

❷ 「명사+to부정사+전치사」

수식을 받는 명사가 전치사의 목적어일 경우 전치사를 to부정사 뒤에 쓴다.

- I need somebody **to talk to.** 나는 이야기할 누군가가 필요하다.
  talk someone (×) / talk **to** someone (o)
- The elderly man wants a chair **to sit on.** 그 노인은 앉을 의자를 원한다.
  sit a chair (×) / sit **on** a chair (o)

> **TIPs**
> something, anyone 등과 같이 '-**thing**', '-**one**', '-**body**'로 끝나는 대명사는 형용사가 뒤에서 수식하여 「-thing/-one/-body + 형용사+ to부정사」의 어순이 된다.
> • **She wants something spicy to eat.**
> 그녀는 매운 어떤 것을 먹길 원한다.

Answers: p.12

Exercise 1 다음 괄호 안에서 알맞은 것을 고르시오.

1 I need some paper (to write / to write on).

2 I would like some bread (to eat / to eat with).

3 He has lots of friends (to play / to play with).

4 I am hungry. Do you have anything (eat / to eat)?

5 Mr. Kim has five kids (to take care / to take care of).

6 Amy bought a book (for read / to read) on the plane.

7 It's really cold outside. You need (something thicker / thicker something) to wear.

Exercise 2 다음 밑줄 친 부분을 바르게 고쳐 쓰시오.

1 Please give me a pen to write. ⇨ ____________

2 It's to say goodbye time already. ⇨ ____________

3 Have you found a house to live? ⇨ ____________

4 I would like hot something to drink. ⇨ ____________

5 Do you have interesting anything to share? ⇨ ____________

6 I bought a black suit wearing to the wedding. ⇨ ____________

7 There's nothing for eat or drink in the refrigerator. ⇨ ____________

8 I want to take a rest. Please give me a chair to sit. ⇨ ____________

Exercise 3 다음 우리말과 같은 뜻이 되도록 〈보기〉의 단어를 이용하여 문장을 완성하시오.

do	talk	live	read	sleep	visit

1 너는 베고 잘 베개가 필요하니?
⇨ Do you need a pillow ________________?

2 우리는 작고, 아늑한 살 집을 원한다.
⇨ We want a small, cozy house ________________.

3 서울에는 가볼 만한 장소가 많다.
⇨ There are many places ________________ in Seoul.

4 그녀는 외로울 때 이야기할 친구가 없다.
⇨ She has no friends ________________ when she feels lonely.

5 Kelly는 심심할 때 읽을 잡지를 샀다.
⇨ Kelly bought a magazine ________________ when she's bored.

6 그들은 쉬는 시간 동안 할 재미있는 무언가를 찾고 있다.
⇨ They are looking for something interesting ________________ during the recess.

Exercise 4 다음 우리말과 같은 뜻이 되도록 주어진 말을 알맞게 배열하여 문장을 완성하시오.

1 마무리하고 집에 갈 시간이다. (wrap up, home, and, to, time, go)
⇨ It's ________________________________.

2 우리는 논의해야 할 두어 가지 문제가 있다. (talk, things, a couple of, about, to)
⇨ We have ________________________________.

3 그 소년은 갖고 놀 새 장난감을 받았다. (play, toy, to, a, with, new)
⇨ The boy got ________________________________.

4 당신은 내 집에 들를 시간이 있나요? (drop by, to, my house, time)
⇨ Do you have ________________________________?

5 누구나 믿고 의지할 친구가 필요하다. (rely on, a friend, to, trust, and)
⇨ Everyone needs ________________________________.

6 우리는 죽기 전에 해야 할 일들이 많다. (things, do, to, many)
⇨ We have ________________________________ before we die.

7 나는 여동생의 생일 선물로 줄 예쁜 무언가를 사야 한다. (pretty, my sister, give, to, something)
⇨ I should buy ________________________________ as a birthday gift.

4-6 to부정사의 부사적 쓰임

to부정사의 부사적 쓰임

to부정사가 부사처럼 동사나 형용사, 또는 부사를 수식하여 목적, 원인, 판단의 근거, 결과 등을 나타낸다.

❶ 목적: '~하기 위해서'

- Jacob went to a bookstore **to buy** some books.
  Jacob은 책을 몇 권 사려고 서점에 갔다.
- I left home early **to have** a cup of coffee before the meeting.
  나는 회의 전에 커피 한 잔 마시기 위해 일찍 집에서 나왔다.

❷ 감정의 원인: '~해서', '~하게 되어서'

- Nice **to meet** you. 만나서 반갑습니다.
- I'm sorry **to hear** that. 그런 이야기를 듣게 되어 유감입니다.

❸ 판단의 근거: '~하는 것을 보니', '~하다니'

- David was brave **to chase away** the thieves. David가 도둑들을 쫓아내다니 용감했구나.
- He must be a nice person **to say** that. 그렇게 말하다니 그는 좋은 사람임이 틀림없다.

❹ 결과: '~해서 …하다'

- He grew up **to be** a talented swimmer. 그는 자라서 재능 있는 수영선수가 되었다.
- Hannah worked hard only **to fail.** Hannah는 열심히 일했으나 결국 실패하고 말았다.

❺ 형용사 수식: '~하기에'

- His theory is difficult **to understand.** 그의 이론은 이해하기 어렵다.
  = It is difficult **to understand** his theory.
- Those words are not easy **to translate** into Korean. 저 단어들은 한국어로 번역하기 쉽지 않다.
  = It is not easy **to translate** those words into Korean.

TIPs
목적을 나타내는 to부정사의 부사적 용법은 **in order to**로 바꿔 쓸 수 있다.
- I came here to meet her.
  = I came here **in order to** meet her.
  나는 그녀를 만나기 위해 이곳에 왔다.

Answers: p.12

Exercise 1 다음 우리말과 같은 뜻이 되도록 〈보기〉의 단어를 이용하여 문장을 완성하시오.

eat	do	keep	be	see

1 다시 뵙게 되어 매우 기쁩니다.
⇒ I'm so happy ______________________ you again.

2 나는 그 비밀을 지키기 위해서 거짓말을 해야만 했다.
⇒ I had to tell a lie ______________________ the secret.

3 너는 이 음식이 먹기 안전하다고 생각하니?
⇒ Do you think this food is safe ______________________?

4 그런 일을 하다니 그는 이기적임이 분명하다.
⇒ He must be selfish ______________________ such things.

5 미운 오리 새끼는 자라서 백조가 되었다.
⇒ The ugly duckling grew up ______________________ a swan.

Exercise 2 다음 문장을 밑줄 친 부분에 유의하여 우리말로 해석하시오.

1 I got up early to catch the train.

⇨ ______________________________

2 I was surprised to hear the news.

⇨ ______________________________

3 Emily grew up to be a good teacher.

⇨ ______________________________

4 You're so kind to help the small boy.

⇨ ______________________________

5 Chuck must be kind to help the poor.

⇨ ______________________________

6 They were excited to watch the game.

⇨ ______________________________

Exercise 3 다음 우리말과 같은 뜻이 되도록 주어진 말을 이용하여 문장을 완성하시오.

1 내가 그의 말을 믿다니 어리석었다. (stupid, believe, what he said)

⇨ I was ______________________________.

2 William은 상을 받게 되어서 아주 기뻤다. (pleased, win, the prize)

⇨ William was ______________________________.

3 그런 것을 생각해 내다니 너는 정말 독창적이구나. (creative, think of, such a thing,)

⇨ You are so ______________________________.

4 이 기계는 사용하기 어렵다. (difficult, use)

⇨ This machine is ______________________________.

5 나는 호주에서 오신 조부모님을 만나게 되어 기뻤다. (happy, meet, my grandparents)

⇨ I was ______________________________ from Australia.

6 우리 할머니는 100세가 되도록 사셨다. (be, one hundred, years, old)

⇨ My grandmother lived ______________________________.

7 그녀는 책을 빌리기 위해 도서관에 갔다. (check out, a book)

⇨ She went to the library ______________________________.

8 Stella는 James를 몇 주 동안 못 본 체하는 것을 보니 그에게 화난 것이 분명하다. (ignore, him, for weeks)

⇨ Stella must be upset with James ______________________________.

4-7 to부정사의 부정

to부정사의 부정

to부정사의 부정형은 「not/never+to+동사원형」의 형태이다.

- She told us **not to go** out tonight. 그녀는 우리에게 오늘 밤 나가지 말라고 했다.
- Be careful **not to touch** the wall. 벽을 건드리지 않도록 조심해라.
- I know what **not to wear** to work. 나는 일하러 갈 때 무엇을 입지 않아야 하는지 알고 있다.

일반부정과 to부정사 부정에는 의미 차이가 있으므로 유의한다.

- I told her **not to meet** him again. 나는 그녀에게 그를 다시는 만나지 말라고 말했다.
- I **didn't** tell her to meet him again. 나는 그녀에게 그를 다시 만나라고 말하지 않았다.

Answers: p.12

Exercise 1 다음 우리말과 같은 뜻이 되도록 〈보기〉의 단어를 이용하여 문장을 완성하시오.

go out　　be　　miss　　tell　　touch

1 어머니는 우리에게 밤늦게 밖에 나가지 말라고 말하셨다.
⇒ Mom told us ______________ late at night.

2 우리는 그 비행을 놓치지 않아서 기뻤다.
⇒ We were pleased ______________ the flight.

3 그녀가 Becky에게 진실을 말하지 않은 것은 현명했다.
⇒ She was wise ______________ Becky the truth.

4 예약시간에 늦지 않도록 유의해라.
⇒ Be careful ______________ late for your reservation.

5 나는 누나에게 다시는 내 물건을 만지지 말라고 말했다.
⇒ I told my sister ______________ my stuff again.

Exercise 2 다음 우리말과 같은 뜻이 되도록 주어진 말을 알맞게 배열하여 문장을 완성하시오.

1 나는 항상 남에게 피해를 주지 않으려고 한다. (trouble, others, not, to)
⇒ I always try ______________.

2 우리는 음악회에 가지 않기로 결정했다. (go, to, not, the concert, to)
⇒ We decided ______________.

3 손으로 눈을 비비지 않도록 주의하세요. (rub, your hands, with, your eyes, to, not)
⇒ Be cautious ______________.

4 네가 그 영화를 본다면 웃지 않는 것은 불가능하다. (not, laugh, to)
⇒ It is impossible ______________ if you see the movie.

4-8 to부정사의 의미상 주어

to부정사의 의미상 주어

to부정사의 행위자를 나타내는 의미상의 주어는 「for/of+행위자」의 형태로 to부정사 앞에 쓴다.

❶ 「for+행위자(목적격)」: difficult, easy, hard, possible 등 일반 형용사

- It was hard **for me to believe** what he said. 나는 그의 말을 믿기 어려웠다.
- Is it really impossible **for Gary to be** in my class? Gary가 우리 반에 오는 것은 정말 불가능한가요?

❷ 「of+행위자(목적격)」: 사람의 성격이나 특성을 나타내는 형용사

kind	nice	wise	smart	polite	generous
silly	foolish	stupid	wrong	selfish	rude …

- It is nice **of you to help** the poor boy.
  그 불쌍한 남자아이를 돕다니 너는 착하구나.
- It was stupid **of me to behave** like that.
  그렇게 행동하다니 나는 어리석었다.

TIPs
to부정사의 의미상 주어가 일반적인 사람을 나타내거나, 문장의 주어나 목적어와 일치할 때 의미상 주어는 따로 쓰지 않는다.
- It's dangerous **to swim** in a deep river. (의미상의 주어 – 일반인)
- She wants **to talk** to you. (she가 talk하는 주체 – 주어와 일치)

Answers: p.13

Exercise 1 다음 괄호 안에서 알맞은 것을 고르시오.

1 It is very nice (for you / of you) to say so.

2 The test will be difficult for (he / him) to pass.

3 It's time (for us / for our) to celebrate our victory.

4 The song won't be hard (for him / of him) to sing.

5 It is hard (to put for me / for me to put) that into words.

6 It's not easy (for children / of children) to express their feelings.

7 It was generous (for you / of you) to take time out of your busy schedule.

Exercise 2 다음 우리말과 같은 뜻이 되도록 주어진 말을 이용하여 문장을 완성하시오.

1 그녀를 돌봐주다니 당신은 좋은 사람입니다. (nice, take care of)
⇨ It is very ______________________________ her.

2 우리가 그렇게 행동한 것은 매우 어리석었다. (stupid, behave)
⇨ It was so ______________________________ like that.

3 네가 더 이상 걷는 것은 불가능해 보인다. (impossible, walk)
⇨ It seems ______________________________ any further.

4 이 화려한 집은 우리가 사기에는 비싸다. (expensive, buy)
⇨ This fancy house is ______________________________.

5 그 질문들은 내가 대답하기에 곤란했다. (difficult, answer)
⇨ The questions were so ______________________________.

4-9 to부정사의 관용 표현

「too+형용사/부사+to부정사」

'너무 ~해서 …할 수 없다'라는 의미로, 「so+형용사/부사+that+주어+can't[couldn't] …」로 바꿔 쓸 수 있다.

- These books are **too heavy to carry** by myself. 이 책들은 너무 무거워서 혼자 들 수 없다.
  = These books are **so heavy that I can't carry** them by myself.
- This movie is **too violent** for children **to watch**. 이 영화는 너무 폭력적이어서 아이들은 볼 수 없다.
  = This movie is **so violent that children can't watch** it.

「형용사/부사+enough+to부정사」

'~할 만큼 충분히 …하다'라는 의미로, 「so+형용사/부사+that+주어+can[could] …」로 바꿔 쓸 수 있다.

- This shirt is **big enough to fit** a giant. 이 셔츠는 거인에게도 맞을 만큼 충분히 크다.
  = This shirt is **so big that it can fit** a giant.
- You are **smart enough to understand** what I mean. 너는 내가 무슨 말을 하는지 알아들을 만큼 충분히 똑똑하다.
  = You are **so smart that you can understand** what I mean.

Answers: p.13

Exercise 1 다음 두 문장이 같은 뜻이 되도록 빈칸에 알맞은 말을 쓰시오.

1 I was so tired that I couldn't move an inch.
⇒ I was ______________________.

2 This soup is so spicy that you can't eat it.
⇒ This soup is ______________________.

3 Mr. Jefferson is rich enough to buy a plane.
⇒ Mr. Jefferson is ______________________.

4 Jack is so smart that he can handle it by himself.
⇒ Jack is ______________________ by himself.

Exercise 2 다음 우리말과 같은 뜻이 되도록 주어진 말을 알맞게 배열하여 문장을 완성하시오.

1 그녀는 하버드대에 갈 만큼 충분히 똑똑하다. (enough, to, get into, smart, Harvard)
⇒ She is ______________________.

2 이 상자는 저 책들을 담을 만큼 충분히 견고해 보인다. (those, to, sturdy, enough, books, hold)
⇒ This box looks ______________________.

3 그는 너무 어려서 상황을 이해할 수 없었다. (understand, too, to, young)
⇒ He was ______________________ the situation.

4 이 책은 너무 지루해서 나는 더 이상 읽을 수가 없다. (boring, for, me, to, read, too)
⇒ This book is ______________________ any longer.

4-10 원형부정사 I

원형부정사
'to가 없는 부정사'로 동사원형을 말하며 「주어+동사+목적어+목적격보어」 어순의 5형식에서 사용된다.

「지각동사+목적어+원형부정사」
feel, see, watch, hear, listen 등의 지각동사와 쓰여 '(목적어가) ~하는 것을 느끼다/보다/듣다'라는 의미로 해석한다.

- We watched Kelly **swim** in the river. 우리는 Kelly가 강에서 수영을 하는 것을 보았다.
- I heard Michael **play** the cello. 나는 Michael이 첼로를 연주하는 것을 들었다.
- She felt somebody **touch** her shoulder. 그녀는 누군가가 자신의 어깨를 만지는 것을 느꼈다.

지각동사의 목적격보어로 분사를 사용하는 경우

❶ 진행되는 순간을 강조할 때: 현재분사

- I saw him **cross** the street. (원형부정사: 동작의 시작부터 끝까지 지켜본 경우)
  나는 그가 길을 건너는 것을 보았다.
- I saw him **crossing** the street. (현재분사: 진행되는 동작에 초점을 맞춘 경우)
  나는 그가 길을 건너고 있는 것을 보았다.

❷ 목적어와 목적격보어의 관계가 수동일 때: 과거분사

- I heard somebody **call** my name. (원형부정사: 누군가가 내 이름을 부르는 것-능동)
  나는 누군가가 내 이름을 부르는 것을 들었다.
- I heard my name **called**. (과거분사: 내 이름이 불리는 것-수동)
  나는 내 이름이 불리는 것을 들었다.

Answers: p.13

Exercise 1 다음 괄호 안에서 알맞은 것을 모두 고르시오.

1 I felt the breeze (touch / to touch / touched) my face.

2 She saw the box (carry / to carry / carried) by two men.

3 We watched the sun (rise / rising / risen) over the mountain.

4 They felt the ground (shook / shake / shaking) when the building collapsed.

5 I heard someone (scream / to scream / screamed) in the middle of the night.

Exercise 2 다음 우리말과 같은 뜻이 되도록 주어진 말을 알맞게 배열하여 문장을 완성하시오.

1 나는 그가 문에 서 있는 것을 보았다. (him, standing, saw, I, at the door)
⇨ ____________________

2 Dylan은 자신의 심장이 빠르게 뛰는 것을 느꼈다. (Dylan, his heart, fast, felt, beating)
⇨ ____________________

3 우리는 구급차가 오는 소리를 들었다. (the ambulance, heard, coming, we)
⇨ ____________________

4 나는 집이 흔들리는 것을 느꼈고 창문이 덜거덕거리는 소리를 들었다.
(I, the house, shake, and, rattle, the windows, felt, heard)
⇨ ____________________

4-11 원형부정사 II

「사역동사+목적어+원형부정사」

make, let, have 등의 사역동사와 쓰여 '(목적어가) ~하도록 시키다'라는 의미로 해석한다.

- She had me **close** my eyes. 그녀는 나의 눈을 감게 하였다.
- The news will make her **smile**. 그 소식이 그녀를 웃게 할 것이다.
- My dad doesn't let me **dye** my hair. 우리 아빠는 내가 염색하지 못하게 하신다.

사역의 의미이지만, 목적격보어로 to부정사나 과거분사를 사용하는 경우

❶ 「get+목적어+to부정사」: (목적어에게) ~하도록 시키다
- I'll get him **to clean** up his room. 나는 그에게 방을 청소하라고 시킬 것이다.

❷ 「help+목적어+to부정사/원형부정사」: (목적어가) ~하는 것을 돕다
- Anne helped me (**to**) **do** my work. Anne은 내가 일하는 것을 도와주었다.

❸ 「have+목적어(대상)+과거분사(상태)」: 목적어와 목적격보어의 관계가 수동일 때
- He had his car **washed**. 그는 자신의 자동차를 세차했다. (그는 자신의 자동차가 세차되도록 했다.)

TIPs

원형부정사의 관용표현
- 「**had better**+원형부정사」: ~하는 것이 더 낫다
  You **had better go** to sleep now.
  너는 지금 잠을 자는 것이 낫겠다.
- 「**cannot but**+원형부정사」: ~하지 않을 수 없다
  I **could not but tell** him a lie.
  그에게 거짓말을 하지 않을 수 없었다.
- 「**would rather**+원형부정사」: 차라리 ~하고 싶다
  I'd rather quit the job.
  나는 차라리 일을 그만두고 싶다.

Exercise 1 다음 괄호 안에서 알맞은 것을 모두 고르시오.

Answers: p.13

1 You'd better (leave / to leave / leaving) early today.
2 I let my children (paint / painted / painting) on the wall.
3 My grandmother had her car (to steal / stealing / stolen).
4 He helped me (pass / to pass / passing) the entrance exam.

Exercise 2 다음 문장에서 어법상 어색한 부분을 찾아 바르게 고치시오.

1 I had my son made his bed. ⇨ ________
2 Rachel helped me finding my dog. ⇨ ________
3 Let me to introduce you to James. ⇨ ________
4 He made her working until late at night. ⇨ ________

Exercise 3 다음 우리말과 같은 뜻이 되도록 주어진 말을 알맞게 배열하여 문장을 완성하시오.

1 Bobby는 이발을 했다. (cut, had, his, hair)
⇨ Bobby ________.

2 우리 엄마는 내가 식탁을 차리게 했다. (set, made, the table, me)
⇨ My mom ________.

3 그녀는 그의 사과를 받아들이지 않을 수 없었다. (could, accept, apology, but, not, his)
⇨ She ________.

4 때때로 내 남자친구는 웃긴 농담으로 나를 웃게 한다. (me, with, laugh, funny jokes, makes)
⇨ Sometimes, my boyfriend ________.

Review Test

[01-04] 다음 빈칸에 알맞은 말을 고르시오.

01 He went to Canada ________ his old friend.

① visit ② visited
③ to visit ④ visiting
⑤ visits

02 It's kind ________ you to help the elderly.

① of ② for
③ to ④ in
⑤ off

03 The boy hurried ________ be late for school.

① in order to ② where to
③ how to ④ not to
⑤ to

04 I saw my neighbor ________ his fence.

① to paint ② paint
③ painted ④ to painting
⑤ have painted

05 다음 밑줄 친 부분과 바꿔 쓸 수 있는 것은?

We are here in the auditorium <u>to</u> have choir practice.

① for ② of
③ with ④ in order to
⑤ due to

[06-07] 다음 빈칸에 들어갈 수 <u>없는</u> 것을 고르시오.

06 I ________ to read two books a week.

① decided ② planned
③ hoped ④ wanted
⑤ made

07 He ________ me clean the dirty floor.

① helped ② made
③ had ④ let
⑤ ordered

08 다음 대화의 빈칸에 들어갈 알맞은 말은?

A Do you know ________ to turn on this machine?
B Just press the red button.

① how ② why
③ where ④ what
⑤ who

09 다음 대화의 빈칸에 들어갈 말이 바르게 짝지어진 것은?

A I broke the window. I don't know ________ to do.
B I think it would be right ________ you to tell the teacher about it.

① what – of
② how – to
③ what – for
④ how – of
⑤ what – to

[10-12] 다음 밑줄 친 to부정사 중 쓰임이 다른 하나를 고르시오.

10 ① I have many things to buy.
② She wants something to drink.
③ Randy has many friends to help him.
④ They came here to meet you.
⑤ I need a book to read.

11 ① To see is to believe.
② I like to travel by train.
③ It is a lot of fun to play tennis.
④ I want something cold to drink.
⑤ My hope is to go abroad and study art.

12 ① I'm happy to meet you.
② You must be so smart to solve the puzzle.
③ You need to take a rest for a while.
④ I went to Africa to travel around.
⑤ He is lucky to meet someone like you.

[13-14] 다음 두 문장이 같은 뜻이 되도록 빈칸에 알맞은 말을 고르시오.

13
Jeff is so tall that he can reach the ceiling.
= Jeff is tall __________ to reach the ceiling.

① too ② not
③ enough ④ so as
⑤ in order

14
To tell a lie is not acceptable.
= __________ is not acceptable to tell a lie.

① It ② This
③ That ④ He
⑤ She

[15-16] 다음 중 어법상 어색한 문장을 고르시오.

15 ① I need a chair to sit on.
② I have a friend to rely on.
③ I have an essay to write on.
④ I have many friends to play with.
⑤ I bought something to write with.

16 ① She got the boy to cut the flowers.
② She let her son read a comic book.
③ I felt something crawled up my back.
④ To take care of children is difficult for me.
⑤ I'm sorry to hear that Jenny broke her leg.

[17-18] 다음 우리말과 같은 뜻이 되도록 빈칸에 알맞은 말을 고르시오.

17
우리는 살기 아늑한 집을 찾고 있다.
= We are looking for __________________.

① a house cozy to live
② a house cozy to live in
③ a cozy house to live
④ a cozy house to live in
⑤ a cozy house living in

18
나는 이번 경기에 참가하지 않기로 결심했다.
= I __________________ this match.

① decided not to take part in
② decided to not take part in
③ decided to take part not in
④ didn't decide to take part in
⑤ haven't decided to take part in

19 다음 문장과 의미가 같은 것은?

The boy is too young to read books.

① The boy is not young, so he reads books.
② The boy is so young that he can read books.
③ The boy is very young, so he can read books.
④ The boy is so young that he can't read books.
⑤ The boy is not young, he doesn't read books.

[20-21] 다음 빈칸에 들어갈 말이 바르게 짝지어진 것을 고르시오.

20

• It was selfish ___________ her to ask you to stay longer.
• Gwen is skillful ___________ to win the competition.

① for – so
② to – that
③ of – enough
④ for – enough
⑤ of – that

21

• We'd like to have the gift ___________, please.
• I had him ___________ this watch.

① wrap – fix
② wrap – fixing
③ wrapped – fix
④ wrapped – fixed
⑤ wrapped – fixing

[22-23] 다음 문장의 밑줄 친 부분과 쓰임이 같은 것을 고르시오.

22

There are many sights to see here.

① I have a lot of things to do.
② It is fun to learn a foreign language.
③ He must be stupid to speak like that.
④ She's practicing hard to win the race.
⑤ He is clever enough to solve the problem.

23

We decided to throw a surprise party for her.

① I'm sorry to hear that.
② I like to read before I go to bed.
③ I have a lot of homework to do.
④ Keith opened the fridge to get some eggs.
⑤ She is not a person to break her promises.

[24-25] 다음 우리말을 영어로 바르게 옮긴 것을 고르시오.

24

나는 Phil이 선생님과 이야기하는 것을 보았다.

① I saw Phil talks with his teacher.
② I saw Phil talked with his teacher.
③ I saw Phil to talk with his teacher.
④ I saw Phil talking with his teacher.
⑤ I saw Phil to have talked with his teacher.

25

그는 이번 주말에 특별히 할 일이 없다.

① He has special nothing to do this weekend.
② He has nothing special to do this weekend.
③ He has special nothing doing this weekend.
④ He has nothing special doing this weekend.
⑤ He doesn't have nothing special to do this weekend.

[26-27] 다음 주어진 문장과 같은 뜻이 되도록 빈칸에 알맞은 말을 쓰시오.

26 To learn hip-hop dance is fun.

⇨ It is fun ________ ________ hip–hop dance.

27 I was so tired that I couldn't do the laundry yesterday.

⇨ I was ________ tired ________ do the laundry yesterday.

28 다음 두 문장을 한 문장으로 만들 때 빈칸에 알맞은 말을 쓰시오.

Mother Teresa went to India. She wanted to help poor people.

⇨ Mother Teresa went to India ________ ________ poor people.

[29-31] 다음 우리말과 같은 뜻이 되도록 주어진 말을 알맞게 배열하여 문장을 완성하시오.

29 아빠는 나에게 수영하는 법을 가르쳐 주었다.

⇨ My dad taught me ________________.
(swim, to, how)

30 Gerald 씨는 우리에게 시끄럽게 하지 말라고 말씀하셨다.

⇨ Mr. Gerald ________________ so much noise. (us, to, make, not, told)

31 많은 부모님들은 그들의 자녀들이 TV를 보지 못하게 한다.

⇨ Many parents don't ________________ TV. (their, watch, children, let)

[32-34] 다음 우리말과 같은 뜻이 되도록 문장을 완성하시오.

32 나는 그녀에게 무슨 말을 해야 할지 몰랐다.

⇨ I didn't know ________________ to her.

33 그 작은 소년은 자라서 위대한 학자가 되었다.

⇨ The little boy grew up ________________ a great scholar.

34 나는 뒤에서 내 이름이 불리는 것을 들었다.

⇨ I heard my name ________________ behind me.

[35-36] 다음 문장 중 어법상 어색한 부분을 찾아 바르게 고쳐 쓰시오.

35 I want to be a singer, but my parents want me becoming a teacher.

⇨ ________________________________

36 I have had my windows to break many times.

⇨ ________________________________

[37-38] 다음 문장을 〈보기〉와 같이 바꿔 쓰시오.

보기 | To have a true friend is a blessing.
⇨ It is a blessing to have a true friend.

37 To send a package by air is expensive.

⇨ ________________________________

38 To keep a journal would be helpful for you.

⇨ ________________________________

보너스 유형별 문제

Answers: p.15

[1-4] 현장학습 유인물을 읽고, 밑줄 친 우리말을 영작하시오. 서술형

Field Trip to Seoraksan National Park

Students are to go to Seoraksan National Park.

When to go: October 11th, Friday

1 가는 장소: Seoraksan National Park

2 가는 방법: By school bus

Don't forget:

- To bring **3** 먹을 것

- To wear a warm jacket, a hat, and hiking boots

* Students must be careful **4** 늦지 않도록 for the school bus.

1 ______________________

2 ______________________

3 ______________________

4 ______________________

5 다음 글의 밑줄 친 부분 중, 어법상 틀린 것은? 수능 대비형

City officials in Clarksville are trying to decide what ① build next. Some people want a new park for their children. ② Others would like a new health center. Residents on the north side of town ③ want a new grocery store, but many young people ④ are asking for a movie theater. The city took a poll ⑤ to see which choice is most popular. The results show there are slightly more supporters for the grocery store than the health center.

* official: 관계자
** resident: 주민

Chapter 5

동명사

5-1 동명사의 역할 I

5-2 동명사의 역할 II

5-3 동명사와 to부정사 I

5-4 동명사와 to부정사 II

5-5 동명사의 관용 표현

Review Test

보너스 유형별 문제

5-1 동명사의 역할 I

동명사

「동사원형+ing」의 형태로 동사의 성질을 그대로 가지고 있으면서 명사와 같이 주어, 목적어, 보어의 역할을 한다.

동명사의 주어 역할

- **Reading** a newspaper is a good way to start a day. 신문을 읽는 것은 하루를 시작하는 좋은 방법이다.
- **Listening** to old music makes me sad. 오래된 음악을 듣는 것은 나를 슬프게 만든다.

동명사의 보어 역할

- My worst habit is **biting** my nails. 내 최악의 습관은 손톱을 물어뜯는 것이다.
- One of his hobbies is **inventing** something interesting.
  그의 취미 중 하나는 재미있는 무언가를 발명하는 것이다.

TIPs
동명사(구)가 문장의 주어로 쓰일 때 동명사(구)는 단수 취급해 단수동사가 온다.
- Reading books is one of my hobbies.
  독서는 내 취미 중 하나이다.

Answers: p.15

Exercise 1 다음 〈보기〉에서 알맞은 동사를 골라 동명사로 문장을 완성하시오.

fly　eat　keep　learn　help

1 ______________ fast food might make you fat.

2 ______________ to drive is easier than I thought.

3 ______________ a diary is helpful for your English.

4 One of my brother's hobbies is ______________ a kite.

5 My job is ______________ people from other countries.

Exercise 2 다음 우리말과 같은 뜻이 되도록 주어진 말을 알맞게 배열하여 문장을 완성하시오.

1 삼촌의 직업은 중고차를 파는 것이다. (uncle's, selling, job, my, is, used, cars)

⇨ ______________________________

2 음악을 크게 듣는 것은 귀에 나쁘다. (loud, your, for, bad, is, listening, ears, to, music)

⇨ ______________________________

3 글을 쓰기 전에 브레인스토밍을 하는 것은 도움이 될 것이다.
(writing, will, brainstorming, helpful, be, before)

⇨ ______________________________

4 나의 건강한 습관은 매일 아침 사과를 먹는 것이다.
(an apple, morning, having, is, every, healthy, my, habit)

⇨ ______________________________

5 Nicole의 취미는 다양한 나라의 엽서를 모으는 것이다.
(postcards, hobby, different, from, Nicole's, countries, collecting, is)

⇨ ______________________________

5-2 동명사의 역할 II

동명사의 목적어 역할

❶ 동사의 목적어

동명사를 목적어로 취하는 동사
enjoy, mind, finish, avoid, give up, keep, quit, stop, suggest ...

- I enjoy **sunbathing** on the beach. 나는 해변에서 일광욕하는 것을 즐긴다.
- Do you mind **opening** the window? 창문을 열어도 괜찮겠습니까?

❷ 전치사의 목적어

- I am afraid of **speaking** in public. 나는 대중 앞에서 말하는 것을 두려워한다.
- That actor is famous for **being** rich. 저 배우는 부유한 것으로 유명하다.

동명사의 부정

동명사의 부정형은 「not/never+동명사」의 형태이다.

- I'm sorry for **not coming** back sooner. 더 빨리 오지 못해 죄송합니다.
- She has a habit of **not knocking** when entering a room.
그녀는 방을 들어올 때 노크를 하지 않는 습관이 있다.

Answers: p.15

Exercise 1 다음 괄호 안에서 알맞은 것을 고르시오.

1 I love (go hiking / going hiking) with my father.

2 Tom is interested in (doing / to do) experiments.

3 Cathy is afraid of (being / to be) left alone at home.

4 My father gave up (smoking / to smoke) a few years ago.

5 I enjoy (getting not up / not getting up) early on Sundays.

6 My brother and I like (watch / watching) movies on Friday nights.

Exercise 2 다음 주어진 동사를 이용하여 문장을 완성하시오.

1 Do you mind ________________ the window? (close)

2 She is thinking about ________________ her job. (change)

3 Dan says he enjoys ________________ science fiction. (read)

4 One of my bad habits is ________________ breakfast. (not, eat)

5 Let's stop ________________, and start doing something. (talk)

6 Are you interested in ________________ something new? (learn)

7 The boys are excited about ________________ a new classmate. (have)

8 If he keeps ________________ late for work, he's going to get fired! (be)

Exercise 3 다음 〈보기〉의 단어를 이용하여 문장을 완성하시오.

turn off	say	write	invite	make	break

1 I finished ____________ the essay yesterday.

2 Nancy left us without ____________ goodbye.

3 Sam is responsible for ____________ the window.

4 Would you mind ____________ the air conditioning?

5 I'm worried about ____________ dinner for ten people.

6 Thank you for ____________ me to your wonderful party.

Exercise 4 다음 문장에서 어법상 어색한 부분을 찾아 바르게 고치시오.

1 Never give up follow your dream. ⇨ ____________

2 She keeps talking not to her parents. ⇨ ____________

3 We are so excited about meet your family. ⇨ ____________

4 I'm sorry not for coming to your wedding. ⇨ ____________

5 Have you already finished eat your breakfast? ⇨ ____________

6 Are you tired of to do the same thing every day? ⇨ ____________

Exercise 5 다음 우리말과 같은 뜻이 되도록 주어진 말을 알맞게 배열하여 문장을 완성하시오.

1 Jason은 우리를 웃기는 것을 잘한다. (is good at, us, laugh, making, Jason)

⇨ ____________

2 우리의 초대에 응해주셔서 감사합니다. (accepting, thank, for, our, invitation, you)

⇨ ____________

3 커튼을 쳐도 괜찮겠습니까? (pulling back, you, would, mind, the curtains)

⇨ ____________

4 때때로 나는 아무것도 하지 않는 것을 즐긴다. (anything, not, enjoy, doing, sometimes, I)

⇨ ____________

5 나의 어머니와 나는 공포 영화 보는 것을 기피한다. (avoid, watching, my mom, horror movies, I, and)

⇨ ____________

5-3 동명사와 to부정사 I

동명사 vs. to부정사

동사에 따라 동명사만을 목적어로 취하거나, to부정사만을 목적어로 취하는 경우가 있다.

동명사를 목적어로 취하는 동사	to부정사를 목적어로 취하는 동사
enjoy, mind, stop, finish, avoid, deny, quit, delay, keep, suggest, practice, give up, put off ...	want, ask, hope, expect, decide, plan, promise, choose, need, learn, refuse, agree, determine ...

- Do you mind **answering** a few questions? 몇 가지 질문에 답변 좀 해 주시겠습니까?
- The baby stopped **crying**. 아기는 우는 것을 멈췄다.
- I'm thirsty. I want **to drink** something cold. 목이 마르다. 차가운 것을 마시길 원해.
- I hope **to meet** you soon. 곧 당신을 만나기를 원합니다.

Answers: p.16

Exercise 1 다음 괄호 안에서 알맞은 것을 고르시오.

1 I decided (to quit / quitting) the job.

2 Kelly denied (having / to have) said like that.

3 The man gave up (to climb / climbing) Mt. Everest.

4 I have avoided (to meet / meeting) her since last week.

Exercise 2 다음 주어진 단어를 이용해 문장을 완성하시오.

1 Mark determined ________________ early. (leave)

2 She doesn't want ________________ anywhere else. (go)

3 Have you finished ________________ that newspaper? (read)

4 My grandmother keeps ________________ about her childhood. (talk)

Exercise 3 다음 우리말과 같은 뜻이 되도록 주어진 말을 이용하여 문장을 완성하시오.

1 나는 정말 집안일 하는 것을 꺼리지 않는다. (mind, do)

⇒ I really ______________________________ the housework.

2 그녀는 평생 나의 동반자가 되기를 약속했다. (promise, be)

⇒ She ______________________________ my partner for life.

3 Mike는 이번에 시험에 합격하기를 바란다. (hope, pass)

⇒ Mike ______________________________ the exam this time.

4 Robert는 2년 전에 미식축구 하는 것을 포기했다. (give up, play)

⇒ Robert ______________________________ football two years ago.

5-4 동명사와 to부정사 II

동명사와 to부정사를 목적어로 취하는 동사

몇몇 동사는 동명사와 to부정사를 모두 목적어로 취할 수 있고 무엇을 취하든지 의미 차이가 없다.

like	love	hate	start	begin	continue …

- I like **playing** soccer. 나는 축구 하는 것을 좋아한다.
  = I like **to play** soccer.
- Anne continued **working** after her retirement. Anne은 은퇴 후에도 일을 계속했다.
  = Anne continued **to work** after her retirement.

동명사와 to부정사를 목적어로 취하지만, 의미 차이가 있는 동사

❶ remember+동명사: ~한 것을 기억하다
remember+to부정사: ~할 것을 기억하다
- I **remember meeting** her at the party. 나는 파티에서 그녀를 만났던 것을 기억한다.
- I **remembered to meet** her after school. 나는 방과 후에 그녀를 만나기로 한 것을 기억했다.

❷ forget+동명사: ~한 것을 잊다
forget+to부정사: ~할 것을 잊다
- I **forgot sending** the letter to him. 나는 그에게 편지를 보냈던 것을 잊어버렸다.
- I **forgot to send** the letter to him. 나는 그에게 편지를 보내야 하는 것을 잊어버렸다.

❸ try+동명사: 시험 삼아 ~해보다
try+to부정사: ~하려고 애쓰다
- We **tried baking** a cake for the first time.
  우리는 처음으로 케이크를 만들어 보았다.
- I always **try to be** honest. 나는 항상 정직하려고 노력한다.

TIPs
stop은 동명사만을 목적어로 취하며, stop뒤에 to부정사가 쓰인 경우는 동사의 목적어가 아닌 문장의 부사(to부정사의 부사적 쓰임- 목적)로 쓰인 경우이다.
- The dog stopped **running.**
  그 개는 뛰는 것을 멈췄다.
- We stopped **to look** for the bank.
  우리는 은행을 찾기 위해 멈췄다.

Answers: p.16

Exercise 1 다음 괄호 안에서 알맞은 것을 모두 고르시오.

1 They all refused (to do / doing) the job.
2 Out of the blue, it began (to rain / raining).
3 The car suddenly started (to move / moving).
4 I would like (to go / going) to the movies tonight.
5 Don't forget (to lock / locking) the door when you leave.
6 I tried (to calm / calming) the crying baby, but I couldn't.
7 I remember (to meet / meeting) her at Will's party last week.
8 Don't forget (to pick up / picking up) the laundry after school.
9 They stopped (to play / playing) baseball when it rained heavily.
10 She quit (to work / working) with him because of his lack of responsibility.

Exercise 2 다음 <보기>와 같이 두 문장이 같은 뜻이 되도록 빈칸에 알맞은 말을 쓰시오.

> You have to turn off the computer before you leave.
> ⇨ Remember to turn off the computer before you leave.

1 I had to buy some milk on my way home, but I forgot.
⇨ I forgot ____________ some milk on my way home.

2 I remember Jake. I met him at summer camp.
⇨ I remember ____________ Jake at summer camp.

3 My sister was a dancer, but she quit because of her weak ankles.
⇨ My sister stopped ____________ because of her weak ankles.

Exercise 3 다음 우리말과 같은 뜻이 되도록 <보기>의 단어를 이용하여 문장을 완성하시오.

> read turn off put on complain

1 그만 투덜대고 그냥 넘어가라.
⇨ Please stop ____________ and move on.

2 나는 지난여름에 그 기사를 읽었던 기억이 난다.
⇨ I remember ____________ the article last summer.

3 그는 그 우스운 핼러윈 의상을 입어보았다.
⇨ He tried ____________ the funny Halloween costume.

4 나는 영화 시작 전에 휴대전화를 끄는 것을 잊었다.
⇨ I forgot ____________ my cell phone before the movie started.

Exercise 4 다음 우리말과 같은 뜻이 되도록 주어진 단어를 이용하여 문장을 완성하시오.

1 그 남자는 나에게 말을 걸기 위해 멈췄다. (stop, talk)
⇨ The man ________________________.

2 당신은 건강을 위해 금주하는 게 좋겠다. (drink, health)
⇨ You'd better ________________________.

3 나는 식물에 물을 준 것을 잊고 또 주었다. (water, the plants)
⇨ I ________________________, and I did it again.

4 내일 오전 9시에 나에게 전화해야 한다는 것을 기억해. (call)
⇨ Please ________________________ at 9 a.m. tomorrow.

5-5 동명사의 관용 표현

- go -ing: ~하러 가다
  - They **go skiing** every winter. 그들은 매년 겨울에 스키 타러 간다.
  - We're **going shopping** for clothes. 우리는 옷을 사러 가고 있다.
- how/what about -ing: ~하는 것이 어때?
  - **How [What] about having** lunch with me today? 오늘 나와 점심 먹는 게 어때?
- feel like -ing: ~하고 싶다
  - I **feel like having** a cup of coffee now. 나는 지금 커피 한 잔 마시고 싶다.
- be busy -ing: ~하느라 바쁘다
  - I **am busy doing** my task. 나는 내 업무를 하느라 바쁘다.
- spend+시간/돈+-ing: ~하는 데 …을 소비하다
  - Tony **spent some money buying** the cake. Tony는 케이크를 사는 데 돈을 좀 썼다.
- cannot help -ing: ~하지 않을 수 없다
  - I **cannot help loving** her. 나는 그녀를 사랑하지 않을 수 없다.
- be used to -ing: ~에 익숙하다
  - I **am used to living** alone. 나는 혼자 사는 것에 익숙하다.
- look forward to -ing: ~을 고대하다
  - He is **looking forward to having** a new car. 그는 새 차를 가지는 것을 고대하고 있다.
- It is no use -ing: ~해도 소용없다
  - **It is no use crying** over spilt milk. 쏟아진 우유 때문에 울어봤자 소용없다.
- be worth -ing: ~할 만한 가치가 있다
  - This book **is worth reading**. 이 책은 읽을 만한 가치가 있다.
- have difficulty/trouble/a hard time -ing: ~하는 데 어려움을 겪다
  - I **had difficulty fixing** the computer. 나는 컴퓨터를 고치는 데 어려움을 겪었다.

TIPs

「go+-ing」형태의 관용 표현:
go shopping: 쇼핑하러 가다
go hiking: 하이킹하러 가다
go fishing: 낚시하러 가다
go skiing: 스키 타러 가다
go walking: 산책하러 가다
go swimming: 수영하러 가다
go camping: 캠핑하러 가다
go climbing: 등산하러 가다

TIPs

「How/What about+-ing」와 바꿔 쓸 수 있는 표현
- Shall we ~?: '우리 ~할까요?'
- Why don't we ~?: '우리 ~게 어때?'
- Let's+동사원형: '~하자'

Answers: p.16

Exercise 1 다음 괄호 안에서 알맞은 것을 고르시오.

1 Sam and I go (to hike / hiking) every Sunday.

2 I am now used to (wear / wearing) a uniform.

3 I don't feel like (to eat / eating) breakfast today.

4 I cannot help (to feel / feeling) sympathy for him.

5 My brother is looking forward (to go / to going) to New York.

6 Jennifer had a hard time (to take / taking) care of the children.

Exercise 2 다음 주어진 동사를 이용하여 문장을 완성하시오.

1 The researcher is busy ________________ her project. (complete)

2 I couldn't help ________________ when I saw him. (laugh)

3 It is no use ________________ about things before they happen. (worry)

4 Mrs. Green looks forward to ________________ her grandson. (meet)

Exercise 3 다음 우리말과 같은 뜻이 되도록 <보기>의 단어를 이용하여 문장을 완성하시오.

use	start	look after	work	try	camp

1 그는 매일 밤 그의 아이를 돌보는 일에 익숙하다.

⇒ He ________________ his baby every night.

2 우리는 미래에 당신과 함께 일하기를 기대하고 있습니다.

⇒ We ________________ with you in the future.

3 나의 부모님은 새로운 사업을 시작하느라 바쁘시다.

⇒ My parents ________________ a new business.

4 내 낡은 컴퓨터는 팔려고 노력할 만한 가치가 있을까?

⇒ Is it ________________ to sell my old computer?

5 우리는 매년 여름 한라산으로 캠핑을 간다.

⇒ We ________________ on Mt. Halla every summer.

6 장애인들은 대중교통을 이용하는 데 여전히 어려움을 겪는다.

⇒ People with disabilities still ________________ public transportation.

Exercise 4 다음 문장을 밑줄 친 부분에 유의하여 해석하시오.

1 I feel like eating spicy food now.

⇒ ________________

2 I couldn't help opening the red box.

⇒ ________________

3 We are used to getting up early every morning.

⇒ ________________

4 Don't spend your precious time playing video games.

⇒ ________________

Review Test

[01-04] 다음 빈칸에 들어갈 알맞은 말을 고르시오.

01 Thank you for ____________ me here.

① invite ② being invited
③ inviting ④ to invite
⑤ invited

02 I go ____________ every year. I love winter sports.

① snowboarding ② skiied
③ to curling ④ ice hockey
⑤ ice skate

03 After he finished ____________ the show, he turned off the TV and went to bed.

① watch ② to watch
③ watching ④ watched
⑤ watches

04 It's no ____________ regretting what you did.

① like ② help
③ worth ④ but
⑤ use

[05-07] 다음 빈칸에 들어갈 수 없는 것을 고르시오.

05 He ____________ writing a letter in English.

① enjoyed ② stopped
③ gave up ④ minded
⑤ wanted

06 I ____________ to buy a new car.

① wanted ② decided
③ would like ④ hoped
⑤ avoided

07 Don't ____________ doing your homework.

① give up ② stop
③ put off ④ delay
⑤ expect

[08-09] 다음 빈칸에 들어갈 말이 바르게 짝지어진 것을 고르시오.

08
- He stopped ____________ for health reasons.
- He stopped ____________ some books at the bookstore.

① smoking – buying
② smoke – to buy
③ smoking – to buy
④ to smoke – to buy
⑤ to smoke – buying

09
- It's raining. I forgot ____________ my umbrella.
- Do you remember ____________ into her at the mall last month?

① bringing – running
② to bring – to run
③ to bring – running
④ bringing – to run
⑤ bring – run

10 다음 빈칸에 공통으로 들어갈 말은?

> • The rain __________ to fall through the weekend.
> • He __________ working until the age of 70.

① continued ② stopped
③ quit ④ finished
⑤ delayed

11 다음 대화의 빈칸에 들어갈 알맞은 말은?

> A I'm so excited. We're going to the beach today!
> B Oh, no. I completely forgot __________ my bathing suit.

① bring ② bringing
③ to bring ④ brought
⑤ be brought

[12-13] 다음 밑줄 친 부분을 바르게 고친 것을 고르시오.

12

> He is tired of do the same old job. So he is thinking about quit.

① to do – to quit
② to do – quitting
③ doing – quitting
④ doing – to quit
⑤ to doing - to quitting

13

> I had difficulty buy a train ticket in Beijing because I couldn't speak Chinese. I'm learning speak Chinese these days.

① to buy – to speak
② to buy – speaking
③ buying – speaking
④ buying – to speak
⑤ to buying – to speaking

[14-16] 다음 우리말을 영어로 바르게 옮긴 것을 고르시오.

14

> 나는 항상 사람들에게 친절하려고 애쓴다.

① I always try be kind to others.
② I always try and am kind to others.
③ I always try being kind to others.
④ I always try to be kind to others.
⑤ I always try to being kind to others.

15

> 당신의 편지에 답장하지 못해 미안합니다.

① I am not sorry for replying to your letter.
② I am sorry not for replying to your letter.
③ I am sorry for not replying to your letter.
④ I am sorry for replying not to your letter.
⑤ I am sorry for replying to your letter not.

16

> 우리는 역에 앉아 하루 종일 시간을 보냈다

① We spent all day to sit at the station.
② We spent all day sitting at the station.
③ We spent all day and sat at the station.
④ We spent all day to sitting at the station.
⑤ We were used to spending all day sitting at the station.

17 다음 두 문장의 의미가 서로 다른 것을 고르시오.

① I forgot calling him today.
= I forgot to call him today.
② I love hanging out with them.
= I love to hang out with them.
③ She hates doing the dishes.
= She hates to do the dishes.
④ When do we begin working together?
= When do we begin to work together?
⑤ The players started practicing yesterday.
= The players started to practice yesterday.

[18-19] 다음 밑줄 친 부분 중 쓰임이 다른 하나를 고르시오.

18 ① I'm having breakfast now.
② I enjoy swimming in the sea.
③ Being honest is the best idea.
④ I like reading books about space.
⑤ I look forward to going to Toronto in Canada.

19 ① Sue's hobby is making unique jewelry.
② They were doing house chores at that time.
③ Love is giving not taking.
④ Her job was teaching children at the kindergarten.
⑤ His biggest mistake was leaving the door unlocked.

[20-21] 다음 중 어법상 어색한 문장을 고르시오.

20 ① I hate being late for something.
② I hope you don't mind inviting her.
③ Once in a while, I go shopping with my dad.
④ She had difficulty to understand his words.
⑤ He is interested in learning foreign languages.

21 ① I'm not used to wearing glasses.
② I'm tired of hearing your excuses.
③ I am afraid of walking alone at night.
④ He suggested to take her to the park.
⑤ Ron decided to give up working as a security guard.

[22-23] 다음 중 어법상 바른 문장을 고르시오.

22 ① I feel like to listen to music.
② She cannot help to love her husband.
③ Sunny had a hard time to master Japanese.
④ I'm worried about running out of money.
⑤ They like to eating fast food for lunch.

23 ① I'm used to living alone in a big apartment.
② He is looking forward to hear from you soon.
③ She tried to avoid to meet her ex–boyfriend.
④ My parents go fishing with me every Sunday.
⑤ Collecting paper dolls were one of my daughter's hobbies.

24 다음 ① ~ ⑤ 중 어법상 어색한 것은?

① Watching movies ② is one of my favorite hobbies. So I spend most of my free time ③ watching movies during weekends. Last weekend, I saw the movie *Shine*. It was rather old, but it was worth ④ watching. The soundtrack is also great. These days, I keep ⑤ to listen to it.

[25-26] 다음 문장에서 어법상 어색한 부분을 찾아 바르게 고치시오.

25 They gave up to chase the thieves.

⇨ ______________________

26 The girls want learning French.

⇨ ______________________

[27-30] 다음 우리말과 같은 뜻이 되도록 〈보기〉에서 알맞은 동사를 골라 문장을 완성하시오. (주어진 단어의 동명사나 to부정사를 쓸 것)

보기	promise think drive take

27 그것에 대해 미리 생각하는 것은 소용없다.

⇨ It's ______________ about it in advance.

28 나는 그에게 그 연극에서 한 역할을 주기로 약속한 것을 기억한다.

⇨ I ______________ him a role in the play.

29 우리 저녁을 먹은 후에 산책을 하는 게 어때?

⇨ ______________ a walk after dinner?

30 Tim은 저 고급 차를 한 번 운전해 보기를 원한다.

⇨ Tim wants to ______________ that fancy car.

31 다음 대화의 밑줄 친 부분을 바르게 고쳐 쓰시오.

A I'm so bored these days. I feel like ① to do something interesting.
B Why don't we go ② ski this weekend?
A That's a good idea. Oh, by the way, I need ③ buying a new pair of ski boots.

① : ______________
② : ______________
③ : ______________

[32-33] 다음 주어진 글과 같은 뜻이 되도록 빈칸에 알맞은 말을 쓰시오.

32 Neil Armstrong is famous because he is the first man to walk on the moon.

⇨ Neil Armstrong is famous for ______________ the first man to walk on the moon.

33 I remember her. I helped her stand up when she fell down on the street.

⇨ I remember ______________ her stand up when she fell down on the street.

[34-36] 다음 우리말과 같은 뜻이 되도록 주어진 말을 알맞게 배열하여 문장을 완성하시오.

34 내 최악의 버릇은 충분한 물을 마시지 않는 것이다.

⇨ My worst habit is ______________.
(enough, drinking, water, not)

35 심호흡을 하는 것은 너의 기분을 나아지게 하는 데 도움이 될 것이다.

⇨ ______________ you feel better.
(deep, will, a, help, breath, taking)

36 우리는 다음 주에 텍사스에 계시는 삼촌을 방문하는 것을 고대하고 있다.

⇨ ______________ our uncle in Texas next week.
(are, forward, visiting, to, we, looking)

보너스 유형별 문제

Answers: p.18

[1-2] 다음 대화를 읽고, 물음에 답하시오. 서술형

A My smartphone keeps ⓐ freeze. I don't know how ⓑ fix it.

B (A) 앱들을 업그레이드 해봐.

A I already did, but it didn't help.

B Then, how about ⓒ ask Felix for help? He is very good at ⓓ repair electronic devices.

A Felix? He is busy ⓔ study for the midterm exam these days.

B Then, let's just take it to the service center.

1 윗글의 ⓐ~ⓔ를 어법에 맞게 고쳐 쓰시오.

ⓐ ________________ ⓑ ________________

ⓒ ________________ ⓓ ________________

ⓔ ________________

2 밑줄 친 (A)를 주어진 말을 이용하여 영작하시오. (update, your apps)

→ ________________________________

3 다음 글의 밑줄 친 부분 중, 어법상 틀린 것은? 수능 대비형

Just two blocks from my office is a little diner called "Joe's Burger." I go there a couple of times a week at lunch or after work ① because it is close and the prices are reasonable. It's not all good, though. The diner ② doesn't have a wide variety of food choices, only burgers, salads, and some beverages. When I don't feel like ③ to have a burger, I have to find someplace else ④ to eat. It's also somewhat small and the service is rather slow. At lunch when there are many customers, the waiting line for a table is quite long. I wish they had a bigger space. It's a 24-hour place, so I can always come here however late I get off work. But the restaurant also has no parking lot so I ⑤ have to walk back to my office building for my car.

* diner: 작은 식당
** reasonable: 적당한, 타당한
*** beverage: 음료

Chapter
6

분사

6-1 분사
6-2 명사를 수식하는 분사
6-3 동사의 활용에 쓰이는 분사
6-4 감정을 나타내는 분사
6-5 현재분사와 동명사
6-6 분사구문
Review Test
보너스 유형별 문제

6-1 분사

분사

동사의 원래 의미를 가지고 있으면서 형용사로 명사를 수식하거나, 보어로 주어나 목적어를 보충 설명하는 역할을 한다. 분사에는 현재분사와 과거분사가 있다.

현재분사와 과거분사의 형태와 역할

현재분사		과거분사	
「동사원형+-ing」		「동사원형+-(e)d」 또는 불규칙 형태	
능동 (~하는)	**shocking** news 놀라운 소식 The movie is **boring.** 그 영화는 지루하다.	수동 (~되어진)	a **shocked** person 놀란 사람 People are **bored.** 사람들이 지루해한다.
진행 (~하고 있는)	**boiling** water 끓고 있는 물 They are **building** a bridge. 그들은 다리를 세우고 있다.	완료 (~된)	**boiled** soup 끓여진 국 They have **built** a bridge. 그들은 다리를 세웠다.

Answers: p.18

Exercise 1 다음 괄호 안에서 알맞은 것을 고르시오.

1 Jacob bought a (using / used) car.

2 Look at the (smiling / smiled) baby.

3 Your grandfather is (standing / stood) over there.

4 The director has (making / made) more than 20 films.

Exercise 2 다음 그림을 보고 주어진 동사를 알맞은 형태로 바꿔 문장을 완성하시오.

❶ 

❹ 

❺ 

❻ 

1 The room has been ________________! (clean)

2 The basket is full of ________________ leaves. (fall)

3 Look at the cat ________________ on the sofa. (sleep)

4 Oh my god! The house is ________________ down. (burn)

5 Be careful with the ________________ glass on the floor. (break)

6 The blue car ________________ in the garage is my aunt's. (park)

6-2 명사를 수식하는 분사

분사의 명사 수식

단독으로 쓰인 분사는 명사 앞에서, 수식어구와 함께 쓰인 분사는 명사 뒤에서 수식한다.

현재분사의 명사 수식

- I feel sorry for the **crying** child. 나는 울고 있는 아이가 가엾게 느껴진다.
- Look at the baby **sleeping** in her arms. 그녀의 품에서 자고 있는 아이를 보아라.

과거분사의 명사 수식

- We all have **hidden** talents. 우리 모두는 숨은 재능을 가지고 있다.
- I fixed the bike **broken** by my son. 나는 아들이 고장 낸 자전거를 고쳤다.

Answers: p.18

Exercise 1 다음 괄호 안에서 알맞은 것을 고르시오.

1 This is a picture of a(n) (flying airplane / airplane flying).

2 We can't eat the fish (catching / caught) in this river.

3 There were already (falling / fallen) leaves on the street.

4 (The girl standing / The standing girl) behind Mike is my sister.

5 The (stolen diamond ring / diamond ring stolen) has not yet been found.

Exercise 2 다음 그림을 보고 주어진 동사를 알맞은 형태로 바꿔 문장을 완성하시오.

❶ 

❷ 

❸ 

❹ 

❺ 

❻ 

1 We watered the ________________ tree. (die)

2 ________________ bread usually tastes bitter. (burn)

3 The door ________________ in green is locked with a padlock. (paint)

4 The boy ________________ on the lawn has hurt his leg. (cry)

5 What does the sign ________________ in Japanese say? (write)

6 The old lady ________________ in the armchair is my grandmother. (sit)

Exercise 3 다음 우리말과 같은 뜻이 되도록 〈보기〉의 단어를 이용하여 문장을 완성하시오.

build	speak	lose	stand	hide	sleep

1 멕시코에서 사용되는 언어는 스페인어다.
⇨ The language ____________ in Mexico is Spanish.

2 Ashley는 조심스럽게 자고 있는 아기를 들어 올렸다.
⇨ Ashley carefully picked up the ____________ baby.

3 벽장 안에 숨어 있는 남자아이들은 나의 친구들이다.
⇨ The boys ____________ in the closet are my friends.

4 Bob 옆에 서 있는 여자아이는 나의 여동생이다.
⇨ The girl ____________ next to Bob is my little sister.

5 어떤 사람이 내 잃어버린 핸드백을 찾아 나에게 돌려줬다.
⇨ Someone found my ____________ purse and returned it to me.

6 이 오래된 성은 백 년도 전에 지어졌다.
⇨ This old castle was ____________ more than a hundred years ago.

Exercise 4 다음 우리말과 같은 뜻이 되도록 주어진 말을 알맞게 배열하여 문장을 완성하시오.

1 저 짖고 있는 개에게 다가가지 마라. (dog, the, barking)
⇨ Don't get closer to ________________________.

2 나는 베이지색으로 페인트가 칠해진 벽이 좋다. (painted, the wall)
⇨ I like ________________________ in beige.

3 우리는 죽어가는 새를 수의사에게 데리고 갔다. (the, bird, dying)
⇨ We took ________________________ to a vet.

4 엄마는 차고 세일에서 중고 텔레비전을 사셨어요. (a, TV, used)
⇨ Mom bought ________________________ at a garage sale.

5 그 탐정은 암호로 쓰인 편지 한 장을 받았다. (written, a, letter)
⇨ The detective received ________________________ in code.

6 파란 모자를 쓰고 있는 남자아이는 같은 반 친구이다. (a, hat, blue, the boy, wearing)
⇨ ________________________ is my classmate.

7 벽에 걸려 있는 그림은 나의 아들이 그린 것이다. (the, hanging, picture, the, wall, on)
⇨ ________________________ was painted by my son.

6-3 동사의 활용에 쓰이는 분사

동사의 활용에 쓰이는 분사

현재분사는 진행시제를, 과거분사는 완료시제와 수동태를 나타내는 데 쓰인다.

❶ **진행시제:** 「be동사+현재분사」

- I **am listening** to the radio. 나는 라디오를 듣고 있다.
- We **were having** lunch at the cafeteria. 우리는 구내식당에서 점심을 먹고 있었다.

❷ **완료시제:** 「have/has/had+과거분사」

- Emma **has gone** to Paris. Emma는 파리에 갔다.
- I **have been** sick since I ate the spoiled meat. 나는 그 상한 고기를 먹은 후부터 아팠다.

❸ **수동태:** 「be동사+과거분사」

- The thief **was caught** two days ago. 그 도둑은 이틀 전에 잡혔다.
- Did you know that glass **is made** from sand? 너는 유리가 모래로 만들어진다는 것을 알았니?

Answers: p.18

Exercise 1 다음 괄호 안에서 알맞은 것을 고르시오.

1 Have you (meeting / met) Mr. Logan?

2 Jennifer was (sitting / sat) next to Henry.

3 The attic was (unlocking / unlocked) by me.

4 My bathroom is (cleaning / cleaned) every day.

5 I am (thinking / thought) of starting a new business.

6 I've (being / been) to lots of places over the last few days.

Exercise 2 다음 우리말과 같은 뜻이 되도록 〈보기〉의 단어를 이용하여 문장을 완성하시오.

drive	play	be	invite	bake

1 나는 오늘 저녁 집들이에 초대받았다.
⇨ I'm ____________ to a house-warming party this evening.

2 여동생과 나는 함께 피아노를 치고 있다.
⇨ My sister and I are ____________ the piano together.

3 너는 오늘 아침부터 조용하구나.
⇨ You have ____________ quiet since this morning.

4 엄마는 주방에서 케이크를 굽고 계셨어.
⇨ Mom was ____________ a cake in the kitchen.

5 너는 전에 운전을 해본 적이 있니?
⇨ Have you ____________ a car before?

6-4 감정을 나타내는 분사

감정을 나타내는 분사

분사가 수식하는 명사가 감정을 일으키는 원인일 경우 현재분사를 쓰고, 감정을 느끼는 주체일 경우 과거분사를 쓴다.

The show on TV now is **interesting**.

People in the concert hall are **excited**.

현재분사 (-ing: 감정을 일으키는)	과거분사 (-ed: 감정을 느끼는)
boring 지루하게 하는	**bored** 지루한
exciting 신나게 하는	**excited** 신난
tiring 지치게 하는	**tired** 지친
interesting 흥미를 일으키는	**interested** 흥미가 있는
shocking 충격적인	**shocked** 충격을 받은
amazing 놀라운	**amazed** 놀란
surprising 놀라운	**surprised** 놀란
satisfying 만족을 주는	**satisfied** 만족한
disappointing 실망시키는	**disappointed** 실망한
pleasing 기쁘게 하는	**pleased** 기쁜
depressing 우울하게 하는	**depressed** 우울한
annoying 귀찮게 하는	**annoyed** 귀찮은

- It was an **exciting** game. 그것은 흥미진진한 경기였다.
- Some **excited** people shouted the name of the player. 일부 흥분한 사람들이 그 선수의 이름을 외쳤다.

- This book contains lots of **interesting** stories. 이 책은 많은 재미있는 이야기를 담고 있다.
- I'm **interested** in both mathematics and science. 나는 수학과 과학 모두에 흥미가 있다.

- The movie was too **shocking** to watch. 그 영화는 너무 충격적이어서 볼 수 없었다.
- The woman was **shocked** at the news. 여자는 그 소식에 충격을 받았다.

Answers: p.19

Exercise 1 다음 괄호 안에서 알맞은 것을 고르시오.

1 Are you (interesting / interested) in fashion?

2 We were (satisfying / satisfied) with the service.

3 You look so (boring / bored). Do you want to play with us?

4 Their first performance was (disappointing / disappointed).

5 It was the most (embarrassing / embarrassed) moment of my life.

6 Matt was (amazing / amazed) when I gave him a surprise present.

Exercise **2** 다음 우리말과 같은 뜻이 되도록 〈보기〉의 단어를 이용하여 문장을 완성하시오.

excite	tire	please	surprise	bore	disappoint

1 나는 너무 피곤해서 아무것도 할 수가 없다.
⇨ I'm so ________________ that I can't do anything.

2 정말 놀라운 광경이다. 나의 눈을 믿을 수가 없구나.
⇨ What a(n) ________________ sight! I can't believe my eyes.

3 Willy가 이 메시지를 받으면 기뻐할 것이다.
⇨ When Willy gets this message, he will be ________________.

4 나는 수업시간에 네가 하품하는 것을 보았어. 수업이 지루했니?
⇨ I saw you yawning during the class. Was it ________________?

5 Lions와 Giants의 경기는 정말 흥미로웠다.
⇨ The game between the Lions and the Giants was really ________________.

6 모든 관중들은 Natalie의 공연에 실망했다.
⇨ All the audience members were ________________ with Natalie's performance.

Exercise **3** 다음 〈보기〉와 같이 빈칸을 채워 각 문장을 완성하시오.

> The news about the tragic accident shocked us.
> ⇨ We were shocked by the news about the tragic accident.
> ⇨ The news about the tragic accident was shocking to us.

1 Big animals frighten little kids.
⇨ Little kids are ________________ of big animals.
⇨ Big animals are ________________ to little kids.

2 The noise from outside annoys me.
⇨ I'm ________________ by the noise from outside.
⇨ The noise from outside is ________________.

3 The unexpected result surprised all of us.
⇨ All of us were ________________ at the unexpected result.
⇨ The unexpected result was ________________.

4 His responsible behavior pleased Wendy.
⇨ His responsible behavior was ________________ to Wendy.
⇨ Wendy was ________________ with his responsible behavior.

6-5 현재분사와 동명사

현재분사와 동명사의 구별

현재분사와 동명사는 「동사원형+-ing」로 형태가 동일하기 때문에 혼동하기 쉽지만, 현재분사는 형용사의 기능을, 동명사는 명사의 기능을 한다.

	현재분사	동명사
「-ing+명사」	· 명사의 행동을 설명 a **sleeping** baby 잠자는 아기 (아기가 잠을 자고 있음) **waiting** people 기다리는 사람들 (사람들이 기다리고 있음)	· 명사의 용도나 목적을 설명 a **sleeping** bag 침낭 (잠자기 위한 가방) a **waiting** room 대기실 (기다리기 위한 방)
「be동사+-ing」	· 진행시제에 쓰임 I'm **listening** to music. 나는 음악을 듣고 있다.	· 보어 역할 My hobby is **listening** to music. 내 취미는 음악을 듣는 것이다.

Answers: p.19

Exercise 1 다음 밑줄 친 부분이 현재분사인지 동명사인지 구분하여 쓰시오.

1 Look at the crying boy. ⇨ ________
2 The roaring lion makes me scared. ⇨ ________
3 We have a big sofa in the living room. ⇨ ________
4 Mom bought a frying pan for ten dollars. ⇨ ________
5 Tim was washing the dishes when I saw him. ⇨ ________
6 You should be careful when you take sleeping pills. ⇨ ________

Exercise 2 다음 우리말과 같은 뜻이 되도록 주어진 말을 알맞게 배열하여 문장을 완성하시오.

1 우리 모두는 그 지루한 영화를 보는 동안 졸았다. (movie, the, during, boring, nodded off)
⇨ All of us ________________.

2 우리 할아버지는 지팡이 없이는 걷지 못하신다. (walking, a, without, walk, cannot, stick)
⇨ My grandfather ________________.

3 남동생과 나는 차고를 청소하고 있었다. (were, the, cleaning up, garage)
⇨ My brother and I ________________.

4 그 호텔은 뒷마당에 거대한 수영장이 있다. (huge, swimming, pool, a, has)
⇨ The hotel ________________ in its backyard.

5 너의 일은 고객이 우리 상점에서 편안함을 느낄 수 있도록 하는 것이다. (feel, customers, is, helping, comfortable)
⇨ Your job ________________ in our store.

6-6 분사구문

분사구문

부사절의 접속사와 주어를 생략하고, 분사를 이용하여 간단히 부사구로 줄여 쓴 구문이다.

분사구문 만들기

When we heard the news, we were shocked.
❶ ❷ ❸

⇒ **Hearing** the news, we were shocked.

❶ 부사절의 접속사를 없앤다.
❷ 부사절과 주절의 주어가 같을 경우 부사절의 주어를 없앤다.
❸ 부사절의 동사를 -ing 형태로 바꾼다.

· After I met Jake, I went to the library. 나는 Jake를 만난 후 도서관에 갔다.
⇒ **Meeting** Jake, I went to the library. (시간)

· Because we were young, we did some silly things. 우리는 어렸기 때문에 어리석은 일을 좀 했다.
⇒ **Being** young, we did some silly things. (이유)

TIPs 부사절을 이끄는 접속사

시간	when, while, after, before, as
이유	because, since, as
조건, 양보	if, unless, although, though

TIPs 분사구문에서 being은 생략할 수 있다.

• Because he was sick, he was absent from school.
= (Being) Sick, he was absent from school.

Exercise 1 다음 문장을 분사구문으로 바꿀 때 빈칸에 알맞은 말을 쓰시오.

Answers: p.19

1 When I watch TV, I usually have snacks.
⇒ ____________ TV, I usually have snacks.

2 When I saw the dog barking at me, I ran away.
⇒ ____________ the dog barking at me, I ran away.

3 Because we had no food, we went grocery shopping.
⇒ ____________ no food, we went grocery shopping.

4 If he shows up in five minutes, he won't be punished.
⇒ ____________ up in five minutes, he won't be punished.

Exercise 2 다음 우리말과 같은 뜻이 되도록 주어진 말을 이용하여 문장을 완성하시오.

1 나는 약을 먹었지만 몸이 더 안 좋아졌다. (take, medicine)
⇒ __________ __________, I felt even worse.

2 점심을 먹고 난 후 우리는 공원으로 산책을 갔다. (have, lunch)
⇒ __________ __________, we went for a walk in the park.

3 나는 어젯밤 피곤해서 일찍 잠자리에 들었다. (tired)
⇒ __________ __________, I went to bed early last night.

4 Timothy는 나를 기다리면서 잡지를 읽었다. (wait, for)
⇒ __________ __________ __________, Timothy read a magazine.

Review Test

[01-05] 다음 빈칸에 들어갈 알맞은 말을 고르시오.

01

The police found the ___________ car.

① steal ② stole
③ stealing ④ stolen
⑤ steals

02

Do you know the woman ___________ outside the door?

① stand ② stood
③ standing ④ to stand
⑤ being standing

03

A new teacher came yesterday. I found him a(n) ___________ person.

① interest ② interested
③ interesting ④ to interest
⑤ be interested

04

She must be ___________ to have failed the entrance exam.

① depress ② depressed
③ depressing ④ to depress
⑤ have depressed

05

___________ left at the corner, you will see the building.

① Turn ② Turning
③ Turned ④ Turns
⑤ Being turned

[06-07] 다음 빈칸에 들어갈 말이 바르게 짝지어진 것을 고르시오.

06

• I found a box ___________ in the bushes.
• Do you know the man ___________ to my sister?

① hiding – talking
② hidden – talked
③ hidden – talking
④ hiding – talked
⑤ hidden – talk

07

• The fences ___________ white look clean.
• ___________ tired, I fell fast asleep as soon as I lay on my bed.

① paint – Feeling
② painted – Feeling
③ painting – Felt
④ painted – Felt
⑤ painting – Feeling

[08-09] 다음 두 문장이 같은 뜻이 되도록 빈칸에 알맞은 말을 고르시오.

08

Being rich, he isn't happy.
= ___________ he is rich, he isn't happy.

① Even though ② Before
③ After ④ Because
⑤ When

09

Forgetting to send the mail, I didn't stop by the post office.
= ___________ I forgot to send the mail, I didn't stop by the post office.

① If ② While
③ After ④ Because
⑤ When

[10-11] 다음 대화의 빈칸에 들어갈 말이 바르게 짝지어진 것을 고르시오.

10

A You look ___________. What's wrong?
B Jenny kept me ___________ for three hours and didn't even show up.

① annoyed – wait
② annoying – waited
③ annoyed – waiting
④ annoying – waiting
⑤ annoy – waiting

11

A I'm so ___________. I'm going to Tokyo for the first time.
B Wow, I've been to Tokyo several times. There are so many ___________ places to visit.

① exciting – interesting
② interesting – exciting
③ excited – interested
④ interested – excited
⑤ excited – interesting

12 다음 밑줄 친 부분의 쓰임이 나머지와 다른 하나는?

① The sleeping dog is very wild.
② The baby is sleeping in peace.
③ I was sleeping when you called.
④ Don't forget to bring a sleeping bag.
⑤ The man sleeping on the bench is homeless.

13 다음 밑줄 친 부분이 어법상 바른 것은?

① A rolled stone gathers no moss.
② My son is excited to see dolphins.
③ Look at the girl worn a strange hat.
④ The monkeys trapping in a cage look sad.
⑤ There are thousands of shined stars in the sky.

[14-15] 다음 밑줄 친 부분과 바꿔 쓸 수 있는 것을 고르시오.

14

Because she had a bad headache, she took a day off.

① Had a bad headache
② Having a bad headache
③ She had a bad headache
④ Having had a bad headache
⑤ Because she having a bad headache

15

While I was taking a bath, I heard the doorbell ring.

① Taking a bath
② I took a bath
③ Being taken a bath
④ While took a bath
⑤ While I taking a bath

[16-17] 다음 문장의 밑줄 친 부분과 쓰임이 같은 것을 고르시오.

16

Who is the boy sitting next to you?

① Do you like reading books?
② One of my hobbies is hunting.
③ Let's go to the swimming pool.
④ Sitting for a long time is hard for me.
⑤ The baby sleeping in her arms is my nephew.

17

The dining car of the train is filled with passengers.

① The man waving to us is my father.
② Your swimming suit looks expensive.
③ The World Cup is a very exciting sport event.
④ The girl wandering the streets has lost her mother.
⑤ Which is more interesting, this movie or that one?

18 다음 밑줄 친 부분을 바르게 고친 것은?

- The statue was beautiful. I was amaze at how well it was made.
- What an amaze concert! This is the greatest performance ever.

① amazed – amazed
② amazing – amazing
③ amazed – amazing
④ amazed – amaze
⑤ amazing – amaze

19 다음 중 어법상 바른 문장은?

① Arriving she home, she washed her hands.
② Listen to the radio, Sean did his homework.
③ After finishing I lunch, I went out for a short walk.
④ Getting up late, he couldn't make it to the meeting.
⑤ Being gone back home, we saw a beautiful sunset.

[20-21] 다음 밑줄 친 부분이 어법상 어색한 것을 고르시오.

20 ① Adam is bored with his job.
② I was surprised at the news.
③ She watched an exciting game.
④ My sister told me a scared story.
⑤ I read the shocking story on the Internet.

21 ① Don't you hear the ringing bell?
② Look at the fallen leaves. It's fall.
③ There is a dancing girl on the stage.
④ There is freshly baking bread on the table.
⑤ We have to do something about the burning house!

[22-23] 다음 우리말을 영어로 바르게 옮긴 것을 고르시오.

22 모두가 그 기쁜 소식에 만족했다.

① Everyone was satisfying with the pleasing news.
② Everyone was satisfied with the pleased news.
③ Everyone was satisfying with the pleased news.
④ Everyone was satisfied with the pleasing news.
⑤ Everyone was satisfied with the news pleasing.

23 나는 산토끼를 사냥하는 독수리를 보았는데 정말 멋졌다.

① I saw a hunting eagle a hare, and it was amazing.
② I saw an eagle hunting a hare, and it was amazing.
③ I saw an eagle hunting a hare, and it was amazed.
④ I saw a hare hunting by an eagle, and it was amazing.
⑤ I saw a hare hunted by an eagle, and it was amazed.

24 다음 중 쓰임이 나머지와 다른 하나는?

Are you interested in a psychology test? Then, how about ① answering this question?

What would you do first in this situation?
- The phone is ② ringing.
- Somebody is ③ knocking at the door.
- There is ④ boiling water on the stove.
- There is a ⑤ crying baby in the bedroom.

[25-28] 다음 우리말과 같은 뜻이 되도록 〈보기〉에서 알맞은 동사를 골라 문장을 완성하시오.

보기	use annoy disappoint excite

25 그 소문을 듣자 우리 부모님은 흥분했다.

⇒ My parents were ____________ when they heard the news.

26 나는 중고차를 살 생각이다.

⇒ I'm thinking of buying a(n) ____________ car.

27 모두가 그의 결정에 실망했다.

⇒ Everyone is ____________ with his decision.

28 공원에서 들려오는 소음을 참을 수가 없다. 정말 성가시다.

⇒ I can't stand the noise coming from the park. It's really ____________.

[29-30] 다음 중 어법상 어색한 부분을 찾아 바르게 고쳐 쓰시오.

29 The girl stood next to Andy is his new girlfriend, Laura.

⇒ ________________________________

30 Ted looked embarrassing when we asked him to sing.

⇒ ________________________________

[31-33] 다음 우리말과 같은 뜻이 되도록 주어진 단어를 알맞게 배열하여 문장을 완성하시오.

31 노란 모자를 쓰고 있는 남자아이는 내 남동생이다.

⇒ ________________________________ is my little brother.
(wearing, a, the, cap, boy, yellow)

32 저 책상 위에 설치된 컴퓨터는 최신 모델이다.

⇒ ________________________________ is a new model.
(set, that, desk, on, up, the, computer)

33 서랍에서 프랑스어로 쓰인 소설을 찾았다.

⇒ I found ________________________ in the drawer. (French, written, in, novel, a)

[34-36] 다음 문장의 밑줄 친 부분이 분사구문이 되도록 빈칸에 알맞은 말을 쓰시오.

34 <u>Because I lost my bike</u>, I walked to school.

⇒ ____________________, I walked to school.

35 <u>If you try hard</u>, you will pass the exam.

⇒ ____________________, you will pass the exam.

36 <u>When I feel nervous</u>, I always say to myself, "I'm the best."

⇒ ____________________, I always say to myself, "I'm the best."

보너스 유형별 문제

Answers: p.20

[1-2] 주어진 단어와 동사의 분사형을 이용하여 밑줄 친 우리말과 같은 뜻이 되도록 대화를 완성하시오. 서술형

A 1 복도에서 너랑 얘기하고 있던 여자애는 누구였어?

B She is Evelyn. She just moved from Chicago.

A What is she like?

B I think she is pretty, smart, and adorable.

A Can you introduce me to her?

B Sure. 2 그녀를 만나면 바로 그녀와 사랑에 빠지게 될 걸.

1 Who was ______________________________ in the hallways? (girl, talk, with)

2 When ______________________, you will instantly fall in love with her. (meet)

3 다음 글의 밑줄 친 부분 중, 어법상 틀린 것은? 수능 대비형

When I was in high school, I was a troubled kid. I wasn't ① interested in studies and skipped classes very often. My father couldn't take it anymore. He wanted me to understand that it is not that easy ② to make it in this world without a proper education. So he got me to work in a shoe factory ③ owning by one of his friends. As I started working, I realized ④ that some illegal activities were going on in the factory and some people were ⑤ arrested and put behind bars. It turned out that one of my coworkers was an undercover cop. He noticed my interest in police work and offered me a position.

* illegal : 불법의
** put behind bars: 감방에 가두다
*** undercover: 비밀리에 하는, 위장 근무의

Chapter
7

대명사

7-1 재귀대명사
7-2 재귀대명사의 관용 표현
7-3 가주어 it
7-4 부정대명사 one, another, other
7-5 부정대명사 표현
7-6 부정대명사 some, any
7-7 부정대명사 each, every, all, both, no
7-8 부정대명사 either, neither
Review Test
보너스 유형별 문제

7-1 재귀대명사

재귀대명사

인칭대명사의 소유격이나 목적격에 -self(단수)나 -selves(복수)를 붙인 형태로 '~자신', '~자체', '스스로', '직접'이라는 의미를 가진다.

	1인칭	2인칭	3인칭
단수	myself	yourself	himself / herself / itself
복수	ourselves	yourselves	themselves

❶ 재귀용법: 문장의 목적어가 주어와 같을 때 목적어를 재귀대명사로 한다.

- Narcissus loved **himself** too much. (Narcissus = himself) 나르시스는 자신을 너무 사랑했다.
- The lady was proud of **herself.** (the lady = herself) 그 여자는 자신이 자랑스러웠다.

❷ 강조용법: 주어, 목적어, 보어의 뜻을 강조하기 위해 쓰인 경우로 강조하고자 하는 (대)명사 바로 뒤 또는 문장의 맨 뒤에 오며 생략할 수 있다.

- I **myself** fixed the car. 내가 직접 차를 고쳤다.
  = I fixed the car **myself**.
- My children **themselves** set the table. 내 아이들이 스스로 상을 차렸다.
  = My children set the table **themselves**.

Answers: p.21

Exercise 1 다음 괄호 안에서 알맞은 것을 고르시오.

1 I want to see Lucy (her / herself).

2 Bruno is looking at (me / myself).

3 Dennis (him / himself) wrote the book.

4 You have to take care of (you / yourself).

5 Angela designs all her dresses (her / herself).

6 Our new teacher introduced (himself / ourselves) to us.

Exercise 2 다음 우리말과 같은 뜻이 되도록 빈칸을 채워 문장을 완성하시오.

1 아버지가 직접 우리를 위해 이 집을 지으셨다.

⇒ My father ______________ built this house for us.

2 우리는 긴장을 풀고 즐길 시간이 없다.

⇒ We don't have time to relax and enjoy ______________.

3 나는 야구 자체를 즐기진 않지만 보는 것은 좋아한다.

⇒ I don't enjoy baseball ______________, but I like watching it.

4 소녀는 거울로 자신의 모습을 보는 데 많은 시간을 보낸다.

⇒ The girl spends a lot of time looking at ______________ in the mirror.

7-2 재귀대명사의 관용 표현

재귀대명사의 관용 표현

by oneself 혼자, 스스로	between ourselves 우리끼리의 이야기로
help oneself (to) (~을) 마음껏 먹다	talk[say] to oneself 혼잣말하다
enjoy oneself 즐거운 시간을 보내다	make oneself at home 편히 하다
teach oneself 독학하다	make oneself understood 이해시키다
by itself 저절로	in itself 본래

- Grace came to see me **by herself.** Grace는 혼자 나를 만나러 왔다.
- **Help yourself** to anything you like. 아무거나 마음껏 드십시오.
- My grandmother often **talks to herself.** 우리 할머니는 종종 혼잣말을 하신다.
- We **enjoyed ourselves** at the party. 우리는 파티에서 즐거운 시간을 보냈다.
- The door opened **by itself.** 문이 저절로 열렸다.

Answers: p.21

Exercise 1 다음 괄호 안에서 알맞은 것을 고르시오.

1 The candle went out (from / by) itself.
2 Did you enjoy (myself / yourself) at the concert?
3 Mr. Gates lives in a big house by (him / himself).
4 We should keep this between (ourself / ourselves).
5 My father taught (herself / himself) three languages.
6 Please help (yourself / ourselves) to the doughnuts.
7 "I will do my best," George said (to himself / for himself).

Exercise 2 다음 우리말과 같은 뜻이 되도록 빈칸을 채워 문장을 완성하시오.

1 어서 들어오세요. 집에서처럼 편안히 계세요.
⇒ Come on in. Please ______________________.

2 우리는 John의 파티에서 즐거운 시간을 보냈다.
⇒ We ______________________ at John's party.

3 나는 부모님을 이해시키는 데 어려움을 겪었다.
⇒ I had trouble ______________________ to my parents.

4 이건 우리끼리 하는 이야기야. 다른 사람에게 말하지 마.
⇒ It's just ______________________. Don't tell anyone about it.

5 Jacob은 그의 임무를 스스로 완수해야 한다.
⇒ Jacob has to carry out his duties ______________________.

7-3 가주어 it

가주어 it

문장에서 주어가 긴 경우, 이를 뒤로 보내고 원래의 주어 자리에 it을 쓴다. 이때 it은 아무런 의미가 없는 주어로 '가주어'라 하고 뒤로 보내진 실질적 주어를 '진주어'라고 한다.

To learn a foreign language is fun. 외국어를 배우는 것은 재미있다.

It is fun to learn a foreign language.
가주어 / 진주어

- **It** is necessary to bring your own food. (to부정사구) 네가 먹을 음식을 가져올 필요가 있다.
  가주어 / 진주어
- **It** is true that he was a famous actor. (명사절) 그가 유명한 배우였다는 것은 사실이다.
  가주어 / 진주어

Answers: p.21

Exercise 1 다음 문장을 가주어 it을 이용하여 다시 쓰시오.

1 To ride a horse is exciting.
⇨ ______________________________

2 That Jamie will marry Gwen is true.
⇨ ______________________________

3 That Kevin lied to me is disappointing.
⇨ ______________________________

4 To wear a hat indoors is considered rude.
⇨ ______________________________

Exercise 2 다음 우리말과 같은 뜻이 되도록 주어진 말을 알맞게 배열하여 문장을 완성하시오.

1 다른 문화를 경험하는 것은 흥미롭다. (other, experience, to, is, it, cultures, exciting)
⇨ ______________________________

2 서울에서 지하철을 타는 것은 편리하다. (to, take, in Seoul, is, it, convenient, the subway)
⇨ ______________________________

3 아무도 나를 믿지 않는다는 것이 나를 속상하게 한다. (makes, no one, me, that, believes, me, upset, it)
⇨ ______________________________

4 그가 이메일 보내는 방법을 모른다는 것은 믿기 어렵다.
(send, know, how to, an e-mail, that, doesn't, unbelievable, is, it, he)
⇨ ______________________________

7-4 부정대명사 one, another, other

one

❶ 앞에서 언급한 명사의 반복을 피하기 위해 사용하는 대명사로, 앞의 명사와 동일한 것이 아닌 같은 종류의 사물을 지칭한다.

- My scarf is too old. I need to buy a new **one**.
  나의 목도리는 너무 낡았다. 나는 새 것을 살 필요가 있다. (one = a scarf)
- The shoes in the window are beautiful. Most of all, I'd like to try on the red **ones**.
  진열장에 있는 신발들은 예쁘다. 그 중에서도 빨간 것을 신어보고 싶다. (ones = shoes)

❷ 일반적인 사람을 지칭한다.

- **One** should respect other people's feelings.
  사람은 다른 사람의 감정을 존중해야 한다.

another

'또 다른 하나', '하나 더'라는 의미로, 같은 종류의 또 다른 하나를 지칭한다.

- I dropped the fork. Can you get me **another**?
  포크를 떨어뜨렸어요. 하나 더 갖다 주시겠습니까?
- Everyone calls him Louis, but he has **another** secret name.
  모두가 그를 Louis라 부르지만 그는 또 다른 비밀 이름을 가지고 있다.

> **TIPs**
> 앞서 언급된 사물과 동일한 것을 지칭할 때는 **it**을 쓴다.
> - Do you have **the book** that I lent you the other day? I want **it** now.
>   너는 내가 저번에 빌려준 책을 가지고 있니? 나는 지금 그것을 원해.

other

❶ others : 불특정한 사람[것]들

- I always try to help **others.** 나는 항상 다른 사람들을 도우려고 한다.

❷ the other : 둘 중 나머지 한 사람[하나]

- There are two different hats. You take one first. I'll take **the other**.
  다른 두 개의 모자가 있다. 네가 먼저 하나를 골라라. 나는 나머지 하나를 할 것이다.

❸ the others : 나머지 전부

- I'll just have one. **The others** are all yours.
  나는 하나만 가질게. 나머지 전부는 너의 것이야.

Exercise 1 다음 괄호 안에서 알맞은 것을 고르시오.

Answers: p.21

1 (One / Ones) should obey the laws of the country.

2 I think this shirt isn't for me. Show me (it / another).

3 The coffee is great. Can I have (other / another) cup?

4 The librarian recommended a book to me. (One / It) was very interesting.

5 This sweater is too small. Do you have a bigger (one / it)?

6 If you're looking for a pen, I have (one / it) in my pencil case.

7 She has two cats. One is black, and (the other, the others) is white.

8 I need a headset, but I don't have enough money to buy (one / it).

Exercise 2 다음 〈보기〉에서 대화의 빈칸에 알맞은 말을 골라 쓰시오.

it	ones	another	others	the other	the others

1 A Which shoes are yours?
B The ________________ with ribbons are mine.

2 A Son, you should listen to ________________.
B OK, Mom. I will keep that in mind.

3 A Can I borrow your car?
B Sure. But you have to return ________________ to me next week.

4 A There are some cookies on the table.
B I will just take three. ________________ are for my brother.

5 A You have two sisters, right?
B Yes. One is a lawyer, and ________________ is a college student.

6 A If you're looking for a dress shirt, how about this one?
B Well, I don't like the color. Can you show me ________________?

Exercise 3 다음 우리말과 같은 뜻이 되도록 주어진 단어를 이용하여 문장을 완성하시오.

1 다른 사람들에게 공손해야 한다. (polite)
⇨ You should be ________________________________.

2 차 한 잔 더 마시겠습니까? (tea)
⇨ Would you like ________________________________?

3 네가 원하는 만큼 가져라. 나머지는 내가 가질 것이다. (have)
⇨ Take as many as you want. I'll ________________________________.

4 이 셔츠는 나에게 맞지 않네요. 더 작은 것을 보여줄 수 있나요? (show)
⇨ This shirt doesn't fit me. Can you ________________________________?

5 장미를 조금 사러 왔습니다. 분홍색 있나요? (pink)
⇨ I'm here to buy some roses. Do you ________________________________?

6 나는 두 마리의 애완동물을 키우고 있다. 하나는 개이고, 나머지 하나는 거북이다. (turtle)
⇨ I have two pets. One is a dog, and ________________________________.

7 진열장에 있는 모자를 써볼 수 있을까요? 중간에 있는 빨간 것 말이에요. (in the middle)
⇨ Can I try on the hat in the window? I mean ________________________________.

7-5 부정대명사 표현

one ~, the other …: (둘 중) 하나는 ~, 나머지 하나는 …

- I have two best friends. **One** is a boy named Jack, and **the other** is a girl named Bella.
  나는 두 명의 절친한 친구가 있다. 한 명은 Jack이라는 이름의 남자아이고, 나머지 한 명은 Bella라는 여자아이다.

one ~, another …, the other ~: (셋 중) 하나는 ~, 다른 하나는 …, 나머지 하나는 ~

- We have three new students. **One** is from Vietnam, **another** is from Canada, and **the other** is from Poland.
  우리는 세 명의 새로 온 학생이 있다. 한 명은 베트남에서 왔고, 다른 한 명은 캐나다에서, 나머지 한 명은 폴란드에서 왔다.

one ~, the others …: (여럿 중에) 하나는 ~, 나머지 전부는 …

- I have four sisters. **One** is older than me, and **the others** are younger.
  나는 네 명의 자매가 있다. 한 명은 언니고, 나머지 전부는 동생이다.

some ~, others …: (여럿 중에) 일부는 ~, 다른 일부는 …

- **Some** like pop music, and **others** like classical music.
  어떤 사람들은 대중음악을 좋아하고, 또 어떤 사람들은 고전음악을 좋아한다.

> **TIPs**
> **each other/one another**: '서로'
> - They love each other.
>   그들은 서로 사랑한다.

some ~, the others …: (여럿 중에) 일부는 ~, 나머지 전부는 …

- There are 15 boys in my class. **Some** are kind, and **the others** are not.
  우리 반에는 열다섯 명의 남학생이 있다. 일부는 착하지만 나머지는 그렇지 않다.

Exercise 1 다음 우리말과 같은 뜻이 되도록 빈칸에 알맞은 말을 쓰시오.

Answers: p.21

1 그들은 어둠 속에서 서로를 찾고 있었다.
⇒ They were looking for ______________ in the dark.

2 두 마리의 강아지가 있다. 한 마리는 흰색이고, 나머지 한 마리는 검은색이다.
⇒ There are two puppies. __________ is white, and __________ is black.

3 어떤 사람들은 잔의 반이 찼다고 말하고, 또 어떤 사람들은 잔의 반이 비었다고 말한다.
⇒ __________ say the glass is half full, and __________ say it is half empty.

4 나는 세 명의 딸이 있다. 한 명은 서울에 살고, 나머지는 부산에 산다.
⇒ I have three daughters. __________ lives in Seoul, and __________ live in Busan.

5 나는 두 개의 휴대전화를 가지고 있다. 하나는 사업용이고, 나머지 하나는 개인적 용도로 쓴다.
⇒ I have two cell phones. __________ is for business, and __________ is for personal use.

6 이 교실에는 여섯 명의 학생이 있다. 몇몇은 책을 읽고 있고, 나머지는 이야기하고 있다.
⇒ There are six students in this classroom. __________ are reading books, and __________ are talking.

7 세 가지 종류의 음료가 있다. 하나는 탄산음료고, 다른 하나는 주스, 나머지 하나는 생수이다.
⇒ There are three types of drinks. __________ is soda, __________ is juice, and __________ is mineral water.

7-6 부정대명사 some, any

some, any

'얼마간', '약간'이라는 의미의 부정대명사로 스스로 쓰이거나, 명사를 꾸며 수량 형용사로 쓰인다.

some	긍정문 또는 권유 · 의뢰를 나타내거나 긍정의 대답을 기대하는 의문문에 쓰임	These muffins are freshly baked. Why don't you have **some**? 이 머핀들은 갓 구워졌다. 조금 먹지 않을래? I have **some** friends to help me. 나는 나를 도와줄 몇 명의 친구가 있다.
any	부정문, 의문문에 쓰임	I went to the market for some peas, but they didn't have **any**. 나는 완두콩을 사러 시장에 갔지만 완두콩은 팔지 않았다. Do you have **any** questions? 질문 있습니까?

some (-body/-one/-thing), any (-body/-one/-thing)

something, anything, someone, anyone, somebody, anybody 등도 some과 any의 쓰임에 준한다.

- He saw **something** in the dark. 그는 어둠 속에서 무엇인가를 보았다.
- Can you introduce **someone** to me? 나에게 누군가를 소개해주겠니?
- Harry doesn't know **anything** about it. Harry는 그것에 대해 아무것도 모른다.
- Does **anyone** want to volunteer? 누군가 자원할 사람 있나요?

TIPs
any는 부정문 · 의문문에 주로 사용하지만, 긍정문에 쓰여 '어떤', '어느 ~라도'라는 의미를 나타낸다.
- **Any** student can use the computer. 어떤 학생도 그 컴퓨터를 사용할 수 있다.

Answers: p.22

Exercise 1 다음 괄호 안에서 알맞은 것을 고르시오.

1 Will you lend me (some / any) money?

2 I don't want (some / any) of these things.

3 Would you like (something / anything) to drink?

4 I don't have (something / anything) in common with John.

5 They didn't show (some / any) interest in my performance.

6 We have plenty of food. Would you like (some / any) more?

7 (Some / Any) people believe in spirits and ghosts.

8 I didn't bring the camera, so we can't take (some / any) pictures.

Exercise 2 다음 <보기>에서 알맞은 것을 골라 문장을 완성하시오.

something anything someone anyone

1 __________ called you last night.

2 Do you know __________ good at math?

3 There isn't __________ in the refrigerator.

4 She mumbled __________ to me, but I couldn't understand.

7-7 부정대명사 each, every, all, both, no

each: '각각의', '각기'라는 의미로, 단독으로 쓰이거나 단수명사를 수식한다.

❶ 「each+단수명사+단수동사」

· **Each** student has to wear a name tag. 각 학생들은 이름표를 달아야 한다.

❷ 「each+of+복수명사+단수동사」

· **Each** of the students has his or her own locker. 각 학생들은 자신의 사물함을 가지고 있다.

every: '모든 ~', '~마다'라는 의미로, 단수명사를 수식하고 단독으로 쓰일 수 없다.

· **Every** player goes through a slump. 모든 선수들은 슬럼프를 겪는다.

· We go to the movies **every** Friday. 우리는 금요일마다 영화 보러 간다.

all: '모든 ~', '모든 것(사람)'이라는 의미로, 단독으로 쓰이거나 명사를 수식한다.

❶ 「all(+of)+복수명사+복수동사」

· **All** the girls in my class like Jake. 우리 반의 여자아이들 모두는 Jake를 좋아한다.

❷ 「all(+of)+셀 수 없는 명사+단수동사」

· **All** my money was stolen from the safe. 금고의 내 모든 돈이 도난됐다.

both: '양쪽 다', '~ 둘 다'라는 의미로, 단독으로 쓰이거나 명사를 수식한다.

❶ 「both+복수명사+복수동사」

· **Both** rooms are big enough for us. 두 방 모두 우리에게는 충분히 크다.

❷ 「both+of+복수명사+복수동사」

· **Both** of them are fluent in English. 그들은 둘 다 영어가 유창하다.

no (= not any): '어떤 ~도 없는', '어떤 ~도 아닌'이라는 의미로, 명사를 수식한다.

· I have **no** questions. 질문 없습니다.
(= I **don't** have **any** questions.)

Exercise 1 다음 괄호 안에서 알맞은 것을 고르시오.

Answers: p.22

1 We have (no / any) paper today.

2 All of my brothers (is / are) very diligent.

3 Every girl (love / loves) to play with dolls.

4 Every (child / children) has to go to school.

5 All of my (friend / friends) are good at sports.

6 Both of the (cap / caps) are too small for me.

7 Each (person / people) must sign up individually.

8 All of the food in the fridge (have / has) gone bad.

9 We are given an assignment every (week / weeks).

10 Both of us (is / are) chosen to play in the big match.

Exercise 2 다음 밑줄 친 부분을 바르게 고쳐 쓰시오.

1 Both of our grandparents is alive. ⇒ ____________

2 Each of the computers need repairing. ⇒ ____________

3 My brother is able to use both hand equally. ⇒ ____________

4 All of my coworker in the office speak Chinese. ⇒ ____________

5 We visit our grandmother almost every weekends. ⇒ ____________

6 The teacher is handing out a sheet to each students. ⇒ ____________

Exercise 3 다음 우리말과 같은 뜻이 되도록 빈칸을 채워 문장을 완성하시오.

1 Logan 부부는 아이가 없다.
⇒ The Logans have ________ ________.

2 각 팀에는 6명의 구성원이 있다.
⇒ There are six members on ________ ________.

3 Lucy는 매달 그녀의 아버지와 캠핑을 간다.
⇒ Lucy goes camping with her father ________ ________.

4 나는 새 차를 사는 데 내 모든 돈을 썼다.
⇒ I spent ________ ________ ________ ________ buying a new car.

5 나는 두 명의 형제가 있고, 둘 다 의사다.
⇒ I have two brothers, and ________ ________ ________ are doctors.

Exercise 4 다음 우리말과 같은 뜻이 되도록 주어진 말을 알맞게 배열하여 문장을 완성하시오.

1 그들은 둘 다 13살이다. (thirteen, them, both, years old, are, of)
⇒ ____________________________

2 나는 일요일마다 교회에 간다. (every, to church, I, Sunday, go)
⇒ ____________________________

3 우리 모두는 같은 학교에 다닌다. (go, the same, school, of, to, all, us)
⇒ ____________________________

4 나의 노크에 아무 대답도 없었다. (no, to my knock, answer, there, was)
⇒ ____________________________

5 각각의 학생들은 각양각색의 재능을 가지고 있다. (talent, a, each, the students, different, has, of)
⇒ ____________________________

7-8 부정대명사 either, neither

either

'(둘 중) 하나'라는 의미로, 단독으로 쓰일 수 있으며 명사를 수식하기도 한다.

❶ 「either+단수명사+단수동사」

A: Which would you like to have, coffee or green tea? 너는 커피와 녹차 중 어느 것을 마시고 싶니?

B: **Either** one is fine. 둘 중 어떤 것이라도 좋아.

❷ 「either+of+복수명사+단수동사」

· **Either** of the answers is correct. 두 대답 중 어느 것이나 정답이다.

> **TIPs**
> **either**는 부정문에서 '둘 중 어느 쪽도 (~아니다)'라는 의미를 가진다.
> • I don't like **either** of the books.
> 나는 그 책 중 어느 쪽도 좋아하지 않는다.

neither

'(둘 중) 어느 쪽도 아닌'이라는 의미로, 단독으로 쓰일 수 있으며 명사를 수식하기도 한다.

❶ 「neither+단수명사+단수동사」

· **Neither** window is open. 두 창문 모두 열려 있지 않다.

❷ 「neither+of+복수명사+단수동사」

· **Neither** of my grandparents is alive. 나의 조부모님 두 분 모두는 살아계시지 않다.

Answers: p.22

Exercise 1 다음 대화의 빈칸에 either나 neither 중 알맞은 것을 쓰시오.

1 A Is Brian British or American?
B ____________. He is French.

2 A Are your parents teachers?
B No. ____________ of them is a teacher.

3 A Choose one of the books. Which one do you want?
B I don't mind ____________ of them.

4 A There are two types of seats, aisle and window. Which would you like?
B ____________. It doesn't matter which one.

Exercise 2 다음 우리말과 같은 뜻이 되도록 주어진 말을 이용하여 문장을 완성하시오.

1 나는 두 명의 아들이 있지만 둘 다 나를 닮지 않았다. (take after)
⇨ I have two sons, but ________________________________.

2 우리 둘 모두 열쇠가 없어서 그 방에 들어갈 수 없었다. (the key)
⇨ We couldn't get into the room because ________________________.

3 판매원이 두 종류의 넥타이를 보여줬지만 둘 중 어느 것도 마음에 들지 않았다. (like)
⇨ The clerk showed me two different ties, but I didn't ____________________.

4 두 명의 새로 온 학생이 있다는 것을 들었지만 그들 중 어느 누구도 만나보지 못했다. (meet)
⇨ I was told that we had two new students, but I haven't ____________________.

Review Test

[01-04] 다음 빈칸에 들어갈 알맞은 말을 고르시오.

01

Fred stayed home and didn't do __________ all day long.

① anyone
② anything
③ nothing
④ somebody
⑤ something

02

This blouse is too large for me. Will you show me __________?

① some
② any
③ another
④ the other
⑤ the others

03

I invited five people to my party, but only Aria and Tom came. __________ didn't show up.

① Some
② Others
③ Another
④ The other
⑤ The others

04

There are two heavy boxes for us to carry. You take one, and I'll take __________.

① another
② one
③ the other
④ the others
⑤ other

05 다음 대화의 빈칸에 들어갈 알맞은 말은?

A Is there a supermarket near here?
B Yes, there's __________ on Main Street.

① one
② it
③ any
④ no
⑤ every

[06-07] 다음 각 문장의 빈칸에 공통으로 들어갈 말을 고르시오.

06

- Do you have __________ good ideas?
- There isn't __________ water in the well.
- __________ questions will be happily answered.

① one
② any
③ some
④ no
⑤ every

07

- There are __________ eggs in the basket.
- Would you like __________ more tea?
- Please lend me __________ money.

① one
② any
③ some
④ no
⑤ every

08 다음 두 문장이 같은 뜻이 되도록 빈칸에 들어갈 알맞은 말은?

You have no problem with your health.
= You don't have __________ problem with your health.

① one
② any
③ some
④ no
⑤ every

09 다음 중 밑줄 친 재귀대명사의 쓰임이 바르지 않은 것은?

① Tim repaired his car himself.
② I finished the report by myself.
③ If you want more milk, help yourself.
④ I bought myself a new laptop computer.
⑤ My parents made this delicious cake herself.

Answers: p.22

[10-11] 다음 문장의 빈칸에 공통으로 들어갈 말을 고르시오.

10

- We helped ___________ to finish the work in time.
- People often give ___________ presents at Christmas.

① another ② others
③ each other ④ the others
⑤ one

11

- Jeff has lost his wallet, so he needs to buy a new ___________.
- We have pizza and hamburgers. Which ___________ would you like?

① it ② that
③ this ④ one
⑤ them

[12-13] 다음 우리말과 같은 뜻일 때 빈칸에 들어갈 알맞은 말을 고르시오.

12

그 아기는 이제 스스로 일어설 수 있다.
= The baby can stand up ___________ himself now.

① by ② with
③ to ④ in
⑤ of

13

사과 주스를 한 잔 더 마시고 싶어요.
= I want to have ___________ glass of apple juice.

① other ② the other
③ another ④ one
⑤ its

[14-15] 다음 대화의 빈칸에 들어갈 말이 바르게 짝지어진 것을 고르시오.

14

A Mom, I want a new smartphone.
B You already have ___________ there.
A But ___________ is too old.

① it – it
② it – some
③ some – one
④ one – one
⑤ one – it

15

A We have ___________ food. We should go grocery shopping.
B You know what? The store we usually go to is closed.
A Don't worry. There's ___________ on Queen Street.

① any – other
② any – the other
③ no – another
④ any – another
⑤ no – other

16 다음 우리말과 같은 뜻일 때 빈칸에 들어갈 알맞은 말이 바르게 짝지어진 것은?

어떤 사람들은 여름을 좋아하고, 또 어떤 사람들은 겨울을 좋아한다.
= ___________ like summer, and ___________ like winter.

① One – others
② Some – other
③ Some – others
④ One – the others
⑤ Another – the others

[17-18] 다음 우리말을 영어로 바르게 옮긴 것을 고르시오.

17

나는 한 손에는 휴대전화를, 다른 한 손에는 컵을 갖고 있다.

① I have my cell phone in one hand, and a cup in the others.
② I have my cell phone in one hand, and a cup in another hand.
③ I have my cell phone in one hand, and a cup in the other hand.
④ I have my cell phone in some hand, and a cup in another hand.
⑤ I have my cell phone in some hand, and a cup in the other hand.

18

Jack은 그들에게 자신의 말을 이해시킬 수 없었다.

① Jack couldn't make it understood to themselves.
② Jack couldn't make him understood to themselves.
③ Jack couldn't make himself understood to themselves.
④ Jack couldn't make himself understood to them.
⑤ Jack couldn't make themselves understood to them.

19 다음 문장의 밑줄 친 one과 쓰임이 같은 것은?

One should keep his promise.

① One of the students is from France.
② One must respect his or her parents.
③ I lost my watch. I have to buy a new one.
④ One fifth of the world's population lives in China.
⑤ I bought two books. One is for my mother, and the other is for myself.

20 다음 중 어법상 어색한 문장은?

① Both of my feet are numb now.
② Neither of the stores are open.
③ All the food in the cooler has gone bad.
④ All the dishes at the restaurant are delicious.
⑤ Each soccer team needs at least 11 players.

21 다음 중 밑줄 친 부분의 쓰임이 다른 하나는?

① Don't blame yourself.
② Please take care of yourself.
③ I myself wouldn't do such a thing.
④ Eddie mumbled to himself for a while.
⑤ My sons enjoyed themselves at the camp.

22 다음 문장의 빈칸에 들어갈 말이 바르게 짝지어진 것은?

________ companies produce goods, and ________ provide services.

① Some – the other
② Some – others
③ One – the other
④ One – others
⑤ Others – some

23 다음 문장의 밑줄 친 it과 쓰임이 같은 것은?

It is hard to focus on work in the morning.

① It is colder than yesterday.
② Is it your car or someone else's?
③ I don't think it is possible to do it by myself.
④ It was still dark when I opened the window.
⑤ Justin recommended the movie, and I liked it very much.

[24-25] 다음 그림을 보고 빈칸에 알맞은 말을 쓰시오.

24
A What is she doing?
B She is looking at ________ in the mirror.

25
A Who is in the classroom?
B There is ________ in there.

[26-28] 다음 중 어법상 어색한 부분을 찾아 바르게 고치시오.

26 Amy has two brothers. Both of them is smart and funny.

⇨ ____________________

27 Suddenly, the door closed in itself with a bang.

⇨ ____________________

28 Each players need to have a bat and glove.

⇨ ____________________

[29-30] 다음 〈보기〉와 같이 가주어 it을 이용하여 문장을 다시 쓰시오.

보기 | To drink too much coffee is bad.
⇨ It is bad to drink too much coffee.

29 That Victoria quit her job is true.

⇨ ____________________

30 To take good pictures is not so easy.

⇨ ____________________

[31-32] 다음 글을 읽고 빈칸에 알맞은 말을 쓰시오.

31 I always carry two things with me. ________ is my smartphone, and ________ is my diary.

32 Mom bought me two different shirts, and ________ of them were black. Though I thanked her, I didn't like ________ of the shirts.

[33-34] 다음 우리말과 같은 뜻이 되도록 빈칸에 알맞은 말을 쓰시오.

33 우리는 어젯밤 **Sam**의 파티에서 즐거운 시간을 보냈다.

⇨ We ________ ________ at Sam's party last night.

34 우리 부모님은 두 분 모두 마법을 믿지 않는다.

⇨ ________ ________ ________ ________ believes in magic.

보너스 유형별 문제

Answers: p.24

[1-2] 다음 대화를 읽고, 물음에 답하시오.

A Are you reading *Oliver Twist* again?

B Yes. It's my favorite book.

A Why do you like it so much?

B Well, it's not interesting in ⓐ it, but I like stories about the dark side of society.

A I see. So, is Charles Dickens your favorite writer?

B Yes. I've read most of ⓑ his book. Some are great, and others are boring, but (A) 각각의 책은 그것만의 교훈이 있어. (its own lesson) His books are worth reading.

1 윗글의 ⓐ와 ⓑ를 어법에 맞게 고쳐 쓰시오.

ⓐ ________________ ⓑ ________________

2 윗글에 주어진 단어를 이용하여 (A)를 영어로 옮기시오.

→ __________ __________ __________ __________ __________ __________

3 다음 글의 밑줄 친 부분 중, 어법상 틀린 것은?

수능 대비형

We ① all make mistakes from time to time, even when dialing a phone number. If the caller ② has reached the wrong number and apologizes, as ③ most people do, all you need to say is "All right." It is rude ④ to hang up on the caller without saying anything. If you dial a wrong number, remember that you have disturbed someone and ⑤ that is only polite to say, "I'm sorry, I have the wrong number."

* hang up on: ~의 전화를 끊어버리다
** disturb: 방해하다

Chapter 8

형용사/부사/ 비교

8-1 형용사의 용법
8-2 주의해야 할 형용사
8-3 형용사의 어순
8-4 주의해야 할 부사 I
8-5 주의해야 할 부사 II
8-6 주의해야 할 부사 III
8-7 원급 비교
8-8 비교급
8-9 최상급
Review Test
보너스 유형별 문제

8-1 형용사의 용법

형용사의 용법

형용사의 용법에는 한정적 용법과 서술적 용법이 있다. 대부분의 형용사는 두 가지 용법 모두로 쓸 수 있지만, 일부 형용사는 한정적 용법으로만, 혹은 서술적 용법으로만 쓰인다.

❶ 한정적 용법: 명사 앞에서 명사를 수식한다.

- Tommy is a **good** dancer. Tommy는 훌륭한 댄서다.
- What's your **favorite** sport? 네가 가장 좋아하는 스포츠는 무엇이니?

❷ 서술적 용법: 주어나 목적어의 성질, 상태를 설명하는 보어로 쓰인다.

- Tiffany is **good** at cheerleading. Tiffany는 치어리딩을 잘한다.
- I found the movie **interesting**. 나는 그 영화가 재미있었다.

TIPs 주격보어로 형용사가 오는 동사

지각동사	look, smell, taste, sound ...
상태동사	remain, keep, hold, stay ...
기타	prove, turn out, seem, appear ...

- The soup **tastes** good.
  그 수프는 맛있다.
- The leaves **turned** yellow.
  나뭇잎이 노랗게 변했다.
- She still **remains** silent.
  그녀는 여전히 침묵을 지키고 있다.

한정적 용법으로만 쓰이는 형용사

live only next lone total extreme drunken elder main ...

- My son brought a **live** chicken home. (o) 아들이 살아 있는 닭을 집으로 가져왔다.
- The chicken is still **live**. (×)
- My **elder** brother is in Canada now. (o) 우리 형은 지금 캐나다에 있다.
- He is **elder** than she is. (×)

TIPs 용법에 따라 의미가 달라지는 형용사

	present	certain	late
한정	현재의	특정한, 어떤	죽은
서술	출석한	확실한	늦은

- I was **present** at the wedding.
  나는 결혼식에 참석했다.
- Write down your **present** address.
  당신의 현주소를 적으세요.

서술적 용법으로만 쓰이는 형용사

alive asleep awake alone afraid ashamed glad sorry upset ...

- The boy is **afraid** of insects. (o) 그 소년은 곤충을 무서워한다.
- The ~~**afraid**~~ boy couldn't touch the cricket. (×) 그 겁먹은 소년은 그 귀뚜라미를 만지지 못했다.
- Our precious baby is **asleep** in my arms. (o) 우리의 사랑스러운 아기가 내 품에 잠들어 있다.
- Don't wake the ~~**asleep**~~ baby. (×) 그 잠들어 있는 아기를 깨우지 마세요.

Answers: p.24

Exercise 1 다음 문장의 밑줄 친 부분이 바르면 O, 어색하면 X로 표시하시오.

1 Both my grandparents are alive. ⇨ ________

2 All my cousins are elder than I am. ⇨ ________

3 Ken looks certain to pass the exam. ⇨ ________

4 He lived an alone life with few friends. ⇨ ________

5 All members are present to rehearse together. ⇨ ________

6 Look at the afraid girl. She is shivering so badly. ⇨ ________

7 I'm getting hungry. Do we have something to eat? ⇨ ________

8 The man must be drunken. He is barely standing up. ⇨ ________

Exercise 2 다음 괄호 안에서 알맞은 것을 고르시오.

1 Those fish are still (live / alive).

2 I was all (lone / alone) in the big room.

3 Fred was (awake / awaken) when I called him.

4 I fell fast (asleep / sleeping) as soon as I laid my head on the pillow.

Exercise 3 다음 문장의 밑줄 친 부분을 우리말로 옮기시오.

1 She was <u>late</u> for the important meeting.

⇒ 그녀는 중요한 회의에 ____________.

2 Our company's <u>present</u> situation is the worst.

⇒ 우리 회사의 ____________ 상황은 최악이다.

3 How many people were <u>present</u> at the meeting?

⇒ 얼마나 많은 사람들이 회의에 ____________?

4 Was the <u>late</u> Queen Elizabeth II a great queen?

⇒ ____________ 엘리자베스 여왕 2세는 훌륭한 여왕이었나요?

5 It is <u>certain</u> that he will succeed in the Premier League.

⇒ 그가 프리미어 리그에서 성공할 것이라는 것은 ____________.

6 <u>Certain</u> students need extra help with schoolwork.

⇒ ____________ 학생들은 학교 수업을 받는 데 추가 도움을 필요로 한다.

Exercise 4 다음 우리말과 같은 뜻이 되도록 주어진 말을 알맞게 배열하여 문장을 완성하시오.

1 너는 달리기를 잘하니? (runner, a, you, are, good)

⇒ ____________________________________

2 우리 모두는 그 책이 지겹게 여겨졌다. (all, the book, boring, we, found)

⇒ ____________________________________

3 나의 남동생은 높은 곳을 무서워한다. (afraid, heights, little, is, my, of, brother)

⇒ ____________________________________

4 모든 학생들이 그 행사에 참석했다. (the event, all, the students, of, were, present, at)

⇒ ____________________________________

5 몇몇의 술 취한 십 대가 창문을 깼다. (a couple of, drunken, broke, teenagers, the window)

⇒ ____________________________________

8-2 주의해야 할 형용사

-ly로 끝나는 형용사

lovely, friendly, lonely, deadly, chilly, daily, likely, lively, silly 등의 형용사는 –ly의 형태로 끝나 부사와 혼동하기 쉽다.

- Look at those **lovely** girls. 저 어여쁜 소녀들을 보아라.
- The disease is **deadly** to animals. 그 질병은 동물에게 치명적이다.

> **TIPs** 장애인을 일컫을 때 '장애'보다는 '사람'에 초점을 두어 the disabled(= disabled people)보다는 people with disabilities 또는 people with special needs라고 표현하는 것이 더 바람직하다.

「the+형용사」

'~ 한 사람들'이라는 의미로, 복수명사로 취급해 복수동사를 취한다.

the poor (= poor people)	**the old** (= old people)	**the living** (= living people)	**the sick** (= sick people)
the rich (= rich people)	**the young** (= young people)	**the dead** (= dead people)	**the disabled** (= disabled people)

- The government must hire more people to look after **the old and sick.**
  정부는 노인들과 아픈 사람들을 돌보기 위해 더 많은 사람들을 고용해야 한다.
- Rachel is devoting herself to helping **the poor.** Rachel은 가난한 사람들을 돕는 데 헌신하고 있다.

Answers: p.24

Exercise 1 다음 괄호 안에서 알맞은 것을 고르시오.

1 You look (lovely / gorgeously) in that hat.

2 You have to be (friendly / kindly) to them.

3 The school has been built for the (blind / blinds).

4 If you ask him (nicely / friendly), he won't say no.

5 I (silly / stupidly) deleted all the contacts on my phone.

6 The young (is / are) interested in the latest electronic products.

Exercise 2 다음 문장의 밑줄 친 부분을 우리말로 옮기시오.

1 How can we use math in our daily life?

⇨ 우리는 ______________________ 수학을 어떻게 활용할 수 있을까?

2 The money will be spent for the poor and sick.

⇨ 그 돈은 ______________________ 위해 쓰일 것이다.

3 The dead cannot stay in the world of the living.

⇨ ______________________ 산 사람들의 세상에 머물 수 없다.

4 I want to buy all of the lovely dolls in the window.

⇨ 나는 진열장에 있는 ______________________ 인형 전부를 사고 싶다.

8-3 형용사의 어순

형용사의 어순

❶ 주로 주관적 생각에 따른 형용사(nice, interesting 등)는 사실에 따른 형용사(round, red 등) 앞에 위치한다.

- Mr. Green is an **interesting young** scientist. Green 씨는 재미있는 젊은 과학자였다.
- I need to buy a **nice cotton** shirt. 나는 질 좋은 면 셔츠를 사야 한다.

❷ 두 개 이상의 형용사(사실에 따른 형용사)가 함께 쓰일 때에는 주로 아래와 같은 어순이 된다.

한정사	주관적 형용사	크기	신구	색깔	국적	재료	명사
a	**nice**	**small**	**new**	**yellow**	**French**	**plastic**	bowl

- I bought some **big wooden** boxes.
  나는 나무로 된 큰 상자 몇 개를 샀다.
- My sister found an **old Chinese** doll in the attic.
  내 여동생은 다락방에서 오래된 중국 인형을 찾았다.

TIPs 한정사는 명사 앞에 쓰이는 형용사 상당 어구를 총칭하는 말이다. 한정사에는 관사, 지시형용사, 대명사의 소유격, 수량형용사 등이 있다.

Answers: p.24

Exercise 1 다음 밑줄 친 부분을 바르게 고쳐 쓰시오.

1 What a sunny beautiful day! ⇨ ____________

2 The Italian old painting was stolen. ⇨ ____________

3 Have you seen my blue favorite tie? ⇨ ____________

4 Black these big bags are not for sale. ⇨ ____________

5 I want to buy a metal nice small vase. ⇨ ____________

6 The stranger was wearing a big fur old coat. ⇨ ____________

7 There are some yellow little pretty flowers over there. ⇨ ____________

Exercise 2 다음 우리말과 같은 뜻이 되도록 주어진 말을 알맞게 배열하여 문장을 완성하시오.

1 어머니는 질 좋은 검정 가죽 재킷을 가지고 계신다. (leather, nice, jacket, a, black)
⇨ My mom has ____________.

2 나는 어젯밤에 슬픈 프랑스 영화를 보았다. (French, a, film, sad)
⇨ I watched ____________ last night.

3 우리는 파티에 쓸 몇 개의 큰 둥근 탁자가 필요하다. (round, tables, some, big)
⇨ We need ____________ for the party.

4 우리 동네에는 이상한 어린 남자아이가 있다. (little, strange, a, boy)
⇨ There is ____________ in my neighborhood.

5 매년 수천 명의 관광객들이 그 오래된 아름다운 탑을 방문한다. (the, old, tower, beautiful)
⇨ Thousands of tourists visit ____________ each year.

8-4 주의해야 할 부사 I

형용사와 형태가 같은 부사

	early	late	only	long	high	fast	well	hard
형용사	이른	늦은	유일한	긴	높은	빠른	건강한	힘든, 단단한
부사	일찍	늦게	오직	오래	높이	빨리	잘	열심히

- Josh gets up **early.** (부사) Josh는 일찍 일어난다.
- Albert is an **early** riser. (형용사) Albert는 일찍 일어나는 사람이다.
- They work **hard** to get what they want. (부사) 그들은 원하는 것을 얻기 위해 열심히 일한다.
- Her family is going through a **hard** time. (형용사) 그녀의 가족은 힘든 시기를 겪고 있다.

-ly가 붙어 전혀 다른 의미가 되는 부사

일반적으로 형용사에 -ly를 붙여 부사를 만들지만 -ly가 붙어 뜻이 완전히 달라지는 부사가 있다.

hard	high	late	near	short	close
어려운, 열심히	높은, 높이	늦은, 늦게	가까운, 가까이	짧은, 짧게	가까운, 가까이
hardly	**highly**	**lately**	**nearly**	**shortly**	**closely**
거의 ~ 않다	대단히, 매우	최근에	거의, 대략	곧, 이윽고	면밀히, 자세히

- Emma studies French very **hard.** Emma는 아주 열심히 프랑스어를 공부한다.
- Dennis **hardly** speaks Portuguese. Dennis는 거의 포르투갈어를 말하지 못한다.
- I have a **close** relationship with Ron. 나는 Ron과 가까운 사이이다.
- Young kids should be **closely** monitored. 어린아이들은 주의 깊게 관찰되어야 한다.

Answers: p.24

Exercise 1 다음 밑줄 친 단어의 품사를 쓰시오.

1 Jackie is a fast runner. ⇨ ____________
2 Raymond can run very fast. ⇨ ____________
3 I go to bed early these days. ⇨ ____________
4 The early bird catches the worm. ⇨ ____________
5 Jenny is known as a hard worker. ⇨ ____________
6 She works very hard for her company. ⇨ ____________

Exercise 2 다음 괄호 안에서 알맞은 것을 고르시오.

1 I haven't seen Mr. Watson (late / lately).
2 Willy works very (hard / hardly) at his new job.
3 I can (hard / hardly) believe what just happened.
4 It took (near / nearly) three minutes to download this program.
5 One of my friends dropped by my house (late / lately) at night.

Exercise 3 다음 중 어법상 어색한 부분을 바르게 고쳐 쓰시오. (바르면 ○표 할 것)

1 Catherine hardly wears jewelry. ⇒ ____________

2 An eagle is flying highly in the air. ⇒ ____________

3 My best friend lives closely to me. ⇒ ____________

4 What movie have you seen recently? ⇒ ____________

5 Near ten thousand people came to the concert. ⇒ ____________

Exercise 4 다음 우리말과 같은 뜻이 되도록 〈보기〉에서 알맞은 말을 골라 문장을 완성하시오.

shortly	hard	close	short	hardly	closely

1 그들은 네가 간 후 바로 나타났다.
⇒ They showed up ____________ after you left.

2 Chris는 며칠 동안 거의 아무것도 먹지 않았다.
⇒ Chris has ____________ eaten anything for several days.

3 나는 공을 세게 쳤고 그것은 펜스를 넘어갔다.
⇒ I hit the ball ____________, and it went over the fence.

4 Ryan이 공을 짧게 던져서 나는 그것을 받지 못했다.
⇒ Ryan threw the ball ____________, and I couldn't catch it.

5 가까이 다가와 봐. 너의 얼굴에 무언가가 묻어 있다.
⇒ Get ____________ to me. You have something on your face.

6 그림을 자세히 보고 난 후, 그는 그것이 가짜임을 깨달았다.
⇒ Looking ____________ at the picture, he realized that it was a fake.

Exercise 5 다음 우리말과 같은 뜻이 되도록 주어진 말을 이용하여 문장을 완성하시오.

1 나는 난간에서 거의 떨어질 뻔했다. (near)
⇒ I ____________ fell off the railings.

2 가까운 미래에 너를 만날 수 있길 바란다. (near)
⇒ I hope to see you in the ____________ future.

3 이 레스토랑이 최근 점점 인기를 끌고 있다. (late)
⇒ This restaurant is becoming popular ____________.

4 모두 Matt가 대단히 성공한 사업가라는 것에 동의한다. (high)
⇒ Everyone agrees that Matt is a(n) ____________ successful businessman.

8-5 주의해야 할 부사 II

so, such

❶ so: 「so+형용사/부사」

'매우', '그만큼'이라는 의미로, 명사를 수식하지 않은 형용사나 부사를 강조한다.

- The play was **so** funny. 그 연극은 매우 재미있었다.
- What I did was **so** stupid. 내가 한 일은 매우 어리석었다.
- Try not to speak **so** fast. 너무 빨리 말하지 않도록 하여라.

❷ such: 「such+(a(n))+형용사+명사」

'매우', '그렇게'라는 의미로, 명사와 함께 쓰이는 형용사를 강조한다.

- That is **such** a sad story. 그것은 매우 슬픈 이야기다.
- We had **such** a good time with the kids. 우리는 아이들과 아주 즐거운 시간을 보냈다.
- I've never met **such** a nice person. 나는 그렇게 좋은 사람을 만나본 적이 없다.

Answers: p.25

Exercise 1 다음 문장의 빈칸에 so 또는 such를 쓰시오.

1 It is ____________ a lovely day.

2 Why are you ____________ late for work?

3 The Andersons are ____________ nice people.

4 We were ____________ tired after the long walk.

5 He has been ____________ quiet for a long time.

6 I couldn't finish my meal after ____________ a big snack.

Exercise 2 다음 우리말과 같은 뜻이 되도록 주어진 단어와 so 또는 such를 이용하여 문장을 완성하시오.

1 나는 그렇게 웃긴 농담은 들어본 적이 없다. (funny, joke)

⇨ I've never heard ________________________________.

2 아기를 돌보는 것은 매우 어려운 일이다. (hard, job)

⇨ Looking after a baby is ________________________________.

3 나는 Klein 씨가 그렇게 나이가 많은지 몰랐다. (old, man)

⇨ I didn't realize Mr. Klein was ________________________________.

4 왜 너는 대중 앞에서 말하는 것을 그렇게 두려워 하니? (afraid)

⇨ Why are you ________________________________ of speaking in public?

5 우리는 이렇게 아침 일찍 찾아오는 사람이 없다. (early)

⇨ We don't have visitors ________________________________ in the morning.

6 그녀는 매우 사랑스럽다. 나는 왜 그녀가 십 대들 사이에서 그렇게 인기가 많은지 알겠다. (popular)

⇨ She is so lovely. I understand why she is ________________________________ among teenagers.

8-6 주의해야 할 부사 III

still, yet, already

❶ still: '여전히', '아직도'라는 의미로, 긍정문과 의문문에 주로 쓰이고, 계속의 의미를 강조할 때는 부정문에도 쓰인다.

- Mom **still** hasn't come home. 엄마는 아직 집에 오시지 않으셨어요.
- Diana is **still** in the hospital after heart surgery.
  Diana는 심장수술 후 여전히 병원에 있다.

❷ yet: 주로 문장의 끝에 위치해, 의문문에서는 '이미', '벌써', '이제'라는 의미로, 부정문에서는 '아직'이라는 의미로 쓰인다.

- Has the train arrived **yet**? 기차가 이미 도착했니?
- I haven't **yet** decided whether to go or not. 나는 아직 갈지 안 갈지 결정하지 못했다.

❸ already: 예상했던 것보다 이를 때 '이미', '벌써'라는 의미로, 긍정문과 의문문에 쓰인다.

- We've **already** had dinner. 우리는 이미 저녁을 먹었다.
- Does she **already** know what happened? 그녀가 벌써 무슨 일이 있었는지 아니?

Answers: p.25

Exercise 1 다음 괄호 안에서 알맞은 것을 고르시오.

1 Have you finished the work (still / yet)?

2 Take an umbrella. It is (still / yet) raining.

3 They have (still / already) left for New York.

4 We are (still / yet) waiting for the missing boys.

5 It's only 11 o'clock, and I'm (already / yet) hungry.

6 I don't know anything about the results (already / yet).

Exercise 2 다음 우리말과 같은 뜻이 되도록 주어진 말을 알맞게 배열하여 문장을 완성하시오.

1 Bill이 이미 새 직업을 구했니? (a, job, found, new, yet, Bill, has)

⇨ ______________________________

2 기차는 이미 정거장을 떠났다. (left, already, has, the station, the train)

⇨ ______________________________

3 너의 남동생은 아직도 자고 있는 거니? (in, your, bed, little, is, still, brother)

⇨ ______________________________

4 Sam은 아직 무엇을 고를지 결정하지 못했다. (decided, what, yet, Sam, hasn't, to, choose)

⇨ ______________________________

5 엄마는 내가 엄마의 가장 아끼는 귀걸이를 잃어버렸다는 것을 이미 아셔.
(her, mom, knows, lost, favorite, I've, earrings, that, already)

⇨ ______________________________

8-7 원급 비교

원급 비교

❶ 「as+형용사/부사의 원급+as」: '~만큼 …한/하게'

- Robert is **as wise as** Solomon (was). Robert는 솔로몬 왕만큼 현명하다.
- I go running **as often as** you (do). 나도 너만큼 자주 달리기를 한다.

❷ 「not+as[so]+형용사/부사의 원급+as」: '~만큼 …하지 않은/않게'

- My hair is**n't as**[so] **long as** yours. 나의 머리카락은 너의 것보다 길지 않다.
  = Your hair is **longer than** mine.
- She does**n't** know **as many** people **as** I do. 그녀는 나보다 많은 사람을 알고 있지는 않다.
  = I know **more** people **than** she does.

❸ 「배수사+as+형용사/부사의 원급+as」: '~보다 …배 ~한/하게'

- China is **three times as big as** India. 중국은 인도보다 세 배 더 크다.
- His car is **twice as expensive as** mine.
  그의 차는 나의 차보다 두 배 비싸다.

> **TIPs**
> 「배수사+as+형/부 원급+as」는 「배수사+비교급+than」으로 바꿔 쓸 수 있다.
> - My bag is **three times as big as** yours.
>   = My bag is **three times bigger than** yours.

❹ 「as+형용사/부사의 원급+as+possible」
'가능한 ~한/하게'라는 의미로, 「as+형용사/부사의 원급+as+주어+can/could」로 바꿔 쓸 수 있다.

- The boys ran up the hill **as fast as possible.** 소년들은 최대한 빨리 그 언덕을 달려 올라갔다.
  = The boys ran up the hill **as fast as** they **could**.
- I'll get in touch with you **as soon as possible.** 가능한 한 빨리 당신에게 연락을 드리겠습니다.
  = I'll get in touch with you **as soon as** I **can**.

Answers: p.25

Exercise 1 다음 그림을 보고 빈칸을 채워 문장을 완성하시오.

❶ 

❷ 

❸ 

❹ 

❺ 

❻ 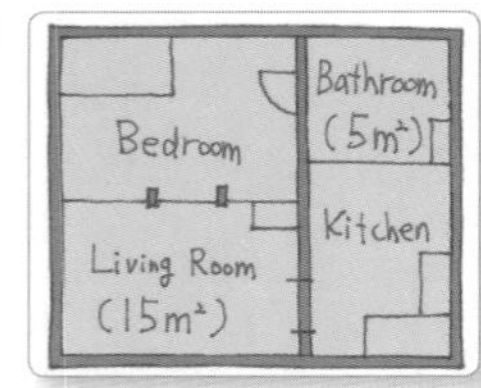

1 Alice is __________ __________ __________ Lucy.

2 Joe has __________ __________ as much money as David does.

3 Evan is __________ __________ __________ __________ Chuck.

4 The mountain on the left is __________ as high as the one on the right.

5 The cassette player is five times __________ __________ the MP3 player.

6 The living room is three times __________ __________ __________ the bathroom.

Exercise 2 다음 괄호 안에서 알맞은 것을 고르시오.

1 Fred spoke to her as clearly as he (can / could).

2 I cannot cook as (well / better) as my mom does.

3 The basketball player is (as twice / twice as) tall as I am.

4 I'll send you the document as (soon / sooner) as possible.

5 Taking the bus is not as fast as (take / taking) the subway.

6 I answered the questions as quickly as (I possible / I could).

7 The necklace is five times (as / more) expensive than I expected.

8 A grasshopper can jump 20 times (as high / higher) as its length.

Exercise 3 다음 두 문장이 같은 뜻이 되도록 원급 비교 구문을 이용하여 문장을 완성하시오.

1 My baby woke up earlier than me.

⇨ I ______________________________ my baby.

2 I have three cookies, and you have nine cookies.

⇨ You have ______________________________ I do.

3 Cold air is heavier than warm air.

⇨ Warm air ______________________________ cold air.

4 This tower is taller than that castle.

⇨ That castle ______________________________ this tower.

5 My sister's room is three times larger than mine.

⇨ My sister's room ______________________________ mine.

Exercise 4 다음 우리말과 같은 뜻이 되도록 주어진 말을 알맞게 배열하여 문장을 완성하시오.

1 나는 최대한 빨리 학교로 달렸다. (I, as, could, fast, as)

⇨ I ran to school ______________________________.

2 나는 가능한 한 자주 운동을 하려고 노력한다. (as, often, can, I, as)

⇨ I try to work out ______________________________.

3 가능한 한 빨리 나에게 알려주세요. (as, soon, possible, as)

⇨ Please let me know ______________________________.

4 LED등은 할로겐등보다 25배 더 오래간다. (long, twenty-five, times, as, as)

⇨ An LED bulb lasts ______________________________ an halogen bulb.

8-8 비교급

「A 비교급+than B」

'A가 B보다 더 ~한/하게'라는 의미로, 원급 비교 「B not as[so]+원급+as A」로 바꿔 쓸 수 있다.

- Platinum is **harder than** gold. 백금은 금보다 더 단단하다.
  = Gold is**n't as**[**so**] **hard as** platinum. 금은 백금만큼 단단하지 않다.
- The bicycle is **more expensive than** my old car. 그 자전거는 내 낡은 자동차보다 더 비싸다.
  = My old car is**n't as**[**so**] **expensive as** the bicycle. 내 낡은 자동차는 그 자전거만큼 비싸지 않다.

「A less+원급+than B」

'A가 B보다 덜 ~한/하게'라는 의미로, 원급 비교 「A not+as[so]+원급+as B」로 바꿔 쓸 수 있다.

- I watch TV **less often than** you do. 나는 너보다 덜 자주 텔레비전을 본다.
  = I do**n't** watch TV **as**[**so**] **often as** you do. 나는 너보다 더 자주 텔레비전을 보지 않는다.
- The injury is **less serious than** it appears. 그 부상은 보이는 것보다 덜 심하다.
  = The injury is**n't as**[**so**] **serious as** it appears. 그 부상은 보이는 것만큼 심하지는 않다.

비교급의 강조

much, even, still, far, a lot 등은 비교급 앞에 쓰여 '훨씬 더'라는 의미로, 비교급을 강조한다.

- Russia is **much bigger** than Korea. 러시아는 한국보다 훨씬 더 크다.
- The problem is getting **far more serious**. 그 문제는 훨씬 더 심각해지고 있다.

Answers: p.25

Exercise 1 다음 〈보기〉와 같이 주어진 단어를 이용하여 문장을 완성하시오.

Jake weighs 130 pounds. Greg weighs 110 pounds. (heavy)
⇒ Jake is heavier than Greg.
⇒ Greg less heavy than Jake.

1 The midterm exam was easy. The final exam was difficult. (difficult)
⇒ The final exam was ______________ than the midterm exam.
⇒ The midterm exam was ______________ than the final exam.

2 I go fishing twice a month. Jeff goes fishing once a month. (often)
⇒ I go fishing ______________ than Jeff does.
⇒ Jeff goes fishing ______________ than I do.

3 There are 30 people on the red bus. There are 10 people on the blue bus. (crowded)
⇒ The red bus is ______________ than the blue bus.
⇒ The blue bus is ______________ than the red bus.

4 This hydrogen vehicle is $60,000. That electric vehicle is $40,000. (expensive)
⇒ This hydrogen vehicle is ______________ than that electric vehicle.
⇒ That electric vehicle is ______________ than this hydrogen vehicle.

Exercise 2 다음 괄호 안에서 알맞은 것을 고르시오.

1 Tom is (so / much) more careful than me.

2 Your scar looks (a lot / very) worse than before.

3 The shirt is (so / more) expensive than I thought.

4 Health is (still / very) more important than wealth.

5 My boss made the work (more / far) easier than it used to be.

Exercise 3 다음 〈보기〉와 같이 문장을 완성하시오.

> I feel math isn't as difficult as science.
> ⇒ I feel science is more difficult than math.
> ⇒ I feel math is less difficult than science.

1 Tommy doesn't have as much money as I do.

⇒ I have ______________________ than Tommy does.

⇒ Tommy has ______________________ than I do.

2 Non-organic food isn't as expensive as organic food.

⇒ Organic food is ______________________ non-organic food.

⇒ Non-organic food is ______________________ organic food.

3 The movie wasn't as interesting as the original.

⇒ The original was ______________________ the movie.

⇒ The movie was ______________________ the original.

Exercise 4 다음 우리말과 같은 뜻이 되도록 주어진 단어를 이용하여 문장을 완성하시오.

1 철이 금보다 더 유용하다. (useful)

⇒ Iron is ______________________ gold.

2 도쿄는 런던보다 훨씬 더 복잡하다. (far, crowded)

⇒ Tokyo is ______________________ London.

3 헬리콥터는 비행기보다 더 낮게 날 수 있다. (low)

⇒ Helicopters can fly ______________________ airplanes.

4 이 공식은 이전 것보다 덜 복잡하다. (complicated)

⇒ This formula is ______________________ the one before.

8-9 최상급

「the+최상급(+명사)+in+장소, 범위를 나타내는 단수명사」: ~에서 가장 …한

- Randy is **the tallest** boy **in** my school. Randy가 우리 학교에서 가장 키가 크다.
- Jupiter is **the biggest** planet **in** the solar system. 목성은 태양계에서 가장 큰 행성이다.

「the+최상급(+명사)+of+기간, 비교 대상이 되는 명사」: ~중에 가장 …한

- I am **the youngest of** three children. 나는 삼 형제 중 막내다.
- It was **the happiest** moment **of** my life.
  그것은 내 생애 가장 행복한 순간이었다.

> **TIPs**
> **much, by far, the very 등으로 최상급을 강조할 수 있다.**
> - James is **by far** the smartest of his brothers.
>   James는 그의 형제들 중 단연 가장 영리하다.

「one of the+최상급+복수명사」: '가장 ~한 … 중 하나'

- She is **one of the most famous singers** in Japan.
  그녀는 일본에서 가장 유명한 가수 중 한 명이다.
- Kayaking is **one of my most favorite outdoor activities.**
  카약은 내가 가장 좋아하는 야외 활동 중 하나이다.

「the+최상급(+that)+주어+have/has ever+과거분사」: '지금까지 ~한 중 가장 …한'

- This book is **the most interesting novel I've ever read.** 이 책은 내가 읽은 소설 중 가장 재미있다.
- What is **the funniest** joke **you've ever heard**? 네가 들어본 것 중 가장 웃긴 농담은 무엇이니?

원급과 비교급을 이용한 최상급 표현

> 「the+최상급」 가장 ~하다
> =「비교급+than any other+단수명사」 ~보다 더 …하다
> =「부정어+비교급+than」 ~보다 더 …한 것은 없다
> =「부정어+as+원급+as」 ~만큼 …한 것은 없다

- Seoul is **the largest** city in Korea. 서울은 한국에서 가장 큰 도시이다.
  ⇨ Seoul is **larger than any other** city in Korea. (비교급) 서울은 한국의 다른 어떤 도시보다 크다.
  ⇨ **No** (**other**) city in Korea is **larger than** Seoul. (비교급) 한국에서 서울보다 큰 도시는 없다.
  ⇨ **No** (**other**) city in Korea is **as large as** Seoul. (원급) 한국에서 서울만큼 큰 도시는 없다.

Answers: p.25

Exercise 1 다음 괄호 안에서 알맞은 것을 고르시오.

1 Your hairpin is the smallest (of / in) all these hairpins.

2 It was the (hotter / hottest) day of the summer.

3 Joe is the brightest boy I've ever (know / known).

4 Jim is (taller / tallest) than any other boy in his class.

5 It is (the very /the most) worst mistake anyone could ever make.

6 No other river in the world is as (long / longer) as the Nile.

7 The little boy was braver than any other (man / men) in the country.

Exercise 2 다음 〈보기〉와 같이 문장을 완성하시오.

> Mt. Everest is the highest mountain in the world.
> ⇒ Mt. Everest is higher than any other mountain in the world.
> ⇒ No other mountain in the world is higher than Mt. Everest.
> ⇒ No other mountain in the world is as high as Mt. Everest.

1 Mr. Wilson is the richest man in the village.
⇒ Mr. Wilson is ______________________________ in the village.
⇒ ______________ in the village is ______________ Mr. Wilson.
⇒ ______________ in the village is ______________ Mr. Wilson.

2 This tower is the tallest building in the city.
⇒ This tower is ______________________________ in the city.
⇒ ______________ in the city is ______________ this tower.
⇒ ______________ in the city is ______________ this tower.

3 The cheetah is the fastest animal on land.
⇒ The cheetah is ______________________________ on land.
⇒ ______________ on land is ______________ the cheetah.
⇒ ______________ on land is ______________ the cheetah.

Exercise 3 다음 우리말과 같은 뜻이 되도록 주어진 말을 이용하여 문장을 완성하시오.

1 Jerry는 내가 만나본 사람 중 가장 재미있는 사람이다. (funny)
⇒ Jerry is ______________________________.

2 나는 우리나라에서 그보다 더 훌륭한 배우는 없다고 생각한다. (actor, than)
⇒ I think ______________________________ him.

3 그는 세상에서 단연 가장 빠른 달리기 선수다. (by far)
⇒ He is ______________________________ in the world.

4 지구상에서 나의 어머니가 어떤 여성보다 현명하다. (wise)
⇒ My mom is ______________________________ on earth.

5 세상에서 바티칸 시국만큼 작은 나라는 없다. (country, as)
⇒ No other ______________________________ Vatican City.

6 프라하는 세상에서 가장 아름다운 도시 중 하나이다. (beautiful)
⇒ Prague is ______________________________ in the world.

Review Test

[01-04] 다음 빈칸에 들어갈 알맞은 말을 고르시오.

01 The baby soon fell ________ in the cradle.

① sleep ② slept
③ sleeping ④ asleep
⑤ sleepy

02 My daughter doesn't know how to swim ________.

① still ② yet
③ too ④ neither
⑤ already

03 Mary has ________ a big mouth. She tells everyone everything!

① so ② such
③ too ④ very
⑤ much

04 Look at those ________ little dolls. I want one of them.

① happily ② luckily
③ truly ④ sadly
⑤ lovely

[05-06] 다음 빈칸에 알맞지 않은 것을 고르시오.

05 It is ________ colder this year than last year.

① much ② very
③ still ④ far
⑤ even

06 A(n) ________ lady got on the bus, and I offered my seat to her.

① old ② pregnant
③ afraid ④ sick
⑤ pretty

07 다음 두 문장의 뜻이 같을 때 빈칸에 들어갈 알맞은 말은?

Mike has 30 dollars, and his brother has 90 dollars.
= Mike's brother has ________ as much money as Mike does.

① much ② very
③ half ④ three times
⑤ better

08 다음 빈칸에 들어갈 알맞은 표현은?

I didn't want to wake anybody. So I tiptoed into the room ________________.

① as quietly as I can
② as quiet as I could
③ as quietly as I could
④ as quietly as I possible
⑤ as quietly as I could possible

09 다음 빈칸에 들어갈 말이 바르게 짝지어진 것은?

It is the ________ book that I've ever read, but it is much ________ interesting than I expected.

① longer – more
② longest – more
③ longer – most
④ longest – most
⑤ long – much

[10-11] 다음 두 문장이 같은 뜻이 되도록 빈칸에 알맞은 말을 고르시오.

10

David doesn't read as many books as I do. = I read ________ David does.

① the most books
② more books than
③ less books than
④ less more books than
⑤ a lot more books than

11

My elder brother is three times as heavy as my younger sister. = My elder brother is three times ________ my younger sister.

① heaviest of
② heavier than
③ as heavy than
④ less heavy than
⑤ much heavier than

12 다음 문장의 괄호 안에 주어진 단어를 알맞게 배열한 것은?

Jess bought (little, Chinese, some, cute) dolls.

① Chinese some little cute
② little cute some Chinese
③ cute little Chinese some
④ some cute little Chinese
⑤ cute some little Chinese

13 다음 밑줄 친 부분 중 성격이 다른 하나는?

① Still water runs deep.
② My mom sings pretty well.
③ No one was late for the party.
④ He hardly ever opens his mouth.
⑤ I've tried hard to make you happy.

14 다음 문장 중 나머지와 의미가 다른 하나는?

① Nothing is as precious as health.
② Health is the most precious thing.
③ Nothing is more precious than health.
④ Health is as precious as any other thing.
⑤ Health is more precious than any other thing.

15 다음 문장의 밑줄 친 부분과 쓰임이 같은 것은?

The live fish in the tank are tropical fish.

① Are you afraid of snakes?
② I was all alone in the room.
③ I'm so glad to finally meet you.
④ Gwen felt ashamed of her selfish thoughts.
⑤ The main subjects are shown in the diagram.

16 다음 밑줄 친 부분 중 의미가 다른 하나는?

① I'm not certain what to do next.
② They are certain to vote for him.
③ Certain students are often late for school.
④ I'm absolutely certain with no doubt.
⑤ It seems certain that Gary will succeed.

17 다음 문장의 밑줄 친 부분과 의미가 같은 것은?

Kelly's late grandfather was one of the bravest generals of the army.

① Why were you so late?
② Don't go out late at night.
③ They were up late last night.
④ I was late for the appointment.
⑤ Mrs. White still misses her late husband.

[18-19] 다음 우리말을 영어로 바르게 옮긴 것을 고르시오.

18 그는 역대 가장 위대한 작가 중 한 명이다.

① He is a great writer of all time.
② He is the greatest writer of all time.
③ He is one of the greatest writers of all time.
④ He is as great as any other writer of all time.
⑤ He is greater than any other writer of all time.

19 그는 요즘 나보다 덜 바쁘다.

① I am not so busy as he is these days.
② He is less busy than I am these days.
③ He is as less busy as I am these days.
④ He is less busier than I am these days.
⑤ I am much busier than he is these days.

20 다음 중 어법상 어색한 문장은?

① I practiced hard to win the contest.
② The poor needs more help than the rich.
③ Jessica jumped high to touch the ceiling.
④ Jasper arrived home shortly after five.
⑤ She is doing well after the surgery.

21 다음 우리말을 영어로 옮긴 것 중 바르지 않은 것은?

① 이미 눈이 그쳤니?
→ Has it stopped snowing yet?
② 너는 왜 그렇게 일찍 일어났니?
→ Why did you get up so early?
③ 나는 아직도 그가 나타나기를 기다리고 있다.
→ I'm still waiting for him to show up.
④ Frank는 그렇게 큰 도시에 가본 적이 없다.
→ Frank has never been to a such big city.
⑤ 너의 아들은 벌써 글을 읽을 줄 아니?
→ Does your son already know how to read?

22 다음 빈칸에 들어갈 말이 바르게 짝지어진 것은?

No other animal in the world is bigger than the blue whale.
⇒ The blue whale is ___________ than any other animal in the world.
⇒ No other animal in the world is as ___________ as the blue whale.
⇒ The blue whale is the ___________ animal in the world.

① big – bigger – biggest
② big – biggest – bigger
③ bigger – biggest – big
④ bigger – big – biggest
⑤ biggest – big – bigger

23 다음 두 문장의 의미가 같지 않은 것은?

① Anna is taller than you.
= You are not so tall as Anna.
② Jason ran away as fast as he could.
= Jason ran away as fast as possible.
③ This question is easier than the last one.
= The last question is as easy as this one.
④ My niece is the smartest girl in her class.
= No other girl in her class is as smart as my niece.
⑤ This car is ten times as expensive as yours.
= This car is ten times more expensive than yours.

[24-25] 다음 문장에서 어법상 어색한 부분을 찾아 바르게 고치시오.

24 Bill speaks Chinese as better as you do.

⇒ ___________________________

25 She hard studies, but she always gets good grades on tests.

⇒ ___________________________

[26-28] 다음 두 문장이 같은 뜻이 되도록 빈칸에 알맞은 말을 쓰시오.

26 You'd better come back as soon as you can.

⇒ You'd better come back as soon as ___________.

27 My oldest brother is twice my age.

⇒ My oldest brother is _________ _________ _________ as I am.

28 I've never seen a more beautiful city than Paris.

⇒ Paris is the __________ __________ city I've ever seen.

[29-32] 다음 우리말과 같은 뜻이 되도록 빈칸에 알맞은 말을 쓰시오.

29 형은 나보다 수영을 훨씬 더 잘한다.

⇒ My brother is much ______________ at swimming than I am.

30 어제 우리는 게를 잡았다. 그리고 그것들은 아직도 살아 있다.

⇒ We caught some crabs yesterday, and they are still ____________.

31 나는 아픈 사람들을 돕기 위해 자선 사업을 시작할 것이다.

⇒ I am going to start a charity to help ____________________________.

32 그녀의 현재 상태는 지난주보다 많이 좋아졌다.

⇒ Her _______________ condition is a lot better than last week.

33 다음 밑줄 친 부분을 우리말로 옮기시오.

A The sky is ① so clear, and the sun is so warm!
B Why don't we go on a picnic?
A That is ② such a good idea. Have you been to Hyde Park ③ lately?
B No, I haven't. But I'm ④ certain that there are lots of people on a beautiful day like this.

① : _______________
② : _______________
③ : _______________
④ : _______________

[34-36] 다음 우리말과 같은 뜻이 되도록 주어진 말을 알맞게 배열하여 문장을 완성하시오.

34 저 큰 빨간 플라스틱 상자는 무엇에 쓰는 것이니?

⇒ What is ____________________ for?
(big, plastic, that, red, box)

35 너는 아직도 그 소식을 듣지 못했니?

⇒ Haven't you ____________________?
(yet, the, heard, news)

36 나는 그렇게 끔찍한 광경을 본 적이 없다.

⇒ I've never seen ____________________.
(horrible, a, sight, such)

보너스 유형별 문제

Answers: p.27

[1-3] 도표를 보고 주어진 단어를 이용하여 문장을 완성하시오. 서술형

Director Gary Whiteman's Last Three Movies

Movie Title	Review	Year released	Running time	Number of tickets sold
The Black Feather	★★★★★	2021	100(mins)	3,000,000
The Gibson's	★★☆☆☆	2022	200(mins)	3,000,000
Why I Left You	★★★☆☆	2019	130(mins)	6,000,000

1 *The Gibson's* is his __________ (late) movie, and it got the __________ (many) stars in the reviews.

2 *The Gibson's* is __________ __________ (two, long) than *The Black Feather*, and it is __________ __________ __________ (popular) *The Black Feather*.

3 *Why I Left You* is __________ __________ (old) movie of the three, but it is __________ __________ __________ (popular) movie.

4 다음 글의 밑줄 친 부분 중, 어법상 틀린 것은? 수능 대비형

Argentina is a ① very large country in the southern part of South America. It is the eighth ② large country in the world. The nation is home to many animal species. In the oceans, ③ there are large populations of seals, penguins, and dolphins. In the northern mountains, cat species, ④ like cougars and jaguars, can be found. Argentina is also a wonderful place ⑤ to see many different types of birds.

* species: 종
** population: 인구[동물들]

Chapter 9

가정법

9-1 가정법 과거
9-2 가정법 과거와 단순 조건문
9-3 가정법 과거완료
9-4 I wish 가정법
9-5 as if 가정법
Review Test
보너스 유형별 문제

9-1 가정법 과거

가정법 과거

가정법 과거는 '~라면[한다면] …일[할] 텐데'라는 의미로, 현재 사실에 반대되는 상황이나 실현 불가능 한 일을 가정하거나 상상할 때 쓰인다.

「If+주어+동사의 과거형 ~, 주어+조동사의 과거형+동사원형 ~」

- If I **won** the lottery, I **would** buy a big mansion.
  내가 복권에 당첨된다면 큰 저택을 살 텐데.
- If we **caught** the 10 o'clock train, we **could** get there earlier.
  우리가 10시 기차를 탄다면 그곳에 더 일찍 도착할 수 있을 텐데.
- What **would** you do if you **were** invisible for a day?
  하루 동안 투명 인간이 될 수 있다면 무엇을 할 거니?

TIPs
가정법 과거에서 if절의 be동사는 인칭이나 수에 관계없이 were를 쓴다. 회화체에서는 was를 쓰기도 한다.
- If it **were** sunny, we could go to the beach. 날씨가 화창하면 우리는 해변으로 갈 수 있을 텐데.

가정법 과거와 직설법

가정법 과거는 현재 사실을 나타내는 직설법 문장으로 표현할 수 있다.

If I had enough money, I could buy a new car. (가정법 과거)

Because[As] I don't have enough money, I can't buy a new car. (직설법)
I don't have enough money, so I can't buy a new car. (직설법)

- **If** I **knew** his phone number, I **could** call him. 내가 그의 전화번호를 안다면 그에게 전화할 텐데.
  ⇒ **Because[As]** I **don't know** his phone number, I **can't** call him.
  ⇒ I **don't know** his phone number, **so** I **can't** call him.
  나는 그의 전화번호를 몰라서 그에게 전화할 수 없다.

Answers: p.27

Exercise 1 다음 괄호 안에서 알맞은 것을 고르시오.

1 If I (go / went) to college, I would study history.
2 Lisa (will / could) meet us if she came earlier.
3 If he (hears / heard) the news, he would be glad.
4 We would travel abroad if we (have / had) more money.
5 If you (was / were) me, you would do the same thing.
6 If I were not sick, I (won't / wouldn't) miss the concert.
7 If I (am / were) him, I would not believe what she says.
8 If I were you, I wouldn't (do / have done) such a thing.
9 We could stay longer in New York if we (have / had) more time.
10 If we had a car, we (won't / wouldn't) have to take the crowded subway.

Exercise 2 다음 주어진 단어를 이용하여 문장을 완성하시오.

1 If it __________ raining, we would go swimming. (be not)

2 If he __________ his car, he could pay the rent. (sell)

3 What would you do if you __________ in my shoes? (be)

4 If he __________ a grown-up, he could see the movie with us. (be)

5 If Brian were not afraid of horses, we __________ go horseback riding. (can)

6 If you listened more carefully, you __________ understand what she is saying. (will)

Exercise 3 다음 우리말과 같은 뜻이 되도록 주어진 단어를 이용하여 문장을 완성하시오.

1 내가 당신이라면 그녀를 고용하는 것을 망설이지 않을 것이다. (hesitate)
⇨ If I __________ you, I __________ __________ to hire her.

2 내가 파리에 산다면 이 아름다운 에펠탑을 매일 볼 수 있을 텐데. (live)
⇨ If I __________ in Paris, I __________ see the beautiful Eiffel Tower every day.

3 Emily가 그 사실을 알면 그녀는 나에게 실망할 텐데. (know)
⇨ If Emily __________ the truth, she __________ __________ disappointed in me.

4 당신이 나라면 그 위험한 제안을 받아들이겠습니까? (accept)
⇨ If you __________ me, __________ __________ __________ the dangerous offer?

Exercise 4 다음 직설법 문장을 가정법 과거 문장으로 전환하시오.

1 As Alex is sick, he can't be with us now.
⇨ ____

2 Anne never keeps her word, so I don't trust her.
⇨ ____

3 As I'm not close to him, I can't tell him what to do.
⇨ ____

4 Because he is not an honest man, he can't be our president.
⇨ ____

5 I don't know her phone number or address, so I can't get in touch with her.
⇨ ____

9-2 가정법 과거와 단순 조건문

가정법 과거와 단순 조건의 비교

	가정법 if	조건의 if
의미	'~라면[한다면] …일[할] 텐데'	'~라면[한다면] …일[할] 것이다'
쓰임	현재 사실과 반대되는 상황이나 실현 가능성이 거의 없는 일을 나타낼 때	현재나 미래에 실현 가능성이 있는 일에 대한 조건을 나타낼 때
형태	「If+주어+동사의 과거형 ~, 주어+조동사의 과거형+동사원형 ~」	「If+주어+동사현재형~, 주어+현재형 또는 미래형 동사 ~」

- **If** it **is** sunny, we **will** go on a picnic. (조건의 if)
  날씨가 화창하면 우리는 소풍을 갈 것이다.
- **If** it **were** sunny, we **would** go on a picnic. (가정법 if)
  날씨가 화창하다면 우리는 소풍을 갈 텐데.

TIPs
미래의 일을 나타낸다고 하더라도 if절의 동사는 현재 시제를 쓴다.
- If he **gets** my message, he will call back. (O)
  그가 나의 메시지를 받으면 내게 다시 전화 줄 거야.
  If he ~~will get~~ my message, he will call back. (X)

Answers: p.27

Exercise 1 다음 괄호 안에서 알맞은 것을 고르시오.

1 If you are tired, you (can / could) leave early today.
2 If it (snows / snowed) tomorrow, the field trip will be canceled.
3 If he were brave enough, he (will / would) face up to his difficulties.
4 If I (have / had) more money, I would buy something for my parents.
5 I would help you with your work if I (am not / weren't) so busy.
6 The children will not go for a walk if it (rains / will rain) in the afternoon.

Exercise 2 다음 우리말과 같은 뜻이 되도록 주어진 단어를 이용하여 문장을 완성하시오.

1 네가 배가 고프면 피자를 주문할 텐데. (order pizza)
⇨ If you were hungry, we ______________________.

2 사람이 더 있으면 음식이 충분하지 않을 텐데. (enough)
⇨ The food ______________________ if we had more people.

3 내가 수영을 할 줄 안다면 그들과 물에서 즐기며 놀 텐데. (how to)
⇨ If I ______________________, I would have fun in the water with them.

4 아버지가 학교에 데려다 주시면 나는 제시간 안에 도착할 수 있을 것이다. (get, there)
⇨ If Dad drives me to school, I ______________________ just in time.

5 Ben을 다시 만나면 당신이 찾고 있다고 전하겠습니다. (see)
⇨ If I ______________________, I will tell him that you are looking for him.

6 우리가 런던에서 저렴한 호텔을 찾으면 계획한 것보다 더 오래 머물 수 있다. (cheap)
⇨ If we ______________________ in London, we can stay longer than we planned.

9-3 가정법 과거완료

가정법 과거완료

가정법 과거완료는 '~이었다면[했다면] …이었을[했을] 텐데'라는 의미로, 과거 사실에 반대되는 상황을 가정할 때 쓰인다.

「If+주어+had+과거분사 ~, 주어+조동사의 과거형+have+과거분사 ~」

- If we **had hurried**, we **wouldn't have missed** the train.
  우리가 서둘렀다면 그 기차를 놓치지 않았을 텐데.
  ⇒ Because [As] we **didn't hurry**, we **missed** the train.
  ⇒ We **didn't hurry**, so we **missed** the train.
  우리가 서두르지 않아서 그 기차를 놓쳤다.
- If you **had come** sooner, you **could have witnessed** the extraordinary sight.
  네가 더 일찍 왔다면 그 놀라운 광경을 목격할 수 있었을 텐데.
  ⇒ Because [As] you **didn't come** sooner, you **couldn't witness** the extraordinary sight.
  ⇒ You **didn't come** sooner, so you **couldn't witness** the extraordinary sight.
  네가 더 일찍 오지 않아서 그 놀라운 광경을 목격할 수 없었다.

Exercise 1 다음 괄호 안에서 알맞은 것을 고르시오.

Answers: p.28

1 If I had tried harder, I would (have passed / had passed) the exam.
2 I wouldn't (be / have been) so upset with him if he had told me the truth.
3 We could have done a better job if we (have had / had had) more time.
4 The concert would (take place / have taken place) outdoors if it hadn't rained.
5 If you (have done / had done) your best, you would have won the competition.
6 If you had behaved yourself, you wouldn't (be / have been) punished.

Exercise 2 다음 직설법 문장을 가정법 과거완료 문장으로 전환하시오.

1 There was a typhoon, so my flight was delayed.
⇒ ______________________________

2 Because I didn't take the subway, I was late for the meeting.
⇒ ______________________________

3 I didn't have time, so I couldn't pick you up at the airport.
⇒ ______________________________

4 As I was so tired, I couldn't get out of bed early this morning.
⇒ ______________________________

5 We didn't have enough money, so we couldn't buy a house with a swimming pool.
⇒ ______________________________

9-4 I wish 가정법

I wish+과거

'~라면[하면] 좋을 텐데'라는 의미로, 현재 이룰 수 없는 일에 대한 소망이나 유감을 나타낸다.

「I wish+주어+동사의 과거형 ~」

- **I wish** I **had** more brothers and sisters. 내게 더 많은 형제자매가 있으면 좋을 텐데.
- **I wish** a lot of people **would** come to my party. 많은 사람들이 나의 파티에 오면 좋을 텐데.

I wish+과거완료

'~였다면[했다면] 좋았을 텐데'라는 의미로, 과거에 이루지 못한 일에 대한 유감을 나타낸다.

「I wish+주어+had+과거분사 ~」

- **I wish** I **had done** my best on the test. 내가 시험에서 최선을 다했으면 좋았을 텐데.
- **I wish** we **had met** each other earlier. 우리가 서로를 더 일찍 만났으면 좋았을 텐데.

Answers: p.28

Exercise 1 다음 괄호 안에서 알맞은 것을 고르시오.

1 I wish I (am / were) tall like a model.

2 I wish I (can / could) be young again.

3 I wish we (don't / didn't) have so much work to do.

4 I wish I (haven't / hadn't) been so rude to my teacher.

5 I wish I (could speak / have spoken) Spanish more fluently.

6 I wish my brother (have / had) left some of the cake for me.

7 I wish you (hadn't done / won't have done) such a silly thing.

Exercise 2 다음 우리말과 같은 뜻이 되도록 주어진 말을 이용하여 문장을 완성하시오.

1 너와 내가 같은 반이면 좋을 텐데. (be the same class)

⇨ I wish you and I ______________________________.

2 내가 좀 더 좋은 성적을 받았다면 좋았을 텐데. (get)

⇨ I wish I ______________________________ a better grade.

3 할머니가 여전히 살아계시면 좋을 텐데. (alive)

⇨ I wish my grandmother ______________________________.

4 나의 실수를 좀 더 일찍 깨달았다면 좋았을 텐데. (realize)

⇨ I wish I ______________________________ my mistake sooner.

5 내가 좀 더 일찍 피아노를 배우기 시작했다면 좋았을 텐데. (start)

⇨ I wish I ____________________ learning to play the piano earlier.

9-5 as if 가정법

as if+과거

'마치 ~인 것처럼'이라는 의미로, 현재 사실에 반대되는 일을 나타낸다.

「as if+주어+동사의 과거형 ~」

- You talk **as if** you **knew** all about me. 너는 마치 나에 대한 모든 것을 아는 것처럼 말한다.
- Mr. Jefferson acts **as if** he **were** my father. Jefferson 씨는 마치 그가 나의 아버지인 것처럼 행동한다.

as if+과거완료

'마치 ~이었던 것처럼'이라는 의미로, 과거 사실에 반대되는 일을 나타낸다.

「as if+주어+had+과거분사 ~」

- They look **as if** they **had had** a fight. 그들은 마치 싸웠던 것처럼 보인다.
- It seems **as if** there **had been** an earthquake in your room. 마치 네 방에 지진이 일어났던 것 같다.

Exercise 1 다음 괄호 안에서 알맞은 것을 고르시오.

Answers: p.28

1 Jack talks as if he (has / had) been to Japan.

2 Don't act as if you (don't / didn't) know about this.

3 You look as if you (hadn't slept / sleep) last night.

4 Evan is nodding as if he (understood / had understood) what I am saying.

Exercise 2 다음 우리말과 같은 뜻이 되도록 주어진 말을 이용하여 문장을 완성하시오.

1 네가 피해자인 것처럼 행동하지 마라. (victim)

⇨ Don't act ______________________.

2 마치 내가 모든 것을 엉망으로 만들었던 것처럼 보인다. (mess up)

⇨ It appears ______________________ everything.

3 나는 지금 마치 집에 있는 것처럼 편안하다. (at home)

⇨ I feel comfortable ______________________ now.

4 Jessica는 마치 뉴욕에서 살았던 것처럼 말한다. (live)

⇨ Jessica talks ______________________ in New York.

5 너는 마치 빙산 위에 앉아 있는 것처럼 떨고 있구나. (sit)

⇨ You're shivering ______________________ on an iceberg.

6 당신은 매일을 생의 마지막 날인 것처럼 살아야 한다. (it, your last day)

⇨ You should live each day ______________________ on earth.

Review Test

[01-06] 다음 빈칸에 들어갈 알맞은 말을 고르시오.

01

If I ___________ on a desert island alone, I would die of loneliness.

① live ② lived
③ have lived ④ had lived
⑤ will live

02

I wish I ___________ wear glasses.

① do ② don't
③ did ④ didn't
⑤ will

03

If it ___________ a home game, the Eagles might have won.

① is ② was
③ were ④ have been
⑤ had been

04

If we had a yacht, we ___________ around the world.

① travel ② traveled
③ will travel ④ would travel
⑤ would have traveled

05

If Jack hadn't scared me, I wouldn't ___________ the vase.

① drop ② dropped
③ have dropped ④ had dropped
⑤ will drop

06

If he ___________ harder, he would reach his goals.

① try ② tries
③ tried ④ has tried
⑤ had tried

[07-09] 다음 대화의 빈칸에 들어갈 알맞은 말을 고르시오.

07

A I can't visit you very often. You live too far from me.
B I know. I wish I ___________ closer to you.

① live ② will live
③ lived ④ have lived
⑤ had lived

08

A How about going to the movies tonight?
B I'm afraid I can't. If I ___________ better, I would go and have fun.

① feel ② felt
③ would feel ④ have felt
⑤ had felt

09

A I can't stand John anymore. I'm tired of his nagging.
B I understand why you are so upset with him. He always acts as if he ___________ our boss.

① is ② were
③ will be ④ would be
⑤ would have been

[10-11] 다음 두 문장이 같은 뜻이 되도록 빈칸에 알맞은 말을 고르시오.

10

> As I lost your number, I couldn't call you.
> = If I __________ your number, I could have called you.

① lose ② didn't lose
③ had lost ④ hadn't lost
⑤ have lost

11

> I don't have a credit card, so I can't buy this coat in installments.
> = If I had a credit card, I __________ this coat in installments.

① buy ② hadn't bought
③ could buy ④ couldn't buy
⑤ could have bought

[12-13] 다음 밑줄 친 부분이 어법상 어색한 것을 고르시오.

12 ① We would help you if we knew how.
② If you asked me, I would have told you what to do.
③ If they told their father about this, he would be very angry.
④ If you go to Australia, you should go whale-watching.
⑤ If they had listened to me, none of this would have happened.

13 ① If you are me, what would you do?
② She'll hear you if you don't stop laughing.
③ They'd go there by bus if they didn't have a car.
④ If it doesn't rain tomorrow, we will go fishing.
⑤ If we don't get tickets for the concert, we'll stay home.

[14-15] 다음 우리말을 영어로 바르게 옮긴 것을 고르시오.

14

> 네가 최선을 다했었다면 대가를 받았을 텐데.

① If you do your best, you will be rewarded.
② If you did your best, you would be rewarded.
③ If you have done your best, you will be rewarded.
④ If you had done your best, you would be rewarded.
⑤ If you had done your best, you would have been rewarded.

15

> 그 소년들은 마치 누군가가 그들의 발을 간질이는 것처럼 낄낄 웃고 있다.

① The boys are giggling as if someone are tickling their feet.
② The boys are giggling as if someone were tickling their feet.
③ The boys are giggling as if someone would be tickling their feet.
④ The boys were giggling as if someone were tickling their feet.
⑤ The boys were giggling as if someone would have been tickling their feet.

16 다음 문장의 빈칸에 들어갈 알맞은 표현은?

> If I had more time, I ____________________.

① will see you more often
② can visit my grandparents
③ could have finished the work
④ would spend it with my kids
⑤ would have written a postcard to you

[17-18] 다음 중 어법상 어색한 문장을 고르시오.

17 ① If you post this letter now, she will receive it tomorrow.
② If I find the ring, I will give it back to you.
③ Peggy will go shopping if she has time in the afternoon.
④ Simon will go to London next week if he gets a cheap flight.
⑤ If Bobby will apologize, she will not leave him.

18 ① If they don't study harder, they will not pass the exam.
② If it rains tomorrow, I would stay home and watch a movie.
③ If you can't fall asleep fast, take a hot bath before you go to bed.
④ If I were rich, I would buy a big house for my parents.
⑤ I would buy a car if I had enough money.

19 다음 글의 내용과 일치하는 것은?

> Jeff hurt his leg when he fell off a roof. If Jeff had not broken his leg, he would have taken part in the contest and would have won first prize.

① Jeff won first prize in the contest.
② Jeff fell off a roof but didn't break his leg.
③ Jeff hurt his leg after he took part in the contest.
④ Jeff took part in the contest but didn't win first prize.
⑤ Jeff couldn't take part in the contest because of his broken leg.

[20-22] 다음 글의 빈칸에 알맞은 말이 바르게 짝지어진 것을 고르시오.

20

> I need to contact my teacher and ask him something now, but I don't have his phone number. If I ________ his phone number, I ________ him.

① know — will call
② knew — will call
③ knew — would call
④ had known — would call
⑤ have known — would have called

21

> My daughter told me that she didn't do such a horrible thing, and I believe her. She ________ me if she ________ it.

① will tell — did
② would tell — did
③ would tell — has done
④ would have told — has done
⑤ would have told — had done

22

> I am trying to reach Mary on the phone now, but I'm afraid she is not in her office. If she ________ there, she ________ the phone.

① was – will answer
② were – would answer
③ had been – would answer
④ were – would have answered
⑤ has been – would have answered

[23-24] 다음 우리말과 같은 뜻이 되도록 주어진 말을 이용하여 문장을 완성하시오.

23

우리가 좀 더 자주 볼 수 있으면 좋을 텐데. (see)

⇒ I wish we ______________ each other more often.

24

내가 그에게 그런 심한 말을 하지 않았더라면 좋을 텐데. (say)

⇒ I wish I ______________ those harsh words to him.

[25-28] 다음 문장에서 어법상 어색한 부분을 찾아 바르게 고치시오.

25

If you ask me earlier, I would have helped you with the problem.

⇒ ______________

26

Mr. Simpson acts as if he is busy whenever I ask him something.

⇒ ______________

27

If it have not started to rain, we would have walked to the museum.

⇒ ______________

28

If my mom will go to the seminar this evening, I will look after my little sister.

⇒ ______________

29 다음 대화의 빈칸에 알맞은 말을 쓰시오.

A I've accidentally broken the window of my classroom. What should I do?
B If I ______________ you, I ______________ tell your teacher straight.

[30-33] 다음 문장과 같은 뜻이 되도록 빈칸에 알맞은 말을 쓰시오.

30

As you didn't listen to me, the accident happened.

⇒ If you ______________ to me, the accident ______________.

31

As I don't have a passport, I can't leave this country.

⇒ If I ______________ a passport, I ______________ this country.

32

We completed the project perfectly, so we could have a break for a couple of days.

⇒ If we ______________ the project perfectly, we ______________ a break for a couple of days.

33

You don't admit your fault because you are not mature enough.

⇒ If you ______________ mature enough, you ______________ your fault.

보너스 유형별 문제

Answers: p.29

[1-2] 다음 글을 읽고, 물음에 답하시오. 서술형

I wish I (A) <u>were</u> born a cat.

It is a rainy day today. I am sitting on the front porch enjoying the spring breeze against my skin. My cat, Fluffy, is taking a nap next to me. Suddenly, I hear my mom calling me. Then I realize that today is house cleaning day. Last night my mom told me that we would clean the whole house and clean our own bedrooms. And she also asked me to clean the basement. Now I have to go clean my room and the basement. I envy Fluffy very much. (B) 만약 내가 Fluffy라면, 어떤 것도 청소하지 않을 텐데. (if, clean, anything) I'd better get to work before my mother gets angry.

1 밑줄 친 (A)를 알맞은 표현으로 고쳐 쓰시오.

→ ____________________

2 (B)에 주어진 단어를 이용하여 우리말에 맞도록 영작하시오.

→ ____________________

3 다음 글의 밑줄 친 부분 중, 어법상 틀린 것은? 수능 대비형

An only child tends to be spoiled ① because their parents give them whatever they want. Even though I'm an only child, my parents are not like that. They are quite strict about proper manners. But they also show ② a lot of affection. They only have me to look after, so they have plenty of time ③ to spend with me. I wouldn't mind, though, if they decide to have another child because I spend more time than I would like by ④ myself. When my parents are at work or all my friends are busy, I wish I ⑤ have a brother. I think it would be nice to have someone my age at home to talk to.

* spoiled: 버릇이 없는
** proper: 올바른
*** affection: 애정

Chapter 10

관계사

10-1 관계대명사와 선행사
10-2 주격 관계대명사
10-3 목적격 관계대명사
10-4 소유격 관계대명사
10-5 관계부사
Review Test
보너스 유형별 문제

10-1 관계대명사와 선행사

관계대명사와 선행사의 개념

관계대명사는 「접속사+대명사」의 역할을 하며, 관계대명사가 이끄는 절은 앞에 있는 명사를 수식하는데 이 명사를 선행사라고 한다. 관계대명사는 선행사와 격에 따라 다음과 같이 나뉜다.

선행사	주격	목적격	소유격
사람	**who**	**who(m)**	**whose**
사물, 동물	**which**	**which**	**whose**
사람, 사물, 동물	**that**	**that**	–

- Mrs. Jones has a son. + He lives in Seoul. (주격)
  ⇒ Mrs. Jones has a son **who** lives in Seoul. Jones 부인은 서울에 사는 아들이 있다.
  선행사
- Joe is my good friend. + I can trust him. (목적격)
  ⇒ Joe is my good friend **whom** I can trust. Joe는 내가 신뢰할 수 있는 좋은 친구이다.
  선행사
- I met a girl. + Her father is a famous TV star. (소유격)
  ⇒ I met a girl **whose** father is a famous TV star.
  선행사
  나는 아버지가 유명한 텔레비전 스타인 소녀를 만났다.

TIPs
관계대명사 that은 사람, 사물, 동물 모두를 선행사로 받을 수 있다.

Answers: p.30

Exercise 1 다음 〈보기〉와 같이 두 문장에서 밑줄 친 부분이 선행사일 때 관계대명사로 바꿔 쓸 수 있는 부분을 표시하시오.

Look at the boy. + (He) is wearing a red cap.

1 I caught a fish. + It was two feet long.

2 I have a daughter. + She is a surgeon.

3 This is the umbrella. + I lost it a few days ago.

4 The boy is my cousin. + He is sleeping in my room.

5 Dave has the tickets. + I gave them to him yesterday.

6 I have a friend. + Her voice is like nails on a chalkboard.

Exercise 2 다음 문장에서 관계대명사 절이 수식하는 선행사에 밑줄 치시오.

1 I know a girl who is from Scotland.

2 The TV that I bought last week is broken.

3 There is the guy whom you've wanted to meet.

4 The girl whose hair is blonde is my classmate.

5 I read a book which is about the nature of good and evil.

6 The building whose height is over 800 meters is the tallest in the world.

10-2 주격 관계대명사

주격 관계대명사

❶ **who**: 선행사가 사람일 때

- **The woman** is my boss. + **She** is standing next to Jim.
  ⇒ The woman **who** is standing next to Jim is my boss.
  Jim의 옆에 서 있는 여자는 나의 상사다.
- I know **a doctor**. + **He** is a specialist in brain injuries.
  ⇒ I know a doctor **who** is a specialist in brain injuries.
  나는 뇌 손상 전문의인 의사 한 명을 안다.

❷ **which**: 선행사가 사물이나 동물일 때

- I bought **a table**. + **It** is made from oak.
  ⇒ I bought a table **which** is made from oak.
  나는 오크나무로 만들어진 탁자 하나를 샀다.
- **The snake** scared all the girls. + **It** was found in the schoolyard.
  ⇒ The snake **which** was found in the schoolyard scared all the girls.
  학교 운동장에서 발견된 그 뱀은 모든 여자아이들을 놀라게 했다.

❸ **that**: 선행사가 사람, 사물, 동물일 때

- He is the man **who**[**that**] saved ten lives in the fire.
  그는 화염 속에서 10명의 목숨을 구한 사람이다.
- My fiancé gave me a ring **which**[**that**] has a big diamond.
  내 약혼자가 나에게 큰 다이아몬드가 박힌 반지를 주었다.
- A dog **which**[**that**] guides the blind is called a "seeing-eye dog."
  앞을 못 보는 사람들을 안내하는 개를 '맹도견'이라고 부른다.

TIPs
주격 관계대명사 절의 동사는 선행사의 수에 일치시킨다.
- Look at those boys who are dancing on the stage.
  무대 위에서 춤추고 있는 저 남자아이들을 보아라.

Exercise 1 다음 괄호 안에서 알맞은 것을 모두 고르시오.

Answers: p.30

1 The car (who / which / that) Jason is driving is not his.
2 We want a room (who / which / that) has an ocean view.
3 A dove is a bird (who / which / that) symbolizes peace.
4 Tony is the boy (who / which / that) is sitting on the bench.
5 The baby (who / which / that) is crying aloud is my little brother.
6 Does anyone know the song (who / which / that) is now playing?
7 Jacob is the student (who / which / that) won the speech contest.
8 The man (who / which / that) lives next door is a baseball player.
9 Have you seen my pants (who / which / that) were in my drawer?
10 I saw a movie (who / which / that) was about a famous ballerina.
11 I often buy books (who / which / that) are easy to read for my kids.
12 Do you have any magazines (who / which / that) were issued in January?
13 The people (who / which / that) are standing over there are all my fans.

Exercise 2 다음 문장에서 어법상 어색한 부분을 찾아 바르게 고쳐 쓰시오.

1 She has two dogs that was well-trained. ⇨ ______________

2 I have a friend who go to Harvard University. ⇨ ______________

3 Is there a bowl who is made of stainless steel? ⇨ ______________

4 The man which is talking to my mother is my uncle. ⇨ ______________

5 What was the name of the person which called me? ⇨ ______________

6 The copy machine which is on the first floor don't work. ⇨ ______________

Exercise 3 다음 우리말과 같은 뜻이 되도록 주어진 단어를 알맞게 배열하여 문장을 완성하시오.

1 어젯밤에 일어난 사고는 끔찍했다. (last, happened, was, that, night, horrible, the accident)

⇨ ______________________________

2 나는 휴대전화를 만드는 회사에서 일한다. (cell phones, that, a company, I, makes, work for)

⇨ ______________________________

3 너는 로스앤젤레스에서 새로 오신 선생님을 만나보았니?
(Los Angeles, met, have, who, you, the new teacher, came from)

⇨ ______________________________

4 나는 James Cameron이 감독한 그 영화가 좋았다.
(was, James Cameron, the movie, I, by, loved, directed, which)

⇨ ______________________________

Exercise 4 다음 두 문장을 관계대명사를 이용하여 한 문장으로 만드시오.

1 An ostrich is a bird. + It cannot fly.

⇨ ______________________________

2 Where is my lunchbox? + It was in the refrigerator.

⇨ ______________________________

3 The thief has been arrested. + He stole my mom's jewelry chest.

⇨ ______________________________

4 I have a smartwatch. + It can last up to 30 days with a single recharge.

⇨ ______________________________

5 Do you know the gentleman? + He is wearing a black hat.

⇨ ______________________________

10-3 목적격 관계대명사

목적격 관계대명사

❶ who(m): 선행사가 사람일 때

· Everyone loves **the teacher**. + I like **him** most.

⇒ Everyone loves the teacher **who(m)** I like most.
모두가 내가 가장 좋아하는 선생님을 좋아한다.

· **The people** were nice. + I met **them** through an online community.

⇒ The people **who(m)** I met through an online community were nice.
온라인 모임을 통해 만난 사람들은 친절했다.

❷ which: 선행사가 사물이나 동물일 때

· Did you read **the book**? + I recommended **it**.

⇒ Did you read the book **which** I recommended?
너는 내가 추천한 책을 읽었니?

· **The medicine** was for my headache. + I took **it** this morning.

⇒ The medicine **which** I took this morning was for my headache.
내가 아침에 먹은 약은 두통약이었다.

❸ that: 선행사가 사람, 사물, 동물일 때

· Do you like the present **that [which]** I gave you?
내가 너에게 준 선물이 마음에 드니?

· He can't forget the girl **that [whom]** he met at the restaurant.
그는 식당에서 만난 소녀를 잊을 수가 없다.

· The little boy wants to have the puppy **that [which]** he saw at the pet shop.
그 어린 소년은 애완동물 가게에서 본 강아지를 갖고 싶어 한다.

TIPs
관계대명사 what은 선행사를 포함하는 관계대명사로, '~한 것'으로 해석하며 the thing(s) that/which로 바꿔 쓸 수 있다.
· This is what I want to have.
→ the thing that/which
이것이 내가 가지고 싶어 하는 것이다.

TIPs
관계대명사 that의 쓰임
· 선행사가 -thing으로 끝나는 말일 때
· 선행사에 최상급이나 서수가 있을 때
· 선행사에 the only, the very, the same 등이 있을 때

목적격 관계대명사의 생략

목적격 관계대명사 who(m), which, that은 생략할 수 있다.

· I've lost the book (which[that]) I borrowed from the library. (생략 가능: 목적격 관계대명사)
나는 도서관에서 빌린 책을 잃어버렸다.

· I've lost the book which[that] was my favorite. (생략 불가: 주격 관계대명사)
나는 내가 가장 좋아하는 책을 잃어버렸다.

Exercise 1 다음 괄호 안에서 알맞은 것을 모두 고르시오.

Answers: p.30

1 Show me (that / what / whom) you have in your bag.
2 I can't understand (that / what / which) you mean exactly.
3 The animal (that / what / which) I like most is a polar bear.
4 Do you have a friend (that / whom / which) you can rely on?
5 It is just a rumor (that / what / whom) I heard from my classmate.
6 Who was the person (what / whom / which) you talked to on the phone?
7 These are the pictures (that / what / which) I took with my own camera.
8 He's a popular actor (that / whom / which) almost all people in England like.

Exercise 2 다음 밑줄 친 관계대명사를 생략할 수 있으면 o, 생략할 수 없으면 x표 하시오.

1 I'm looking for a boy <u>who</u> is taller than me. ⇨ ________
2 Love is a feeling <u>which</u> nobody can describe. ⇨ ________
3 The people <u>who</u> we met at the party were very friendly. ⇨ ________
4 I bought the same book <u>that</u> you were reading the other day. ⇨ ________
5 If you give your children everything <u>that</u> they want, you will spoil them. ⇨ ________
6 We will visit the palace <u>which</u> opened to the public last week. ⇨ ________

Exercise 3 다음 중 어법상 어색한 부분에 밑줄을 치고 알맞게 고치시오.

1 I still have all the letters of which you sent me. ⇨ ________
2 The chair of which I was sitting on was too hard. ⇨ ________
3 The earrings that I'm wearing now is my mother's. ⇨ ________
4 Aren't they the boys whose you were looking for? ⇨ ________
5 I found the watch whom I had lost the other day. ⇨ ________
6 The thing what you should do first is to turn off your computer. ⇨ ________

Exercise 4 다음 우리말과 같은 뜻이 되도록 주어진 단어를 알맞게 배열하여 문장을 완성하시오.

1 그는 내가 추천한 게임기를 샀다. (which, to, I, him, a game console, recommended)
⇨ He bought ________________________________.

2 나는 아직도 그가 이야기하고자 했던 것을 이해하지 못한다. (he, meant, what, to say)
⇨ I still don't understand ________________________________.

3 그들이 이야기하던 남자아이는 나의 친구이다. (talking about, that, were, they, the boy)
⇨ ________________________________ is my friend.

4 프랑스어는 나의 조부모님이 쓰시는 언어다. (my grandparents, which, the language, speak)
⇨ French is ________________________________.

5 당신은 나의 삶을 함께 나누고 싶은 유일한 사람이다.
(want to, I, share my life with, that, the only person)
⇨ You are ________________________________.

6 이것은 나의 아버지가 내 생일선물로 사주신 핸드백과 같은 것이다.
(for my birthday, bought, my dad, the same purse, me, that)
⇨ This is ________________________________.

10-4 소유격 관계대명사

소유격 관계대명사

소유격 관계대명사에는 whose가 있으며, 선행사가 사람, 사물, 동물일 때 사용한다.

· We are looking for **a girl.** + **Her name** is Jennifer.
⇨ We are looking for a girl **whose** name is Jennifer.
우리는 이름이 Jennifer인 소녀를 찾고 있다.

· Bill has **an old car.** + **Its color** is blue.
⇨ Bill has an old car **whose** color is blue.
Bill은 파란색 낡은 차를 가지고 있다.

· Mrs. Brown has **a pet dog.** + **His tail** is very short.
⇨ Mrs. Brown has a pet dog **whose** tail is very short.
Brown 여사에게는 꼬리가 매우 짧은 애완견이 한 마리 있다.

TIPs
관계대명사 that은 소유격으로 쓰이지 않는다.
• I have a friend **whose** brother is a composer. (○)
I have a friend **that** brother is a composer. (×)

Exercise 1 다음 괄호 안에서 알맞은 것을 고르시오.

Answers: p.30

1 I have a cat (which / whose) tail is long.
2 Abbie lives in a house (which / whose) front door is red.
3 This is the man (whom / whose) I told you about yesterday.
4 The room (which / whose) was painted yesterday is still drying.
5 We helped a woman (whose / which) car had broken down.
6 A woman (who / whose) voice sounded like a sheep answered my call.
7 We need to help families (whom / whose) houses were destroyed in the flood.
8 Tobacco is a plant (which / whose) leaves are used in making cigarettes and cigars.

Exercise 2 다음 우리말과 같은 뜻이 되도록 주어진 단어를 알맞게 배열하여 문장을 완성하시오.

1 지붕이 빨간 그 집은 우리 삼촌의 집이다. (red, roof, whose, the house, is)
⇨ ______________________________ is my uncle's.

2 나는 부인이 명성 높은 작가인 한 남자를 안다. (wife, a famous author, is, whose, a man)
⇨ I know ______________________________.

3 높이가 50미터가 넘는 그 탑은 중세시대에 지어졌다. (50 meters, height, the tower, whose, over, is)
⇨ ______________________________ was built in medieval times.

4 나는 형이 잘 알려진 작곡가인 친구 한 명이 있다. (whose, a well-known, composer, brother, is, a friend)
⇨ I have ______________________________.

5 깃털이 화려하고 우아한 저 아름다운 새를 보아라. (the, beautiful, feathers, colorful, and, are, whose, elegant, bird)
⇨ Look at ______________________________.

10-5 관계부사

관계부사

관계부사는 「접속사+부사」의 역할을 하며, 선행사를 수식하는 절을 이끈다. 선행사의 종류에 따라 다음과 같이 나뉜다.

	선행사	관계부사	전치사+관계대명사
시간	the year, the time, the day ...	**when**	at /on /in + which
장소	the place, the house, the city ...	**where**	at /on /in + which
이유	the reason	**why**	for which
방법	the way	**how**	in which

❶ when : 선행사가 시간을 나타낼 때

- Do you remember **the day**? + We adopted our first cat **on that day**.
  - ⇒ Do you remember the day **when** we adopted our first cat?
  - ⇒ Do you remember the day **on which** we adopted our first cat?

  당신은 우리가 첫 고양이를 입양한 날을 기억하세요?

❷ where : 선행사가 장소를 나타낼 때

- This is **the place.** + I was born **in that place.**
  - ⇒ This is the place **where** I was born.
  - ⇒ This is the place **in which** I was born.

  이 곳이 내가 태어난 곳이다.

❸ why : 선행사가 이유를 나타낼 때

- I want to know **the reason.** + She left me **for that reason.**
  - ⇒ I want to know the reason **why** she left me.
  - ⇒ I want to know the reason **for which** she left me.

  나는 그녀가 나를 떠난 이유를 알고 싶다.

❹ how : 선행사가 방법을 나타낼 때

(선행사 the way와 how는 함께 쓸 수 없기 때문에 둘 중 하나만 쓴다.)

- This is **the way.** + I tie my shoelaces **in that way.**
  - ⇒ This is **how** I tie my shoelaces.
  - ⇒ This is **the way** I tie my shoelaces.
  - ⇒ This is the way **in which** I tie my shoelaces.

  이것이 내가 신발 끈을 묶는 방법이다.

TIPs

선행사가 the time, the reason, the place 등 일반적인 경우에 관계부사 또는 선행사를 생략할 수 있다.

- I remember the place we first met.
  = I remember where we first met.

  나는 우리가 처음 만난 곳을 기억하고 있다.

Answers: p.30

Exercise 1 다음 괄호 안에서 알맞은 것을 고르시오.

1 This is the place (how / where) I keep my money.

2 Saturday is the day (when / where) we go out for dinner.

3 No one likes (for which / the way) Tommy shows off his wealth.

4 Do you understand the reason (why / how) some people dislike cats?

5 I'll show you the way (how / in which) you can share large data files.

Exercise 2 다음 〈보기〉에서 알맞은 것을 골라 문장을 완성하시오.

when	where	why	how

1 Can you explain the reason ___________ you skipped school last week?

2 I'd like to know ___________ you could come up with the perfect idea.

3 September 2, 2008 was the day ___________ my parents got married.

4 Qatar is the country ___________ the 2022 World Cup was held.

Exercise 3 다음 두 문장을 관계부사를 이용하여 한 문장으로 만들 때 빈칸에 알맞은 말을 쓰시오.

1 The city is the second biggest in Korea. + I was born in that city.
⇒ The city ___________ I was born is the second biggest in Korea.
⇒ The city ___________ ___________ I was born is the second biggest in Korea.

2 Tell me the way. + You could get such a good grade on the test.
⇒ Tell me ___________ you could get such a good grade on the test.
⇒ Tell me ___________ ___________ you could get such a good grade on the test.

3 I know the reason. + There was no one on the street for that reason.
⇒ I know the reason ___________ there was no one on the street.
⇒ I know the reason ___________ ___________ there was no one on the street.

4 My mother misses the days. + She was in her hometown on the days.
⇒ My mother misses the days ___________ she was in her hometown.
⇒ My mother misses the days ___________ ___________ she was in her hometown.

Exercise 4 다음 우리말과 같은 뜻이 되도록 주어진 말을 알맞게 배열하여 문장을 완성하시오.

1 너는 내가 중고 자전거를 살 수 있는 곳을 알고 있니? (where, can, I, a place, buy, a used bike)
⇒ Do you know ____?

2 나는 내 남동생을 처음 안아 보았던 순간을 잊지 못한다. (first, held, I, the moment, when)
⇒ I can't forget ______________________________________ my little brother.

3 나는 Anne이 모든 사람들에게 사랑받는 이유를 안다. (why, loved, Anne, everyone, by, the reason, is)
⇒ I know ____.

4 Franklin 씨는 그 잠긴 교실로 아이들이 들어간 방법을 모른다.
(got into, how, the kids, the locked classroom)
⇒ Mr. Franklin doesn't know ______________________________________.

Review Test

[01-04] 다음 빈칸에 알맞은 것을 고르시오.

01 This is the bank ________ was robbed yesterday.

① who ② whom
③ whose ④ that
⑤ what

02 Look at the girl ________ is playing the violin on the stage.

① who ② whom
③ which ④ whose
⑤ what

03 I clearly remember the day ________ we first met.

① who ② when
③ which ④ where
⑤ why

04 Do you remember ________ you did last night?

① who ② whom
③ which ④ whose
⑤ what

05 다음 밑줄 친 부분이 어법상 어색한 것은?

There are ① a lot of people ② who ③ needs our help, and there are ④ lots of things ⑤ that we can do for them.

[06-07] 다음 두 문장을 한 문장으로 만들 때 빈칸에 알맞은 것을 고르시오.

06 Mom ordered a pair of boots. + They are made of leather.
⇨ Mom ordered a pair of boots ________ are made of leather.

① who ② whom
③ which ④ whose
⑤ what

07 I don't know the reason. + He keeps lying to me.
⇨ I don't know the reason ________ he keeps lying to me.

① when ② where
③ how ④ why
⑤ what

[08-09] 다음 밑줄 친 부분을 바르게 고친 것으로 알맞은 것을 모두 고르시오.

08 I tried to repair the copier, but I couldn't. Please teach me where you fix it.

① how ② whose
③ the way ④ whom
⑤ which

09 There is the girl whose I want to introduce to you.

① what ② that
③ which ④ what
⑤ whom

[10-11] 다음 대화의 빈칸에 알맞은 것을 고르시오.

10

A Do you know the boy over there?
B You mean the one ___________ is wearing a tuxedo?

① who ② whom
③ which ④ whose
⑤ what

11

A Oh, no. I always have trouble tying a tie.
B I'll show you ___________ you can do it easily.

① who ② where
③ when ④ why
⑤ how

12 다음 두 문장이 같은 뜻이 되도록 할 때 빈칸에 알맞은 것은?

Everybody liked the meal that I cooked.
= Everybody liked ___________ I cooked.

① when ② where
③ who ④ how
⑤ what

13 다음 밑줄 친 부분을 생략할 수 없는 것은?

① The car which we are going to buy is blue.
② Do you know someone who I can ask for advice?
③ The first thing that you should do is to call 911.
④ The old couple whom we stayed with was very kind.
⑤ A man who used to be an astronaut moved in next door.

[14-15] 다음 빈칸에 알맞은 말이 바르게 짝지어진 것을 고르시오.

14

• Look at the lizard ___________ tail is twice as long as its body.
• I want to know the reason ___________ he left me without a word.

① who – that
② whom – who
③ whose – how
④ whose – why
⑤ whom – what

15

• I visited the house ___________ George Washington was born.
• We still remember the day ___________ we had our first fight.

① which – when
② where – how
③ which – when
④ on which – when
⑤ where – on which

16 다음 중 어법상 어색한 것은?

① The flowers that grow in your garden is beautiful.
② I could hardly understand what you were saying.
③ The film that we watched last night was very interesting.
④ This is the park where I used to play with my brothers.
⑤ He is an artist whose paintings are very popular.

17 다음 밑줄 친 what의 쓰임이 나머지 넷과 다른 것은?

① What is your favorite activity?
② Give me what is in your hand.
③ Tell me what you really want.
④ What I know about him is true.
⑤ What makes him happy is his daughter.

[18-19] 다음 우리말을 바르게 옮긴 것을 고르시오.

18

보스턴은 내가 태어난 도시이다.

① Boston is the city which I was born.
② Boston is the city when I was born.
③ Boston is the city what I was born in.
④ Boston is the city where I was born in.
⑤ Boston is the city in which I was born.

19

네가 어떻게 답을 맞혔는지 나에게 얘기해 줄래?

① Can you tell me what you got this answer?
② Can you tell me at which you got this answer?
③ Can you tell me the way which you got this answer?
④ Can you tell me the way how you got this answer?
⑤ Can you tell me the way in which you got this answer?

20 다음 문장의 밑줄 친 that과 쓰임이 같은 것은?

This is the first letter that I got from him.

① What is that tall building?
② You didn't tell me that it's yours.
③ Can you show me that one over there?
④ I know that girl who is wearing a white dress.
⑤ Is this your bag that you lost the other day?

[21-22] 다음 빈칸에 들어갈 말이 나머지와 다른 하나를 고르시오.

21 ① That is not ________ I meant.
② That was just ________ I needed.
③ Just do ________ you want to do.
④ I didn't like ________ my brother bought at the store.
⑤ Think about the thing ________ you should do first.

22 ① I know a woman ________ children are studying abroad.
② Daisy is a girl ________ eyes are as bright as stars.
③ Carnival is a festival ________ a lot of people take part in.
④ She gave me an umbrella ________ handle was broken.
⑤ A shark is a fish ________ jaws are stronger than those of the crocodile.

23 다음 두 문장을 한 문장으로 연결한 것으로 바르지 않은 것은?

① I know a man. He is a journalist.
⇒ I know a man who is a journalist.
② Do you have the book? I lent you the book the other day.
⇒ Do you have the book I lent you the other day?
③ I miss the town. I was born in that town.
⇒ I miss the town where I was born in.
④ Let me know the reason. You were absent yesterday for that reason.
⇒ Let me know the reason why you were absent yesterday.
⑤ I will never forget the days. I was with Daniel on the days.
⇒ I will never forget the days when I was with Daniel.

24 다음 밑줄 친 부분이 어법상 어색한 것을 고르시오.

① This is the ring that I found in the cave.
② I miss the small town in which I grew up.
③ I still have the picture of which we took in Paris.
④ I don't understand why Susie was chosen for the part.
⑤ The museum which we visited last month is closed now.

[25-26] 다음 두 문장을 한 문장으로 바꿀 때 빈칸에 알맞은 말을 쓰시오.

25 The vet cured a panda. + Its life was in danger.

⇨ The vet cured a panda __________ life was in danger.

26 Do you remember the day? + We had so much fun playing with the snow on that day.

⇨ Do you remember the day __________ we had so much fun playing with the snow?

[27-28] 다음 문장에 어법상 어색한 부분을 찾아 바르게 고치시오.

27 The man who live on the corner is a taxi driver.

⇨ ______________________________

28 There are lots of things whom you need for the baby.

⇨ ______________________________

29 다음 대화를 읽고, 빈칸에 각각 들어갈 말을 쓰시오.

A Good afternoon! What can I do for you?
B I lost my bag yesterday.
A __________ did you lose it?
B I think I lost it in the shopping center.
A I see. Could you tell me its size and color?
B It is a small, black handbag which has a zipper on the back.
A I'll check for it. Is this __________ you're looking for?
B Yes, that's mine. Thank you!

[30-31] 다음 두 문장을 관계사를 이용하여 한 문장으로 바꿔 쓰시오.

30 The bananas are rotten. + We bought them from the market.

⇨ ______________________________
____

31 I know the reason. + Gary was absent today for that reason.

⇨ ______________________________

[32-33] 다음 우리말과 같은 뜻이 되도록 주어진 말을 알맞게 배열하여 문장을 완성하시오.

32 빨간 셔츠를 입고 있는 카우보이는 매우 재미있다.
(who, the red shirt, is, wearing, the cowboy)

⇨ ______________________________ is very funny.

33 나는 처음 그를 본 순간을 잊을 수 없다.
(when, first, saw, I, the moment, him)

⇨ I can never forget __________.

보너스 유형별 문제

Answers: p.32

[1-2] 다음 글을 읽고, 물음에 답하시오. 서술형

When they were children, the Wright brothers always wanted to understand (A) the way that things could fly. One day, their father gave them a toy helicopter. After they got the helicopter, they kept trying to make things like it. Even though they failed lots of times, they never gave up. They knew exactly what they really wanted to make. (B) 그들은 마침내 최초로 비행기를 날린 사람들이 되었다. (eventually, become, the first, fly, an airplane) Their great invention changed not only their lives but also ours.

1 한 단어로 밑줄 친 (A)와 의미가 같은 말을 쓰시오.

→ ______________________

2 (B)에 주어진 단어를 이용하여 우리말에 맞도록 영작하시오.

→ ______________________

3 다음 글의 밑줄 친 부분 중, 어법상 틀린 것은? 수능 대비형

① While it may be true that a pretty girl is asked out more on average, being "attractive" depends on things ② other than good looks. One group of high school boys ③ who were asked what they liked and disliked about girls agreed ④ that enthusiasm was much more important than beauty. They like girls ⑤ whose are fun to be with, have a good sense of humor, and try to see the amusing side of things.

* attractive: 매력적인
** enthusiasm: 열정

Chapter 11

전치사와 접속사

11-1 시간을 나타내는 전치사
11-2 장소 · 방향을 나타내는 전치사
11-3 기타 전치사
11-4 명사절을 이끄는 접속사
11-5 간접의문문
11-6 시간을 나타내는 접속사
11-7 이유 · 양보를 나타내는 접속사
11-8 조건을 나타내는 접속사
11-9 상관접속사
11-10 선택의문문
Review Test
보너스 유형별 문제

11-1 시간을 나타내는 전치사

from vs. since

from	'~이래, ~부터'라는 의미로, 시간, 순서 등의 기점, 시발점을 나타냄	The stores open **from** nine to five. 저 상점들은 9시에서 5시까지 영업한다.
since	'~이래로'라는 의미로, 주로 완료시제와 함께 쓰여 과거에 시작된 사건이 현재에도 영향이 있음을 나타냄	Josh and Kate have been together **since** last year. Josh와 Kate는 지난해 이래로 함께해왔다.

by vs. until: '~까지'

by	일회성의 동작이나 상태가 완료되는 시점을 나타냄	You have to submit the report **by** Friday. 너는 금요일까지 보고서를 제출해야 한다.
until	계속되던 동작이나 상태가 완료되는 시점을 나타냄	The concert tickets are available **until** June. 음악회 티켓은 6월까지 유효하다.

for vs. during: '~동안'

for	「for+시간, 기간을 나타내는 명사(구)」	I've been waiting for her response **for** two hours. 나는 두 시간 동안 그녀의 응답을 기다리고 있다.
during	「during+특정 기간」	They played hide-and-seek **during** recess. 그들은 쉬는 시간 동안 숨바꼭질을 했다.

Answers: p.32

Exercise 1 다음 빈칸에 알맞은 말을 보기에서 골라 쓰시오.

1 James has returned (from / since) his tour of Africa.

2 My family was in Hawaii (for / during) the summer.

3 Jerry has been sick in bed (for / during) three weeks.

4 My husband and I have been married (from / since) September 2020.

5 Please let me know (by / until) next Wednesday if you want this ticket.

Exercise 2 다음 우리말과 같은 뜻이 되도록 빈칸에 알맞은 말을 <보기>에서 골라 쓰시오.

since　　by　　until　　during

1 Jim은 지난달부터 쭉 병원에 있다.
⇒ Jim has been in the hospital __________ last month.

2 청중 몇 명은 강의 중에 졸았다.
⇒ Some of the audience dozed off __________ the lecture.

3 나는 이 파일을 오늘까지 그에게 전달해야 한다.
⇒ I need to hand over this file to him __________ today.

4 크리스마스까지 며칠이나 남았니?
⇒ How many more days are there __________ Christmas?

11-2 장소 · 방향을 나타내는 전치사

above vs. below

The clock is **above** the entrance door. 시계가 출입구 위에 있다.
The entrance door is **below** the clock. 출입구가 시계 아래에 있다.

above	'(~보다) 위에'	There are dark clouds **above** the mountains. 산 위에 먹구름이 있다.
below	'(~보다) 아래에'	The bottle sank **below** the surface of the water. 병이 수면 아래로 가라앉았다.

to vs. for

to	'~로', '~에'라는 의미로, go, come 등의 동사와 함께 도착지를 나타냄	Can you come **to** my office after work? 퇴근 후에 나의 사무실로 와주실 수 있나요? I'm on my way **to** the bank. 나는 은행에 가는 길이다.
for	'~로', '~을 향해'라는 의미로, leave, start 등의 동사와 함께 방향을 나타냄	The Smiths are leaving **for** Switzerland soon. Smith 가족은 곧 스위스로 떠난다. The train **for** Las Vegas runs every day. 라스베이거스 행 열차는 매일 운행한다.

Exercise 1 다음 괄호 안에서 알맞은 것을 고르시오.

Answers: p.32

1 Can you come (to / for) my party tonight?

2 Please do not write (for / below) this line.

3 The moon has risen (to / above) the mountain.

4 Vanessa has gone (to / for) Italy to study music.

5 What time do you leave (to / for) work in the morning?

Exercise 2 다음 우리말과 같은 뜻이 되도록 빈칸에 알맞은 전치사를 쓰시오.

1 당신은 언제 뮌헨으로 떠나십니까?
⇒ When are you leaving ________ Munich?

2 태양이 수평선 아래로 사라지고 있다.
⇒ The sun is disappearing ________ the horizon.

3 나는 학교 가는 길에 Jill과 우연히 마주쳤다.
⇒ I bumped into Jill on my way ________ school.

4 에베레스트 산은 해발 8,848 미터이다.
⇒ Mt. Everest stands at 8,848 meters ________ sea level.

11-3 기타 전치사

수단을 나타내는 전치사

by	(교통수단) ~으로 ~의 단위로	**by** taxi, **by** bus, **by** subway **by** the liter, **by** the kilometer
in	(언어, 색) ~으로 (의류, 색) ~을 입고 있는	**in** English, **in** German, **in** red **in** a raincoat, **in** a yellow cap, **in** black
for	~의 가격으로	**for** 5 dollars, **for** 5000 won, **for** free
with	(도구, 재료) ~을 가지고	**with** scissors, **with** a hammer, **with** flour
through	(경로, 중계) ~을 통해	**through** books, **through** the Internet

- I usually go to work **by** bus. 나는 주로 버스로 출근한다.
- Buy this fine wallet **for** just 10 dollars. 단돈 10달러로 이 질 좋은 지갑 사세요.
- It's hard to learn to cook **through** books. 책으로 요리를 배우는 것은 어렵다.

원인을 나타내는 전치사

at / of	(감정의 원인) ~으로, ~에	angry **at** me, tired **of** life
with	(두려움, 흥분 등의 감정) ~으로	**with** fear, **with** anger, **with** excitement
for	(행위의 이유) ~ 때문에	**for** many reasons
from / of	(질병, 부주의 등) ~으로 인해	die **of** cancer, die **from** hunger

- I don't know why he is so angry **at** me. 나는 그가 왜 그렇게 나에게 화가 났는지 모르겠다.
- The little boy was shaking **with** fear. 그 어린 소년은 공포로 떨고 있었다.
- You deserve to be punished **for** your behavior. 너는 네 자신의 행동 때문에 벌 받아 마땅하다.

as vs. like

as	~이라고 (자격) ~로서	She was very famous **as** a singer in Korea. 그녀는 한국에서 가수로 매우 유명하다. We regard him **as** a genius. 우리는 그를 천재라고 여긴다.
like	~와 같이 ~처럼	Put your hands on your head **like** this. 이렇게 너의 손을 머리에 올려라. Mrs. Roberts cried **like** a child when she talked about her late mother. Roberts 부인은 돌아가신 어머니에 대해 이야기할 때 어린아이처럼 울었다.

Answers: p.32

Exercise 1 다음 괄호 안에서 알맞은 것을 고르시오.

1 I know there's no one (of / like) him.

2 They got the news (at / through) the morning paper.

3 Do you know the man (in / like) the blue suit?

4 They tore down the wall (by / with) a hammer.

5 Many children in Africa die (of / as) hunger every day.

6 The boys and girls screamed out (with / through) excitement.

Exercise 2 다음 빈칸에 알맞은 말을 〈보기〉에서 골라 쓰시오.

of	in	through	for	with

1 I'm so tired __________ his arrogance.

2 The old man shouted at the nurse __________ anger.

3 The instructions are written __________ French.

4 Ben had to leave his job __________ mental health reasons.

5 Tickets for the musical are being sold __________ the Internet.

Exercise 3 다음 밑줄 친 부분을 바르게 고치시오.

1 We will fix your computer with free. ⇨ __________

2 How long does it take to get to the airport on taxi? ⇨ __________

3 Why do people dress as black at a funeral? ⇨ __________

4 My mom works of a counselor at a high school. ⇨ __________

5 My grandfather died for lung cancer because of smoking. ⇨ __________

Exercise 4 다음 우리말과 같은 뜻이 되도록 빈칸에 알맞은 전치사를 쓰시오.

1 Daniel은 속도위반 때문에 딱지를 떼였다.

⇨ Daniel got a ticket __________ speeding.

2 나는 친구로서 너에게 이런 충고를 하는 것이다.

⇨ I give you this advice __________ a friend.

3 어머니는 아직도 나를 어린애 취급하신다.

⇨ My mother still treats me __________ a child.

4 콘서트 표는 각각 50달러의 가격에 판매되고 있다.

⇨ The concert tickets are being sold __________ $50 each.

5 미국에서 휘발유는 리터 단위로 팔리나요?

⇨ Is gasoline sold __________ the liter in the U.S.A?

6 Jamie는 부끄러워서 얼굴이 붉어졌다.

⇨ Jamie's face turned red __________ embarrassment.

11-4 명사절을 이끄는 접속사

명사절을 이끄는 접속사

❶ that

접속사 that이 이끄는 명사절은 문장에서 주어, 목적어, 보어 역할을 한다.

- **That** Greg is leaving for Germany is true. (주어)
  Greg가 독일로 떠난다는 것은 사실이다.
- No one knows **that** I am in love with Julie. (목적어)
  아무도 내가 Julie를 사랑한다는 것을 모른다.
- The truth is **that** happiness exists in simple things. (보어)
  진실은 행복이 단순한 것들에 존재한다는 것이다.

❷ whether / if

접속사 whether와 if는 '~인지 아닌지'라는 의미로, 명사절을 이끈다.

- You should decide **whether** you support me (or not).
  너는 나를 지지할지 안 할지를 결정해야 한다.
- Mr. Collins asked me **if** I knew the correct answer (or not).
  Collins 씨는 내게 정답을 알고 있는지 물었다.
- I wonder **if or not** you can help me. (x)
  나는 네가 나를 도와줄 수 있는지 알고 싶다.

TIPs
목적어절을 이끄는 접속사 that은 생략할 수 있다.
- I think (**that**) she is telling a lie.
  나는 그녀가 거짓말을 하고 있다고 생각한다.

TIPs
whether / if와 함께 쓰이는 or not은 주로 whether / if절의 끝에 위치하지만, whether의 바로 뒤에 와서 whether or not으로 쓰이기도 한다.
- I don't know **whether/if** Michael loves me **or not**.
  = I don't know **whether or not** Michael loves me.
  나는 Michael이 나를 사랑하는지 안 하는지 모르겠어.

Answers: p.33

Exercise 1 다음 밑줄 친 that절의 역할을 쓰시오.

1 The point is that we all live in one world. ⇨ ______
2 Everyone thinks that the man is innocent. ⇨ ______
3 My father doesn't know that I quit my job. ⇨ ______
4 That he didn't tell me about it made me upset. ⇨ ______
5 The problem is that I don't have her phone number. ⇨ ______
6 He told me that you can speak Chinese fluently. ⇨ ______

Exercise 2 다음 빈칸에 whether와 that 중 알맞은 것을 넣으시오.

1 I don't know ______ he is a college student or not.
2 I can hardly believe ______ Fred got first place.
3 We know ______ the celebrity couple broke up.
4 I'll ask Billy ______ he knows anything about the broken jar.
5 We're not sure ______ Emily played the violin in the orchestra.
6 The problem is ______ she and I don't speak the same language.

Exercise 3 다음 〈보기〉와 같이 두 문장을 that이나 whether를 이용하여 한 문장으로 바꿔 쓰시오.

> We have no time to waste. That is the point.
> ⇒ The point is that we have no time to waste.

1 Is the boy Henry's cousin? I'm not sure.

⇒ ______________________________

2 He is always late for the meeting. That is the problem.

⇒ ______________________________

3 Do you have a partner for the prom? I was wondering.

⇒ ______________________________

4 We accomplished what we wanted. That is the most important thing.

⇒ ______________________________

Exercise 4 다음 우리말과 같은 뜻이 되도록 주어진 말을 알맞게 배열하여 문장을 완성하시오.

1 나는 Emma가 어린 나이에 어머니를 여의었다는 것을 들었다. (Emma, her mother, lost, at an early age, that)

⇒ I heard ______________________________.

2 나는 네가 다른 학교로 전학 간다고 들었다. (to another school, are, that, you, transferring)

⇒ I was told ______________________________.

3 나의 의견은 네가 스스로 결정을 내려야 한다는 것이다. (your own decision, have to, make, that, you)

⇒ My opinion is ______________________________.

4 여동생이 내 물건을 계속 쓰는 것이 나를 신경 쓰이게 한다. (my sister, my stuff, keeps, using, that)

⇒ It really bothers me ______________________________.

5 너는 그에게 수영을 할 수 있는지 없는지 물어보는 게 좋겠다. (can, swim or not, whether, he)

⇒ You'd better ask him ______________________________.

6 위원회는 그 아이를 벌할지 말지를 결정하려고 한다. (whether, decide, the child, they, punish, or not)

⇒ The committee is about to ______________________________.

11-5 간접의문문

간접의문문: 의문문이 문장에서 주어, 목적어, 보어 역할을 하여 문장의 일부가 되는 것을 말한다.

의문사가 있는 간접의문문: 의문사가 접속사 역할을 하며 「의문사+주어+동사」의 어순으로 쓴다.

- Can you tell me? + What time is it now?
  ⇨ Can you tell me **what time it is** now? 지금이 몇 시인지 얘기해 줄래?
- I don't know. + How did he make it?
  ⇨ I don't know **how he made** it. 나는 그가 그것을 어떻게 만들었는지 모른다.

❶ 의문사가 주어인 간접의문문의 경우에는 「의문사+동사」의 어순이 된다.

- Do you know?+Who moved my chair?
  ⇨ Do you know **who moved** my chair? 너는 누가 내 의자를 옮겼는지 알고 있니?
- Tell me.+What made him so happy?
  ⇨ Tell me **what made** him so happy. 무엇이 그를 행복하게 하는지 말해 줘.

❷ 주절에 동사 think, believe, imagine, guess, suppose 등의 동사가 올 경우 의문사가 문두로 이동해 「의문사+주절+주어+동사?」의 어순이 된다.

- Do you think? + Where does she live?
  ⇨ Do you think where she lives? (×)
  ⇨ **Where** do you think **she lives**? (○) 너는 그녀가 어디에 산다고 생각하니?
- Do you guess? + What is the correct answer?
  ⇨ Do you guess what the correct answer is? (×)
  ⇨ **What** do you guess **the correct answer is**? (○) 너는 정답이 무엇인 것 같니?

TIPs 일반동사가 있는 의문문을 간접의문문으로 만들 경우 종속절의 동사를 시제와 인칭에 알맞게 바꿔야 한다.
- Tell me.+Where did you stay last night?
  → Tell me where you stayed last night. 어젯밤에 어디에서 묵었는지 내게 말해 줘.

의문사가 없는 간접의문문: 의문사가 없는 문장의 간접의문문은 접속사 if나 whether를 이용해서 만들며 「접속사+주어+동사」의 어순이 된다. 이 때 if나 whether를 '~인지 아닌지'라고 해석한다.

- I'm not sure. + Is David married?
  ⇨ I'm not sure if[whether] **David is** married. 나는 David가 결혼했는지 안 했는지 잘 모른다.
- Can you tell me? + Did you meet Jason last night?
  ⇨ Can you tell me if[whether] **you met** Jason last night?
  네가 어젯밤 Jason을 만났는지 말해 줄 수 있니?

Answers: p.33

Exercise 1 다음 괄호 안의 주어진 단어를 알맞게 배열하여 문장을 완성하시오.

1 I'm not sure ______________________ my letter. (if, received, she)
2 Do you know ______________________? (Amanda, is, how old)
3 I wonder ______________________. (what, is, your brother's job)
4 Can you tell me ______________________ right? (is, my answer, if)
5 Do you remember ______________________ my car key? (I, where, put)
6 I want to know ______________________. (when, will, come back, she)
7 Rick asked me ______________________ him last night. (I, called, whether)
8 Tell me ______________________ late for school this morning. (you, were, why)

Exercise 2 다음 문장에서 어법상 어색한 부분을 찾아 바르게 고치시오.

1 He asked me if I did like it. ⇨ ____________

2 Can you tell me why is she crying? ⇨ ____________

3 Do you think which is more expensive? ⇨ ____________

4 I have no idea how does he feel about Isabella. ⇨ ____________

5 He asked me where did I study last weekend. ⇨ ____________

6 I wonder that whether she will come to my birthday party. ⇨ ____________

Exercise 3 다음 두 문장을 한 문장의 간접의문문으로 바꿀 때 빈칸에 알맞은 말을 쓰시오.

1 Can you tell me? + Who do you like most?

⇨ Can you tell me ____________?

2 Do you imagine? + What did Melissa say to me?

⇨ What do you imagine ____________?

3 Does she know? + What does he want for his birthday gift?

⇨ Does she know ____________?

4 He wonders. + Does she work for a law firm?

⇨ He wonders ____________.

5 I'm not sure. + Can you go to the amusement park tomorrow?

⇨ I'm not sure ____________ tomorrow.

Exercise 4 다음 우리말과 같은 뜻이 되도록 주어진 말을 알맞게 배열하여 문장을 완성하시오.

1 우리는 그들이 오늘 밤 저녁 식사로 무엇을 원하는지 모른다.
(what, want, dinner, for, tonight, they, we, know, don't)

⇨ ____________

2 나는 그녀가 학생인지 아닌지 궁금하다. (wonder, I, whether, a student, she, is, or not)

⇨ ____________

3 너는 그가 언제 공항에 도착하는지 아니? (do, arrives, you, when, know, airport, he, at, the)

⇨ ____________

4 그녀는 내가 어제 회의에 참석했는지 나에게 물었다.
(asked, me, she, attended, yesterday, the meeting, whether, I)

⇨ ____________

11-6 시간을 나타내는 접속사

시간을 나타내는 접속사

❶ when: '~할 때'

- **When** Anthony called me yesterday, I was having dinner.
  Anthony가 나에게 어제 전화 했을 때 나는 저녁을 먹던 중이었다.

❷ while: '~하는 동안', '~하던 중에'

- I kept making eye contact with Josh **while** I was talking to him.
  나는 Josh와 이야기 하면서 계속 눈을 맞췄다.

❸ as: '~할 때', '~하면서'

- **As** I walked down the street, I saw a car accident.
  내가 거리를 걸어갈 때, 자동차 사고를 목격했다.

❹ before: '~하기 전에'

- Please make sure all the windows are locked **before** you go to bed.
  잠자리에 들기 전에 모든 창문이 잠겼는지 확인해주세요.

❺ after: '~한 후에'

- **After** you finish reading the book, put it on my desk.
  그 책을 다 읽고 나서 내 책상 위에 올려놓아라.

❻ until: '~할 때 까지'

- I couldn't fall asleep **until** you came back.
  나는 네가 돌아올 때까지 잠들지 못했다.

❼ since: '~한 이래로'(현재완료 문장에서 사용)

- Mrs. Jackson has known me **since** I was a kindergartner.
  Jackson 부인은 내가 유치원생일 때부터 나를 알았다.

시간을 나타내는 부사절의 시제

시간을 나타내는 접속사가 이끄는 부사절에서는 현재시제가 미래시제를 대신한다.

- I'll deliver your message when my boss **comes** back in the afternoon. (o)
  상사가 오후에 돌아오면 당신의 메시지를 전하겠습니다.
- I'll deliver your message when my boss ~~**will come**~~ back in the afternoon. (x)

Answers: p.33

Exercise 1 다음 괄호 안에서 알맞은 것을 고르시오.

1 Wait inside (since / until) the rain stops.

2 It gets hotter and hotter (as / until) the day goes on.

3 (While / Since) I was doing the dishes, Sam did the laundry.

4 Wash your hands (before / until) you sit down at the dinner table.

5 Brian has wanted to visit England (when / since) he was very young.

6 When you (will grow up / grow up), you will understand what it means.

7 Jack returned to Korea (after / since) he graduated from a college in Sydney.

8 They will ask you some questions after you (are / will be) done with your presentation.

Exercise 2 다음 빈칸에 알맞은 말을 〈보기〉에서 골라 쓰시오.

while	before	after	since

1 I called 911 right ____________ the accident occurred.

2 Compare the fuel efficiency ____________ you buy a car.

3 I have had a stomachache ____________ I ate too much at the buffet.

4 ____________ you were away, there was another robbery in town.

Exercise 3 다음 우리말과 같은 뜻이 되도록 빈칸에 알맞은 접속사를 쓰시오.

1 나는 모든 돈을 다 쓸 때까지 여행할 계획이다.
⇨ I plan to travel ____________ all my money runs out.

2 Dennis가 창문을 열었을 때 참새 한 마리가 날아들어 왔다.
⇨ ____________ Dennis opened the window, a sparrow flew in.

3 내가 사흘 전 이곳에 도착한 후부터 계속 비가 오고 있다.
⇨ It has been raining ____________ I arrived here three days ago.

4 그 도둑들은 그 큰 개가 자고 있는 동안 그 집 안으로 몰래 들어갔다.
⇨ The thieves sneaked into the house ____________ the big dog was asleep.

5 톨게이트에 닿기 전에 충분한 잔돈이 있는지 확인해라.
⇨ Make sure we have enough change ____________ we reach the toll gate.

Exercise 4 다음 우리말과 같은 뜻이 되도록 주어진 말을 이용하여 문장을 완성하시오.

1 나는 여동생이 태어난 후부터 그녀를 돌봐왔다. (be born)
⇨ I have looked after my little sister ______________________________.

2 당신이 사무실을 나간 후 누군가가 전화했습니다. (leave the office)
⇨ Someone called ______________________________.

3 내가 문을 열었을 때 강당에는 아무도 없었다. (open, the door)
⇨ There was no one in the auditorium ______________________________.

4 여름이 오기까지 얼마 남지 않았다. (summer, come)
⇨ It won't be long ______________________________.

5 우리가 저녁을 먹는 도중에 Rebecca가 갑자기 웃기 시작했다. (in the middle of, dinner)
⇨ Rebecca suddenly began to laugh ______________________________.

11-7 이유 · 양보를 나타내는 접속사

이유를 나타내는 접속사

because, since, as 등이 있고, '~ 때문에', '해서, ~하니'로 해석한다.

- I don't want to go shopping **because** I am so tired now.
  나는 지금 너무 피곤하기 때문에 쇼핑하고 싶지 않다.
- **Since** the music outside was so loud, we couldn't concentrate on reading.
  밖의 음악 소리가 너무 시끄러워서 우리는 책 읽는 것에 집중할 수가 없었다.
- **As** you are honest with me, I'll be honest with you, too.
  네가 나에게 솔직하니, 나도 너에게 정직해야겠다.

TIPs
접속사 because 다음에는 주어+동사가 오지만, 전치사구 because of는 뒤에 명사(구)가 온다.
- The train has been delayed **because of** heavy snow.
  기차는 폭설로 연착되었다.

양보를 나타내는 접속사

though, although, even though 등이 있고, '~에도 불구하고', '비록 ~일지라도'로 해석한다.

- **Although** this stereo is expensive, it is worth it.
  비록 이 스테레오는 비싸지만 그만한 가치가 있다.
- Fred and Jeff are brothers **even though** they look nothing alike.
  Fred와 Jeff는 전혀 닮은 점이 없어 보이지만 형제이다.

Answers: p.33

Exercise 1 다음 괄호 안에서 알맞은 것을 고르시오.

1 I can't hear you (because / because of) the noise.

2 (Even though / Because) Greg is deaf, he can speak and read lips.

3 (Since / Though) Jason lives near my house, I have never visited him.

4 I drank the water right from the tap (since / though) I was very thirsty.

5 (Although / Since) we come from different countries, we have a lot in common.

Exercise 2 다음 우리말과 같은 뜻이 되도록 주어진 말을 이용하여 문장을 완성하시오.

1 나는 경주에서 우승하지 못할 것을 알았지만 결코 포기하지 않았다. (although, win the race)

⇨ ______________________, I never gave up.

2 너의 무책임 때문에 누군가는 고통 받아야 한다. (lack of responsibility)

⇨ Someone has to suffer ______________________.

3 비록 우리가 경기는 졌지만 참된 삶의 교훈을 얻었다. (even though, lose)

⇨ ______________________, it was a true life lesson.

4 비록 나는 그를 좋아하지는 않지만 그가 좋은 가수임은 사실이다. (even though, like)

⇨ It's true that he is a good singer ______________________.

5 나는 밤새 기침하느라 어젯밤에 한숨도 못 잤다. (because, cough, constantly)

⇨ I couldn't sleep a wink last night ______________________.

11-8 조건을 나타내는 접속사

조건을 나타내는 접속사

❶ if: '만약 ~라면'

· **If** you help us, we can complete the mission. 당신이 우리를 도와준다면 우리는 임무를 완수할 수 있다.

· We will go out for dinner **if** the snow stops.
눈이 그치면 우리는 저녁을 먹으러 나갈 것이다.

❷ unless(= if ~ not): '만약 ~가 아니라면'

· **Unless** you tell me all about it, I cannot trust you any more.
만약 네가 그것에 대한 모든 것을 말하지 않는다면, 나는 너를 더 이상 믿을 수 없다.
= **If** you do**n't** tell me all about it, I cannot trust you any more.

TIPs

접속사 unless는 이미 부정의 의미를 포함하고 있기 때문에 부정어와 함께 쓰지 않는다.

• Unless you get a job soon, you'll be in big trouble. (o)
Unless you don't get a job soon, you'll be in big trouble.(x)
곧 직장을 얻지 못하면 너는 큰 곤경에 빠질 것이다.

if/unless 조건문의 명령문 전환

❶ if 조건문: 「명령문, and ~」로 바꿔 쓸 수 있고 '~해라, 그러면 …'으로 해석한다.

· **If you turn left at the corner**, you will see the building you're looking for.
= **Turn left at the corner, and** you will see the building you're looking for.
모퉁이에서 왼쪽으로 돌면 네가 찾고 있는 건물이 보일 것이다.

❷ unless(= if ~ not) 조건문: 「명령문, or ~」로 바꿔 쓸 수 있고 '~해라, 그렇지 않으면 …'으로 해석한다.

· **Unless you put on a thick coat**, you will catch a cold.
= **If you don't put on a thick coat**, you will catch a cold.
= **Put on a thick coat, or** you will catch a cold. 두꺼운 코트를 입지 않으면 감기에 걸릴 것이다.

조건을 나타내는 부사절의 시제

조건을 나타내는 접속사가 이끄는 부사절에서는 현재시제가 미래시제를 대신한다.

· The concert will be rescheduled if it **rains** on that day. (o)
그날 비가 오면 콘서트는 일정이 변경될 것이다.

· The concert will be rescheduled if it **will rain** on that day. (x)

Exercise 1 다음 괄호 안에서 알맞은 것을 고르시오.

Answers: p.34

1 (If / Unless) we hurry, we will miss the bus.

2 Don't get any closer to me, (and / or) I'll call the police.

3 Take a deep breath, (and / or) you'll feel better.

4 (If / Unless) you are late for my class, you'll be kicked out of my classroom.

Exercise 2 다음 문장에서 어법상 어색한 부분을 찾아 바르게 고치시오.

1 We'll go fishing if it will be sunny in the afternoon. ⇒ ________

2 If my dad will come from Indonesia, we will be very happy. ⇒ ________

3 Be nice to your employees, or they will treat you well. ⇒ ________

4 Unless we don't save fossil fuels, they'll run out in 50 years. ⇒ ________

Exercise 3 다음 우리말과 같은 뜻이 되도록 빈칸에 알맞은 말을 쓰시오.

1 조용히 하지 않으면 선생님이 화낼 것이다.

⇨ The teacher will get angry __________ you are quiet.

2 별다른 일이 없으면 우리는 정시에 출발할 것이다.

⇨ We will start right on time __________ something happens.

3 어떤 급한 일이 있으면 언제든지 전화해라.

⇨ Feel free to call me anytime __________ you have something urgent.

4 지금 바쁘지 않으면 이것을 좀 도와주겠니?

⇨ __________ you are not busy now, can you give me a hand with this?

5 사람들에게 예의를 갖춰라, 그렇지 않으면 아무도 너를 정중히 대하지 않을 것이다.

⇨ Be polite to others, __________ no one will treat you with respect.

6 성급히 결정하면 너의 선택을 후회하게 될 것이다.

⇨ __________ you rush your decision, you will regret it.

7 네가 하는 모든 일에 최선을 다해라, 그러면 당신은 성공할 것이다.

⇨ Try your best in everything you do, __________ you will be successful.

8 경제적 여유가 없다면 저 비싼 드레스를 살 생각은 하지 마라.

⇨ Don't even think about buying that expensive dress __________ you can afford it.

Exercise 4 다음 문장이 모두 같은 뜻이 되도록 빈칸을 채우시오.

1 If you go straight on, you will see the church.

⇨ Go straight on, __________ you will see the church.

2 If you don't take a taxi, you'll be late for the examination.

⇨ Take a taxi, __________ you'll be late for the examination.

3 Unless you pay your debt, they will take some legal action.

⇨ __________ you __________ pay your debt, they will take some legal action.

⇨ Pay your debt, __________ they will take some legal action.

4 Unless you avoid late-night snacks, you'll have a swollen face next day.

⇨ Avoid late-night snacks, __________ you'll have a swollen face next day.

⇨ __________ you __________ avoid late-night snacks, you'll have a swollen face next day.

11-9 상관접속사

상관접속사: 두 개 이상의 어구가 짝을 이뤄 접속사 역할을 하는 것을 말한다.

❶ both A and B: 'A와 B 둘 다'

· Dave is good at playing **both** the guitar **and** the drums. Dave는 기타와 드럼 둘 다에 능하다.

❷ either A or B: 'A와 B 둘 중 하나'

· **Either** Harry **or** you have to take this part. Harry와 너 중 한 명이 이 역할을 맡아야 한다.

❸ neither A nor B: 'A와 B 둘 다 아닌'

· I want **neither** the red shoes **nor** the pink ones.
나는 빨간 신발과 분홍 신발 둘 다 원하지 않는다.

❹ not A but B: 'A가 아니라 B'

· **Not** you **but** I have to take the responsibility for it.
네가 아닌 내가 그것에 대한 책임을 져야 한다.

❺ not only A but (also) B(= B as well as A): 'A뿐만 아니라 B도'

· Jamie can speak **not only** English **but** (**also**) Spanish.
= Jamie can speak Spanish as well as English.
Jamie는 영어뿐만 아니라 스페인어도 할 줄 안다.

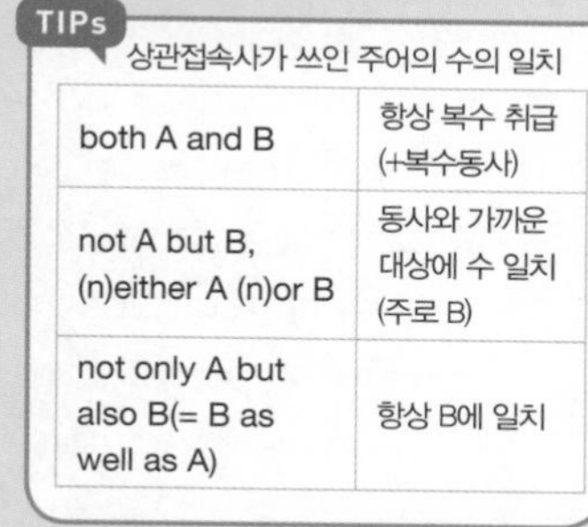
TIPs 상관접속사가 쓰인 주어의 수의 일치

both A and B	항상 복수 취급 (+복수동사)
not A but B, (n)either A (n)or B	동사와 가까운 대상에 수 일치 (주로 B)
not only A but also B(= B as well as A)	항상 B에 일치

Exercise 1 다음 괄호 안에서 알맞은 것을 고르시오.

Answers: p.34

1 Steven is not a musician (and / but) a poet.

2 (Neither / Either) you nor I am on the list.

3 Both Jennifer and Monica (is / are) coming to my party.

4 I as well as my friends (am / are) satisfied with the result.

5 You have to choose either the new version (or / and) the old one.

6 David is (either / not only) the tallest but also the best-looking boy in my school.

Exercise 2 다음 우리말과 같은 뜻이 되도록 빈칸에 알맞은 말을 쓰시오.

1 개구리는 물에서나 육지에서나 살 수 있다.
⇨ Frogs can live ________ in the water ________ on land.

2 당신은 메시지를 남기거나 나중에 다시 전화를 주시면 됩니다.
⇨ You can ________ leave a message ________ call back later.

3 나의 남편과 아들 둘 다 나의 생일을 기억하지 못한다.
⇨ ________ my husband ________ my son remembers my birthday.

4 Jeff는 총명할 뿐 아니라 창의력이 매우 뛰어나다.
⇨ Jeff is ________ ________ intelligent ________ ________ very creative.

11-10 선택의문문

선택의문문: or를 사용하여 상대방에게 어느 한쪽을 선택하여 대답하게 하는 의문문으로, Yes나 No로 답하지 않는다.

❶ 의문사가 없는 선택의문문: 의문사가 없는 의문문에 or를 사용하여 질문한다.

- Do you like **soccer or baseball**? 너는 축구를 좋아하니, 야구를 좋아하니?
  ⇒ I like soccer. 나는 축구를 좋아해.
- Should I take **a bus or a train**? 제가 버스를 타야 할까요, 아니면 기차를 타야 할까요?
  ⇒ You should take a train. 기차를 타셔야 해요.

❷ 의문사가 있는 선택의문문: 「의문사+(명사)+동사+주어 ~, A or B?」의 어순이 된다.

- Who did you go there with, **Jen or Amy**? Jen과 Amy 중 너는 누구와 거기에 갔니?
  ⇒ I went there with Jenny. 나는 Jenny와 거기에 갔어.
- Which color do you like, **blue or red**? 파랑과 빨강 중 너는 어떤 색을 좋아하니?
  ⇒ I like both of them. 나는 둘 다 좋아해.
- Which do you want to have, **coffee or tea**? 커피와 차 중 어떤 것을 마실래?
  ⇒ I don't want to have either of them. 나는 둘 다 마시고 싶지 않아.

TIPs 선택의문문의 억양은 or 앞을 올리고 맨 뒤 물음표에서 내린다.

- Is this your pen↗ or his pen↘?
  선택의문문
- Is this your pen↗?
  일반의문문

TIPs 의문사가 있는 선택의문문은 either나 both를 사용해 대답할 수 있다.

A: Which food do you like better, Italian or Chinese?
이탈리아 음식과 중국 음식 중에서 어떤 것을 더 좋아해?
B: I don't like either of them.
둘 다 좋아하지 않아.
I like both of them.
둘 다 좋아해.

Answers: p.34

Exercise 1 다음 우리말과 같은 뜻이 되도록 빈칸에 알맞은 말을 쓰시오.

1 너희 아버지가 그것을 만드셨니 아니면 사셨니?
⇒ ________ your father make it ________ buy it?

2 Mike와 Brian 중 누가 너의 가장 친한 친구니?
⇒ ________ is your best friend, Mike ________ Brian?

3 너희 어머니는 가정주부시니 아니면 일을 하시니?
⇒ ________ your mother a housewife ________ a career woman?

4 일본과 프랑스 중 너는 휴가 때 어디에 가고 싶니?
⇒ ________ do you want to go for your vacation, Japan ________ France?

Exercise 2 다음 두 문장을 선택의문문으로 바꿔 쓰시오.

1 Is this your mother? + Is this your aunt?
⇒ ________________________________

2 Would you like to stay here? + Would you like to go home?
⇒ ________________________________

3 Does she study English? + Does she study Spanish?
⇒ ________________________________

4 Do you want to be a doctor? + Do you want to be an entertainer?
⇒ ________________________________

Exercise 3 다음 그림을 보고 질문에 답하시오.

❶ ❷ ❸ ❹ ❺ ❻

1 Is she cooking or cleaning?

⇨ ______________________________

2 Does he live in America or England?

⇨ ______________________________

3 How do you go to school, by bus or by subway?

⇨ ______________________________

4 Which season do you like better, summer or winter?

⇨ ______________________________

5 Who broke your computer, your sister or your brother?

⇨ ______________________________

6 Which is taller, the Empire State Building or the Statue of Liberty?

⇨ ______________________________

Exercise 4 다음 우리말과 뜻이 같도록 주어진 말을 알맞게 배열하여 문장을 완성하시오.

1 너의 자동차는 흰색이었니 검은색이었니? (your, black, white, car, or, was)

⇨ ______________________________

2 지구와 태양 중 어느 것이 더 큽니까? (is, bigger, the sun, or, the earth, which)

⇨ ______________________________

3 쇠고기와 닭고기 중 무엇으로 드시겠습니까? (beef, or, would, which, like, have, to, you, chicken)

⇨ ______________________________

4 창문 좌석을 원하십니까 아니면 통로 좌석을 원하십니까? (you, want, a window seat, do, an aisle seat, or)

⇨ ______________________________

Review Test

[01-05] 다음 빈칸에 들어갈 알맞은 말을 고르시오.

01 There might be no one in the dorms ___________ the winter break.

① at ② by
③ with ④ during
⑤ above

02 He introduced himself ___________ a police officer.

① in ② by
③ as ④ for
⑤ with

03 I'm not sure ___________ Ken comes back today or tomorrow.

① that ② after
③ until ④ since
⑤ if

04 ___________ you hurry, you won't get to the station in time.

① If ② As
③ Unless ④ Since
⑤ For

05 How would you like to pay, cash ___________ charge?

① and ② but
③ or ④ so
⑤ nor

[06-07] 다음 빈칸에 공통으로 들어갈 말을 고르시오.

06
- I heard that you are leaving ___________ New Zealand this Saturday.
- I really want to thank you ___________ your help.

① in ② for
③ with ④ to
⑤ by

07
- I was wondering ___________ you could give me some suggestions.
- We will go sledding ___________ it snows this weekend.

① so ② that
③ whether ④ if
⑤ because

[08-09] 다음 대화의 빈칸에 들어갈 알맞은 말을 고르시오.

08
A Don't speak loudly in public places, ___________ people might think you are rude.
B Okay, Mom. I'll be more careful.

① and ② but
③ or ④ if
⑤ so

09
A Where do you ___________ they will meet?
B They will meet at the bus stop.

① see ② know
③ like ④ tell
⑤ think

[10-11] 다음 빈칸에 들어갈 말이 바르게 짝지어진 것을 고르시오.

10

- Nick heard an enormous bang ____________ he was listening to the radio.
- I haven't had any trouble taking the subway ____________ I moved into this area.

① so – because ② although – as
③ while – since ④ as – because of
⑤ because – until

11

- Look at the girls who are all dressed up ____________ pink.
- The man was arrested ____________ hit-and-run last Tuesday.

① in – of ② in – for
③ on – of ④ on – with
⑤ with – in

12 다음 대화의 빈칸에 들어갈 말로 알맞은 것은?

A Which day is better for you, Monday or Tuesday?
B ______________________________

① I'll just have a steak.
② Either is okay with me.
③ Monday is my birthday.
④ That sounds like a better idea.
⑤ I'll be home next weekend.

13 다음 밑줄 친 부분과 바꾸어도 의미가 변하지 않는 것은?

Since it was hot during the day, I was wearing a sleeveless shirt.

① Although ② While
③ Because ④ After
⑤ When

[14-15] 다음 밑줄 친 부분이 어법상 어색한 것을 고르시오.

14 ① Hundreds of people die of heart attacks every day.
② What is the bruise above your left eye?
③ The Dead Sea is below sea level.
④ Eric was in the hospital during a week.
⑤ I waited for Tiffany until 3 o'clock.

15 ① Both Tom and I are good swimmers.
② Take a rest, or you will feel better.
③ Not only you but I am interested in art.
④ You should either take the bus or just walk.
⑤ Although you are my best friend, I can't help you every time.

16 다음 밑줄 친 that 중 생략할 수 없는 것은?

① I know that you tried your best.
② No one thinks that I am stubborn.
③ That's the reason why I came here.
④ I still can't believe that you cheated on me.
⑤ Bob doesn't think that he did something wrong.

17 다음 문장의 밑줄 친 that과 쓰임이 다른 것은?

I hope that he will get over the shock soon.

① I'm sure that Gwen is an honest girl.
② He insisted that I should see a doctor.
③ Paul told me that he would come at noon.
④ This is the best movie that I have ever seen.
⑤ I think that Michael is the best musician in the world.

18 다음 두 문장이 같은 뜻일 때 빈칸에 들어갈 알맞은 말은?

> Robert has been not only to Mexico but also to Brazil.
> = Robert has been to Brazil ___________ to Mexico.

① as well as ② as good as
③ as many as ④ as much as
⑤ as long as

[19-21] 다음 중 어법상 어색한 문장을 고르시오.

19 ① Do you know why he is running?
② Do you imagine where the birds go?
③ I wonder if she still likes chocolate.
④ I don't know why he was absent today.
⑤ Ask her if she will come here tomorrow.

20 ① Whether you believe it or not, it is true.
② I have known Chris since he was a child.
③ Neither you or I need to tell them what is right.
④ As you are quite smart, you may understand it.
⑤ Although Mr. Gibson is rich, he doesn't spend much money.

21 ① I have stayed in a cheap hotel for three days.
② Somebody knocked on the door while I was taking a shower.
③ Try to finish the task by the end of this month.
④ Unless you don't pay attention, you will miss your turn.
⑤ Betty thinks she is fat even though she is skinny.

22 다음 주어진 문장과 의미가 같은 것은?

> Ben was very tired, but he couldn't get any sleep.

① Because Ben was very tired, he couldn't get any sleep.
② Ben was very tired, so he couldn't get any sleep.
③ If Ben was very tired, he couldn't get any sleep.
④ Although Ben was very tired, he couldn't get any sleep.
⑤ Unless Ben was very tired, he couldn't get any sleep.

23 다음 문장의 as와 쓰임이 같은 것은?

> I saw Gary as I was getting off the bus.

① Everybody treats me as a child.
② Harry is twice as strong as I am.
③ As your teacher, I have to say this to you.
④ I heard someone calling my name as I was watching TV.
⑤ I can speak Chinese and write it as well.

24 다음 밑줄 친 that 중 쓰임이 다른 하나는?

① I found that the building was destroyed by the earthquake.
② Diana told me that she would always help me.
③ Everyone thinks that Samuel is very generous.
④ Look at the monkeys that are playing on the ground.
⑤ I'm sure that she will do a great job.

25 다음 문장의 when과 쓰임이 다른 하나는?

What do you want to be when you grow up?

① I remember the day when you asked me to marry you.
② When I saw her, she was standing next to Mike.
③ When it snows, I feel like staying home.
④ Don't forget to turn off the TV when you leave.
⑤ I'm very sad when you say such things.

[26-28] 다음 중 어법상 어색한 부분을 찾아 바르게 고치시오.

26

We canceled our plan to go on a picnic because of it rained heavily.

⇒ ______________________________

27

The factory has been in my town for the early 1950s.

⇒ ______________________________

28

I want to know whether does he like my present.

⇒ ______________________________

[29-30] 다음 문장과 같은 뜻이 되도록 빈칸에 알맞은 말을 쓰시오.

29

If you don't work harder, you may get fired.

⇒ __________ you work harder, you may get fired.

30

We ordered not only a pizza but also some fresh salad.

⇒ We ordered some fresh salad __________ __________ __________ a pizza.

[31-33] 다음 우리말과 같은 뜻이 되도록 빈칸에 알맞은 말을 쓰시오.

31

너는 그녀가 왜 말도 없이 나를 떠나갔는지 아니?

⇒ Do you know __________ __________ __________ me without a word?

32

나는 배가 불렀지만 초콜릿 머핀을 먹지 않을 수가 없었다.

⇒ __________ __________ I was full, I couldn't resist the chocolate muffin.

33

Phillip은 어젯밤에 잠을 거의 못 자서 오늘 아침 늦게 일어났다.

⇒ Phillip got up late this morning __________ he hardly slept last night.

[34-35] 다음 두 문장을 한 문장으로 바꿔 쓰시오.

34

Do you think? + What will happen tomorrow?

⇒ ______________________________

35

Could you tell me? + What's your favorite fruit?

⇒ ______________________________

보너스 유형별 문제

Answers: p.35

[1-3] 다음 표를 읽고, 주어진 단어를 이용하여 문장을 완성하시오. 서술형

Name	Favorite Activities
Ezra	swimming, playing soccer
Sebastian	playing computer games, cooking
Zachary	watching movies, reading
Charlotte	playing tennis, rock climbing
Rory	reading, gardening

1 ________ Sebastian ________ Zachary ________ playing sports. (neither, like)

2 ________ Ezra ________ Charlotte ________ outdoor activities. (both, like)

3 ________ ________ Zachary ________ ________ Rory ________ reading. (not only, enjoy)

4 다음 글의 밑줄 친 부분 중, 어법상 틀린 것은? 수능 대비형

Hi, Anna! ① Because Amy's ballet recital in the afternoon, I won't be able to meet you at the airport. Sorry! Come to the house. You know where the keys are. Michelle and I will be at home around 6 ② after dropping Amy off at my parents'. Then we will take you to the restaurant I ③ told you about on the phone. I know you've only got 4 hours ④ until your connecting flight to L.A. Don't worry. After dinner, we will get you back to the airport in no time. Let me know ⑤ if there is anything else you need!

* recital: 발표회
** connecting flight: 연결 항공편

★ NEW EDITION ★

GRAMMAR BRIDGE

Level

2

Workbook

Answers: p.36

A 주어진 단어를 이용하여 현재 시제 문장을 완성하시오.

1 My grandmother ______________ about my future, but I ______________ about her health. (worry)

2 My twin sister and I ______________ our homework after dinner, but my brother ______________ his homework before dinner. (do)

3 Jessica ______________ golf every weekend, and we ______________ soccer every Sunday. (play)

4 I ______________ business at Harvard, and Erin ______________ biology at Stanford. (study)

5 Many teenagers ______________ spicy food, but Jeremy ______________ sweet food. (love)

6 Kelly ______________ working with us, and we ______________ working with her. (miss)

7 Mr. Richardson and I ______________ mathematics, and Ms. Taylor ______________ chemistry. (teach)

B 〈보기〉에서 알맞은 것을 골라 현재 시제 문장을 완성하시오.

catch　　wink　　fry　　eat　　hate　　mix

1 The music artist ______________ all kinds of music.

2 The movie star ______________ at his fans.

3 The cook usually ______________ potatoes for 10 minutes.

4 The early bird ______________ the worm.

5 Some people never ______________ after 8 pm.

6 Sally and her sister ______________ doing the dishes.

C 주어진 단어를 이용하여 과거 시제로 문장을 완성하시오.

1 The elevator suddenly ______________ at the second floor. (stop)

2 Jessica ______________ me early in the morning. (call)

3 Ava ______________ you at the party. (see)

4 He ______________ to me in a low voice. (speak)

5 Nobody ______________ the kid leaving the building. (watch)

6 Your dog ______________ across the river and ran into the woods. (swam)

D 밑줄 친 부분을 과거 시제로 바르게 고쳐 쓰시오.

1 My boss and I respectted each other.

⇨ ______________

2 I meeted an old friend of mine on my way here.

⇨ ______________

3 Alice growd up in a small city.

⇨ ______________

4 We seen him at the museum two days ago.

⇨ ______________

5 The tourist taked the first train for Busan.

⇨ ______________

E 주어진 단어를 현재진행형으로 바꿔 대화를 완성하시오.

1 **A** Are you going to take a taxi?

B No. Jake ______________________ me home. (drive)

2 **A** Hey, ______________ you ______________ to the radio? (listen)

B No. You can turn it off.

3 **A** Look. Casper ______________________ a hole in the sand. (dig)

B I think he wants to hide my stuff again.

4 **A** Where are Mom and Dad?

B They ______________________ overtime. (work)

5 **A** What are the boys doing?

B They ______________________ in the pool. (swim)

F 주어진 단어를 이용하여 과거진행 시제 문장을 완성하시오. [부정문은 축약형으로 쓸 것]

1 You ______________________ so fast. (talk)

2 We ______________________ a movie. (watch)

3 They ______________________ attention. (not, pay)

4 My dad ______________________ up the mess. (clean)

5 Tyler ______________________ until late last night. (not, study)

G 밑줄 친 부분을 어법에 맞게 고쳐 쓰시오.

1 Tim has <u>leave</u> his bag on the subway.

⇨ ______________________

2 How long <u>do</u> you known Ashley?

⇨ ______________________

3 I <u>have never try</u> to play golf before.

⇨ ______________________

4 Jennie <u>not has spoken</u> to me for a week.

⇨ ______________________

H 두 문장을 현재완료를 이용한 한 문장으로 바꿔 쓰시오.

1 Jessica was sick last Sunday. She is still sick.

⇨ Jessica ______________________ since last Sunday.

2 Dylan went to Paris to study. He is still in Paris.

⇨ Dylan ______________________ to study.

3 My mother lost her watch. She doesn't have it now.

⇨ My mother ______________________.

4 Jean played the cello when she was young. She still plays it.

⇨ Jean ______________________ since she was young.

5 I started wearing glasses when I was a little kid. I still wear them.

⇨ I ______________________ since I was a little kid.

I 우리말과 같은 뜻이 되도록 주어진 단어를 이용하여 문장을 완성하시오.

1 마침내 겨울이 왔다. (come)

⇨ Finally, winter ______________________.

2 나는 우리 졸업식 이후로 그녀를 본 적이 없다. (see, her)

⇨ I ______________________ since our graduation.

3 전에 눈에 문제가 있었나요? (have, problems)

⇨ ______________________ with your eyes before?

4 Kevin은 배낭을 잃어버렸다. (lose, his backpack)

⇨ Kevin ______________________.

5 그들은 약 5년 동안 소를 기르고 있다. (raise, cattle)

⇨ They ______________________ for about 5 years.

6 나는 그에게서 어떤 메시지도 받지 않았다. (receive, any messages)

⇨ I ______________________ from him.

Chapter 2 조동사

Answers: p.36

A 밑줄 친 부분을 어법에 맞게 고쳐 쓰시오.

1 Will I go to the bathroom, please?

⇒ ______________

2 Look at the clouds. It may to rain soon.

⇒ ______________

3 Sophie is able repair your computer.

⇒ ______________

4 They will making a special announcement.

⇒ ______________

5 Cathy can speaks Japanese but can't speak Chinese.

⇒ ______________

6 She will can win another gold medal.

⇒ ______________

7 May you tell us how your YouTube channel became so popular?

⇒ ______________

B 주어진 문장을 의문문으로 바꿔 쓰시오.

1 I may ask several questions.

⇒ ____

2 We should keep quiet.

⇒ ____

3 She must log in to her account.

⇒ ____

4 You can download old songs for free.

⇒ ____

C 〈보기〉에서 알맞은 조동사를 골라 주어진 동사를 이용하여 문장을 완성하시오.

must	might	can't	may not

1 You even worked on the weekend. You ______________ very tired. (be)

2 I have only $10 in my bank account. This ______________ real. (be)

3 There are so many subway lines. I ______________ lost. (get)

4 He was raised in an American family. He ______________ Korean. (understand)

D 우리말과 같은 뜻이 되도록 주어진 단어를 이용하여 문장을 완성하시오.

1 오늘 밤에 눈이 내릴지도 모른다. (snow)

⇨ ____________________ tonight.

2 도와드릴까요? (help)

⇨ ____________________ you?

3 다음 달이면 그 아기는 걸을 수 있을 것이다. (walk)

⇨ The baby ____________________ next month.

4 Eric은 작곡을 아주 잘 할 수 있다. (write songs)

⇨ Eric ____________________ very well.

5 제가 여기에 앉아도 될까요? (sit)

⇨ ____________________ here?

6 내가 어릴 적에 Bolt만큼 빨리 달릴 수 있었다. (run)

⇨ I ____________________ as fast as Bolt when I was younger.

7 사진 올리는 법 좀 내게 알려줄 수 있니? (teach)

⇨ ____________________ how to post photos?

E 밑줄 친 부분에 유의하여 해석을 완성하시오.

1 It is not sweet enough. You should add more sugar.

⇨ 그것이 충분히 달지가 않네. 너는 설탕을 더 ____________________________________.

2 Ellie must be smart.

⇨ Ellie는 ____________________________________.

3 Sienna doesn't have to come to work today.

⇨ Sienna는 오늘 ____________________________________.

4 We had better ask for help.

⇨ 우리는 ____________________________________.

F 〈보기〉에서 단어를 골라 주어진 조동사를 이용하여 문장을 완성하시오.

leave	use	take	watch

1 This painting is very unique. ____________ I ____________ a picture of it? (may)

2 You ____________________ any time you want. (may)

3 There is no one in the bathroom. You ____________________ it now. (can)

4 I just finished my homework. ____________ I ____________ TV now? (can)

G have to를 이용한 문장으로 바꿔 쓰시오.

1 They must follow the school rules.

⇒ ______________________________

2 Must I keep it a secret?

⇒ ______________________________

3 James must put away his smartphone.

⇒ ______________________________

H 두 문장의 의미가 통하도록 〈보기〉에서 알맞은 말을 골라 문장을 완성하시오. (중복 사용 가능)

would like to	had better	used to

1 I watched American TV shows, but not anymore.

⇒ I ____________ watch American TV shows, but not anymore.

2 The journalist wants to interview you.

⇒ The journalist ____________ interview you.

3 Henry got up at 6 every morning.

⇒ Henry ____________ get up at 6 every morning.

4 I don't think I should touch the cat.

⇒ I ____________ not touch the cat.

5 I think you should stop playing the mobile game.

⇒ You ____________ stop playing the mobile game.

I 우리말과 같은 뜻이 되도록 주어진 단어를 알맞게 배열하시오.

1 중학생 시절에 수업을 빼먹곤 하셨나요? (use to, did, classes, you, skip)

⇒ ______________________________ when you were in middle school?

2 너는 그들과 어울리지 않는 것이 좋겠다. (not, with, hang out, them, better, had)

⇒ You ______________________________.

3 뭐 하고 재미있게 놀고 싶나요? (would, do, like to, what, you)

⇒ ______________________________ for fun?

4 그 환자는 하루 더 머무는 게 좋겠네요. (for, stay, day, had better, another)

⇒ The patient ______________________________.

5 우리는 그를 위해 생일 파티를 열어주는 게 좋겠다. (for, a birthday party, had better, him, throw)

⇒ We ______________________________.

6 강 위로 다리가 하나 있었는데 이제는 없어졌다. (a bridge, the river, be, used to, there, over)

⇒ ______________________________, but it's gone now.

Chapter 3 수동태

Answers: p.37

A 주어진 단어를 과거분사로 바꿔 수동태 문장을 완성하시오.

1 Was this e-mail ______________ automatically? (send)

2 This novel was ______________ by a Korean immigrant. (write)

3 The drunk was ______________ by a police officer. (arrest)

4 Were these products ______________ in China? (make)

5 The museum is ______________ by numerous tourists from all over the world. (visit)

B 밑줄 친 부분을 어법에 맞게 고쳐 쓰시오.

1 Your clothes were folded up not by Mom.

⇒ ______________________

2 She was seen ride your bike.

⇒ ______________________

3 Did the paintings painted by your son?

⇒ ______________________

4 Those awful comments should delete immediately.

⇒ ______________________

5 Music is taught for us by the new teacher.

⇒ ______________________

C 능동태 문장을 수동태 문장으로 바꿔 쓰시오.

1 The student didn't tell the truth.

⇒ The truth ____.

2 He doesn't water the plants.

⇒ The plants ____.

3 We should make a quick decision on this issue.

⇒ A quick decision on this issue ____.

4 Did Russia attack Ukraine?

⇒ ______________ Ukraine ____________________________?

D 주어진 단어를 어법에 맞게 바꿔 문장을 완성하시오. (시제는 과거로 할 것)

1 sell (a) The girl ______________ lemonade after school.
(b) The masterpiece ______________ to a rich man.

2 invite (a) They ______________ many friends to their anniversary party.
(b) The Lees ______________ to the thanksgiving dinner as well.

3 take (a) I ______________ some pictures of the flowers.
(b) These photos ______________ during the thunder storm.

4 raise (a) Mrs. Smith ______________ three beautiful children.
(b) The student ______________ in a middle-class family.

5 break (a) Lucas ______________ his leg while playing soccer.
(b) When they returned home, they noticed that the windows ______________.

E 빈칸에 알맞은 말을 〈보기〉에서 골라 쓰시오. (한 번씩만 쓸 것)

[1~4]

with	in	from	at

1 What is balsamic vinegar made ______________?

2 You won't be pleased ______________ my exam results.

3 We were all surprised ______________ his reaction.

4 Is Mark interested ______________ K-pop?

[5~8]

about	with	to	of

5 These accidents are not related ______________ one another.

6 This beautiful photo frame is made ______________ crystal.

7 Why is the mountain always covered ______________ snow?

8 I'm really excited ______________ the field trip.

F 우리말과 같은 뜻이 되도록 주어진 단어를 이용하여 문장을 완성하시오.

1 에베레스트산이 우주에서도 보이나요? (see)
⇨ Can Mt. Everest ______________________ from outer space?

2 그 죄수는 조용히 있게 되었다. (make, keep)
⇨ The prisoner ______________________ quiet.

3 라면 한 그릇이 내 형에 의해서 요리되었다. (cook)
⇨ A bowl of ramen ______________________ by my brother.

4 너의 보고서는 내일까지 제출되어야 한다. (must, hand in)
⇨ Your report ______________________ by tomorrow.

5 당신의 아들이 도난당한 자동차를 운전하는 게 목격되었습니다. (see, drive)
⇨ Your son ______________________ a stolen vehicle.

6 그 약국은 일요일마다 문을 닫아요. (close)
⇨ The pharmacy ______________________ every Sunday.

7 우리에게 아무것도 주어지지 않았다. (give)
⇨ Nothing ______________________.

G 우리말과 같은 뜻이 되도록 주어진 단어를 배열하시오.

1 이 약은 매 식사 후에 복용해야 한다. (each meal, taken, after, be, should)
⇨ This medicine ________________________________.

2 그 교회는 2년 전에 파괴되었나요? (destroyed, the church, was)
⇨ ________________________________ two years ago?

3 그 승객은 자리에 앉으라고 요청을 받았다. (asked, sit down, was, to)
⇨ The passenger ________________________________.

4 그 공포 영화는 내가 감독한 것이 아니에요. (directed, me, not, by, was)
⇨ The horror movie ________________________________.

5 그 선물은 잘못 보내졌다. (sent, the wrong person, to, was)
⇨ The gift ________________________________.

6 내 음식은 로봇이 나에게 가져온 것이었다. (brought, a robot, me, was, to, by)
⇨ My food ________________________________.

7 Matthew가 개를 산책시키는 것을 보았다. (walking, seen, was, a dog)
⇨ Matthew ________________________________.

Answers: p.37

A 밑줄 친 부분을 바르게 고쳐 쓰시오.

1 She tried to be not lazy.
⇨ ______________

2 Many students hope to being influential streamers.
⇨ ______________

3 Iris wrote down his phone number to not forget it.
⇨ ______________

4 They want something to drinking.
⇨ ______________

5 I like to going fishing.
⇨ ______________

6 We decided order more fries.
⇨ ______________

B 밑줄 친 to부정사가 문장에서 주어, 목적어, 보어 중 어떤 역할을 하는지 쓰시오.

1 I hope to see you guys again soon. ⇨ ______________
2 Her plan is to turn the place into a luxury hotel. ⇨ ______________
3 Tiffany wants to be a celebrity. ⇨ ______________
4 To work alone takes a lot of courage. ⇨ ______________
5 Your job is to keep our website safe. ⇨ ______________
6 To trust someone is difficult. ⇨ ______________

C 〈보기〉와 같이 우리말과 같은 뜻이 되도록 문장을 완성하시오.

> **나는 너에게 말할 이야기가 있다. (a story, tell)**
> **⇨ I have a story to tell you.**

1 나는 마실 탄산음료 하나를 샀다. (a soda, drink)
⇨ I bought ______________________________.

2 너의 알약을 먹어야 할 시간이다. (time, take, pills)
⇨ It is ______________________________.

3 우리는 모두 대화를 나눌 누군가가 필요하다. (someone, talk with)
⇨ We all need ______________________________.

4 우리 언니는 할 일이 많아. (many things, do)
⇨ My sister has ______________________________.

5 Tim은 플레이할 게임을 좀 다운로드했다. (some games, play)
⇨ Tim downloaded ______________________________.

D 〈보기〉와 같이 두 문장의 뜻이 통하도록 문장을 완성하시오.

> He wanted to buy a bottle of water. So he went to the convenience store.
> ⇨ He went to the convenience store to buy a bottle of water.

1 She wants to buy a new smartwatch. So she is saving some money.
⇨ ______________________________

2 I was disappointed. I saw him leave.
⇨ ______________________________

3 James wanted to catch the train. So he got up early.
⇨ ______________________________

4 They were pleased. They received your message.
⇨ ______________________________

E 두 문장이 같은 의미가 되도록 문장을 완성하시오.

1 To charge my phone is necessary.
⇨ __________ is necessary ______________________________.

2 To live without my parents is impossible.
⇨ __________ is impossible ______________________________.

3 To learn how to edit videos is very useful.
⇨ __________ is very useful ______________________________.

4 To bite your fingernails is a bad habit.
⇨ __________ is a bad habit ______________________________.

5 To travel alone in Korea is not dangerous.
⇨ __________ is not dangerous ______________________________.

F 주어진 단어를 이용하여 빈칸에 알맞은 의미상의 주어를 쓰시오.

1 It was generous __________ to share your toys with Mike. (you)

2 It was foolish __________ to lie to Ms. Anderson. (he)

3 It was polite __________ to use both of his hands to receive the money. (he)

4 It is necessary __________ to stay focused. (they)

5 It was careless __________ to insult the lady. (you)

6 It was impossible __________ to calm down. (she)

7 It wasn't easy __________ to work for Mr. Park. (we)

8 It is hard __________ to speak in public. (I)

G 두 문장의 의미가 통하도록 that을 써서 문장을 완성하시오.

1 We all studied hard enough to pass the math test.

⇒ We all studied ______________________________ the math test.

2 The queen was strong enough to invade another country.

⇒ The queen was ______________________________ another country.

3 My parents are too busy to go shopping with me.

⇒ My parents ______________________________ with me.

4 Patrick was too sick to come to the party.

⇒ Patrick was ______________________________ to the party.

H 우리말과 같은 뜻이 되도록 주어진 단어를 배열하시오.

1 Claire는 너무 이기적이라서 자신의 친구들과 같이 놀지 못한다. (hang out, too, to, her, with, selfish, friends)

⇒ Claire is ______________________________.

2 18세의 사람들은 선거에서 투표할 만큼 충분히 나이를 먹었다. (elections, in, vote, enough, old, to)

⇒ 18-year-olds are ______________________________.

3 그 얇은 얼음에서 스케이트를 타다니 그는 부주의했구나. (the thin ice, on, careless, to, of, skate, him)

⇒ It was ______________________________.

4 우리가 매일 비타민을 섭취하는 것은 중요하다. (every day, for, take, us, to, important, vitamins)

⇒ It is ______________________________.

5 내가 아침에 일찍 일어나는 것은 쉽다. (in the morning, for, get up, me, easy, to, early)

⇒ It is ______________________________.

6 그 피자는 아이들이 먹기에 너무 매워요. (to, spicy, children, for, too, eat)

⇒ The pizza is ______________________________.

I 우리말과 같은 뜻이 되도록 to부정사와 주어진 단어를 이용하여 문장을 완성하시오.

1 Amy는 몸매를 유지하기 위해 매일 아침 달린다. (order, keep in shape)

⇒ Amy runs every morning ______________________________.

2 그 퍼즐은 풀기에 충분히 쉽다. (easy, solve)

⇒ The puzzle is ______________________________.

3 날씨가 너무 더워서 밤잠을 잘 잘 수가 없었다. (hot, get, a good night's sleep)

⇒ It was ______________________________.

4 나는 결승전까지 진출할 만큼 충분히 운이 있었다. (lucky, make it, to the finals)

⇒ I was ______________________________.

Answers: p.38

A 주어진 단어를 동명사로 바꿔 문장을 완성하시오.

1 We love ______________ movies. (talk about)

2 I enjoy ______________ alone. (work)

3 ______________ sweets is not good for your teeth. (eat)

4 One of my hobbies is ______________ drones. (fly)

5 Kate is interested in ______________ clothes. (make)

B 밑줄 친 동명사가 문장에서 주어, 목적어, 보어 중 어떤 역할을 하는지 쓰시오.

1 Do you mind slowing down? ⇨ ______________

2 Learning about a new culture is interesting. ⇨ ______________

3 My favorite thing to do is watching Marvel movies. ⇨ ______________

4 My biggest mistake was not listening to your advice. ⇨ ______________

5 Riding my bike always makes me happy. ⇨ ______________

6 Ivy began reading the book out loud. ⇨ ______________

C 두 문장의 의미가 통하도록 〈보기〉와 같이 바꿔 쓰시오.

> **Mrs. Simmons teaches science. It is her job.**
> ⇨ Mrs. Simmons's job is teaching science.

1 He plays soccer with his friends. It is his favorite thing to do.
⇨ His favorite thing to do is ______________________________.

2 I can't talk to girls. It is difficult for me.
⇨ ______________________________ is difficult for me.

3 Don't eat too much ice cream. It is bad for your stomach.
⇨ ______________________________ is bad for your stomach.

4 Daisy writes computer programs. She is interested in it.
⇨ Daisy is interested in ______________________________.

5 I want to fly a KF-21. It is my dream.
⇨ I have a dream of ______________________________.

6 Meg listens to K-pop. She enjoys it.
⇨ Meg enjoys ______________________________.

D 〈보기〉에서 알맞은 것을 골라 지시대로 바꿔 문장을 완성하시오.

[1-3] 동명사

break	build	meet

1 Her job is ______________ houses.

2 ______________ new people is fun and exciting.

3 They are exciting about ______________ the world record.

[4-6] 동명사의 부정

get	be	tell

4 I am sorry for ______________________ careful enough.

5 Because of ______________________ to the airport on time, we missed the flight.

6 I apologize for ______________________ the truth.

E 주어진 동사를 알맞은 형태로 바꿔 문장을 완성하시오.

1 They need ______________ more milk. (buy)

2 Aria finished ______________ up the laundry. (fold)

3 I don't mind ______________ the air conditioner on. (keep)

4 Kelly quit ______________ as a violinist. (work)

5 Sarah hopes ______________ sushi someday. (try)

6 When do you plan ______________ her out? (ask)

F 두 문장의 의미가 통하도록 〈보기〉와 같이 바꿔 쓰시오.

> **Remember that you should turn off the lights on your way out.**
> ⇨ Remember to turn off the lights on your way out.

1 Ryan wanted to pick up the $10 bill from the sidewalk, so he stopped.

⇨ Ryan stopped ____.

2 Don't forget that you should take out the trash.

⇨ Don't forget ____.

3 We remember that we saw Matilda hanging out at the mall last Saturday.

⇨ We remember ____.

4 Remember that you should return the books to the library by tomorrow.

⇨ Remember ____.

5 I forgot that I borrowed a pencil from Elliot.

⇨ I forgot ____.

G 〈보기〉에서 알맞은 단어를 골라 어법에 맞게 바꿔 문장을 완성하시오.

attract	become	read	pay	see	learn

1 Eva decided ____________________ a writer. She is reading a lot of novels these days.
2 The salesclerk was very rude. I asked ____________________ the store manager.
3 My brothers enjoy ____________________ foreign languages. They want to study overseas.
4 We spent another $100,000 on advertising. We expect ____________________ more visitors.
5 If you are having trouble getting to sleep, I suggest ____________________ the bible.
6 The landlord kicked him out because he delayed ____________________ his rent.

H 우리말과 같은 뜻이 되도록 주어진 단어를 이용하여 문장을 완성하시오.

1 시장은 자신이 옳다는 것을 증명하려고 노력 중이다. (try, prove)
⇨ The mayor is ____ that he is right.

2 나는 언니의 원피스를 한번 입어보았다. (try, put on, dress)
⇨ I ____.

3 그들은 그들의 회의를 연기하기로 동의했다. (agree, postpone, meeting)
⇨ They ____.

4 그는 자신의 가족에게 장난치는 것을 매우 좋아한다. (love, pull, pranks)
⇨ He ____ on his family.

5 유튜브 동영상 좀 그만 봐. 시간 낭비야. (quit, watch, YouTube videos)
⇨ ____ It is a waste of time.

I 우리말과 같은 뜻이 되도록 주어진 단어를 배열하시오.

1 나는 저녁 식사 전에 내 리포트 쓰는 것을 끝내야 한다. (essay, I, finish, writing, dinner, my, should, before)
⇨ ____

2 나와 눈 마주치는 것을 피하지 마세요. (eye contact, avoid, me, making, Don't, with)
⇨ ____

3 한국인들은 술 마시고 노래하는 것을 좋아한다. (singing, like, drinking, Koreans, and)
⇨ ____

4 그 학생은 답을 아는 척했다. (pretended, to, the answer, know, the student)
⇨ ____

5 Rosie는 9시까지 돌아오겠다고 약속했다. (Rosie, to, be, by, back, promised, 9)
⇨ ____

6 갑자기 그 여자아이는 반 친구들에게 소리지르기 시작했다. (her, the girl, screaming, started, at, classmates)
⇨ Suddenly, ____.

Chapter 6 분사

Answers: p.39

A 주어진 단어를 과거분사나 현재분사로 바꿔 문장을 완성하시오.

1 We can't live without products ____________ in China. (make)

2 I saw them ____________ chocolate bars at the store. (steal)

3 The photos ____________ by Ella Smith are very rare. (take)

4 Alex told us something very ____________ last night. (interest)

5 The boy ____________ alone at the table is my son. (sit)

6 I stood by the window listening to the sound of the ____________ rain. (fall)

B 〈보기〉와 같이 문장을 완성하시오.

> **Tommy is driving a truck. It is filled with rocks.**
> ⇨ Tommy is driving a truck filled with rocks.

1 Maria is reading a novel. It is written in Spanish.
⇨ Maria is reading a novel ____________________.

2 The teenage girl is talking on the phone. She is my niece, Amelia.
⇨ The teenage girl ____________________ is my niece, Amelia.

3 Look at the dog. It is barking at the kids.
⇨ Look at the dog ____________________.

4 The hotel is over one hundred years old. It was built by the lake.
⇨ The hotel ____________________ is one hundred years old.

C 우리말과 같은 뜻이 되도록 주어진 단어와 분사를 이용하여 문장을 완성하시오.

1 Toby가 너무 짜증나게 해서 난 방에서 나왔다. (so, annoy)
⇨ ______________________________ that I left the room.

2 우리 아빠는 1990년 대에 찍은 영화를 수집하고 계셔. (movies, film, in the 1990s)
⇨ My dad has a collection of ______________________________.

3 나는 the Ice라고 불리는 한 남자를 찾고 있어요. (a man, call, the Ice)
⇨ I am looking for ______________________________.

4 이 그림에서 보이는 구조물은 남아메리카에서 발견되었습니다. (the structure, show, in this picture)
⇨ ______________________________ was discovered in South America.

5 Leah는 자신의 도난 당한 핸드백을 찾아야 한다. (steal, purse)
⇨ Leah has to get ______________________________ back.

D 우리말과 같은 뜻이 되도록 주어진 말을 알맞게 배열하시오.

1 Ethan은 그 오래된 사진을 보며 울고 있어. (crying, old, the, photo, looking at, is)
⇒ Ethan ____.

2 Lucy는 모든 마을 사람들에게 알려진 약사이다. (everyone, known, a pharmacist, to)
⇒ Lucy is ____ in town.

3 그 끓고 있는 물에 너의 손가락을 넣지 마. (the, water, boiling)
⇒ Do not put your finger in ____.

4 공을 가지고 공연하는 저 물개를 봐. (performing, the seal, a ball, with)
⇒ Look at ____.

5 수영장에서 수영을 하고 아이들은 누구야? (swimming, the kids, the pool, in)
⇒ Who are ____?

6 경찰관 한 명이 버스정류장에 주차된 차에 접근하고 있다. (at, the car, the bus stop, parked)
⇒ A police officer is approaching ____.

7 우리 부모님은 파티에서 모든 친척들을 보고서 놀라워하셨다. (see, to, amazed, were)
⇒ My parents ______________________________ all their relatives at the party.

E 두 문장이 같은 의미가 되도록 분사구문을 이용하여 문장을 완성하시오.

1 As he listened to the radio, Joshua lay on the floor.
⇒ ______________________________, Joshua lay on the floor.

2 If you turn around the corner, you will find the bank.
⇒ ______________________________, you will find the bank.

3 Because she was tired, she went straight to bed.
⇒ ______________________________, she went straight to bed.

4 Although she works alone, she never gets lonely.
⇒ ______________________________, she never gets lonely.

5 Because he had a toothache, George went to the dentist.
⇒ ______________________________, George went to the dentist.

6 While I was taking a shower, I found a bruise on my chest.
⇒ ______________________________, I found a bruise on my chest.

7 As he cried like a baby, my son kept looking for me.
⇒ ______________________________, my son kept looking for me.

F 주어진 접속사를 이용하여 두 문장의 의미가 통하도록 부사절을 완성하시오.

1 Hearing about Dylan's accident, Molly began to cry. (when)

⇨ ______________________________, Molly began to cry.

2 Taking the bus, you will get there on time. (if)

⇨ ______________________________, you will get there on time.

3 Ruby stood up, yelling at us. (as)

⇨ Ruby stood up ______________________________.

4 Winning the race, we screamed with excitement. (after)

⇨ ______________________________, we screamed with excitement.

G 우리말과 같은 뜻이 되도록 주어진 단어와 분사구문을 이용하여 문장을 완성하시오.

1 거울을 보면 네가 얼마나 아름다운지 볼 수 있을 거야. (look, the mirror, in)

⇨ ______________________, you see see will how beautiful you are.

2 그 마라톤선수는 부상을 당했음에도 계속 달렸다. (be, injured)

⇨ ______________________, the marathoner kept running.

3 자신의 친구들과 얘기를 나누면 그녀는 생기를 느낀다. (talk, to, friends)

⇨ ______________________, she feels alive.

4 저녁을 준비하면서 나는 클래식 음악을 들었다. (prepare, dinner)

⇨ ______________________, I listened to classical music.

5 그의 손을 흔든 후, 그는 버스를 탔다. (wave, hand)

⇨ ______________________, he got on the train.

H 우리말과 같은 뜻이 되도록 주어진 말을 알맞게 배열하시오.

1 매일 흡연을 하면 너의 상태는 더 악화될 거야. (get, every day, conditions, smoking, worse, will, your)

⇨ ____

2 순찰차를 보자 그 강도는 도망치기 시작했다. (to run away, the robber, seeing, the patrol car, started)

⇨ ____

3 그는 최선을 다했지만, 그는 여전히 상대방을 이길 수 없었다. (his opponent, he, his best, beat, doing, still couldn't)

⇨ ____

4 야근을 하는 중에 나는 누군가 소리지르며 도움을 요청하는 것을 들었어요. (overtime, for help, someone, heard, working, I, screaming)

⇨ ____

5 의사는 너무 놀랐기 때문에 얼굴이 창백해졌다. (so shocked, turned, the doctor, pale, being)

⇨ ____

6 그 소식을 들었을 때 그 병사들은 자신의 소총을 떨어뜨렸다. (the news, their, dropped, rifles, hearing, the soldiers)

⇨ ____

Answers: p.39

A 빈칸에 알맞은 재귀대명사를 쓰시오.

1 She cut ______________ while she was playing with a knife.

2 I will never be able to forgive ______________.

3 We made the birthday cake ______________.

4 Can they finish the project ______________?

5 History repeats ______________.

6 David can take care of ______________.

7 Emily, you should learn to love ______________.

B 〈보기〉에서 알맞은 말을 골라 문장을 완성하시오.

by myself	help yourself	enjoyed ourselves
taught herself	introduced themselves	hurt himself

1 Evelyn ______________________________ to play the drums.

2 Please ______________________________ to the cookies.

3 We ______________________________ at the school dance.

4 William ______________________________ during the morning practice.

5 I live ______________________________ in this old house.

6 The new students ______________________________ to us.

C 주어진 문장을 가주어 It를 이용한 문장으로 바꿔 쓰시오.

1 To understand his southern accent was impossible.
⇨ ____

2 To collect more data is necessary.
⇨ ____

3 To get an A in this course is not hard.
⇨ ____

4 To see their reactions was interesting.
⇨ ____

5 To go jogging late at night is dangerous.
⇨ ____

D 〈보기〉에서 알맞은 것을 골라 대화를 완성하시오. (중복 사용 가능)

another	ones	one	it

1 Seth bought a brand new bike. ______________ is really expensive.

2 Where did you put the remote control? I can't find ______________.

3 Nina left her umbrella in the taxi. She needs a new ______________.

4 My feet hurt in these sneakers. Could you show me bigger ______________?

5 We waited two weeks for the results. They said we have to wait ______________ two weeks.

6 Jasper was drank a glass of water, but he was very thirsty. So he drank ______________ glass of water.

E 우리말과 같은 뜻이 되도록 빈칸에 알맞은 말을 쓰시오.

1 어떤 사람들은 화창한 날씨를 좋아한다. 또 다른 사람들은 비 오는 날씨를 좋아한다.
⇨ ______________ people like sunny days. ______________ like rainy days.

2 Freya는 두 종류의 자동차를 소유하고 있다. 하나는 픽업트럭이고 나머지 하나는 미니밴이다.
⇨ Freya owns two types of cars. ______________ is a pickup truck, and ______________ is a minivan.

3 나에게는 세 명의 외국인 친구가 있다. 한 명은 미국인이고, 또 다른 한 명은 캐나다인이며, 나머지 한 명은 중국인이다.
⇨ I have three foreign friends. ______________ is American, ______________ is Canadian, and ______________ is Chinese.

4 Grace는 세 명의 아이들이 있다. 하나는 고등학교에 다니고, 나머지는 유치원에 다닌다.
⇨ Grace has three children. ______________ is in high school, and ______________ are in kindergarten.

F 빈칸에 some이나 any 중 알맞은 것을 써넣으시오.

1 Daisy added ______________ pepper in the soup.

2 Would you like ______________ coffee?

3 She needed to borrow ______________ money from her parents.

4 What are we going to do about it? Do you have ______________ good ideas?

5 I really wanted to buy a popsicle, but I didn't have ______________ cash on me.

6 Luckily, he doesn't have ______________ plans for Thanksgiving.

G 〈보기〉에서 알맞은 단어를 골라 우리말과 같은 뜻이 되도록 문장을 완성하시오.

somebody	something	anyone	anything	nothing	no one

1 가족보다 중요한 것은 없다.
⇨ ______________ is more valuable than family.

2 그것엔 아무런 문제가 없어 보입니다.
⇨ I can't find ______________ wrong with it.

3 그녀는 사내연애를 하고 있어.
⇨ She is dating ______________ from work.

4 아무도 그 사고가 어떻게 일어났는지 못 봤다.
⇨ ______________ saw how the accident happened.

5 멋있는 거 보여줄까?
⇨ Do you want to see ______________ cool?

6 질문 있는 사람 있나요?
⇨ Does ______________ have questions?

H 밑줄 친 부분을 어법에 맞게 고쳐 쓰시오.

1 Every men loves adventure. ⇨ ______________

2 All the guests at the party was having fun. ⇨ ______________

3 Each of the students need to participate. ⇨ ______________

4 Don't play with the ball. One doesn't belong to us. ⇨ ______________

I 주어진 동사를 알맞은 형태로 바꿔 문장을 완성하시오. (현재 시제로 쓸 것)

1 Either Mike or Jason ______________ going to pay for the damage soon. (be)

2 Not only she but also her daughters ______________ proud of me. (feel)

3 Neither my wife nor I ______________ a special plan for Christmas. (have)

4 Both Eva and her brother ______________ watching K-dramas. (love)

J 우리말과 같은 뜻이 되도록 주어진 단어를 이용하여 문장을 완성하시오.

1 감자튀김이나 치킨너겟을 선택하실 수 있어요. (either, French fries, chicken nuggets)
⇨ You can choose ____.

2 Hannah는 네덜란드어와 독일어 둘 다 유창하게 한다. (Dutch, German)
⇨ Hannah can speak ____ fluently.

3 나의 부모님과 조부모님 모두 서울대학교를 나오셨어. (both, parents, grandparents)
⇨ ____ graduated from Seoul National University.

4 그 손님은 현찰도 신용카드도 소지하고 있지 않았다. (cash, credit cards)
⇨ The customer carried ____.

Chapter 8 형용사/부사/비교

Answers: p.40

A 짝지어진 두 문장이 같은 뜻이 되도록 빈칸에 알맞은 말을 쓰시오.

1 Rich people do not always live longer.
⇒ ____________ do not always live longer.

2 The city needs to help homeless people.
⇒ The city needs to help ____________.

3 The number of unemployed people has increased again.
⇒ The number of ____________ has increased again.

B 주어진 단어를 이용하여 밑줄 친 단어를 수식하는 문장을 다시 쓰시오.

1 The actress has long hair. (blonde)
⇒ ____________

2 How much is that vase? (large, crystal)
⇒ ____________

3 Maria is a girl. (smart)
⇒ ____________

4 The class is full of students. (bright)
⇒ ____________

C 밑줄 친 부분을 바르게 고쳐 쓰시오.

1 Not surprising, Alice was late for class again. ⇒ ____________
2 Time goes fastly. ⇒ ____________
3 This mango tastes bitter so. ⇒ ____________
4 I got a highly score in physical education. ⇒ ____________
5 She plays the piano good. ⇒ ____________
6 Please move the boxes careful. ⇒ ____________
7 James worked hardly to support his family. ⇒ ____________
8 My sister came home earlily from school. ⇒ ____________

D 우리말과 같은 뜻이 되도록 <보기>에서 알맞은 단어를 골라 원급 비교 문장을 완성하시오.

intelligent	popular	lazy	well	effective	early

1 미니밴은 SUV만큼 인기가 있지 않다.
⇨ Minivans are not ______________________ SUVs.

2 그녀는 나만큼 아침에 일찍 일어나지 않는다.
⇨ She doesn't get up ______________________ I do.

3 Holly는 나만큼 게으르지는 않다.
⇨ Holly is not ______________________ I am.

4 이 백신은 다른 것만큼 효과가 있다.
⇨ This vaccine is ______________________ other ones.

5 어떤 개들은 원숭이만큼 똑똑하다.
⇨ Some dogs are ______________________ monkeys.

6 우리 아버지는 전문요리사만큼 요리를 잘 하신다.
⇨ My father cooks ______________________ a professional chef.

E 두 문장의 의미가 통하도록 원급 비교 문장을 완성하시오.

1 Bob has $50. Andrew has $70. (not, much money)
⇨ Bob ______________________ Andrew does.

2 This box is 10 kg. That box is 15 kg. (not, heavy)
⇨ This box ______________________ that one.

3 Sean is 178 cm tall. His father is 178 cm tall. (tall)
⇨ Sean ______________________ his father.

4 David reads five books a month. Cindy reads seven books a month. (not, many)
⇨ David ______________________ Cindy does.

5 Janet runs 100 m in 14 seconds. Kate also runs 100 m in 14 seconds. (fast)
⇨ Janet ______________________ Kate does.

F 밑줄 친 부분을 어법에 맞게 고쳐 쓰시오.

1 This book is as thickest as that one. ⇨ ____________

2 I cannot sing as well than the soprano. ⇨ ____________

3 The exhibition was crowded than I expected. ⇨ ____________

4 His conditions are worse much than before. ⇨ ____________

5 Amelia is married to the richer man in town. ⇨ ____________

G 우리말과 같은 뜻이 되도록 주어진 단어를 이용하여 문장을 완성하시오.

1 그 배우는 실제보다 더 키가 커 보인다. (look, tall)
⇨ The actor ____________________ he really is.

2 역사는 다른 어떤 과목보다 더 중요하다. (be, important)
⇨ History ____________________ any other subject.

3 나의 유튜브 구독자들은 인스타그램 팔로워들보다 더 충성심이 강하다. (be, loyal)
⇨ My YouTube subscribers ____________________ my Instagram followers.

4 Anna는 쌍둥이 여동생보다 3분 일찍 태어났다. (three minutes, early)
⇨ Anna was born ____________________ her twin sister.

5 Harper는 공포 영화보다 액션 영화를 더 좋아한다. (like, action movies, much)
⇨ Harper ____________________ horror movies.

6 신호등 덕분에 자동차사고가 전보다 덜 빈번하게 발생한다. (happen, frequently)
⇨ Thanks to the traffic lights, car accidents ____________________ before.

H 문장의 의미가 통하도록 괄호 안의 지시대로 문장을 완성하시오.

1 Russia is the largest country in the world.
⇨ Russia ____________________. (비교급)
⇨ No ____________________. (비교급)
⇨ No ____________________. (원급)

2 Nora is the smartest employee in the office.
⇨ Nora ____________________. (비교급)
⇨ No ____________________. (비교급)
⇨ No ____________________. (원급)

I 우리말과 같은 뜻이 되도록 주어진 단어를 배열하시오.

1 우리는 마을에서 가장 맛있는 빵을 구워요. (bake, we, bread, the, delicious, most)
⇨ ____________________ in town.

2 오늘은 그녀의 일생에서 가장 중요한 날이다. (day, today, important, is, most, the)
⇨ ____________________ of her life.

3 루브르 박물관에서 가장 비싼 그림은 무엇입니까? (is, painting, what, expensive, most, the)
⇨ ____________________ in the Louvre?

4 Logan은 모든 학생들 중에서 가장 큰 집에서 살아요. (lives, house, Logan, the, in, biggest)
⇨ ____________________ of all the students.

5 그는 한국에서 가장 힘 있는 회사를 운영한다. (the, company, he, powerful, most, runs)
⇨ ____________________ in Korea.

Answers: p.41

A 주어진 단어를 이용하여 문장을 완성하시오.

1 If they ______________ me, I could have gone to the party. (not, see)

2 If the weather were nice, she wouldn't ______________ so disappointed. (be)

3 If she weren't sick, she would ______________ shopping with us. (go)

4 If I ______________ up earlier, I wouldn't have missed the first train. (get)

5 If you ______________ harder, you could have gotten an 'A.'(try)

6 If I ______________ more money, I would help the poor. (have)

7 If the food ______________ delicious, we would order some more. (be)

B 두 문장이 같은 뜻이 되도록 가정법 문장을 완성하시오.

1 As he doesn't know how to speak English, he doesn't live in Australia.
⇒ If he ______________________________, he ______________________________.

2 As it wasn't rainy yesterday, we didn't just stay at home.
⇒ If it ______________________________, we ______________________________.

3 As I don't own several buildings downtown, I can't stop working.
⇒ If I ______________________________, I ______________________________.

4 As Eric didn't do his best, he didn't become the champion.
⇒ If Eric ______________________________, he ______________________________.

5 As I am injured, I can't play in the finals.
⇒ If I ______________________________, I ______________________________.

6 As they didn't hurry, they couldn't watch the opera.
⇒ If they ______________________________, they ______________________________.

7 As Noah didn't show up on time, his girlfriend was so angry.
⇒ If Noah ______________________________, his girlfriend ______________________________.

C 밑줄 친 부분을 어법에 맞게 고쳐 쓰시오.

1 If he has his phone with him, he would call 911 now. ⇒ ______________

2 If Luna is nice to me, we would make good friends. ⇒ ______________

3 If you eat more often, you would gain some weight. ⇒ ______________

4 If it not snow, the students could go on the field trip. ⇒ ______________

5 If I am you, I would forgive her. ⇒ ______________

6 If James makes $100,000 a year, he would be much happier. ⇒ ______________

D 우리말과 같은 뜻이 되도록 주어진 단어를 이용하여 문장을 완성하시오.

1 어제 비가 오지 않았다면, 우리는 수영하러 갔을 텐데. (rain, go)
⇨ If it ____________ yesterday, we ____________ swimming.

2 Millie가 잉글랜드에 없다면 우리는 여기서 매우 즐거운 시간을 보낼 텐데. (be, have)
⇨ If Millie ____________ in England, we ____________ so much fun here.

3 내가 만약 자전거가 있다면 학교에 걸어 다니지 않을 텐데. (have, walk)
⇨ If I ____________ a bike, I ____________ to school.

4 그가 조금 더 주의를 쏟았다면, 그의 아이는 넘어지지 않았을 텐데. (pay, fall)
⇨ If he ____________ more attention, his kid ____________ down.

5 Jeremy가 좀 더 관대했더라면 더 많은 인기를 얻을 수 있었을 텐데. (be, become)
⇨ If Jeremy ____________ more generous, he ____________ more popular.

E 주어진 단어를 이용하여 문장을 완성하시오.

1 It snowed a lot yesterday. I wish it ____________. (not, snow)
2 Leah has a cold. She wishes she ____________ home last night. (stay)
3 Max studies until 11 pm. He wishes he ____________ that late. (not, study)
4 The musical was fantastic! I wish you ____________ there with us. (be)
5 Aiden has never learned Taekwondo but he talks as if he ____________ a black belt. (have)
6 Emma and Leo hate each other, but they act as if they ____________ best friends. (be)

F 두 문장의 의미가 통하도록 가정법 문장을 완성하시오.

1 In fact, I haven't seen her in person before.
⇨ I feel as if I ____________________.

2 In fact, he has lung cancer.
⇨ He acts as if he ____________________.

3 I'm sorry I didn't make an apology to her.
⇨ I wish I ____________________.

4 In fact, the guard didn't lock the doors.
⇨ The guard talks as if he ____________________.

5 I'm sorry I'm not as young as you.
⇨ I wish I ____________________.

6 I'm sorry my husband doesn't love me unconditionally.
⇨ I wish my husband ____________________.

G **우리말과 같은 뜻이 되도록 주어진 단어를 이용하여 문장을 완성하시오.**

1 Aaron은 마치 군인인 것처럼 보이지만, 그는 군인이 아니다. (as if, be)
⇒ Aaron looks ______________________ a soldier, but he isn't.

2 너는 지금 떠나야 해? 더 머무를 수 있으면 좋을 텐데. (wish, stay)
⇒ Do you have to leave now? I ______________________ longer.

3 마치 강당에 라이브 콘서트가 열렸던 것 같다. (as if, there, be)
⇒ It seems ______________________ a live concert in the auditorium.

4 그들은 그 경기에서 졌어. 그들이 더 연습했었더라면 좋았을 텐데. (wish, practice)
⇒ They lost the match. I ______________________ more.

5 James는 마치 이해한 것처럼 고개를 끄덕였지만, 이해하지 못했다. (as if, understand)
⇒ James nodded his head ______________________, but he didn't.

6 나는 고양이를 안 키워. 한 마리 키우면 좋을 텐데. (wish, have)
⇒ I don't have a cat. I ______________________ one.

H **우리말과 같은 뜻이 되도록 주어진 단어를 배열하시오.**

1 Adam은 자신이 세상을 구한 것처럼 말한다. (had, the world, as if, saved, he)
⇒ Adam talks ______________________________________.

2 나는 도시에 산다. 교외에 살면 좋을 텐데. (lived in, wish, the suburbs, I)
⇒ I live in the city. I ______________________________________.

3 Liam은 마치 무서운 것을 본 것처럼 얼굴이 창백해졌다. (seen, as if, had, something, he, scary)
⇒ Liam turned pale ______________________________________.

4 내가 그녀에게 그 바보 같은 말들을 하지 않았으면 좋았을 텐데. (said, things, those, wish, hadn't, stupid, I)
⇒ I ______________________________________ to her.

5 내 친구들이 나를 두고 부산으로 떠났다. 그들이 나를 좀만 더 기다렸으면 좋았을 텐데. (waited, they, a little longer, wish, for me, had)
⇒ My friends left for Busan without me. I ______________________________________.

6 그의 질환에 대해서 알았더라면 좋았을 텐데. (had, his, about, known, wish, illness)
⇒ I ______________________________________.

7 그는 프로 축구선수처럼 축구를 정말 잘한다. (a, he, professional, as if, were, soccer player)
⇒ He is really good at soccer ______________________________________.

Answers: p.42

A 빈칸에 who(m), which, whose 중 알맞은 것을 써넣으시오.

1 The car ______________ she bought last week is very cool.

2 What happened to the driver ______________ was sending text messages?

3 My daughter is the girl ______________ is standing by Mr. Choi.

4 I need a smartwatch ______________ can last longer than a week.

5 Some of the employees ______________ we work with are from Vietnam.

6 The house ______________ walls are painted yellow is put up for sale.

7 The umbrella ______________ he was carrying is worth a lot of money.

B 두 문장을 관계대명사를 이용하여 한 문장으로 만드시오.

1 I have some friends. I haven't seen them in years.
⇒ I have some friends ____.

2 I didn't get the text. He sent it to me.
⇒ I didn't get the text ____.

3 Violet is driving an electric car. The electric car is her mother's.
⇒ Violet is driving an electric car ____.

4 The sneakers look really cool. Kyle is wearing them.
⇒ The sneakers ____ look really cool.

5 Mr. Bates is the new manager. He studied at Harvard.
⇒ Mr. Bates is the new manager ____.

6 Bella is the student. Her father is a politician.
⇒ Bella is the student ____.

7 Chloe is the scientist. She solved the mystery.
⇒ Chloe is the scientist ____.

C 〈보기〉에서 알맞은 관계대명사를 골라 문장을 완성하시오. (한 번씩만 쓸 것)

who whom which that what

1 Please show us ______________ you did to pass the test.

2 Do you remember the flight attendant ______________ asked us to be quiet?

3 The man ______________ you are talking about is my brother's homeroom teacher.

4 Is this the bench on ______________ we should sit?

5 How much is the tablet computer ______________ Teddy wants for his birthday?

D 밑줄 친 부분을 생략할 수 있으면 ○, 생략할 수 없으면 ×표 하시오.

1 It's hard to find a restaurant that is open until midnight. ⇨ ____________

2 We found the cave into which the children went. ⇨ ____________

3 Did you throw away the device which had many problems? ⇨ ____________

4 Esme is the one that I want to hang out with. ⇨ ____________

5 Look at the boys who are helping the old lady. ⇨ ____________

E 우리말과 같은 뜻이 되도록 관계대명사와 주어진 단어를 이용하여 문장을 완성하시오.

1 내가 지난주에 만든 로봇에게 무슨 일이 생긴 거지? (make)
⇨ What happened to the robot ______________________ last week?

2 네가 반한 그 남자애가 누구야? (have)
⇨ Who is the boy ______________________ a crush on?

3 나는 그녀가 처리하고 있는 프로젝트가 걱정 돼. (work)
⇨ I am worried about the project ______________________ on.

4 우리는 우리가 믿을 수 있는 프로그래머를 고용해야 해요. (can, trust)
⇨ We need to hire a programmer ______________________.

5 Brantley 선생님이 네게 챙겨오라고 요청하신 책을 갖고 왔니? (Mr. Brantley, ask)
⇨ Did you bring the book ______________________ you to bring?

6 나의 사촌은 러시아 미사일이 파괴한 마을에서 살고 있었다. (the Russian missiles, destroy)
⇨ My cousin was living in the town ______________________.

F 밑줄 친 부분을 바르게 고쳐 쓰시오.

1 It is a trick whose makes you look attractive. ⇨ ____________

2 Pizza is something whom is loved all over the world. ⇨ ____________

3 Oliver wears glasses which lenses are really thick. ⇨ ____________

4 I know a guy who brother is a famous news anchor. ⇨ ____________

5 This is a Korean TV show whom everyone can enjoy watching. ⇨ ____________

G 두 문장을 관계대명사 whose를 이용하여 한 문장으로 만드시오.

1 I know a man. His voice is deep and strong.
⇒ I know a man ______________________________.

2 We teach students. Their first language is not English.
⇒ We teach students ______________________________.

3 Ivy bought a pen. Its body is made of stainless steel.
⇒ Ivy bought a pen ______________________________.

4 Nathan wants to marry someone. Her hobbies are related to art.
⇒ Nathan wants to marry someone ______________________________.

5 There are many actors. Their parents are also actors.
⇒ There are many actors ______________________________.

H 빈칸에 〈보기〉에서 알맞은 것을 골라 써넣으시오. (한 번씩만 쓸 것)

when	where	how	why

1 Tell me the reason ____________ you are not talking to me.

2 I still remember the day ____________ we went on a first date.

3 What other stores are there in the building ____________ you work?

4 We wonder ____________ Koreans make the best home appliances.

I 밑줄 친 부분을 어법에 맞게 고쳐 문장을 다시 쓰시오.

1 Is this the right way how you print documents?
⇒ ______________________________

2 Do you know about the restaurant why your parents had dinner last night?
⇒ ______________________________

3 She will never forget the moment how she saw the car accident.
⇒ ______________________________

4 Nobody knows the reason where Jake quit his job.
⇒ ______________________________

5 I live close to the store when the police arrested the teenagers.
⇒ ______________________________

Chapter 11 전치사와 접속사

Answers: p.42

A at, on, in 중 알맞은 것을 골라 빈칸에 써넣으시오.

1 Let's go camping ______________ the summer.

2 Will it snow ______________ Christmas Day?

3 The last train leaves ______________ midnight.

4 Many Americans enjoy fireworks ______________ Independence Day.

5 The festival starts ______________ Sunday evening.

6 Lyla gets up ______________ 7 in the morning.

7 Because of the pandemic, the 2020 Olympics was held ______________ 2021.

8 What is the weather like ______________ October?

B 밑줄 친 부분을 어법에 맞게 고쳐 쓰시오.

1 Your report must be handed in <u>until</u> Dec. 10th. ⇨ ______________

2 Hazel has worked as an English tutor <u>during</u> six months. ⇨ ______________

3 My friends waited for me <u>by</u> lunch. ⇨ ______________

4 The singer got injured <u>for</u> the rehearsal. ⇨ ______________

5 I didn't hear anything <u>for</u> the night? ⇨ ______________

6 You should stay focused <u>for</u> class. ⇨ ______________

7 Make sure you get back home <u>until</u> 7 p.m. ⇨ ______________

8 I watch TV <u>during</u> two hours every day. ⇨ ______________

C 두 문장에 공통으로 들어갈 알맞은 전치사를 써넣으시오.

1 • Isabella keeps something mysterious ______________ her locker.
• Is the Eiffel Tower located ______________ Paris?

2 • Who hung the clock ______________ the kitchen wall?
• I put the stapler back ______________ your desk.

3 • Why are you standing ______________ the door? Come in.
• We like to hang out ______________ the library.

4 • The last train ______________ Busan has just left.
• Luke hates me ______________ many reasons.

D 우리말과 같은 뜻이 되도록 주어진 단어를 배열하시오.

1 Charlie가 스크루드라이버로 그 탁자를 고쳤어요. (a screwdriver, the table, repaired, Charlie, with)
⇨ ______________________________

2 Jacob은 여름에 구조요원으로 일해요. (works, the summer, as, in, Jacob, a lifeguard)
⇨ ______________________________

3 많은 사람들이 피부암으로 죽나요? (skin cancer, many, do, die, people, of)
⇨ ______________________________

4 Clarkson 선생님은 펭귄처럼 걸으셔. (walks, Mr. Clarkson, a penguin, like)
⇨ ______________________________

5 검은 색 옷을 입은 여자가 수상해 보입니다. (looks, in, the woman, black, suspicious)
⇨ ______________________________

6 대개 자원봉사자들은 무료로 일을 해. (usually, for, volunteers, work, free)
⇨ ______________________________

E 빈칸에 that 또는 whether를 넣어 문장을 완성하시오.

1 Sam asked my sister ____________ she wanted to go to the movies with him.

2 I am sure ____________ Julie is married.

3 Nobody realized ____________ the meeting was so important.

4 Why can't you see ____________ I'm trying my best?

5 I wonder ____________ Mia is interested in sports.

F 두 문장을 한 문장의 간접의문문으로 바꿔 쓰시오.

1 Do you know? + Where was Emily hiding?
⇨ Do you know ______________________________?

2 I wonder. + Do you like Sophia?
⇨ I wonder ______________________________.

3 We're not sure. + Are those passengers alive?
⇨ We're not sure ______________________________.

4 Please tell me. + When can I see my parents?
⇨ Please tell me ______________________________.

G 〈보기〉에서 알맞은 말을 골라 빈칸에 써넣으시오. (한 번씩만 쓸 것)

before	because	when	if

1 ______________ you know the answer, raise your hand.

2 How did you feel ______________ you found out about him?

3 We decided to give you a raise ______________ you have worked so hard.

4 Let's clean up this mess ______________ someone comes in.

H 우리말과 같은 뜻이 되도록 주어진 단어를 배열하시오.

1 Myles는 배가 불렀음에도 그 피자를 계속 먹었다. (he, full, although, was)

⇒ Myles kept eating the pizza ______________________________.

2 Fatima는 외동이라서 종종 외로움을 탄다. (she, since, only child, an, is)

⇒ Fatima often feels lonely ______________________________.

3 네가 내게 사과할 때까지는 나는 너랑 말 안 해. (apologize, me, until, you, to)

⇒ I am not talking to you ______________________________.

4 그들은 영화를 하나 보고 나서 식료품을 사러 갔다. (watched, after, a movie, they)

⇒ They went grocery shopping ______________________________.

5 Finley는 공을 내게 패스하면서 나의 이름을 외쳤다. (to me, as, passed, the ball, he)

⇒ Finley shouted out my name ______________________________.

I 두 문장의 의미가 통하도록 주어진 접속사를 이용하여 문장을 완성하시오.

1 My friends came to visit me, and my neighbors also came to visit me.

⇒ ______________________________ came to visit me. (not only ~ but also)

⇒ ______________________________ came to visit me. (as well as)

2 Olga is from Ukraine, and Oksana is from Ukraine, too.

⇒ ______________________________ are from Ukraine. (both)

3 The lecture was not interesting, and it was not boring, either.

⇒ The lecture was ______________________________. (neither ~ nor)

4 Go down the street, and you will see the hospital on your right.

⇒ ______________________________, you will see the hospital on your right. (if)

5 Take my bike, or you won't get there on time.

⇒ ______________________________, you won't get there on time. (unless)

⇒ ______________________________, you won't get there on time. (if ~ not)

MEMO

MEMO

NEXUS Edu

LEVEL CHART

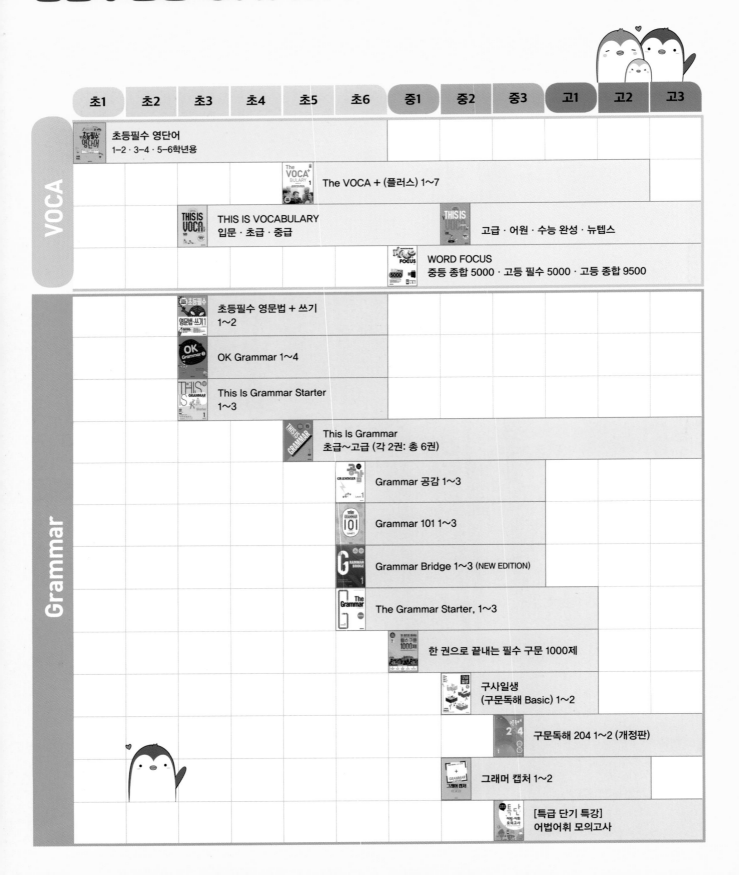

	초1	초2	초3	초4	초5	초6	중1	중2	중3	고1	고2	고3
VOCA	 초등필수 영단어 1-2 · 3-4 · 5-6학년용											
VOCA					 The VOCA + (플러스) 1~7							
VOCA			THIS IS VOCABULARY 입문 · 초급 · 중급					고급 · 어원 · 수능 완성 · 뉴텝스				
VOCA							 WORD FOCUS 중등 종합 5000 · 고등 필수 5000 · 고등 종합 9500					
Grammar			 초등필수 영문법 + 쓰기 1~2									
Grammar			 OK Grammar 1~4									
Grammar			 This Is Grammar Starter 1~3									
Grammar					 This Is Grammar 초급~고급 (각 2권: 총 6권)							
Grammar						 Grammar 공감 1~3						
Grammar						Grammar 101 1~3						
Grammar						 Grammar Bridge 1~3 (NEW EDITION)						
Grammar						 The Grammar Starter, 1~3						
Grammar							 한 권으로 끝내는 필수 구문 1000제					
Grammar								 구사일생 (구문독해 Basic) 1~2				
Grammar									 구문독해 204 1~2 (개정판)			
Grammar								 그래머 캡처 1~2				
Grammar									 [특급 단기 특강] 어법어휘 모의고사			

★ NEW EDITION ★

GRAMMAR BRIDGE

넥서스영어교육연구소 · 김경태 지음

Level 2

정답 및 해설

NEXUS Edu

★ NEW EDITION ★

GRAMMAR BRIDGE

넥서스영어교육연구소 · 김경태 지음

Level

2

정답 및 해설

NEXUS Edu

Chapter 1

1-1 현재시제 p.12

Exercise 1

1 starts
2 begins
3 goes
4 looks
5 are

Exercise 2

1 sounds
2 arrives
3 departs
4 live
5 work out

1-2 동사의 변화 p.14

Exercise 1

1 died, died
2 fought, fought
3 caught, caught
4 replied, replied
5 stopped, stopped
6 worried, worried
7 found, found
8 lent, lent
9 told, told
10 hopped, hopped
11 hurried, hurried
12 washed, washed
13 paid, paid
14 hoped, hoped
15 taught, taught
16 broke, broken
17 arrived, arrived
18 married, married
19 kept, kept
20 read, read
21 met, met
22 hurt, hurt
23 danced, danced
24 rang, rung
25 let, let
26 stole, stolen
27 bit, bitten
28 passed, passed
29 heard, heard
30 decided, decided
31 studied, studied
32 felt, felt
33 sang, sung
34 chose, chosen
35 carried, carried
36 threw, thrown
37 hit, hit
38 applied, applied
39 prepared, prepared
40 rose, risen

Exercise 2

1 threw
2 cut
3 tried
4 hopped
5 read
6 stood

1-3 과거시제 p.15

Exercise 1

1 bought
2 goes
3 rises
4 invented
5 left
6 played
7 dropped
8 took

Exercise 2

1 broke out
2 bought
3 went
4 lost
5 shook
6 had

1-4 진행시제 p.16

Exercise 1

1 feel
2 smell
3 has
4 are having
5 were

Exercise 2

1 is doing
2 was coming
3 is reading
4 was sleeping

1-5 현재완료 p.17

Exercise 1

1 heard
2 studied
3 met
4 been
5 seen
6 eaten

Exercise 2

1 Have, seen
2 has, gone
3 has, been
4 has, not, spoken

1-6 현재완료의 용법 p.18

Exercise 1

1 have, forgotten
2 have, not, finished
3 have, gone
4 has, lived
5 has, been

Exercise 2

1 gone
2 been
3 been
4 gone

1-7 현재완료: 주의해야 할 표현 p.19

Exercise 1

1 ever
2 did you meet
3 saw
4 has played
5 haven't received
6 have never been

1 have not[haven't] seen
2 has not[hasn't] stopped
3 have not[haven't] slept
4 had dinner

Review Test

p.20

01 ②	02 ②	03 ④	04 ②	05 ①	06 ③
07 ⑤	08 ③	09 ③	10 ⑤	11 ①	12 ⑤
13 ④	14 ②	15 ①	16 ⑤	17 ①	18 ④
19 ④	20 ③	21 ③	22 ④	23 ②	24 ③
25 ②	26 ④				

27 for
28 since
29 yet
30 been
31 Has Sam found a new place to live?
32 I have not[haven't/have never] heard the song before.
33 has, lost
34 has, lived
35 has, wanted
36 Have, thought

01 play는 규칙 변화 동사이며, 「모음+y」로 끝나는 동사는 「동사+-ed」의 형태로 나타낸다. 따라서 동사 변화가 played-played-played이다.

02 win은 불규칙 변화 동사로, 동사 변화가 win-won-won이다.

03 '나는 아직 그 프로젝트를 끝내지 못했다.'라는 의미로, 현재완료의 완료 용법에 해당한다. 현재완료 부정문에 사용되어 '아직'이라는 의미로 쓰이는 부사 yet을 고른다. '~ 동안'이라는 의미의 for와 '~ 이래로'라는 의미의 since는 계속 용법과, '이미', '벌써'라는 의미의 already는 완료 용법과, '여태까지'라는 의미의 ever는 경험 용법과 함께 쓰인다.

04 'Amanda는 어제 학교에 결석했다.'라는 의미이며, yesterday가 특정한 과거 시점을 나타내는 부사이기 때문에 과거시제 was를 고른다.

05 동사의 형태가 「have/has+과거분사」로 현재완료 문장임을 알 수 있다. 따라서 현재완료 문장에서 쓸 수 있는 부사구 for three years를 고른다. 'Rebecca는 3년 동안 이탈리아에 머물고 있다.'라는 의미로, 과거에 시작된 일이 현재까지 계속되는 것을 나타내는 현재완료의 계속 용법에 해당한다. ②, ③, ④, ⑤는 특정한 과거 시점을 나타내는 부사구로 과거시제와 함께 쓰일 수 있다.

06 '내 다리가 부러졌다. 아프다.'라는 의미로, 과거에 일어난 일이 현재까지 영향을 미치는 현재완료 문장이다. 현재완료는 「have/has+과거분사」의 형태로 나타내며 break는 불규칙 변화 동사로, 동사 변화가 break-broke-broken이다.

07 '나는 이미 군청색 코트를 골랐다.'라는 의미로, 현재완료의 완료 용법에 해당한다. 따라서 「have/has+과거분사」의 형태인 ⑤를 고른다. '이미'라는 의미의 부사 already는 주로 have/has와 과거분사 사이에 위치하거나, 문장 맨 뒤에 위치한다.

08 주어진 문장은 '내 남편은 지금 집에 없다. 산책하러 나갔다.'라는 의미이다. 따라서 '가 버렸다(현재 여기에 있지 않음)'라는 의미로 현재완료의 결과 용법을 나타내는 「has+gone」을 고른다.

09 주어진 문장이 'Peter는 5년 전에 태권도를 배우기 시작했다. 그는 아직도 그것을 배우고 있다.'라는 의미이므로 과거의 한 시점에서 시작된 일이 현재까지 계속되는 것을 나타내는 현재완료의 계속 용법에 해당하는 문장을 고른다. for는 '~ 동안'이라는 의미로 뒤에 기간을 나타내는 말이 오며, 현재완료의 계속 용법과 함께 쓰인다.

10 '그녀가 문을 노크했을 때 너는 무엇을 하고 있었니?'라는 의미로, 「was/were+-ing」 형태의 과거진행시제 문장이다. 과거진행시제로 물으면 과거진행시제로 답한다.

11 '너는 어제 무엇을 했니?'라는 의미로, 과거에 이미 끝난 동작을 나타내는 과거시제 문장이다. 과거시제로 물으면 과거시제로 답한다.

12 A 질문의 대답이 '아니, 나는 그를 전에 만나 본 적이 없어.'라는 의미로, 과거부터 현재까지의 경험을 나타내는 현재완료 경험 용법 문장이다. 따라서 현재완료로 물어야 하며, 현재완료 의문문은 「Have/Has+주어+과거분사 ~?」 형태로 나타낸다.

13 ① '~로 가 버렸다'라는 의미의 「has+gone+to+장소」는 3인칭 주어와 함께 쓰인다. ② '너는 귀신을 본 적 있니?'라는 의미의 현재완료 경험 용법 문장이 되어야 하므로 Did는 Have가 되어야 한다. ③ 과거 시점을 나타내는 부사구 last year가 있기 때문에 have ridden은 rode가 되어야 한다. ⑤ 과거 시점을 나타내는 부사 yesterday가 있기 때문에 has bought는 bought가 되어야 한다.

14 ① '나는 그를 한 번 만난 적 있다.'라는 의미로, 과거부터 현재까지의 경험을 나타내는 현재완료의 경험 용법, ② 'Miyuki는 일본으로 돌아가 버렸다.'라는 의미로, 과거에 일어난 일이 현재까지 영향을 미치고 있음을 나타내는 현재완료의 결과 용법, ③ '나는 이처럼 당황스러워 본 적이 없다.'라는 의미로, 현재완료의 경험 용법, ④ '너는 직접 유명인사를 본 적 있니?'라는 의미로, 현재완료의 경험 용법, ⑤ '너는 새로 생긴 이탈리아 식당에서 식사를 해 본 적 있니?'라는 의미로, 현재완료의 경험 용법이다.

15 ① '나는 막 푸짐한 점심을 먹었다.'라는 의미로, 과거에 일어난 일이 현재에 완료된 것을 나타내는 현재완료의 완료 용법, ② '너는 서울에서 얼마나 오래 살았니?'라는 의미로, 과거에 시작된 일이 현재까지 계속되는 것을 나타내는 현재완료의 계속 용법, ③ '그들은 며칠 동안 샤워를 하지 못했다.'라는 의미로, 현재완료의 계속 용법, ④ '나는 Serena와 약 10년 동안 알고 지냈다.'라는 의미로, 현재완료의 계속 용법, ⑤ 'Carol과 James는 2020년부터 결혼생활을 해오고 있다.'라는 의미로, 현재완료의 계속 용법이다.

16 '우리 삼촌은 지난주 토요일에 차 사고를 당했다. 그는 그때 이후로 입원해 계신다.'라는 의미이다. 첫 번째 빈칸에는 특정한 과거 시점을 나타내는 부사구 last Saturday가 있으므로 과거시제 had가 와야 한다. 두 번째 빈칸에는 과거에 시작된 일이 현재까지 계속되는 것을 나타내는 현재완료의 계속 용법이 되어야 하므로 has been이 와야 한다. since는 '~ 이래로'라는 의미로, 현재완료의 계속 용법과 함께 쓰이는 전치사이며 since 뒤에는 시작 시점이 온다.

17 '나는 브라질에 가본 적이 없다. 내가 남아메리카로 여행하는 것은 이번이 처음이다.'라는 의미이다. 첫 번째 빈칸에는 과거부터 현재까지의 경험을 나타내는 현재완료의 경험 용법이 되어야 하므로 been이, 두 번째 빈칸에는 현재의 사실이나 상태를 나타내고 있기 때문에 현재시제 is가 와야 한다.

18 ④ 특정한 과거 시점을 나타내는 부사구 last week가 있기 때문에 has driven이 drove가 되어야 한다.

19 ④ like는 상태 동사이므로 진행시제로 쓰지 않는다. 따라서 are liking이 like가 되어야 한다.

20 ③ 특정 시점을 묻는 의문사 when은 과거시제와 함께 사용해야 하므로 have you woken이 did you wake가 되어야 한다.

21 ① '무엇을 하고 있니?'라는 의미이며, 현재 진행 중인 동작을 나타내는 진행시제이다. 진행시제로 물으면 진행시제로 답해야 한다. ② '어젯밤 콘서트는 어땠니?'라는 의미이며, 과거에 이미 끝난 동작이나 상태, 습관을 나타내는 과거시제 문장으로 과거시제로 답해야 한다. ④ '해변에서 재미있게 놀았니?'라는 의미이며, 과거에 이미 끝난 동작이나 상태, 습관을 나타내는 과거시제 문장으로 과거시제로 답해야 한다. ⑤ '네 오빠는 언제 스코틀랜드로 떠나니?'라는 의미이며, 현재진행시제로 이미 확정된 일정이나 계획을 나타내고 있기 때문에 현재진행시제로 답해야 한다.

22 과거부터 현재까지의 상태를 표현하고 있으므로 현재완료 「have/has+과거분사」 문장이 되어야 한다.

23 이미 확정된 일정이나 계획은 현재진행시제로 나타낼 수 있다. 현재진행시제는 「am/is/are+-ing」의 형태로 나타낸다.

24 주어진 문장은 '나는 도쿄에 가본 적 없다.'라는 의미로, 과거부터 현재까지의 경험을 나타내는 현재완료의 경험 용법에 해당한다. ① '나는 이미 리포트를 다 썼다.'라는 완료 용법, ② '나는 막 역에 도착했다.'라는 의미로 완료 용법, ③ 나는 전에 그 영화배우를 만난 적 있다.'라는 의미로 경험 용법, ④ '너는 이 도시에 얼마나 오랫동안 살고 있니?'라는 의미로 계속 용법, ⑤ Jill과 나는 고등학교 때부터 알고 지내왔다.'라는 의미로 계속 용법이다.

25 주어진 문장은 'Sandra는 자신의 지갑을 잃어버렸다.(아직 찾지 못함)'라는 의미로, 과거에 일어난 일이 현재까지 영향을 미치고 있음을 나타내는 현재완료의 결과 용법에 해당한다. ① '나는 그 책을 두 번 읽었다.'라는 의미로 경험 용법, ② '아이들은 도서관에 갔다.(현재 여기에 있지 않음)'이라는 의미로 결과 용법, ③ '그는 10년 동안 교사로 일해 왔다.'라는 의미로 계속 용법, ④ 'Jessica는 강에서 수영해 본 적이 없다.'라는 의미로 경험 용법, ⑤ '나는 열여덟 살 이후로 George를 사랑해 왔다.'라는 의미로 계속 용법에 해당한다.

26 ④ '너는 왜 기침을 심하게 하고 있니?'라는 질문에 '감기에 걸렸어.(지금도 감기를 앓고 있는 상태)'라고 대답하는 것이 적절하다. 따라서 과거에 일어난 일이 현재까지 영향을 미치고 있음을 나타내는 현재완료 문장으로 답해야 하며, 특정한 과거 시점을 나타내는 last week가 삭제되어야 한다.

27 'Scott은 3년 동안 스페인어를 공부하고 있다.'라는 의미이다. 빈칸에는 '~ 동안'이라는 의미로, 뒤에 기간을 나타내는 말이 오는 for를 고른다.

28 '우리 이모는 작년부터 런던에 살고 계신다.'라는 의미이다. 빈칸에는 '~ 이래로'라는 의미로, 뒤에 시작 시점을 나타내는 말이 오는 since를 고른다.

29 'Jeremy는 몇 달 전에 일을 그만두었고 아직 다른 일을 찾지 못했다.'라는 의미이다. 빈칸에는 부정문에 쓰여 '아직'이라는 의미를 나타내는 yet을 고른다.

30 '너 싱가포르에 가 본 적 있니?', '당연하지. 우리 부모님이 거기에 살고 계서 몇 번 가 본 적 있어.'라는 의미가 되어야 하므로 '~에 갔다 왔다', '~에 다녀온 경험이 있다'라는 의미의 「have+been」을 사용한다. 따라서 빈칸에는 been이 와야 한다.

31 현재완료 의문문은 「Have/Has+주어+과거분사 ~?」의 형태로 나타낸다.

32 현재완료 부정문은 「have/has+not/never+과거분사」의 형태로 나타낸다.

33 'Kevin은 어제 자신의 애완 뱀을 잃어버렸다. 그는 그것이 어디 있는지 모른다.'라는 의미로, 과거에 일어난 일이 현재까지 영향을 미치고 있다. 따라서 현재완료로 나타내야 하며 현재완료는 「have/has+과거분사」의 형태로 나타낸다.

34 'Alice는 6개월 전에 자신의 부모님 집에서 분가했다. 그녀는 지금 자립해서 산다.'라는 의미로, 과거에 시작된 일이 현재까지 계속되고 있기 때문에 현재완료로 나타낸다.

35 과거에 시작된 일이 현재까지 계속되는 것을 나타내는 현재완료의 계속 용법에 해당한다.

36 과거부터 현재까지의 경험을 나타내는 현재완료의 경험 용법에 해당하며 현재완료 의문문은 「Have/Has+주어+과거분사~?」의 형태로 나타낸다.

보너스 유형별 문제 p.24

1 has played
2 have left my driver's license
3 has been sick

1 Oscar는 5년 전에 축구를 시작했다. 그는 여전히 지금도 축구를 한다.
→ Oscar는 5년 동안 축구를 하고 있다.
과거에 시작된 일이 현재까지 계속되는 것을 나타내는 현재완료 (have+p.p.)의 '계속' 용법

2 나는 집에 내 운전면허증을 놓고 왔다. 그래서 나는 지금 그것이 없다.
→ 나는 집에 내 운전면허증을 놓고 와 버렸다.
과거에 일어난 일이 현재까지 영향을 미치므로 현재완료의 '결과'

3 Cora는 지난주에 아팠다. 그녀는 지금도 여전히 아프다.
→ Cora는 지난주부터 아팠다.
과거에 시작된 일이 현재까지 계속되는 것을 나타내는 현재완료 (have+p.p.)의 '계속' 용법

4 갤러리 개관식에 초대해 주셔서 대단히 감사합니다. 작업에 도움을 주셨던 분들을 모두 초대하신다고 어젯밤에 제 조교 Kate에게서 들었습니다. 보내 주신 편지에 적힌 정성 어린 말씀을 통해 깊은 감사의 마음을 느꼈습니다. 안타깝지만 저는 그날 참석하지 못할 것 같습니다. 가서 도움을 드리고 싶은 마음만큼이나 꼭 참석해야 하는 중요한 학회가 있습니다. 학회의 기조 연설자가 저의 오랜 친구입니다. 돌아와서 더 자세히 말씀드리겠습니다.
특정한 과거의 시점(last night)을 나타내는 부사구와 현재완료는 함께 쓸 수 없으므로 과거형인 heard를 써야 옳다.

Chapter 2

2-1 조동사 p.26

Exercise 1

1 can
2 do
3 look
4 be
5 snow
6 be able to
7 have to
8 smell
9 answer
10 not go
11 have to
12 go

Exercise 2

1 spoke → speak
2 jumps → jump
3 not may → may not
4 has → have
5 musts → must

Exercise 3

1 She may not be in her office.
2 We must not tell Jake the truth.
3 I cannot [can't] see the stars from the window.
4 You should not [shouldn't] be proud of yourself.
5 Emma will not [won't] tell you what happened.

Exercise 4

1 Can Aaron drive a car?
2 Will Jennifer be happy to see you?
3 Can you dive in deep seas?
4 Would you like to come to my party?
5 Can you call me before you come to my office?

2-2 can p.28

Exercise 1

1 May
2 can
3 could
4 is not able to
5 can
6 was able to
7 is able to

Exercise 2

1 can
2 be able to
3 can
4 be able to
5 can

Exercise 3

1 허가
2 요청
3 추측
4 요청
5 허가
6 능력

Exercise 4

1 Can[Could], open
2 couldn't, understand
3 can, leave
4 were, able, to, escape
5 can't, be
6 will, be, able, to, take, off

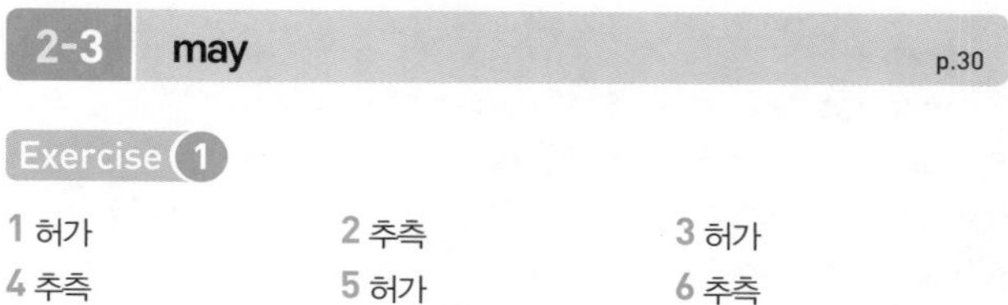

2-3 may p.30

Exercise 1

1 허가
2 추측
3 허가
4 추측
5 허가
6 추측

Exercise 2

1 May I have your attention
2 may [might] not be ready
3 may open the letter
4 may [might] help you
5 may [might] go back

2-4 will / be going to p.31

Exercise 1

1 Are you going to buy the book online?
2 The exam is not [isn't] going to be easy for you.
3 It will not [won't] take a long time to find a perfect house.
4 Will you invite all your classmates to the party?

Exercise 2

1 Will you give me some water
2 There will be a lot of people
3 is going to study for the math test
4 is going to play the violin

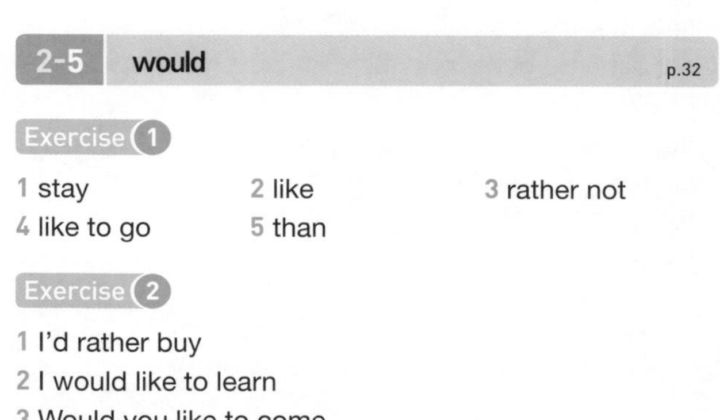

2-5 would p.32

Exercise 1

1 stay
2 like
3 rather not
4 like to go
5 than

Exercise 2

1 I'd rather buy
2 I would like to learn
3 Would you like to come
4 We would like to thank you

5 I'd like a tuna sandwich
6 I'd rather work extra hours than

2-6 must / have to p.33

Exercise 1

1 have	2 must	3 have
4 to go	5 have to	6 have
7 had	8 have	9 don't have to
10 must	11 must	12 had to

Exercise 2

1 must not lie to me
2 must [have to] correct the problem
3 must [have to] go
4 had to tell him
5 doesn't have to bring
6 Do I have to return
7 can't be late
8 must be sisters

Exercise 3

1 He doesn't have to go to the hospital.
2 Did Jacob have to pay for the damage?
3 Juliet will have to tell her mom the truth.
4 She had to treat them very carefully.
5 Does Gary have to wear a suit and tie to work?
6 You must not open the box when you're alone.

2-7 should / had better p.35

Exercise 1

1 should	2 had better not
3 had better	4 should
5 ought to	

Exercise 2

1 should go not → should not [shouldn't] go
2 finding → find
3 not better → better not
4 would → had
5 ought respect → ought to respect
6 ought to not → ought not to
7 to finish → finish
8 remembers → remember

Exercise 3

1 should be at school
2 should do something
3 should go to bed early
4 should take some medicine

Exercise 4

1 had better not cut
2 had better not walk
3 had better not invite her
4 had better call
5 had better be on time

Exercise 5

1 You shouldn't eat too much.
2 You ought not to press the button.
3 We ought not to lose this chance.
4 I think you should buy those jeans.

2-8 used to / would p.37

Exercise 1

1 used to have	2 used to be
3 used to eat	4 used to live
5 used to smoke	

Exercise 2

1 used to [would] eat a lot of fast food
2 used to work at the zoo
3 used to be fat
4 used to [would] play hockey
5 used to be a big auditorium

Review Test p.38

01 ③	02 ①	03 ②	04 ①	05 ③	06 ①
07 ③	08 ③	09 ④	10 ⑤	11 ④	12 ②
13 ③	14 ③	15 ⑤	16 ④	17 ③	18 ③
19 ②	20 ①	21 ②	22 ④	23 ④	24 ⑤
25 ①	26 ④				

27 used to
28 had better
29 would rather
30 don't need to [don't have to]
31 used to
32 wants to study
33 had better leave early
34 ought not to walk
35 Can I join you?
36 Fred will be able to go home for the holidays.
37 We had to get up early to catch the flight.
38 May [Can/Could] I invite him to the party?
39 You don't have to apologize to her. / You don't need to [need not] apologize to her.

01 '너는 도서관에서 조용히 해야 한다.'라는 의미가 되어야 하므로 '~해야 한다'라는 의미로, 의무를 나타내는 must를 고른다.

02 '그는 항상 우리에게 거짓말을 한다. 그래서 그가 하는 말은 사실일 리가 없다.'라는 의미가 되어야 한다. 따라서 '~일 리가 없다'라는 의미로, 부정적 추측을 나타내는 can't를 고른다.

03 '우리 이번 주말에 낚시하러 갈까요?'라는 의미가 되어야 하므로 제안 · 권유를 나타내는 shall을 고른다.

04 '너는 집에 있는 것이 좋겠다.'라는 의미가 되어야 한다. '~하는 게 낫다'라는 의미로, 충고나 경고를 나타내는 had better 다음에는 동사원형이 온다.

05 '제가 창문을 닫아도 될까요?'라는 의미가 되어야 하므로 '~해도 좋다'라는 의미로, 허가를 나타내는 can을 고른다.

06 '너는 그것에 대해 걱정할 필요가 없다.'라는 의미가 되어야 하므로 '~할 필요 없다'라는 의미로, 불필요를 나타내는 don't have to를 고른다.

07 '그것은 소파 아래에 있을지도 몰라.'라는 의미가 되어야 하므로 '~일지도 모른다'라는 의미로, 불확실한 추측을 나타내는 may를 고른다.

08 '너는 어제 늦게까지 일을 해야만 했다. 그러니 집에 일찍 들어가서 휴식을 취하는 것이 좋겠다.'라는 의미가 되어야 한다. '~해야 한다'라는 의미의 조동사 have to의 과거형 had to, '~하는 게 낫다'라는 의미의 had better를 이용한 구문으로 공통으로 들어갈 말은 had이다.

09 '영화관에 가면 휴대전화를 전원을 꺼야 한다. 또한, 네 앞좌석을 발로 차지 말아야 한다.'라는 의미가 되어야 한다. '~해야 한다'라는 의미의 should, '~하지 말아야 한다'는 의미의 should not을 이용한 구문으로 공통으로 들어갈 말은 should이다.

10 '이곳에 주차하면 안 된다[할 수 없다/하지 않는 게 좋겠다].'라는 의미가 되어야 하므로 불확실한 추측을 나타내는 might는 적절하지 않다.

11 '제가 그 책을 빌려도 될까요?'라는 의미로, 허가를 구하는 질문에 ④ '안 돼, 그렇게 해야만 해.'라는 대답은 적절하지 않다.

12 '너는 우산을 가져갈 필요 없다.'라는 의미이다. '~할 필요 없다'라는 의미로, 불필요를 나타내는 don't have to는 need not 또는 don't need to로 바꿔 쓸 수 있다.

13 '나는 어렸을 때 아버지와 캠핑을 가곤 했다.'라는 의미이다. '~하곤 했다'라는 의미로, 과거의 반복적인 행동이나 습관을 나타내는 used to는 would와 바꿔 쓸 수 있다. (단, would는 used to와 달리 과거의 상태를 나타내지 못하기 때문에 used to가 '~이 있었다'라는 의미로 과거의 상태를 나타낼 때에는 would와 바꿔 쓸 수 없다.)

14 'A 하느니 차라리 B하겠다'라는 의미의 조동사 표현은 「would rather B than A」이다.

15 '~할 필요 없다'라는 의미로, 불필요를 나타내는 조동사는 don't have to이다.

16 '~일 리가 없다'는 의미로, 부정적 추측을 나타내는 조동사는 can't이다.

17 can은 '~할 수 있다'라는 의미로 능력 · 가능성, '~해 주시겠어요?'라는 의미로 요청, 그리고 '~해도 좋다'라는 의미로 허가를 나타낸다. 주어진 문장의 밑줄 친 부분은 '저를 도와주실래요?'라는 의미로 요청을 나타낸다. ① '나는 내가 날 수 있다고 믿는다.'라는 의미로 능력 · 가능성, ② '너는 빨리 수영할 수 있니?'라는 의미로 능력 · 가능성, ③ '문을 좀 열어 주시겠어요?'라는 의미로 요청, ④ '네가 원하면 언제든지 나를 방문해도 돼.'라는 의미로 허가, ⑤ '그는 내년에 캐나다에 갈 수 있다.'라는 의미로 능력 · 가능성을 나타낸다.

18 must는 '~해야 한다'라는 의미로 의무, '~임에 틀림없다'라는 의미로, 강한 추측을 나타낸다. 주어진 문장은 '너는 10시 이전에 돌아와야 한다.'라는 의미로 의무를 나타낸다. ① '나는 오늘 밤에 공부를 해야 한다'라는 의미로 의무, ② '우리는 에너지를 절약해야 한다.'라는 의미로 의무, ③ '그는 나에게 화가 난 것임에 틀림없다.'라는 의미로 강한 추측, ④ '모든 학생들은 교복을 입어야 한다.'라는 의미로 의무, ⑤ '그는 내일 치과에 가야 한다.'라는 의미로, 의무를 나타낸다.

19 may는 '~일지도 모른다'라는 의미로 불확실한 추측, '~해도 좋다'라는 의미로 허가를 나타낸다. 주어진 문장은 '너는 질문을 하나 더 해도 된다.'라는 의미로 허가를 나타낸다. ① '들어가도 될까요?'라는 의미로 허가, ② '내일 비가 올지도 모른다.'라는 의미로 불확실한 추측, ③ '너는 그것들 중 하나를 가져도 된다.'라는 의미로 허가, ④ '내가 네 휴대전화를 써도 될까?'라는 의미로 허가, ⑤ '네 친구들과 나가도 된다.'라는 의미로 허가를 나타낸다.

20 ② 조동사를 중복해서 사용할 수 없고, '그는 내일 낚시하러 가도 된다.'라는 의미로, 허가를 나타내기 때문에 can이나 may 둘 중 하나를 삭제해야 한다. ③ '~하는 게 낫다'라는 의미의 had better 다음에는 동사원형이 오므로 to stay가 stay가 되어 한다. ④ 조동사의 의문문은 「조동사+주어+동사원형 ~?」의 형태로 나타낸다. 따라서 played가 play가 되어야 한다. ⑤ '~할 것이다'라는 의미의 be going to 다음에는 동사원형이 오기 때문에 visits가 visit이 되어야 한다.

21 ① '~하는 게 더 낫다'라는 의미의 had better의 부정은 had better not이다. ③ '~하곤 했었다', '~이 있었다'라는 의미의 조동사는 used to이다. 따라서 use가 used가 되어야 한다. ④ '~할 수 있다'라는 의미는 「be able to + 동사원형」으로 나타낸다. 따라서 able 다음에 to가 와야 한다. ⑤ 조동사의 부정문은 「주어+조동사+not+동사원형 ~」의 형태로 나타낸다. 따라서 likes가 like가 되어야 한다.

22 ④ 조동사를 중복해서 사용할 수 없기 때문에 can이 be able to가 되어야 한다.

23 ④ '~해야 한다'라는 의미로, 의무나 충고를 나타내는 ought to의 부정형은 ought not to이다.

24 ⑤ '제가 여기에 앉아도 될까요?'라는 의미의 질문에 '사양하겠습니다.'라는 대답은 부자연스럽다.

25 주어진 문장은 '제가 난로를 끄길 원하시나요?'라는 의미의 문장으로 상대방의 의향을 묻는 표현이다. ① '제가 난로를 끌까요?'라는 의미로 상대방의 의향을 묻는 표현, ② '우리 난로를 끌까요?'라는 의미로 제안 · 권유하는 표현, ③ '난로를 꺼줄래?'라는 의미로 요청을 나타내는 표현, ④ '난로를 꺼주시겠나요?'라는 의미로 요청을 나타내는 표현, ⑤ '난로를 꺼주시겠나요?'라는 의미로 요청을 나타내는 표현

26 '~할 필요 없다'라는 의미로 불필요를 나타내는 don't have to는 don't need to 또는 need not으로 바꿔 쓸 수 있다.

27 '~이 있었다'라는 의미로, 과거의 상태를 나타내는 used to를 고른다.

28 '~하지 않는 것이 좋겠다'라는 표현은 had better not으로 빈칸 뒤에 not이 있기 때문에 had better를 고른다.

29 'A 하느니 차라리 B하겠다'라는 의미를 나타내는 표현은 「would rather B than A」로 빈칸에는 would rather가 적절하다.

30 '너는 서두를 필요 없다.'라는 의미이다. need not은 '~할 필요가 없다'는 의미로, don't have to 또는 don't need to로 바꿔 쓸 수 있다.

31 '어릴 적엔 안경을 썼지만, 지금은 쓰지 않다.'라는 의미이다. (더 이상은 그렇지 않은) 과거의 상태를 나타내고 있기 때문에 used to를 쓴다.

32 'Dorothy는 대학에서 생물학을 공부하고 싶어 한다.'라는 의미이다. would like to는 want to로 바꿔 쓸 수 있고 주어가 3인칭 단수이므로 wants to가 적절하다.

33 '너 몸이 안 좋아 보여. 오늘은 일찍 가는 게 낫겠다.'라는 의미가 되어야 하므로 '~하는 게 낫다'라는 의미의 had better가 와야 하며 had better 다음에는 동사원형이 온다.

34 '~해야 한다'라는 의미의 ought to의 부정형은 ought not to로 나타낸다.

35 조동사의 의문문은 「조동사+주어+동사원형 ~?」의 형태로 나타낸다.

36 can의 미래시제는 will be able to로 나타낸다.

37 must의 과거시제는 had to로 나타낸다.

38 조동사의 의문문은 「조동사+주어+동사원형 ~?」의 형태로 나타내며, '~해도 된다'라는 의미로, 허가를 나타내는 조동사 may/can/could를 이용한다.

39 '~할 필요가 없다'라는 의미로, 불필요를 나타내는 경우에는 don't have to이며, don't have to는 need not 또는 don't need to로 바꿔 쓸 수 있다.

보너스 유형별 문제 p.42

1 would you like to have for dinner
2 you must be very hungry
3 ④

[1-2] A 저녁으로 무엇을 먹고 싶니?
B 저에게 스파게티를 만들어 주실래요?
A 물론이지. 학교에서 재미있었니?
B 네. 수업 끝나고 반 친구들과 농구를 했어요.
A 그럼, 너 틀림없이 배가 많이 고프겠구나. 하지만 저녁식사 전에 숙제를 끝내는 게 좋을걸.
B 알겠어요, 엄마.

1 would like to+동사원형: ~하고 싶다
2 강한 추측을 나타내는 조동사 must

3 그날 Frank는 직장에서 평범한 하루를 보냈다. 열심히 일하고, 밤늦게까지 친구들과 즐거운 금요일 저녁 식사를 했다. 아파트에 도착했을 때, 그는 노부부가 사는 아래층에서 연기가 나는 걸 보았다. 처음에는 믿을 수가 없었고 무엇을 해야 할지 몰랐다. 911에 전화할까 생각했지만, 구조대원들이 도착하려면 시간이 좀 걸릴 것이라는 생각이 들었다. 그들을 기다릴 시간이 없었다. 당장 뭔가를 해야 한다는 것을 깨닫고 문을 부숴 노부부를 깨우기 위해 연기로 가득 찬 방으로 뛰어들어갔다. 그들은 이미 의식이 없었고, Frank는 그들을 한 명씩 집 밖으로 끌어냈다. 이 젊은 영웅은 자신의 행동에 대해 매우 겸손해 하며, 그저 "그분들이 다치지 않아서 다행이에요"라고 말할 뿐이었다.
주절이 과거시제이므로 이에 따라 has to의 과거형인 had to로 써야 옳다.

Chapter 3

3-1 수동태 p.44

Exercise 1

1 was born
2 bitten
3 by
4 stung
5 are used
6 is delivered
7 by
8 loved by
9 are bought
10 were brought

Exercise 2

1 were, done
2 was, stopped
3 by, her
4 was, destroyed
5 were, made
6 is, respected
7 was, composed, by

Exercise 3

1 were made by
2 is spoken
3 is loved by
4 was made
5 is trusted by
6 is surrounded by
7 was caused by

3-2 수동태의 시제 p.46

Exercise 1

1 was, invented
2 will, be, watered
3 is, used
4 have, been, helped

Exercise 2

1 is being used by
2 will be rescheduled
3 been remodeled by
4 were taken by

3-3 조동사가 쓰인 수동태 p.47

Exercise 1

1 must, be, finished
2 can, be, solved
3 should, be, painted
4 will, be, loved

Exercise 2

1 should be prepared
2 might be sent
3 will be accepted
4 can be seen
5 must be paid

3-4 수동태의 부정문 p.48

Exercise 1

1 Tobacco is not sold
2 hasn't been fixed yet
3 the door was not locked
4 Your letter won't be delivered

Exercise 2

1 The bridge was not[wasn't] built in 2001.
2 The trash can has not[hasn't] been emptied.
3 The door cannot[can't] be closed automatically.
4 My sons are not[aren't] being taught by Ms. Parker.

3-5 수동태의 의문문 p.49

Exercise 1

1 were, you, born
2 will, be, completed
3 Was, written, by
4 Can, be, paid

Exercise 2

1 Was the window broken by Bill?
2 Will the event be held on Saturday?
3 Was the camera invented in the 19th century?
4 Have you been robbed twice in the last three months?

3-6 by 이외의 전치사를 쓰는 수동태 p.50

Exercise 1

1 of
2 with
3 with
4 at/by
5 to
6 with

Exercise 2

1 is satisfied with
2 is covered with
3 are excited about
4 was surprised at/by

3-7 동사구의 수동태 p.51

Exercise 1

1 is taken good care of by
2 has to be finished (by them)
3 was taken away by
4 is made use of (by us)
5 were brought up

Exercise 2

1 is looked up to by
2 were taken care of by
3 was turned on by
4 was put off

3-8 4형식의 수동태 p.52

Exercise 1

1 was told an interesting story
2 was served to us
3 were bought for her
4 were sent to me
5 was written to me
6 were made for us

3-9 5형식의 수동태 p.53

Exercise 1

1 is called Little Giant
2 was made famous
3 was made to take piano lessons
4 were kept busy

Exercise 2

1 Laura was seen dancing with Jack at the party (by us).
2 We were told to keep on trying by Ms. Miller.
3 My little brother was made to run an errand by me.
4 Mr. Hanson was elected chairman of the board (by us).

Review Test p.54

01 ②	02 ③	03 ④	04 ③	05 ④	06 ②
07 ①	08 ③	09 ④	10 ④	11 ⑤	12 ①
13 ⑤	14 ③	15 ③	16 ①	17 ④	18 ③
19 ②	20 ④	21 ④	22 ②	23 ②	24 ④

25 are, spoken
26 be, used
27 be, decorated
28 was, brought, to
29 was, bought, for
30 were, given, to
31 for → of
32 in → with
33 The computer is being repaired.
34 My parents were satisfied with my grades.
35 I was made to mow the lawn by Dad.
36 Some buildings in the city were damaged by the earthquake.

01 '그 반지는 내 약혼자를 위해 구매되었다.'라는 의미로, 주어가 행위를 당하는 수동태 문장이다. I bought my fiancée the ring.의 4형식 문장을 수동태로 전환하였다. 4형식의 직접목적어를 주어로 하는 수동태 문장을 만들 때는 간접목적어 앞에 전치사를 써야 한다. 동사가 bought이므로 전치사 for가 와야 한다.

02 '그 노인은 자신의 외아들의 보살핌을 받는다.'라는 의미로, 주어가 행위를 당하는 수동태 문장이다. 「동사+전치사」 형태로 동사 역할을 하는 동사구는 하나의 동사로 취급해 수동태 문장을 만들기 때문에 is looked after를 고른다.

03 '정말 불쌍한 개야! 그 개는 어제 차에 치였어.'라는 의미의 수동태 문장이다. 과거 시점을 나타내는 yesterday가 있기 때문에 과거 수동태가 되어야 하며, 과거 수동태는 「was/were+과거분사(+by+행위자)」로 나타낸다.

04 '내 자동차가 운전을 하는 도중에 갑자기 멈췄어. 지금 당장 검사를 받아야 해.'라는 의미로, 조동사가 있는 수동태 문장이다. 조동사가 있는 수동태는 「조동사+be+과거분사(+by+행위자)」로 나타낸다. 조동사 must가 빈칸 앞에 있으므로 be checked를 고른다.

05 '엄마와 아빠가 내 성과에 기뻐하셨다.'라는 의미이며, '~에 기뻐하다'라는 의미의 「be pleased with ~」를 쓴다.

06
- '그는 그 시험 결과에 실망했다.'라는 의미이며, '~에 실망하다'라는 의미의 「be disappointed with ~」는 by 이외의 전치사를 쓰는 수동태이다.
- '그 소년은 몇몇 비열한 아이들에게 멸시를 당했다.'라는 의미로, 수동태 문장이다. 수동태의 행위자는 「by+행위자(목적격)」으로 나타낸다.

07
- '그 경기장은 큰 환호성으로 가득 차 있었다.'라는 의미이며, '~로 가득 차 있다'라는 의미의 「be filled with ~」는 by 이외의 전치사를 쓰는 수동태이다.
- '내 딸은 현대 미술에 아주 관심이 많다.'라는 의미이며, '~에 관심이 있다'라는 의미의 「be interested in ~」은 by 이외의 전치사를 쓰는 수동태이다.

08 '그것은 세탁기에서 세탁되는 중이야.'라는 의미로, 주어(It)가 행위를 당하는 수동태 문장인데, 문맥상 수동태 진행형이 적절하므로 is being washed를 고른다.

09 '그 그림을 너 혼자 그렸니?'라는 질문에 '언니의 도움을 받았어.'라는 의미의 수동태 문장으로 답해야 한다. 과거의 일을 묻고 있기 때문에 과거 수동태 「was/were+과거분사」 형태, 즉 was helped를 고른다.

10 진행시제 수동태 문장으로 「be동사+being+과거분사(+by+행위자)」의 형태로 나타낸다.

11 과거시제 수동태 문장으로 「was/were+과거분사(+by+행위자)」의 형태로 나타낸다.

12 ① 주어가 행위를 당하는 수동태 문장이며 조동사가 있는 수동태는 「조동사+be+과거분사(+by+행위자)」의 형태로 나타낸다. 따라서 must obey는 must be obeyed가 되어야 한다.

13 ⑤ 수동태 의문문은 「be동사+주어+과거분사 ~?」의 형태로 나타낸다. 따라서 Does는 Is가 되어야 한다.

14 '그것은 고급 면으로 만들어졌어.'라는 의미가 되어야 한다. '~로 만들어지다'라는 의미의 「be made of[from] ~」는 by 이외의 전치사를 쓰는 수동태이다.

15 '터널은 지난달에 폭우로 파괴되었다.'라는 의미가 되어야 하므로 빈칸에 과거 수동태가 와야 한다. 과거 수동태는 「was/were+과거분사(+by+행위자)」의 형태로 나타낸다.

16 ① 수동태의 행위자는 「by+행위자(목적격)」으로 나타내기 때문에 to Brian은 by Brian이 되어야 한다.

17 call off는 「동사+전치사」 형태로 동사 역할을 하는 동사구이다. 동사구는 하나의 동사로 취급해 수동태 문장을 만들기 때문에 was called off by them을 고른다.

18 「주어+동사+목적어+목적격보어」의 어순으로 5형식이다. 5형식 수동태는 목적어를 주어로 만들고 목적격보어는 그대로 두면 된다. (단, 목적격보어가 동사원형인 경우 목적격보어 앞에 to를 붙인다.) 따라서 was seen talking to the principal을 고른다.

19 주어진 문장은 과거시제 능동태 의문문으로 과거시제 수동태 의문문으로 전환하면 되는데 과거시제 수동태 의문문은 「Was/Were+주어+과거분사(+by+행위자)?」의 형태로 나타낸다.

20 「주어+동사+목적어+목적격보어」의 어순으로 5형식이다. 5형식 수동태는 목적어를 주어로 만들고 목적격보어가 wait로 동사원형이기 때문에 wait 앞에 to를 붙인다.

21 「주어+동사+간접목적어+직접목적어」의 어순으로 4형식이다. 4형식은 직접목적어, 간접목적어를 모두 주어로 하는 수동태 문장을 만들 수 있으며, 직접목적어를 주어로 하는 수동태 문장을 만들 때는 간접목적어 앞에 전치사를 쓰면 된다. 동사가 give이므로 전치사 to를 사용한다. 주어진 문장을 수동태로 만들면 'I was given the letter by Norah.' 또는 'The letter was given to me by Norah.'가 된다.

22 주어진 문장은 미래시제로 미래시제 수동태로 전환하면 된다. 미래시제 수동태는 「will+be+과거분사(+by+행위자)」의 형태로 나타낸다.

23
- '도심은 항상 많은 사람과 차량들로 붐빈다.'라는 의미이다. '~로 붐비다'라는 의미의 「be crowded with ~」는 by 이외의 전치사를 쓰는 수동태이다.
- '그 벽장은 오래된 책으로 가득 차 있다.'라는 의미이다. '~로 가득 차 있다'라는 의미의 「be filled with ~」는 by 이외의 전치사를 쓰는 수동태이다.

24
- '나는 그 배의 크기에 놀랐다.'라는 의미이다. '~에 놀라다'라는 의미의 「be surprised at ~」은 by 이외의 전치사를 쓰는 수동태이다.
- 'Jason은 우스꽝스러운 모자를 썼다는 이유로 동료의 비웃음을 샀다.'라는 의미이다. 「laugh at ~」은 '~을 비웃다'라는 의미의 동사구로, 동사구는 하나의 동사로 취급해 수동태 문장을 만든다.

25 주어가 동작의 대상이 되는 수동태 문장으로 현재시제 수동태는 「am/are/is+과거분사(+by+행위자)」의 형태로 나타낸다. 주어(Both English and French)가 복수이므로 are spoken이 되어야 한다.

26 조동사가 있는 수동태 문장으로 「조동사+be+과거분사(+by+행위자)」의 형태로 나타낸다. 빈칸 앞에 can이 있으므로 be used가 되어야 한다.

27 조동사가 있는 수동태 문장으로 「조동사+be+과거분사(+by+행위자)」의 형태로 나타낸다. 빈칸 앞에 has to가 있으므로 be decorated가 되어야 한다.

28 「주어+동사+간접목적어+직접목적어」의 어순으로 4형식이다. 4형식 수동태로 직접목적어 a wrong dish가 주어로 왔기 때문에 간접목적어 앞에 전치사를 써야 한다. 동사 bring은 수동태로 전환할 때 간접목적어 앞에 전치사 to를 쓴다.

29 4형식 수동태로 직접목적어 a smartphone이 주어로 왔기 때문에 간접목적어 앞에 전치사를 써야 한다. 동사 buy는 수동태로 전환할 때 간접목적어 앞에 전치사 for를 쓴다.

30 4형식 수동태로 직접목적어 two tickets to the concert가 주어로 왔

기 때문에 간접목적어 앞에 전치사를 써야 한다. 동사 give는 수동태로 전환할 때 간접목적어 앞에 전치사 to를 쓴다.

31 4형식 수동태로 직접목적어 a lot of questions가 주어로 왔기 때문에 간접목적어 앞에 전치사를 써야 한다. 동사 ask는 수동태로 전환할 때 간접목적어 앞에 전치사 of를 쓴다. 따라서 for는 of가 되어야 한다.

32 '~로 가득 차 있다'라는 의미의 「be filled with ~」는 by 이외의 전치사를 쓰는 수동태이므로 in은 with가 되어야 한다.

33 진행시제 수동태 문장으로 「be동사+being+과거분사(+by+행위자)」의 형태로 나타낸다.

34 '~에 만족해하다'라는 의미의 「be satisfied with ~」는 by 이외의 전치사를 쓰는 수동태이다.

35 주어진 문장이 5형식이므로, 수동태를 만들 때 목적어를 주어로 만들고 목적격보어 mow가 동사원형이기 때문에 앞에 to를 붙인다.

36 과거시제 수동태 문장으로 「was/were+과거분사(+by+행위자)」의 형태로 나타낸다.

보너스 유형별 문제 p.58

1 should be shared with others
2 must be followed
3 shouldn't be used
4 ②

[1-3] 교칙
복도에서 뛰지 마라.
항상 공손하게 행동하라.
서로를 도와라.
안전하게 놀아라.
1 너의 교구를 친구들과 공유해라.
2 선생님의 지시 사항을 따르라.
3 수업 중에는 스마트폰을 사용하지 마라.

1-3 조동사의 수동태 「조동사 + be + p.p. (+ by 행위자)」

4 이곳은 Sycamore의 좋은 지역에 위치한 단독 주택으로 침실 4개, 욕실 3개, 원목 마루가 있으며, 중앙 거실에는 벽난로가 갖춰져 있습니다. 주방은 1년 전에 최신식으로 고쳐서, 새 오븐, 가스레인지, 식기세척기가 설치되어 있습니다. 이곳은 새로 지어진 집들과 함께 조용한 거리에 자리 잡고 있으며, 학교, 상가, 대중교통과 가까운 거리에 위치해 있습니다. 주택 공개는 예정되어 있지 않지만, 개별적으로 집을 보시고 싶으면 요청하실 수 있습니다.
주방이 1년 전에 최신식으로 고쳐진 것이므로 update를 수동태로 쓰는 것이 옳다. 따라서 과거분사인 updated로 고쳐야 한다.

Chapter 4

4-1 to부정사의 명사적 쓰임: 주어 역할 p.60

Exercise 1

1 To see, to believe
2 to see
3 to do
4 to get, to eat
5 to hear
6 to take, to see

Exercise 2

1 is
2 to swim
3 to understand
4 To become
5 It

Exercise 3

1 It is not good to watch TV too much.
2 It is important to keep your promises.
3 It is interesting to learn new languages.
4 It is necessary to wash fruits and vegetables.
5 It is not good behavior to bully weak people.
6 It is not easy to take a risk and try something new.
7 It is very helpful to use visual aids in your presentation.

Exercise 4

1 To invent something new
2 impossible to arrive there
3 difficult to finish the work
4 pleasant to drive
5 To know your enemy

4-2 to부정사의 명사적 쓰임: 보어 역할 p.62

Exercise 1

1 to lose
2 to share
3 to get
4 to water
5 to visit

Exercise 2

1 to sort out letters and parcels
2 want me to turn off
3 would like you to meet
4 asked my son to bathe the cat
5 asked me to take care of
6 allow me to go to the restroom

4-3 to부정사의 명사적 쓰임: 목적어 역할 p.63

Exercise 1

1 to have
2 to move
3 to speak
4 to look
5 to think through

Exercise 2

1 hopes to succeed
2 planning to go
3 needs to meet
4 agreed to cancel
5 want to be friends
6 learn to overcome
7 decided to go

4-4 의문사+to부정사 p.64

Exercise 1

1 who(m) to vote for
2 when to stop by
3 what to say
4 where to stay
5 how to turn on

Exercise 2

1 how to bake
2 what to do
3 how to speak
4 how to play
5 what to wear

4-5 to부정사의 형용사적 쓰임 p.65

Exercise 1

1 to write on
2 to eat
3 to play with
4 to eat
5 to take care of
6 to read
7 something thicker

Exercise 2

1 to write with
2 time to say goodbye
3 to live in
4 something hot to
5 anything interesting to share
6 a black suit to wear
7 to eat or drink
8 to sit on

Exercise 3

1 to sleep on
2 to live in
3 to visit
4 to talk to/with
5 to read
6 to do

Exercise 4

1 time to wrap up and go home
2 a couple of things to talk about
3 a new toy to play with
4 time to drop by my house
5 a friend to trust and rely on
6 many things to do
7 something pretty to give my sister

4-6 to부정사의 부사적 쓰임 p.67

Exercise 1

1 to see
2 to [in order to] keep
3 to eat
4 to do
5 to be

Exercise 2

1 나는 그 기차를 타기 위해 일찍 일어났다.
2 그 소식을 듣고[듣게 되어서] 나는 매우 놀랐다.
3 Emily는 자라서 좋은 선생님이 되었다.
4 그 작은 소년을 돕다니 너는 매우 친절하구나.
5 가난한 사람들을 돕는 것을 보니 Chuck은 친절한 사람임이 틀림없다.
6 그들은 그 게임을 보게 되어 흥분했다.

Exercise 3

1 stupid to believe what he said
2 pleased to win the prize
3 creative to think of such a thing
4 difficult to use
5 happy to meet my grandparents
6 to be one hundred years old
7 to [in order to] check out a book
8 to ignore him for weeks

4-7 to부정사의 부정 p.69

Exercise 1

1 not to go out
2 not to miss
3 not to tell
4 not to be
5 not to touch

Exercise 2

1 not to trouble others
2 not to go to the concert
3 not to rub your eyes with your hands
4 not to laugh

4-8 to부정사의 의미상 주어 p.70

Exercise 1

1 of you 2 him 3 for us 4 for him
5 for me to put 6 for children 7 of you

Exercise 2

1 nice of you to take care of
2 stupid of us to behave
3 impossible for you to walk
4 expensive for us to buy
5 difficult for me to answer

4-9 to부정사의 관용 표현 p.71

Exercise 1

1 too tired to move an inch
2 too spicy for you to eat
3 so rich that he can buy a plane
4 smart enough to handle it

Exercise 2

1 smart enough to get into Harvard
2 sturdy enough to hold those books
3 too young to understand
4 too boring for me to read

4-10 원형부정사 I p.72

Exercise 1

1 touch 2 carried
3 rise, rising 4 shake, shaking
5 scream

Exercise 2

1 I saw him standing at the door.
2 Dylan felt his heart beating fast.
3 We heard the ambulance coming.
4 I felt the house shake and heard the windows rattle.

4-11 원형부정사 II p.73

Exercise 1

1 leave 2 paint
3 stolen 4 pass, to pass

Exercise 2

1 made → make
2 finding → find/to find
3 to introduce → introduce
4 working → work

Exercise 3

1 had his hair cut
2 made me set the table
3 could not but accept his apology
4 makes me laugh with funny jokes

Review Test p.74

01 ③ 02 ① 03 ④ 04 ② 05 ④ 06 ⑤
07 ⑤ 08 ① 09 ③ 10 ④ 11 ④ 12 ③
13 ③ 14 ① 15 ③ 16 ③ 17 ④ 18 ①
19 ④ 20 ③ 21 ③ 22 ① 23 ② 24 ④
25 ②
26 to, learn
27 too, to
28 to, help
29 how to swim
30 told us not to make
31 let their children watch
32 what to say
33 to be
34 called
35 becoming → to become
36 to break → broken
37 It is expensive to send a parcel by air.
38 It would be helpful for you to keep a journal.

01 '그는 자신의 옛 친구를 만나기 위해 캐나다로 갔다.'라는 의미이며, 목적을 나타내는 to부정사의 부사적 쓰임이 와야 한다. to부정사는 「to+동사원형」으로 나타낸다.

02 '네가 노인들을 돕다니 친절하구나.'라는 의미로, to부정사의 의미상 주어 형태를 고르는 문제이다. to부정사 의미상의 주어는 일반 형용사의 경우 「for+목적격」의 형태로, 사람의 성질이나 성격을 나타내는 형용사의 경우 「of+목적격」의 형태로 to부정사 앞에 쓴다. kind는 사람의 성질이나 성격을 나타내는 형용사이므로 of를 고른다.

03 '그 소년은 학교에 늦지 않기 위해 서둘렀다.'라는 의미가 되어야 하므로 to부정사의 부정형이 와야 한다. to부정사의 부정형은 「not/never+to+동사원형」으로 나타낸다.

04 '나는 내 이웃이 울타리를 칠하는 것을 보았다.'라는 의미로 「주어+지각동사+목적어+목적격보어」 어순의 5형식 문장이다. 지각동사는 목적격보어로 원형부정사가 오거나, 진행의 의미를 강조할 때는 현재분사가 온다.

05 '우리는 합창 연습을 하기 위해 여기 강당에 왔다.'라는 의미이다. to have choir practice는 '연습을 하기 위하여'라는 의미로, 목적을 나타내는 to

부정사의 부사적 쓰임에 해당한다. 목적을 나타내는 to부정사의 부사적 쓰임은 in order to로 바꿔 쓸 수 있다.

06 목적어로 to read가 왔기 때문에 빈칸에는 to부정사를 목적어로 취하는 동사가 와야 한다. 따라서 made는 적절하지 않다.

07 「주어+동사+목적어+목적격보어」 어순의 5형식 문장으로 목적격보어로 원형부정사가 왔기 때문에 빈칸에는 목적격보어로 원형부정사를 취하는 동사가 와야 한다. 따라서 to부정사가 목적격보어로 오는 ordered는 적절하지 않다.

08 '이 기계를 어떻게 켜는지 알고 있니?'라는 의미가 되어야 하므로 '어떻게 ~하는지'라는 의미의 「how+to부정사」가 되어야 한다. 따라서 how를 고른다.

09 '무엇을 해야 할지 모르겠어', '그것을 네가 선생님께 말씀 드리는 게 옳은 것 같아.'라는 의미가 되어야 하므로 '무엇을 해야 할지'라는 의미의 「what+to부정사」가 되어야 하며, 두 번째 빈칸 앞에 일반 형용사 right이 왔기 때문에 의미상의 주어는 「for+목적격」으로 나타낸다. 따라서 빈칸에는 what과 for가 적절하다.

10 ① '사야 할 많은 것'이라는 의미로, 명사를 수식하는 형용사적 쓰임, ② '마실 것'이라는 의미로, 형용사적 쓰임, ③ '그를 도와줄 많은 친구들'이라는 의미로, 형용사적 쓰임, ⑤ '읽을 책'이라는 의미로, 형용사적 쓰임에 해당한다. ④ '너를 만나기 위해서'라는 의미로, 목적을 나타내는 to부정사의 부사적 쓰임이다.

11 ① '보는 것이'라는 의미로, 문장에서 주어 역할을 하는 명사적 쓰임, ② '기차 여행을 하는 것을 좋아한다.'라는 의미로, 문장에서 목적어 역할을 하는 명사적 쓰임, ③ '테니스를 치는 것은 정말 재미있다.'라는 의미로, to play tennis가 문장의 진주어로 명사적 쓰임, ⑤ '해외로 가서 미술 공부를 하는 것'이라는 의미로, 문장에서 보어 역할을 하는 명사적 쓰임에 해당한다. ④ '차가운 마실 것'이라는 의미로, something을 수식하는 형용사적 쓰임이다.

12 ① '당신을 만나게 되어 기쁩니다.'라는 의미로, 감정의 원인을 나타내는 부사적 쓰임, ② '그 퍼즐을 풀다니 영리한 게 틀림없구나.'라는 의미로, 판단의 근거를 나타내는 부사적 쓰임, ④ '여행을 하기 위해 아프리카에 갔다.'라는 의미로, 목적을 나타내는 부사적 쓰임, ⑤ '너 같은 사람을 만나다니 운이 좋다.'라는 의미로, 판단의 근거를 나타내는 부사적 쓰임에 해당한다. ③ '휴식을 취해야 한다.'라는 의미로, 문장에서 목적어 역할을 하는 명사적 쓰임이다.

13 「so+형용사/부사+that+주어+can[could]」는 '~할 만큼 충분히 …하다'라는 의미의 관용 표현 「형용사/부사+enough+to부정사」로 바꿔 쓸 수 있다.

14 to부정사가 주어로 오는 경우 주어(to부정사)를 뒤로 보내고 가주어 it을 주어 자리에 쓴다.

15 ③ '써야 할 에세이가 있다.'라는 의미로, an essay to write이 되어야 한다. 따라서 on이 삭제되어야 한다.

16 ③ 「주어+지각동사+목적어+목적격보어」 어순의 5형식 문장에서 지각동사는 목적격보어로 원형부정사를 취하거나, 진행되는 순간을 강조할 때는 현재분사를 취한다. 또한 목적어와 목적격보어의 관계가 수동일 때는 과거분사를 취한다. '무언가가 내 등 위를 기어가는 것을 느꼈다.'라는 의미로, 목적어가 something, 목적격보어가 crawl로 능동의 관계가 되어야 한다. 따라서 crawled가 원형부정사 crawl 또는 crawling(진행의 의미를 강조하는 경우)이 되어야 한다.

17 수식을 받는 명사 a house가 전치사 in의 목적어 역할을 해야 하므로 a cozy house to live in을 고른다.

18 to부정사의 부정은 「not/never+to+동사원형」으로 나타낸다.

19 '그 소년은 너무 어려서 책을 읽을 수 없다.'라는 의미이다. '너무 ~해서 …할 수 없다'라는 의미의 관용 표현 「too+형용사/부사+to부정사」는 「so+형용사/부사+that+주어+can't[couldn't]」로 바꿔 쓸 수 있다.

20 • '그녀가 너에게 더 오래 머물도록 요청한 것은 이기적이었다.'라는 의미이며, selfish가 사람의 성질이나 성격을 나타내는 형용사이므로 의미상의 주어를 「of+목적격」으로 나타낸다.
• 'Gwen은 그 경기에서 우승할 만큼 충분히 숙련되어 있다.'라는 의미이다. '~할 만큼 충분히 …하다'라는 의미의 관용 표현은 「형용사/부사+enough+to부정사」이므로 enough이다.

21 • '선물을 포장해 주세요.'라는 의미이며, 「주어+동사+목적어+목적격보어」 어순의 5형식 문장에서 동사가 사역동사 have, 목적어가 gift로 '선물이 포장되는'이라는 수동의 의미가 되어야 하므로 목적격보어로 과거분사 wrapped가 와야 한다.
• '나는 그에게 이 시계를 고치게 했다.'라는 의미이며 「주어+동사+목적어+목적격보어」 어순의 5형식 문장에서 동사가사역동사로 have, 목적어가 him으로 그가 시계를 고치도록 시키다라는 능동의 의미가 되어야 하므로 목적격보어로 원형부정사 fix가 와야 한다.

22 주어진 문장의 밑줄 친 부분은 '구경할 많은 곳'이라는 의미로, 명사를 수식하는 to부정사의 형용사적 쓰임에 해당한다. ① '해야 할 많은 일'이라는 의미로, 명사를 수식하는 형용사적 쓰임, ② '외국어를 배우는 것'이라는 의미로, 문장에서 진주어 역할을 하는 명사적 쓰임, ③ '그렇게 말하다니 정말 어리석음이 틀림없다.'라는 의미로, 판단의 근거를 나타내는 to부정사의 부사적 쓰임, ④ '경기에서 이기기 위해서'라는 의미로, 목적을 나타내는 to부정사의 부사적 쓰임, ⑤ '그 문제를 풀만큼 충분히 똑똑하다.'라는 의미로, 판단의 근거를 나타내는 to부정사의 부사적 쓰임에 해당한다.

23 주어진 문장의 밑줄 친 부분은 '깜짝 파티를 열기로 했다.'라는 의미로, decided의 목적어 역할을 하는 명사적 쓰임에 해당한다. ① '그 소식을 들어서 유감입니다.'라는 의미로, 감정의 원인을 나타내는 부사적 쓰임, ② '책을 읽는 것을 좋아한다.'라는 의미로, like의 목적어 역할을 하는 명사적 쓰임, ③ '해야 할 숙제'라는 의미로, 명사를 수식하는 형용사적 쓰임, ④ '달걀을 꺼내기 위해서'라는 의미로, 목적을 나타내는 to부정사의 부사적 쓰임, ⑤ '자신의 약속을 어기는 사람'이라는 의미로, 명사를 수식하는 형용사적 쓰임에 해당한다.

24 「주어+지각동사+목적어+목적격보어」 어순의 5형식 문장에서 지각동사는 목적격보어로 원형부정사를 취하거나, 진행되는 순간을 강조할 때 현재분사를, 목적어와 목적격보어의 관계가 수동일 때 과거분사를 취한다.

25 -thing/-one/-body로 끝나는 대명사는 수식하는 형용사가 대명사 뒤에 위치하게 되는데 이를 다시 to부정사가 수식하면 「-thing/-one/-body+형용사+to부정사」의 어순이 된다.

26 가주어·진주어 구문으로 만들 때 주어(to부정사)를 뒤로 보내고 그 자리에 가주어 it을 쓴다.

27 '너무 ~해서 …할 수 없다'라는 의미의 관용 표현 「too+형용사/부사+to부정사」는 「so+형용사/부사+that+주어+can't[couldn't]」로 바꿔 쓸 수 있다.

28 '테레사 수녀는 인도에 갔다. 그녀는 가난한 사람을 도와주고 싶었다.'라는 의미이다. 목적을 나타내는 to부정사로 '~하기 위하여'라는 의미를 나타낼 수 있다.

29 '어떻게 ~하는지'라는 의미는 「how+to부정사」로 나타낸다.

30 to부정사의 부정은 「not/never+to+동사원형」으로 나타낸다.

31 「주어+동사+목적어+목적격보어」 어순의 5형식 문장에서 사역동사 let은 목적격보어로 원형부정사를 취한다.

32 '무엇을 해야 할지'라는 의미는 「what+to부정사」로 나타낸다.

33 '~해서 …하다'라는 의미는 결과를 나타내는 to부정사의 부사적 쓰임을 사용한다.

34 「주어+지각동사+목적어+목적격보어」 어순의 5형식 문장으로 목적어가 my name이며 '불리는'이라는 수동의 의미가 되어야 하므로 목적격보어로 과거분사 called가 와야 한다.

35 '우리 부모님께서는 내가 선생님이 되길 원하신다.'라는 의미로, want는 목적격보어로 to부정사를 취하는 동사이다. 따라서 becoming이 to become이 되어야 한다.

36 「주어+동사+목적어+목적격보어」 어순의 5형식 문장이며, 동사는 사역동사로 have이다. 목적어로 my windows가 왔고, '창문이 깨졌다'라는 수동의 의미가 되어야 하기 때문에 목적격보어 to break는 broken이 되어야 한다.

37 가주어 · 진주어 구문으로 전환하는 문제이다. 가주어 · 진주어 구문을 만들 때 주어(to부정사)를 뒤로 보내고 그 자리에 가주어 it을 쓴다. '항공 우편으로 소포를 보내는 것은 비싸다.'라는 의미이다.

38 가주어 · 진주어 구문으로 만들 때 주어(to부정사)를 뒤로 보내고 그 자리에 가주어 it을 쓴다. '일기를 쓰는 것은 너에게 도움이 될 것이다.'라는 의미이다.

보너스 유형별 문제 p.78

1 where to go
2 how to go
3 something to eat
4 not to be late
5 ①

[1-4] 설악산국립공원 현장학습
학생들은 설악산국립공원에 갈 예정입니다.
때: 10월 11일
가는 장소: 설악산국립공원
가는 방법: 스쿨버스
잊지 마세요:
– 먹을 것 챙겨오기
– 따뜻한 겉옷을 입고, 모자 쓰고, 등산화 착용하기
학생들은 스쿨버스를 타는 데 늦지 않도록 주의해야 합니다.

1 '어디로 ~할지'라는 의미는 「where+to부정사」로 나타낸다.
2 '어떻게 ~하는지'라는 의미는 「how+to부정사」로 나타낸다.
3 '~할 것'이라는 의미는 「something+to부정사」로 나타낸다.
4 to부정사의 부정형은 「not + to + 동사원형」으로 쓰고 여기서는 부사적 용법으로 쓰여 '~하지 않기 위해서'로 해석한다.

5 Clarksville의 시 관계자들은 다음에 무엇을 지을지 결정하려고 합니다. 어떤 사람들은 어린이들을 위한 새 공원을 원합니다. 또 어떤 사람들은 새 건강 센터를 바라고 있습니다. 도시 북쪽에 사는 주민들은 새 식료품점을 원하지만, 많은 젊은이들이 극장을 요구하고 있습니다. 시에서는 어떤 것이 가장 인기 있는지 알아보기 위해 여론 조사를 실시하였습니다. 그 결과 건강 센터보다 식료품점을 원하는 사람들이 조금 더 많은 것으로 나왔습니다.
문맥상 '무엇을 ~할지'라는 말을 써야하는데 이는 「what+to부정사」로 나타낸다. 따라서 build를 to build로 써야 옳다.

Chapter 5

5-1 동명사의 역할 I p.80

Exercise 1

1 Eating 2 Learning 3 Keeping
4 flying 5 helping

Exercise 2

1 My uncle's job is selling used cars.
2 Listening to loud music is bad for your ears.
3 Brainstorming before writing will be helpful.
4 My healthy habit is having an apple every morning.
5 Nicole's hobby is collecting postcards from different countries.

5-2 동명사의 역할 II p.81

Exercise 1

1 going hiking 2 doing
3 being 4 smoking
5 not getting up 6 watching

Exercise 2

1 closing 2 changing
3 reading 4 not eating
5 talking 6 learning
7 having 8 being

Exercise 3

1 writing 2 saying
3 breaking 4 turning off
5 making 6 inviting

Exercise 4

1 follow → following
2 talking not → not talking
3 meet → meeting
4 not for coming → for not coming
5 eat → eating
6 to do → doing

Exercise 5

1 Jason is good at making us laugh.
2 Thank you for accepting our invitation.
3 Would you mind pulling back the curtains?
4 Sometimes I enjoy not doing anything.
5 My mom and I avoid watching horror movies.

5-3 동명사와 to부정사 I p.83

Exercise 1

1 to quit
2 having
3 climbing
4 meeting

Exercise 2

1 to leave
2 to go
3 reading
4 talking

Exercise 3

1 don't mind doing
2 promised to be
3 hopes to pass
4 gave up playing

5-4 동명사와 to부정사 II p.84

Exercise 1

1 to do
2 to rain, raining
3 to move, moving
4 to go
5 to lock
6 to calm
7 meeting
8 to pick up
9 playing
10 working

Exercise 2

1 to buy
2 meeting
3 dancing

Exercise 3

1 complaining
2 reading
3 putting on
4 to turn off

Exercise 4

1 stopped to talk to me
2 stop drinking for your health
3 forgot watering the plants
4 remember to call me

5-5 동명사의 관용 표현 p.86

Exercise 1

1 hiking
2 wearing
3 eating
4 feeling
5 to going
6 taking

Exercise 2

1 completing
2 laughing
3 worrying
4 meeting

Exercise 3

1 is used to looking after
2 are looking forward to working
3 are busy starting
4 worth trying
5 go camping
6 have difficulty [trouble/a hard time] using

Exercise 4

1 나는 지금 매운 음식을 먹고 싶다.
2 나는 그 빨간 상자를 열어보지 않을 수 없었다.
3 우리는 매일 아침 일찍 일어나는 것에 익숙하다.
4 너의 소중한 시간을 비디오 게임을 하면서 소비하지 마라.

Review Test p.88

01 ③ 02 ① 03 ③ 04 ⑤ 05 ⑤ 06 ⑤
07 ⑤ 08 ③ 09 ③ 10 ① 11 ③ 12 ③
13 ④ 14 ④ 15 ③ 16 ② 17 ① 18 ①
19 ② 20 ④ 21 ④ 22 ④ 23 ① 24 ⑤
25 to chase → chasing
26 learning → to learn
27 no use thinking
28 remember promising
29 How [What] about taking
30 try driving
31 ①: doing ②: skiing ③: to buy
32 being
33 helping
34 not drinking enough water
35 Taking a deep breath will help
36 We are looking forward to visiting

01 '저를 여기 초대해 주셔서 감사합니다.'라는 의미로, 전치사 for의 목적어 역할을 하는 동명사를 고른다. 동명사는 「동사원형 +ing」의 형태로 나타낸다.

02 '매년 스노보드를 타러 간다.'라는 의미로, '~하러 가다'라는 뜻의 관용 표현은 「go+-ing」로 나타낸다. 따라서 snow-boarding을 고른다.

03 '그 쇼를 보고 난 후, 그는 TV를 끄고 잠자리에 들었다.'라는 의미이며, finish는 목적어로 동명사를 취한다.

04 '네가 한 일을 후회해도 소용없다.'라는 의미로, '~해도 소용없다'라는 뜻의 관용 표현은 「It is no use+-ing」로 나타낸다.

05 writing이 문장의 목적어로, 빈칸에는 목적어로 동명사를 취하는 동사가 와야 한다. want는 목적어로 to부정사를 취하는 동사로 적절하지 않다.

06 to buy가 문장의 목적어로, 빈칸에는 to부정사를 목적어로 취하는 동사가 와야 한다. avoid는 목적어로 동명사를 취하는 동사로 적절하지 않다.

07 doing이 문장의 목적어로, 빈칸에는 목적어로 동명사를 취하는 동사가 와야 한다. expect는 목적어로 to부정사를 취하는 동사로 적절하지 않다.

08 • '그는 건강상의 이유로 담배를 끊었다.'라는 의미가 되어야 하므로 '~하는 것을 멈추다'라는 의미의 「stop+동명사」를 고른다.
• '그는 서점에서 책을 사기 위해 멈췄다.'라는 의미가 되어야 하므로 '~하기 위해서 멈추다'라는 의미의 「stop+to부정사」를 고른다.

09 • forget은 to부정사와 동명사를 모두 취할 수 있지만, 「forget+to부정사」는 '~할 것을 잊다'라는 의미이고, 「forget+동명사」는 '~한 것을 잊다'라는 의미이다. '우산을 가져오는 것을 잊었다.'라는 의미가 되어야 하므로 to bring을 고른다.
• remember는 to부정사와 동명사를 모두 취할 수 있지만, 「remember+to부정사」는 '~할 것을 기억하다'라는 의미이고, 「remember+동명사」는 '~한 것을 기억하다'라는 의미이다. '지난달에 쇼핑몰에서 그녀를 만난 것을 기억하니?'라는 의미가 되어야 하므로 동명사 running을 고른다.

10 '비가 주말 내내 계속 내렸다.', '그는 70세까지 계속 일했다.'라는 의미이며, 문장의 목적어가 to fall, working으로 빈칸에는 목적어로 to부정사와 동명사를 모두 취하는 동사가 와야 한다. stop, quit, finish, delay는 목적어로 동명사를 취하는 동사이다.

11 A 나 정말 신 나! 오늘 우리 수영하러 가잖아.
B 오, 안 돼. 나 수영복을 가져오는 걸 완전히 잊어버렸어.
'수영복을 가져 오는 것을 잊다'라는 의미가 되어야 하므로 '~할 것을 잊다'라는 뜻의 to bring을 고른다.

12 '그는 늘 똑같은 일을 하는 데 지쳤다. 그래서 그는 일을 그만둘까 생각중이다.'라는 의미이다. 전치사 of, about의 목적어 역할을 할 수 있는 동명사, doing과 quitting을 고른다.

13 '내가 중국어를 할 수 없었기 때문에 베이징에서 기차표를 사는 데 어려움을 겪었다. 나는 요즘 중국어를 배우고 있다.'라는 의미이다. 「have difficulty+-ing」는 '~하는 데 어려움을 겪다'라는 의미의 관용 표현으로 buy가 buying이 되어야 한다. learn은 목적어로 to부정사를 취하는 동사로 speak이 to speak이 되어야 한다.

14 try는 목적어로 to부정사와 동명사를 취할 수 있지만, 「try+to부정사」는 '~하려고 애쓰다'라는 의미이고, 「try+동명사」는 '시험 삼아 ~해보다'라는 의미이다.

15 동명사의 부정은 「not/never+동명사」의 형태로 나타낸다.

16 '~하는 데 …을 소비하다'라는 의미의 동명사 관용 표현은 「spend+시간/돈+-ing」이다.

17 love, hate, begin, start는 to부정사와 동명사를 모두 목적어로 취하고 무엇을 취하든 의미 변화가 없는 동사이다. ① forget은 to부정사와 동명사를 모두 취할 수 있지만, 「forget+to부정사」는 '~할 것을 잊다', 「forget+동명사」는 '~한 것을 잊다'라는 의미이다.

18 ① '아침을 먹고 있다.'라는 의미이며, 「be동사+-ing」의 형태로 진행을 나타내는 현재분사, ② '수영하는 것을 즐긴다.'라는 의미로, enjoy의 목적어 역할을 하는 동명사, ③ '정직한 것'이라는 의미로, 문장에서 주어 역할을 하는 동명사, ④ '책 읽는 것을 좋아한다.'라는 의미로, like의 목적어 역할을 하는 동명사, ⑤ '토론토에 가는 것을 고대한다.'라는 의미로, 「look forward to+-ing」는 '~하는 것을 고대하다'라는 의미의 관용 표현이다. 따라서 ①은 현재분사, ②, ③, ④, ⑤는 동명사이다.

19 ① '독특한 장신구를 만드는 것'이라는 의미로, 문장에서 보어 역할을 하는 동명사, ② '집안일을 하고 있었다.'라는 의미로, 「be동사+-ing」의 형태로 진행을 나타내는 현재분사, ③ '사랑을 주는 것'이라는 의미로, 문장에서 보어 역할을 하는 동명사, ④ '유치원에서 아이들을 가르치는 것'이라는 의미로, 문장에서 보어 역할을 하는 동명사, ⑤ '문을 잠그지 않은 채로 둔 것'이라는 의미로, 문장에서 보어 역할을 하는 동명사이다. 따라서 ②는 현재분사, ①, ③, ④, ⑤는 동명사이다.

20 ④ 「have difficulty+-ing」는 '~하는 데 어려움을 겪다'라는 의미의 관용 표현으로 to understand가 understanding이 되어야 한다.

21 ④ suggest는 목적어로 동명사를 취하는 동사이다. 따라서 to take는 taking이 되어야 한다.

22 ① 「feel like+-ing」는 '~하고 싶다'라는 의미의 관용 표현으로 to listen이 listening이 되어야 한다. ② 「cannot help+-ing」는 '~하지 않을 수 없다'라는 의미의 관용 표현으로 to love가 loving이 되어야 한다. ③ 「have a hard time+-ing」는 '~하는 데 어려움을 겪다'라는 의미의 관용 표현으로 to master가 mastering이 되어야 한다. ⑤ like는 목적어로 to부정사와 동명사를 취하는 동사로, to eating이 to eat 또는 eating이 되어야 한다.

23 ② 「look forward to+-ing」는 '~하는 것을 고대하다'라는 의미의 관용 표현으로 hear가 hearing이 되어야 한다. ③ avoid는 동명사를 목적어로 취하는 동사로 to meet이 meeting이 되어야 한다. ④ 「go+-ing」는 '~하러 가다'라는 의미의 관용 표현으로 to fish가 fishing이 되어야 한다. ⑤ 동명사(구)가 문장의 주어로 쓰였을 경우 동명사(구)는 단수 취급해 단수 동사가 온다. 따라서 were는 was가 되어야 한다.

24 ⑤ '계속해서 그것을 듣고 있다.'라는 의미로, keep은 목적어로 동명사를 취하는 동사이다.

25 '그들은 절도범을 추적하는 것을 포기했다.'라는 의미로, give up은 목적어로 동명사를 취하는 동사이다. 따라서 to chase가 chasing이 되어야 한다.

26 '그 소녀들은 프랑스어를 배우고 싶어 한다.'라는 의미로, want는 목적어로 to부정사를 취하는 동사이다. 따라서 learning은 to learn이 되어야 한다.

27 「It is no use+-ing」는 '~해도 소용없다'라는 의미의 동명사 관용 표현이다.

28 remember는 to부정사와 동명사를 모두 취할 수 있지만, 「remember+to부정사」는 '~할 것을 기억하다', 「remember+동명사」는 '~한 것을 기억하다'라는 의미이다.

29 「how/what about+-ing」는 '~하는 것이 어때?'라는 의미의 관용 표현이다.

30 try는 목적어로 to부정사와 동명사를 취할 수 있지만, 「try+to부정사」는 '~하려고 애쓰다'라는 의미이고, 「try+동명사」는 '시험 삼아 ~해보다'라는 의미이다.

31 ① 「feel like+-ing」는 '~하고 싶다'라는 의미의 관용 표현으로 do가 doing이 되어야 한다. '무언가 재미있는 것을 하고 싶어.'라는 의미이다.

② 「go+-ing」는 '~하러 가다'라는 의미의 관용 표현으로 ski가 skiing이 되어야 하며, '스키 타러 가는 게 어때?'라는 의미이다. ③ '~할 필요가 있다'라는 의미로 need는 to부정사를 취하므로 buying이 to buy가 되어야 하며 '나는 새 스키 부츠 한 켤레를 사야 해.'라는 의미이다.

32 'Neil Armstrong이 유명한 이유는 그가 달 위를 걸은 최초의 인간이기 때문이다.'라는 의미이며 '처음 달 위를 걸은 것으로 유명하다.'라는 의미로 바꿔 쓸 수 있다. 따라서 전치사 for의 목적어 역할을 하는 동명사 being이 와야 한다.

33 '도와준 것을 기억한다.'라는 의미가 되어야 하므로 '~한 것을 기억하다'라는 의미의 「remember+동명사」가 되어야 한다.

34 동명사의 부정은 「not/never+동명사」의 형태로 나타낸다.

35 동명사는 '~하는 것', '~하기'라는 의미로, 주어, 목적어, 보어 역할을 하며 「동사원형+-ing」의 형태로 나타낸다.

36 「look forward to+-ing」는 '~하는 것을 고대하다'라는 의미의 관용 표현이다.

보너스 유형별 문제 p.92

1 ⓐ freezing ⓑ to fix ⓒ asking
ⓓ repairing ⓔ studying

2 Try updating your apps.

3 ③

[1-2] A 내 스마트폰이 자꾸 먹통이 돼. 어떻게 고쳐야 하는지 모르겠어.
B 앱들을 업그레이드 해봐.
A 벌써 그렇게 했어. 그런데 소용없었어.
B 그럼, Felix에게 도움을 청하는 게 어때? 그는 전자기기를 아주 잘 고쳐.
A Felix? 그는 요즘 중간고사를 준비하느라고 바빠.
B 그러면 그냥 서비스센터에 맡기자.

1 ⓐ '계속 ~하다'라는 의미의 표현은 「keep + -ing」 ⓑ '~하는 법'이라는 의미로 「how to + 동사원형」 ⓒ '~하는 게 어때?'라는 의미의 표현은 「how[what] about -ing」 ⓓ 전치사의 목적어로 동명사가 필요하므로 repairing ⓔ '~ 하느라 바쁘다'라는 의미의 표현은 「be busy -ing」

2 '시험 삼아 (한번) ~하다'라는 의미의 표현은 「try + -ing」

3 사무실에서 불과 두 블록 떨어진 곳에 Joe's Burger라는 작은 식당이 있다. 가깝고 가격도 적당해서 일주일에 몇 번은 점심시간이나 퇴근길에 간다. 하지만 좋은 점만 있는 것은 아니다. 이 식당은 메뉴가 다양하지 않아서 햄버거와 샐러드, 음료 몇 가지만 판다. 햄버거를 먹을 기분이 아니면 다른 식당을 찾아야 한다. 공간도 협소하고 서비스도 다소 느린 편이다. 손님이 많은 점심때는 자리에 앉으려고 줄을 길게 서야 한다. 식당이 좀 더 컸으면 좋겠다. 24시간 운영하는 식당이라 늦게 퇴근해도 항상 들를 수 있긴 하지만, 주차장이 없어서 차를 가지러 사무실 건물로 다시 가야 한다.
'~하고 싶다'라는 말을 「feel like -ing」로 나타내므로 to have를 having으로 써야 옳다.

Chapter 6

6-1 분사 p.94

Exercise 1

1 used
2 smiling
3 standing
4 made

Exercise 2

1 cleaned
2 fallen
3 sleeping
4 burning
5 broken
6 parked

6-2 명사를 수식하는 분사 p.95

Exercise 1

1 flying airplane
2 caught
3 fallen
4 The girl standing
5 stolen diamond ring

Exercise 2

1 dying
2 burned
3 painted
4 crying
5 written
6 sitting

Exercise 3

1 spoken
2 sleeping
3 hiding
4 standing
5 lost
6 built

Exercise 4

1 the barking dog
2 the wall painted
3 the dying bird
4 a used TV
5 a letter written
6 The boy wearing a blue hat
7 The picture hanging on the wall

6-3 동사의 활용에 쓰이는 분사 p.97

Exercise 1

1 met
2 sitting
3 unlocked
4 cleaned
5 thinking
6 been

Exercise 2

1 invited
2 playing
3 been
4 baking
5 driven

6-4 감정을 나타내는 분사 p.98

Exercise 1

1 interested
2 satisfied
3 bored
4 disappointing
5 embarrassing
6 amazed

Exercise 2

1 tired
2 surprising
3 pleased
4 boring
5 exciting
6 disappointed

Exercise 3

1 frightened, frightening
2 annoyed, annoying
3 surprised, surprising
4 pleasing, pleased

6-5 현재분사와 동명사 p.100

Exercise 1

1 현재분사
2 현재분사
3 동명사
4 동명사
5 현재분사
6 동명사

Exercise 2

1 nodded off during the boring movie
2 cannot walk without a walking stick
3 were cleaning up the garage
4 has a huge swimming pool
5 is helping customers feel comfortable

6-6 분사구문 p.101

Exercise 1

1 Watching
2 Seeing
3 Having
4 Showing

Exercise 2

1 Taking, medicine
2 Having, lunch
3 Being, tired
4 Waiting, for, me

Review Test p.102

01 ④	02 ③	03 ③	04 ②	05 ②	06 ③
07 ②	08 ①	09 ④	10 ③	11 ⑤	12 ④
13 ②	14 ②	15 ①	16 ⑤	17 ②	18 ③
19 ④	20 ④	21 ④	22 ④	23 ②	24 ①

25 excited
26 used
27 disappointed
28 annoying
29 stood → standing
30 embarrassing → embarrassed
31 The boy wearing a yellow cap
32 The computer set up on that desk
33 a novel written in French
34 Losing my bike
35 Trying hard
36 Feeling nervous

01 '도난당한'이라는 수동의 의미로, car를 수식하는 과거분사 stolen이 와야 한다.

02 '문 밖에 서 있는 여자'라는 능동의 의미로, woman을 수식하는 현재분사 standing이 와야 한다.

03 '재미있는 사람'이라는 능동의 의미로, person을 수식하는 현재분사 interesting이 와야 한다.

04 '우울함에 틀림없다.'라는 의미로, 'She'가 감정을 느끼는 주체이기 때문에 과거분사 depressed가 와야 한다.

05 부사절 If you turn left at the corner를 분사구문으로 바꾼 문장이므로 빈칸에는 Turning이 와야 한다. '왼쪽으로 돌면'이라는 의미이다.

06
- '풀숲에 숨겨진 상자'라는 수동의 의미가 되어야 하므로 과거분사 hidden이 와야 한다.
- 내 언니와 얘기를 나누는 남자'라는 능동의 의미가 되어야 하므로 현재분사 talking이 와야 한다.

07
- '흰색으로 칠해진 울타리'라는 수동의 의미가 되어야 하므로 과거분사 painted가 와야 한다.
- Because[As/Since] I felt tired를 분사구문으로 바꾼 문장이므로 빈칸에는 Feeling이 와야 한다. '나는 피곤했기 때문에'라는 의미이다.

08 분사구문을 부사절로 바꿀 때 빈칸에 알맞은 접속사를 고르는 문제이다. '그는 부유하지만, 행복하지 않다.'라는 의미로, 빈칸에는 '~임에도 불구하고'라는 뜻의 양보 접속사가 와야 한다.

09 분사구문을 부사절로 바꿀 때 빈칸에 알맞은 접속사를 고르는 문제이다. '우편물을 보내는 것을 잊어버렸기 때문에 나는 우체국에 들르지 않았다.'라는 의미로, 빈칸에는 '~ 때문에'라는 뜻의 이유를 나타내는 접속사가 와야 한다.

10 A 넌 짜증이 난 것처럼 보인다. 무슨 일이니?
B Jenny가 나를 세 시간이나 기다리게 해놓고 심지어 나오지도 않았어.

'짜증이 난 것처럼 보인다.'라는 의미로, 'You'가 감정을 느끼는 주체이기 때문에 과거분사 annoyed, '세 시간 동안 나를 기다리게 했다.'라는 의미로, 목적어와 목적격보어의 관계가 능동이므로 현재분사 waiting이 되어야 한다.

11 A 나 정말 신 나. 나 처음으로 도쿄에 가게 됐어.
B 우와, 나 여러 번 도쿄에 갔다 왔어. 정말 가볼 만한 흥미로운 곳이 많아.

'정말 흥분된다.'라는 의미로, 'I'가 감정을 느끼는 주체이기 때문에 과거분사 excited, '재미있는 곳'이라는 의미로, places가 감정을 일으키는 원인이기 때문에 현재분사 interesting이 되어야 한다.

12 ① '잠을 자고 있는 개'라는 의미로, dog를 수식하는 현재분사, ② '아기가 편히 잠을 자고 있다.'라는 의미로, 진행시제를 나타내는 현재분사, ③ '잠을 자고 있었다.'라는 의미로, 진행시제를 나타내는 현재분사, ④ '잠자기 위한 가방'이라는 의미로, sleeping은 bag의 용도나 목적을 나타내는 동명사, ⑤ '벤치에서 잠을 자고 있는 남자'라는 의미로, man을 수식하는 현재분사이다.

13 ① '구르는 돌'이라는 능동의 의미로, 현재분사가 와야 한다. 따라서 rolled가 rolling이 되어야 한다. ③ '이상한 모자를 쓰고 있는 여자'라는 능동의 의미로, 현재분사가 와야 한다. 따라서 worn이 wearing이 되어야 한다. ④ '우리에 갇힌 원숭이들'이라는 수동의 의미로, 과거분사가 와야 한다. 따라서 trapping이 trapped가 되어야 한다. ⑤ '빛나는 별'이라는 능동의 의미로, shined가 shining이 되어야 한다.

14 부사절 Because she had a bad headache를 분사구문으로 알맞게 바꾼 것을 고르는 문제이다. 부사절을 분사구문으로 만들 때 부사절의 접속사(Because)를 없애고, 부사절과 주절의 주어가 같을 경우 부사절의 주어(she)를 없앤 다음, 부사절의 동사(had)를 -ing 형태로 바꾸면 된다. 따라서 Having a bad headache를 고른다.

15 부사절 While I was taking a bath를 분사구문으로 알맞게 바꾼 것을 고르는 문제이다. 부사절을 분사구문으로 만들 때 부사절의 접속사(While)를 없애고, 부사절과 주절의 주어가 같을 경우 부사절의 주어(I)를 없앤 다음, 부사절의 동사(was taking)를 -ing 형태로 바꾸면 된다. 따라서 Being taking a bath가 되는데 분사구문에서 being은 생략할 수 있다.

16 주어진 문장의 밑줄 친 부분은 '네 옆에 앉아 있는 소년'이라는 의미로, 명사를 수식하는 현재분사이다. ① '책을 읽는 것을 좋아한다.'라는 의미로, like의 목적어 역할을 하는 동명사, ② '취미 중 하나가 사냥이다.'라는 의미로, 문장에서 보어 역할을 하는 동명사, ③ '수영장'이라는 의미로, 용도나 목적을 나타내는 동명사, ④ '오랫동안 앉아 있는 것'이라는 의미로, 문장에서 주어 역할을 하는 동명사, ⑤ '잠자고 있는 아기'라는 의미로, 명사를 수식하는 현재분사이다.

17 주어진 문장의 밑줄 친 부분은 '식당칸'이라는 의미로, 용도나 목적을 나타내는 동명사이다. ① '우리에게 손을 흔들고 있는 남자'라는 의미로, man을 수식하는 현재분사, ② '수영복'이라는 의미로, 용도나 목적을 나타내는 동명사, ③ '신나는 스포츠 행사'이라는 의미로, 명사를 수식하는 현재분사, ④ '길거리를 헤매고 있는 소녀들'이라는 의미로, 명사를 수식하는 현재분사, ⑤ '어느 것이 더 재미있니?'라는 의미로, 감정을 일으키는 원인을 나타내는 현재분사이다.

18 • '어떻게 그렇게 잘 만들어졌는지에 대해 놀랐다.'라는 의미로, 'I'가 감정을 느끼는 주체이기 때문에 amaze는 과거분사 amazed가 되어야 한다.
• '정말 멋진 공연이야!'라는 의미로, 'concert'가 감정을 일으키는 원인이기 때문에 amaze는 현재분사 amazing이 되어야 한다.

19 부사절을 분사구문으로 만들 때 부사절의 접속사를 없애고, 부사절과 주절의 주어가 같을 경우 부사절의 주어를 없앤 다음, 부사절의 동사를 -ing 형태로 바꾸면 된다. 따라서 ① Arriving she home은 Arriving home, ② Listen은 Listening, ③ After finishing I는 Finishing, ⑤ Being gone은 Going이 되어야 한다.

20 ④ '무서운 이야기'라는 의미로, story가 감정을 일으키는 원인이기 때문에 scared는 scaring이 되어야 한다.

21 ④ '막 구워진 빵'이라는 의미로, bread와 수동의 관계이므로 baking이 baked가 되어야 한다.

22 'Everyone'이 감정을 느끼는 주체이기 때문에 과거분사 satisfied를, news가 감정을 일으키는 원인이기 때문에 현재분사 pleasing을 고른다.

23 「주어+지각동사+목적어+목적격보어」 어순의 5형식에서 진행의 의미를 강조하는 경우에는 현재분사가 오기 때문에 목적격보어로 hunting을, it은 감정을 일으키는 원인이기 때문에 현재분사 amazing을 고른다.

24 ① '이 문제에 답을 해보는 건 어떨까?'라는 의미로, 전치사 about의 목적어 역할을 하는 동명사, ② '전화벨이 울리고 있다.'라는 의미로, be동사와 함께 진행시제를 나타내는 현재분사, ③ '누군가가 문을 두드리고 있다.'라는 의미로, be동사와 함께 진행시제를 나타내는 현재분사, ④ '끓고 있는 물'이라는 의미로, 명사를 수식하는 현재분사, ⑤ '울고 있는 아이'라는 의미로, 명사를 수식하는 현재분사이다.

25 'My parents'가 감정을 느끼는 주체이기 때문에 과거분사 excited가 와야 한다.

26 '중고차'라는 수동의 의미가 되어야 하므로 과거분사 used가 와야 한다.

27 'Everyone'이 감정을 느끼는 주체이기 때문에 과거분사 disappointed가 와야 한다.

28 'It'이 감정을 일으키는 원인이기 때문에 현재분사 annoying이 와야 한다.

29 'Andy 옆에 서 있는 소녀'라는 능동의 의미이므로 stood가 standing이 되어야 한다.

30 'Ted는 당황해 하는 것처럼 보였다.'라는 의미로, 'Ted'가 감정을 느끼는 주체이기 때문에 embarrassing이 embarrassed가 되어야 한다.

31 분사가 수식어구와 함께 명사를 수식하는 경우에는 명사 뒤에서 수식한다. 따라서 The boy wearing a yellow cap이 되어야 한다.

32 분사가 수식어구와 함께 명사를 수식하는 경우에는 명사 뒤에서 수식한다. 따라서 The computer set up on that desk가 되어야 한다.

33 분사가 수식어구와 함께 명사를 수식하는 경우에는 명사 뒤에서 수식한다. 따라서 a novel written in French가 되어야 한다.

34 부사절을 분사구문으로 만들기 위해 부사절의 접속사 Because를 없애고, 부사절과 주절의 주어가 같기 때문에 부사절의 주어 I를 없앤 다음, 부사절의 동사 lost를 -ing 형태로 바꾼다. '자전거를 잃어버려서 나는 학교에 걸어갔다.'라는 의미이다.

35 접속사 If를 없애고, 부사절과 주절의 주어가 같기 때문에 부사절의 주어 you를 없앤 다음, 부사절의 동사 try를 -ing 형태로 바꾼다. '열심히 노력하면 너는 그 시험에 합격할 것이다.'라는 의미이다.

36 접속사 When을 없애고, 부사절과 주절의 주어가 같기 때문에 부사절의 주어 I를 없앤 다음, 부사절의 동사 feel을 -ing 형태로 바꾼다. '나는 초조할 때 항상 "내가 최고다."라고 혼잣말을 한다.'라는 의미이다.

보너스 유형별 문제

p.106

1 the girl talking with you

2 meeting her

3 ③

[1-2] A 복도에서 너랑 얘기하고 있던 여자애는 누구였어?
B 그녀는 Evelyn이야. 얼마 전에 시카고에서 이사 왔어.
A 그녀는 어때?
B 그녀는 예쁘고, 똑똑하고, 사랑스러운 것 같아.
A 그녀에게 날 소개해 줄 수 있어?
B 당연하지. 그녀를 만나면 바로 그녀와 사랑에 빠지게 될 걸.

1 분사가 수식어구(with you)와 함께 쓰여 명사 뒤에서 꾸며주어야 한다. '~하고 있는'이라는 능동적 의미를 나타내기 위해 현재분사를 쓴다.

2 When you meet her를 분사구문으로 바꿔 쓸 때 meeting her로 쓰고 더 확실한 의미를 전달하기 위해 접속사를 그대로 남겨둘 수 있다.

3 고등학생 때 나는 문제아였다. 공부에는 관심이 없었고 수업도 자주 빼먹었다. 아버지는 더 이상 참지 않으셨다. 아버지는 내가 제대로 교육도 받지 못한 채 이 세상에서 성공하기가 그리 쉽지 않다는 것을 깨닫길 바라셨다. 그래서 친구분이 소유하고 계신 구두 공장에서 나를 일하게 하셨다. 일을 하기 시작하면서 나는 몇 가지 불법 행위가 공장 안에서 일어나서 일부 직원이 체포되어 수감되었음을 알게 되었다. 나중에 알고 보니 동료 중 한 명이 잠입 수사관이었던 것이다. 그는 내가 경찰 업무에 관심이 있다는 것을 알고 나에게 잠입 수사관직을 제안했다.
공장(factory)은 친구에 의해 소유되는 것이므로 현재분사가 아닌 과거분사(owned)로 수식해야 옳다.

Chapter 7

7-1 재귀대명사 p.108

Exercise 1

1 herself
2 me
3 himself
4 yourself
5 herself
6 himself

Exercise 2

1 himself
2 ourselves
3 itself
4 herself

7-2 재귀대명사의 관용 표현 p.109

Exercise 1

1 by
2 yourself
3 himself
4 ourselves
5 himself
6 yourself
7 to himself

Exercise 2

1 make yourself at home
2 enjoyed ourselves
3 making myself understood
4 between ourselves
5 by himself

7-3 가주어 it p.110

Exercise 1

1 It is exciting to ride a horse.
2 It is true that Jamie will marry Gwen.
3 It is disappointing that Kevin lied to me.
4 It is considered rude to wear a hat indoors.

Exercise 2

1 It is exciting to experience other cultures.
2 It is convenient to take the subway in Seoul.
3 It makes me upset that no one believes me.
4 It is unbelievable that he doesn't know how to send an e-mail.

7-4 부정대명사 one, another, other p.111

Exercise 1

1 One
2 another
3 another
4 It
5 one
6 one
7 the other
8 one

Exercise 2

1 ones
2 others
3 it
4 The others
5 the other
6 another

Exercise 3

1 polite to others
2 another cup of tea
3 have the others
4 show me a smaller one
5 have pink ones
6 the other is a turtle
7 the red one in the middle

7-5 부정대명사 표현 p.113

Exercise 1

1 each other[one another]
2 One, the other
3 Some, others
4 One, the others
5 One, the other
6 Some, the others
7 One, another, the other

7-6 부정대명사 some, any p.114

Exercise 1

1 some	2 any
3 something	4 anything
5 any	6 some
7 some	8 any

Exercise 2

1 Someone	2 anyone
3 anything	4 something

7-7 부정대명사 each, every, all, both, no p.115

Exercise 1

1 no	2 are
3 loves	4 child
5 friends	6 caps
7 person	8 has
9 week	10 are

Exercise 2

1 are	2 needs
3 hands	4 coworkers
5 weekend	6 student

Exercise 3

1 no, children	2 each, team
3 every, month	4 all, of, my, money
5 both, of, them	

Exercise 4

1 Both of them are thirteen years old.
2 I go to church every Sunday.
3 All of us go to the same school.
4 There was no answer to my knock.
5 Each of the students has a different talent.

7-8 부정대명사 either, neither p.117

Exercise 1

1 Neither	2 Neither
3 either	4 Either

Exercise 2

1 neither of them takes after me
2 neither of us had the key
3 like either of them
4 met either of them

Review Test p.118

01 ②	02 ③	03 ⑤	04 ③	05 ①	06 ②
07 ③	08 ②	09 ⑤	10 ③	11 ④	12 ①
13 ③	14 ⑤	15 ③	16 ③	17 ③	18 ④
19 ②	20 ②	21 ③	22 ②	23 ③	

24 herself
25 no one [nobody]
26 is → are
27 in → by
28 players need → player needs
29 It is true that Victoria quit her job.
30 It is not so easy to take good pictures.
31 One, the other
32 both, either
33 enjoyed, ourselves
34 Neither, of, my, parents

01 '온종일 아무것도 하지 않았다.'라는 의미가 되어야 하므로 부정문에 쓰여 '아무것'이라는 의미를 나타내는 anything을 고른다. something은 '어떤 것'이라는 의미로, 긍정문에 쓰이고, nothing은 '아무것도 없음'이라는 의미로, 그 자체에 부정의 의미가 포함되어 있기 때문에 not 등의 다른 부정어와 함께 사용하지 않는다.

02 '다른 것을 보여 주시겠어요?'라는 의미가 되어야 하므로 '(같은 종류의) 또 다른 하나'라는 의미의 부정대명사 another가 와야 한다.

03 '나머지는 모두 오지 않았다.'라는 의미가 되어야 하므로 '나머지 전부'라는 의미의 부정대명사 the others를 고른다.

04 '네가 하나를 옮기면 나머지 하나는 내가 옮길 것이다.'라는 의미가 되어야 하므로 '(둘 중) 나머지 다른 하나'라는 의미의 부정대명사 the other를 고른다.

05 '시내 중심가에 하나 있어.'라는 의미가 되어야 하므로 같은 종류의 사물을 나타내는 부정대명사 one이 와야 한다.

06
- '좋은 생각 있니?'라는 의미가 되어야 하므로 '얼마간', '약간'이라는 의미로 의문문에 쓰이는 any가 와야 한다.
- '우물에는 물이 없다.'라는 의미가 되어야 하므로 부정문에 쓰이는 any가 와야 한다.
- '어떤 질문도 기꺼이 응답해 드리겠습니다.'라는 의미가 되어야 하므로 긍정문에 쓰여 '어떤 ~라도'라는 의미를 나타내는 부정대명사 any가 와야 한다.

07
- '바구니에 달걀 몇 개가 있다.'라는 의미가 되어야 하므로 '얼마간', '약간'이라는 의미로, 긍정문에 쓰이는 some이 와야 한다.
- '차를 좀 더 드실래요?'라는 의미로, 권유 · 의뢰를 나타내는 문장에서는 부정대명사 some이 와야 한다.
- '나에게 돈을 좀 빌려줘.'라는 의미로 some이 와야 한다.

08 '어떤 ~도 아닌[없는]'이라는 의미로, 명사를 수식하는 no는 not any로 바꿔 쓸 수 있다. 따라서 any가 와야 한다. '당신의 건강에는 아무런 문제도 없다.'라는 의미이다.

09 ⑤ '나의 부모님께서 이 맛있는 케이크를 직접 만드셨다.'라는 의미로, 주어를 강조하는 재귀대명사의 강조용법이다. 주어가 My parents, 즉 3인칭 복수로 herself는 themselves가 되어야 한다.

10 • '우리는 제 시간에 그 일을 끝내기 위해 서로 도와주었다.'라는 의미가 되어야 한다.
• '사람들은 종종 크리스마스 때 서로 선물을 준다.'라는 의미가 되어야 한다. 따라서 빈칸에 공통으로 들어갈 말은 '서로'의 의미를 가진 each other를 고른다.

11 • '지갑을 잃어버려서 새 것을 사야 한다.'라는 의미로, 같은 종류의 사물을 나타내는 부정대명사 one이 와야 한다.
• '어느 것을 원하시나요?'라는 의미로, which와 함께 쓰여 특정한 것[사람]을 나타내는 대명사 one이 와야 한다.

12 '스스로'라는 의미의 재귀대명사 관용 표현은 「by+oneself」이다.

13 '하나 더', '또 다른 하나'라는 의미의 부정대명사 another를 고른다.

14 A 엄마, 저 새 스마트폰을 사고 싶어요.
B 넌 벌써 거기 하나 가지고 있잖니.
A 하지만 그건 너무 구형이잖아요.

첫 번째 빈칸에는 같은 종류의 사물을 나타내는 부정대명사 one, 두 번째 빈칸에는 앞에서 언급된 동일한 사물을 나타내는 it이 와야 한다.

15 A 우리는 먹을 것이 없어. 식료품을 사러 가야 해.
B 너 그거 아니? 우리가 주로 가는 상점이 문을 닫았어.
A 걱정하지 마. 퀸즈 가에 또 하나가 있어.

첫 번째 빈칸에는 '어떤 ~도 없는'이라는 의미를 나타내는 no, 두 번째 빈칸에는 '또 다른 하나'라는 의미의 another가 와야 한다.

16 '(여럿 중) 일부는 ~, 다른 일부는 …'라는 의미의 부정대명사 표현은 「some ~, others …」이다.

17 '(둘 중) 하나는 ~, 나머지 하나는 …'라는 의미의 부정대명사 표현은 「one ~, the other …」이다.

18 '이해시키다'라는 의미의 재귀대명사 관용 표현은 「make oneself understood」이다.

19 주어진 문장이 '사람들은 자신의 약속을 지켜야 한다.'라는 의미로, 밑줄 친 one은 일반적인 사람을 지칭한다. ① '그 학생들 중 한 명이 프랑스 출신이다.'라는 의미로, one은 '(한 집단 중) 하나[한 명]'이라는 의미의 한정사이다. ② '사람들은 자신의 부모를 공경해야 한다.'라는 의미로, one은 일반적인 사람을 지칭한다. ③ '나는 시계를 잃어버렸다. 그래서 새것을 사야 한다.'라는 의미로, 같은 종류의 사물을 나타내는 부정대명사이다. ④ '세계 인구의 5분의 1이 중국에 산다.'라는 의미로, 숫자를 나타내는 한정사이다. ⑤ '나는 책을 두 권 샀다. 한 권은 엄마를 위한 것이고, 다른 한 권은 내 것이다.'라는 의미로, one은 둘 중 하나를 지칭하는 부정대명사이다.

20 ② neither는 '(둘 중) 어느 것도 아닌'이라는 의미이며 「neither+단수명사+단수동사」 또는 「neither+of+복수명사+단수동사」의 형태로 나타낸다. 따라서 are는 is가 되어야 한다.

21 ① '너 자신을 자책하지 마라.'라는 의미의 명령문이다. 명령문은 앞에 주어 you를 생략하여 동사원형을 시작하기 때문에 yourself는 주어와 목적어가 같은 대상임을 나타내는 재귀대명사의 재귀용법, ② '몸조심하세요.'라는 의미의 명령문으로 yourself는 주어와 of의 목적어가 같은 대상임을 나타내는 재귀대명사의 재귀용법, ③ '나는 그런 일을 하지 않겠다.'라는 의미로, 주어를 강조하는 재귀대명사의 강조용법, ④ 'Eddie는 한동안 혼잣말로 중얼거렸다.'라는 의미로, 주어와 to의 목적어가 같은 대상임을 나타내는 재귀대명사의 재귀용법, ⑤ '내 아들들은 캠프에서 즐거운 시간을 보냈다.'라는 의미로, 「enjoy oneself」는 '즐거운 시간을 보내다'라는 의미의 재귀대명사 관용 표현이며, themselves는 주어와 목적어가 같은 대상임을 나타내는 재귀대명사의 재귀용법이다.

22 '어떤 회사는 물건을 판매하고, 어떤 회사는 서비스를 제공한다.'라는 의미가 되어야 하므로 '(여럿 중) 일부는 ~, 다른 일부는 …'라는 의미의 부정대명사 표현 「some ~, others …」를 고른다.

23 주어진 문장은 '아침에 업무에 집중하는 것은 힘들다.'라는 의미로, 밑줄 친 it은 문장에서 주어(to focus on work in the morning)를 뒤로 보내고 원래 주어 자리에 쓰는 가주어 it이다. ① '오늘은 어제보다 더 춥다.'라는 의미로, 시간, 날짜, 날씨, 계절, 온도 등을 나타내는 비인칭 대명사 it, ② 앞서 언급된 동일한 사물을 나타내는 대명사 it, ③ '혼자 그것을 하는 것은 불가능한 것 같아.'라는 의미로, 주어(to do it by myself)를 뒤로 보내고 주어 자리에 쓴 가주어 it, ④ '내가 창문을 열었을 때 여전히 어두웠다.'라는 의미로 시간, 날짜, 날씨, 계절, 온도 등을 나타내는 비인칭 대명사 it, ⑤ 'Justin이 그 영화를 추천했고, 나는 그 영화가 정말 좋았다.'라는 의미로, it은 앞에 언급된 the movie를 가리키는 대명사 it이다.

24 '그녀는 지금 거울에 비친 자신을 보고 있다.'라는 의미가 되어야 하므로 주어와 목적어가 같은 대상임을 나타내는 재귀대명사가 와야 한다. she의 재귀대명사는 herself이다.

25 '거기에는 아무도 없다.'라는 의미가 되어야 하므로 '어떤 ~도 없는'이라는 의미로 명사를 수식하는 no를 사용하여 no one, 또는 '아무도 ~ (아니다)'라는 의미의 nobody가 와야 한다.

26 '그들 둘 다 똑똑하고 재미있다.'라는 의미의 문장이다. both는 '둘 다'라는 의미로, 명사를 수식하거나 단독으로 쓰이는 부정대명사로 「both+복수명사+복수동사」 또는 「both+of+복수명사+복수동사」의 형태로 사용된다. 따라서 is는 are가 되어야 한다.

27 '갑자기, 문이 쾅하며 저절로 닫혔다.'라는 의미로, '저절로'라는 의미의 재귀대명사 관용 표현은 by itself이다. 따라서 in은 by가 되어야 한다.

28 '각 선수들은 배트와 글러브를 필요로 한다.'라는 의미이고, each는 「each+단수명사+단수동사」 또는 「each+of+복수명사+단수동사」의 형태로 사용된다. 따라서 players need는 player needs가 되어야 한다.

29 That Victoria quit her job이 문장의 주어로, 문장의 주어가 긴 경우 이를 뒤로 보내고 그 자리에 가주어 it을 쓰는 가주어 · 진주어 구문이다. 가주어 it을 문장 앞에 쓰고, 진주어(That Victoria quit her job)를 문장 뒤로 보내면 된다.

30 To take good pictures가 문장의 주어로, 문장의 주어가 긴 경우 이를 뒤로 보내고 그 자리에 가주어 it을 쓰는 가주어 · 진주어 구문이다. 가주어 it을 문장 앞에 쓰고, 진주어(To take good pictures)를 문장 뒤로 보내면 된다.

31 '하나는 휴대전화이고, 나머지 하나는 다이어리이다.'라는 의미가 되어야 하므로 '(둘 중) 하나는 ~, 나머지 하나는 …'이라는 의미의 부정대명사 표현 「one ~, the other …」가 와야 한다.

32 '엄마가 내게 두 종류의 셔츠를 사주셨고, 둘 다 검은색이었다. 엄마에게 고맙다고 했지만, 나는 둘 중 어느 쪽도 마음에 들지 않았다.'라는 의미가 되어야 한다. 따라서 첫 번째 빈칸에는 '둘 다'라는 의미의 부정대명사 both, 두 번째 빈칸에는 부정문에서 쓰여 '둘 중 어느 쪽도 ~ (아니다)'라는 의미의 either가 와야 한다.

33 '즐거운 시간을 보내다'라는 의미의 재귀대명사 관용 표현은 「enjoy oneself」이다.

34 내용상 '(둘 중) 어느 쪽도 아닌'이라는 의미의 부정대명사가 와야 하기 때문에 「neither+of+복수명사」를 써서 나타낸다.

보너스 유형별 문제 p.122

1 ⓐ itself ⓑ his books
2 each book has its own lesson
3 ③

[1-2] A 너 또 '올리버 트위스트'를 읽고 있니?
B 응, 이건 내가 가장 좋아하는 책이야.
A 너는 왜 그렇게 그것을 좋아하니?
B 음, 그것이 그 자체로는 재미있지 않지만, 나는 사회의 어두운 부분에 관한 이야기를 좋아하지.
A 알겠어. 그러면 찰스 디킨스가 네가 가장 좋아하는 작가야?
B 응, 나는 그의 책들 대부분을 읽었어. 어떤 것은 훌륭하고 어떤 것들은 지루해. 하지만 각각의 책은 그것만의 교훈이 있어. 그의 책은 읽을 만한 가치가 있어.

1 ⓐ in itself: 본래, 그 자체로
ⓑ all 뒤에 셀 수 있는 명사가 올 경우, 복수형으로 써야 한다.

2 「each + 단수명사 + 단수동사」

3 우리는 모두 때로 실수를 한다. 심지어 전화번호를 누를 때에도 말이다. 전화를 건 사람이 잘못 걸어서 사과를 한다면 대부분의 사람들처럼 "괜찮아요"라고 하면 된다. 아무 말도 하지 않고 전화를 끊어버리는 것은 무례한 것이다. 전화를 잘못 건다면 당신은 다른 사람을 방해한 것이므로 "죄송합니다, 잘못 걸었습니다"라고 말하는 것이 예의이다.
진주어 'to say ~'를 대신하여 가주어를 쓸 수 있는데 that이 it을 써야 옳다.

Chapter 8

8-1 형용사의 용법 p.124

Exercise 1

1 o　2 ×　3 o　4 ×
5 o　6 ×　7 o　8 ×

Exercise 2

1 alive　2 alone
3 awake　4 asleep

Exercise 3

1 늦었다　2 현재　3 출석했나요
4 고인이 된　5 확실하다　6 어떤

Exercise 4

1 Are you a good runner?
2 We all found the book boring.
3 My little brother is afraid of heights.
4 All of the students were present at the event.
5 A couple of drunken teenagers broke the window.

8-2 주의해야 할 형용사 p.126

Exercise 1

1 lovely　2 friendly　3 blind
4 nicely　5 stupidly　6 are

Exercise 2

1 일상생활에서　2 가난하고 아픈 사람들을
3 죽은 사람들은　4 귀여운

8-3 형용사의 어순 p.127

Exercise 1

1 a beautiful sunny
2 The old Italian
3 my favorite blue
4 These big black
5 nice small metal
6 big old fur
7 pretty little yellow

Exercise 2

1 a nice black leather jacket
2 a sad French film
3 some big round tables
4 a strange little boy
5 the beautiful old tower

8-4 주의해야 할 부사 I p.128

Exercise 1

1 형용사　2 부사　3 부사
4 형용사　5 형용사　6 부사

Exercise 2

1 lately　2 hard　3 hardly
4 nearly　5 late

Exercise 3

1 o　2 high　3 close
4 o　5 Nearly

Exercise 4

1 shortly　2 hardly　3 hard
4 short　5 close　6 closely

Exercise 5

1 nearly　2 near
3 lately　4 highly

8-5 주의해야 할 부사 II p.130

Exercise 1

1 such
2 so
3 such
4 so
5 so
6 such

Exercise 2

1 such a funny joke
2 such a hard job
3 such an old man
4 so afraid
5 so early
6 so popular

8-6 주의해야 할 부사 III p.131

Exercise 1

1 yet
2 still
3 already
4 still
5 already
6 yet

Exercise 2

1 Has Bill found a new job yet?
2 The train has already left the station.
3 Is your little brother still in bed?
4 Sam hasn't decided what to choose yet.
5 Mom already knows that I've lost her favorite earrings.

8-7 원급 비교 p.132

Exercise 1

1 as, tall, as
2 ten, times
3 not, as, heavy, as
4 twice
5 cheaper, than
6 as, big[large], as

Exercise 2

1 could
2 well
3 twice as
4 soon
5 taking
6 I could
7 more
8 as high

Exercise 3

1 didn't wake up as early as
2 three times as many cookies as
3 is not as heavy as
4 is not as tall as
5 is three times as large as

Exercise 4

1 as fast as I could
2 as often as I can
3 as soon as possible
4 twenty-five times as long as

8-8 비교급 p.134

Exercise 1

1 more difficult, less difficult
2 more often, less often
3 more crowded, less crowded
4 more expensive, less expensive

Exercise 2

1 much
2 a lot
3 more
4 still
5 far

Exercise 3

1 more money, less money
2 more expensive than, less expensive than
3 more interesting than, less interesting than

Exercise 4

1 more useful than
2 far more crowded than
3 lower than
4 less complicated than

8-9 최상급 p.136

Exercise 1

1 of
2 hottest
3 known
4 taller
5 the very
6 long
7 man

Exercise 2

1 richer than any other man, No other man, richer than, No other man, as rich as
2 taller than any other building, No other building, taller than, No other building, as tall as
3 faster than any other animal, No other animal, faster than, No other animal, as fast as

Exercise 3

1 the funniest man (that) I have[I've] ever met
2 no other actor in our country is greater than
3 by far the fastest runner
4 wiser than any other woman
5 country in the world is as small as
6 one of the most beautiful cities

Review Test

p.138

01 ④ 02 ② 03 ② 04 ⑤ 05 ② 06 ③
07 ④ 08 ③ 09 ② 10 ② 11 ② 12 ④
13 ③ 14 ④ 15 ⑤ 16 ③ 17 ⑤ 18 ③
19 ② 20 ② 21 ④ 22 ④ 23 ③

24 better → well
25 hard → hardly
26 possible
27 twice, as, old
28 most, beautiful
29 better
30 alive
31 the sick [sick people]
32 present
33 ①: 매우 ②: 대단히, 매우 ③: 최근 ④: 확실한
34 that big red plastic box
35 heard the news yet
36 such a horrible sight

01 빈칸에는 서술적 용법으로 쓰는 형용사가 와야 한다. 따라서 동사 fall과 함께 '잠이 들다'라는 의미를 나타내는 asleep을 고른다.

02 '어떻게 수영하는지 아직 모른다.'라는 의미가 되어야 하므로 부정문에서 '아직'이라는 의미를 나타내는 부사 yet을 고른다.

03 'Mary는 매우 수다스럽다'라는 의미가 되어야 하므로 a big mouth 앞에 위치할 수 있는 부사를 고른다. such는 '매우', '대단히'라는 의미로, 명사와 함께 쓰인 형용사를 강조하여 「such+(a(n))+형용사+명사」의 어순으로 쓰인다.

04 '저 귀여운 작은 인형들 좀 봐.'라는 의미로, 명사 dolls를 수식하는 형용사를 고르는 문제이다. '귀여운'이라는 의미로, -ly로 끝나는 형용사인 lovely가 적절하며, happily, luckily, truly, sadly는 부사이므로 빈칸에 들어갈 수 없다.

05 '올해가 작년보다 훨씬 더 춥다.'라는 의미로, '훨씬'이라는 뜻으로, 비교급을 강조하는 표현이 와야 한다. 비교급 강조 표현에는 much, still, a lot, far, even 등이 있다. very는 비교급을 강조할 수 없기 때문에 적절하지 않다.

06 빈칸에는 명사 앞에서 명사를 수식하는 한정적 용법의 형용사가 와야 한다. afraid는 서술적 용법으로 쓰이는 형용사로 적절하지 않다.

07 'Mike의 형은 Mike보다 세 배나 많은 돈을 가지고 있다.'라는 의미가 되어야 하므로 '~보다 …배 ~한/하게'라는 의미의 「배수사+as+형용사/부사의 원급+as」의 형태가 되어야 하므로 three times가 적절하다.

08 '방으로 가능한 한 조용히 살금살금 들어갔다.'라는 의미가 되어야 하므로 '가능한 한 ~하게'라는 의미의 「as+형용사/부사의 원급+as+possible」 또는 「as+형용사/부사의 원급+as+주어+can/could」의 형태가 와야 한다.

09 '그것은 내가 이제껏 읽어본 책 중에 가장 길지만, 내가 기대했던 것보다 훨씬 더 재미있다.'라는 의미가 되어야 한다. '지금까지 ~ 한 것 중 가장 …한'이라는 의미의 표현은 「the+최상급(+that)+주어+have/has ever+과거분사」로 첫 번째 빈칸에는 longest가 적절하다. much는 비교급 앞에 쓰여 '훨씬'이라는 의미로 비교급을 강조하는 표현이기 때문에 두 번째 빈칸에는 비교급 more가 적절하다.

10 'David는 나만큼 많은 책을 읽지 않는다.'라는 의미이다. 「A not as[so]+원급+as B」는 「B 비교급+than A」로 바꿔 쓸 수 있다.

11 '우리 오빠는 여동생보다 세 배나 몸무게가 많이 나간다.'라는 의미이다. 「배수사+as+형용사/부사의 원급+as」는 「배수사+비교급+than」으로 바꿔 쓸 수 있다.

12 형용사의 어순을 묻는 문제로 「한정사(some)+주관적 형용사(cute)+크기(little)+국적(Chinese)」의 어순이 되어야 한다.

13 ① '고요한 물이 깊게 흐른다.'라는 의미이며, deep은 '깊게'라는 뜻으로, 동사 runs를 수식하는 부사, ② '우리 엄마는 노래를 꽤 잘 부르신다.'라는 의미이며, well은 '잘'이라는 뜻으로, 동사 sings를 수식하는 부사, ③ '아무도 그 파티에 늦지 않았다.'라는 의미이며, late는 '늦은'이라는 뜻으로, 보어 역할을 하는 형용사, ④ '그는 자신의 입을 거의 열지 않는다.'라는 의미이며, hardly는 '거의 ~아니다'라는 뜻으로, 동사 opens 수식하는 부사, ⑤ '나는 너를 행복하게 하기 위해 열심히 노력했다.'라는 의미이며, hard는 '열심히'라는 뜻으로, 동사를 수식하는 부사이다.

14 최상급은 「the+최상급(+명사)」로 나타내며, 「비교급+than any other+단수명사」, 「부정어+비교급+than」, 「부정어+as+원급+as」로 바꿔 쓸 수 있다.

15 주어진 문장의 밑줄 친 부분 live는 명사 fish를 수식하는 형용사로 한정적 용법에 해당한다. ①, ②, ③, ④ 주어의 상태를 보충 설명하는 보어로 쓰인 서술적 용법에 해당하고, ⑤ 명사 subjects를 수식하는 한정적 용법에 해당한다.

16 certain은 한정적 용법으로 '특정한', '어떤'이라는 의미로, 서술적 용법으로 '확실한'이라는 의미로 쓰인다. ①, ②, ④, ⑤ 서술적 용법으로 쓰여 확실한'이라는 의미, ③ 명사를 수식하는 한정적 용법으로 쓰여 '특정한'이라는 의미이다.

17 late는 한정적 용법으로 '죽은'이라는 의미로, 서술적 용법으로 '늦은'이라는 의미로 쓰인다. 또한 부사로 '늦게'라는 의미로 쓰이기도 한다. ①, ④ 형용사의 서술적 용법으로 쓰여 '늦은'이라는 의미, ②, ③ 부사로 쓰여 '늦게'라는 의미, ⑤ 형용사의 한정적 용법으로 쓰여 '죽은'이라는 의미이다.

18 '가장 ~한 것 중 하나'라는 의미의 최상급 관용 표현은 「one of the+최상급+복수명사」이다.

19 'A가 B보다 덜 ~한/하게'라는 의미의 비교급 표현은 「A less+원급+than B」로 나타낸다.

20 ② 「the+형용사」는 '~한 사람들'이라는 의미로, 복수명사로 취급해 복수동사를 취한다. 따라서 needs는 need가 되어야 한다. '가난한 사람들은 부유한 사람들보다 더 많은 도움을 필요로 한다.'라는 의미이다.

21 '매우', '대단히'라는 의미로, 명사와 함께 쓰이는 형용사를 강조하는 such는 「such+(a(n))+형용사+명사」의 어순으로 쓰인다.

22 「부정어+비교급+than」은 '~보다 더 …한 것은 없다'라는 의미로, 비교급을 이용한 최상급 표현이다. 최상급 표현 「the+최상급(+명사)」는 비교급을 이용한 최상급 표현 「비교급+than any other+단수명사」, 원급을 이용한 최상급 표현 「부정어+as+원급+as」로 바꿔 쓸 수 있다. 따라서 각 빈칸에는 bigger, big, biggest가 와야 한다.

23 「A 비교급+than B」의 비교급 표현은 「B not as[so]+원급+as A」의 원급 표현으로 바꿔 쓸 수 있다. 따라서 'The last question is not as[so] easy as this one.'이 되어야 한다.

24 '~만큼 …한/하게'라는 의미의 원급 비교는 「as+형용사/부사의 원

급+as」로 나타낸다. 따라서 비교급 better는 원급 well이 되어야 한다.

25 '그녀는 거의 공부를 하지 않지만, 항상 시험에서 좋은 성적을 받는다.'라는 의미가 되어야 하므로 hard는 '거의 ~하지 않는'이라는 의미의 부사 hardly가 되어야 한다.

26 '가능한 한 ~하게'라는 의미의 「as+형용사/부사의 원급+as+주어+can/could」는 「as+형용사/부사의 원급+as+possible」로 바꿔 쓸 수 있다.

27 '우리 맏오빠는 내 나이의 두 배나 나이가 많다.'라는 의미로, '~보다 …배 ~한/하게'라는 의미의 「배수사+as+형용사/부사의 원급+as」의 형태로 나타낸다.

28 '나는 파리보다 더 아름다운 도시를 본 적 없다.'라는 의미로, '지금까지 ~ 한 것 중 가장 …한'이라는 의미의 표현 「the+최상급(+that)+주어+have/has ever+과거분사」를 사용한다.

29 'A가 B보다 ~한/하게'라는 의미의 비교급 표현은 「A 비교급+than B」으로 나타낸다.

30 빈칸에는 '살아 있는'이라는 의미로 주어 they를 보충 설명하는 서술적 용법의 형용사가 와야 하기 때문에 alive가 적절하다. live는 한정적 용법으로 쓰이는 형용사이므로 빈칸에 적절하지 않다.

31 「the+형용사」는 '~한 사람들'이라는 의미를 나타낸다. 따라서 빈칸에는 the sick 또는 sick people이 와야 한다.

32 빈칸에는 '현재의'라는 의미로 명사 condition을 수식하는 한정적 용법의 형용사가 와야 하기 때문에 present가 적절하다. present는 서술적 용법으로 '출석한'이라는 의미를 나타낸다.

33 ① so는 「so+형용사/부사」의 형태로 사용되어 '매우', '그 만큼'이라는 의미를 나타낸다. ② such는 「such+(a(n))+형용사+명사」의 어순으로 쓰여 '매우', '대단히'라는 의미이며, 명사와 함께 쓰이는 형용사를 강조한다. ③ lately는 '최근'이라는 의미의 부사이다. ④ certain은 한정적 용법으로 '특정한', '어떤'이라는 의미로, 서술적 용법으로 '확실한'이라는 의미로 쓰인다. 이 문장에서는 서술적 용법으로 쓰였다.

34 형용사의 어순을 묻는 문제로 「한정사(that)+크기(big)+색깔(red)+재료(plastic)」의 어순이 되어야 한다. 따라서 that big red plastic box가 적절하다.

35 yet은 주로 의문문 끝에 위치하여 '이미,' '벌써'라는 뜻으로 쓰인다.

36 such는 '매우', '대단히'라는 의미로 명사와 함께 쓰인 형용사를 강조하며, 「such+(a(n))+형용사+명사」의 어순으로 쓰인다.

보너스 유형별 문제 p.142

1 latest, most
2 twice longer, as popular as
3 the oldest, the most popular
4 ②

1 「The Gibson's」가 그의 가장 최근 영화이고, 서평에서 가장 많은 별을 받았다.
가장 최근 영화이고 가장 많은 별을 받았음으로 late과 more의 최상급을 써야 한다.

2 「The Gibson's」는 「The Black Feather」보다 두 배 더 길고, 「The Black Feather」만큼 인기가 있다.
'~보다 …배 ~한/하게'라는 의미의 「배수사+형용사/부사의 비교급」의 형태로 나타내고 '~만큼 …한/하게'라는 의미의 원급 비교는 「as+형용사/부사의 원급+as」로 나타낸다.

3 「Why I Left You」는 세 권 중에서 가장 인기 있는 영화이다.
'가장 ~한'이라는 의미의 최상급은 「the+최상급」으로 나타낸다.

4 아르헨티나는 남미의 남쪽에 있는 매우 광대한 나라로, 전 세계에서 여덟 번째로 가장 큰 나라이다. 이곳은 많은 동물들의 고향이기도 한데, 바다에는 바다표범, 펭귄, 돌고래가 많이 살고, 북쪽 산악 지대에는 퓨마와 재규어 같은 고양이과 동물들을 볼 수 있다. 또한 아르헨티나는 다양한 종류의 새들을 볼 수 있는 멋진 곳이다.
의미상 가장 큰 나라임을 표현해야 하므로 large의 최상급인 largest로 써야 옳다.

Chapter 9

9-1 가정법 과거 p.144

Exercise 1

1 went
2 could
3 heard
4 had
5 were
6 wouldn't
7 were
8 do
9 had
10 wouldn't

Exercise 2

1 were not [weren't]
2 sold
3 were
4 were
5 could
6 would

Exercise 3

1 were, wouldn't, hesitate
2 lived, would [could]
3 knew, would, be
4 were, would, you, accept

Exercise 4

1 If Alex were not sick, he could be with us now.
2 If Anne kept her word, I would trust her.
3 If I were close to him, I could tell him what to do.
4 If he were an honest man, he could be our president.
5 If I knew her phone number or address, I could get in touch with her.

9-2 가정법 과거와 단순 조건문 p.146

Exercise 1

1 can
2 snows

3 would　　4 had
5 weren't　　6 rains

Exercise 2

1 would order pizza
2 wouldn't be enough
3 knew how to swim
4 can get there
5 see Ben again
6 find a cheap hotel

9-3 가정법 과거완료

p.147

Exercise 1

1 have passed　　2 have been
3 had had　　4 have taken place
5 had done　　6 have been

Exercise 2

1 If there hadn't been a typhoon, my flight wouldn't have been delayed.
2 If I had taken the subway, I wouldn't have been late for the meeting.
3 If I had had time, I could have picked you up at the airport.
4 If I hadn't been so tired, I could have gotten out of bed early this morning.
5 If we had had enough money, we could have bought a house with a swimming pool.

9-4 I wish 가정법

p.148

Exercise 1

1 were　　2 could
3 didn't　　4 hadn't
5 could speak　　6 had
7 hadn't done

Exercise 2

1 were in the same class
2 had gotten
3 were still alive
4 had realized
5 had started

9-5 as if 가정법

p.149

Exercise 1

1 had　　2 didn't
3 hadn't slept　　4 understood

Exercise 2

1 as if you were a victim
2 as if I had messed up
3 as if I were at home
4 as if she had lived
5 as if you were sitting
6 as if it were your last day

Review Test

p.150

01 ②　02 ④　03 ⑤　04 ④　05 ③　06 ③
07 ③　08 ②　09 ②　10 ④　11 ③　12 ②
13 ①　14 ⑤　15 ②　16 ④　17 ⑤　18 ②
19 ⑤　20 ③　21 ⑤　22 ②
23 could see
24 had not [hadn't] said
25 ask → had asked
26 is → were
27 it have → it had
28 will go → goes
29 were, would
30 had listened, would not [wouldn't] have happened
31 had, could leave
32 had not [hadn't] completed, could not [couldn't] have had
33 were, would admit

01 가정법 과거 문장으로 if절의 시제는 과거가 되어야 하므로 빈칸에는 lived가 와야 한다.

02 의미상 안경을 쓰지 않았으면 하는 현재의 이룰 수 없는 소망을 나타내고 있으므로 빈칸에는 didn't가 와야 한다.

03 주절의 문장이 「조동사의 과거형(might)+have+과거분사」이므로 if절은 가정법 과거완료가 되어야 한다. 따라서 빈칸에는 had been이 적절하다.

04 가정법 과거 문장으로 주절은 「주어+조동사의 과거형+동사원형」의 형태가 되어야 한다. 따라서 빈칸에는 would travel이 와야 한다.

05 if절이 과거완료 시제이므로, 주절은 「주어+조동사의 과거형+have+과거분사」의 형태가 되어야 한다. 따라서 빈칸에는 have dropped가 적절하다.

06 주절이 「주어+조동사의 과거형+동사원형」의 형태를 가지고 있으므로, if절은 가정법 과거가 되어야 한다. 따라서 빈칸에는 tried가 적절하다.

07 I wish 가정법으로, 가까이 살았으면 한다는 현재의 이룰 수 없는 소망을 나타내고 있으므로 빈칸에는 과거시제가 와야 한다. 따라서 빈칸에는 lived가 적절하다.

08 '몸이 괜찮으면 같이 가서 즐긴 텐데.'라는 의미로, 현재의 이룰 수 없는 소망을 나타내고 있다. 따라서 if절은 가정법 과거를 나타내는 과거시제가 되어야 하므로 felt가 와야 한다.

09 「as if+주어+동사의 과거형」은 '마치 ~인 것처럼'이라는 뜻으로 현재 사실에 반대되는 일을 나타낼 때 쓰인다.

10 전화번호를 잃어버려서 전화할 수 없었다는 과거의 일을 나타내고 있으므로 if절은 「had+과거분사」의 형태가 되어야 한다. 전화번호를 잃어버리지 않았다면'이라는 뜻이 되어야 하므로 hadn't lost가 적절하다.

11 '카드가 있다면'이라는 뜻으로, 현재 사실과 반대되는 사실을 나타내는 가정법 과거이므로 주절은 「조동사의 과거형+동사원형」의 형태가 되어야 하고, '코트를 살 수 있을 텐데'라는 긍정의 의미가 되어야 한다. 따라서 빈칸에는 could buy가 와야 한다.

12 ② 주절이 「조동사의 과거형+have+과거분사」의 형태이므로 if절은 가정법 과거완료를 나타내는 「had+과거분사」의 형태가 되어야 한다. 따라서 asked는 had asked가 되어야 한다.

13 ① '당신이 나라면 어떻게 하겠습니까?'라는 의미로, 가정법 과거 문장이므로 if절의 동사는 과거가 되어야 한다. 따라서 are는 were로 바꿔야 한다.

14 의미상 가정법 과거완료의 형태인 「If+주어+had+과거분사 ~, 주어+조동사의 과거형+have+과거분사 ~」가 되어야 한다.

15 「as if+주어+과거형」은 '마치 ~인 것처럼'이라는 의미로 현재 사실에 반대되는 일을 나타낸다.

16 if절이 '시간이 좀 더 있다면'이라는 뜻으로, 현재 이룰 수 없는 소망을 나타내는 가정법 과거이므로 주절은 「조동사의 과거형+동사원형」의 형태가 되어야 한다.

17 ⑤ 조건을 나타내는 부사절에서는 현재시제가 미래시제를 대신한다. 따라서 If Bobby will apologize를 If Bobby apologizes로 바꿔야 한다.

18 ② 가정법과 직설법을 구분하는 문제이다. if절을 기준으로 할 때 if절의 시제가 현재이므로 가정법이 아닌 직설법이다. 따라서 주절의 시제는 현재 또는 미래가 되어야 하므로 would는 will이 되어야 한다.

19 ⑤ Jeff가 지붕에서 떨어져 다리를 다쳐 콘테스트에 참가하지 못했다는 과거의 사실을 나타내고 있다.

20 ③ 현재 선생님의 전화번호를 몰라 전화를 할 수 없다는 내용으로 현재 이룰 수 없는 소망을 나타내는 가정법 과거가 적절하다.

21 ⑤ '딸이 그런 일을 했으면 나에게 말을 했을 텐데.'라는 의미로, 과거 사실에 반대되는 상황을 가정하는 가정법 과거완료가 적절하다.

22 ② '지금 그녀가 사무실에 있다면 전화를 받을 텐데.'라는 의미로, 현재 사실에 반대되는 상황을 나타내야 하므로 가정법 과거가 적절하다.

23 「I wish+주어+과거형」은 현재 이룰 수 없는 일에 대한 소망이나 유감을 나타낸다. 따라서 빈칸에는 가능을 나타내는 조동사 can의 과거형 could가 쓰여 could see가 와야 한다.

24 「I wish+주어+had+과거분사」는 과거에 일어난 일에 대한 유감을 나타낸다. 의미상 과거 사실에 반대되는 상황을 나타내야 하므로 빈칸에는 had not[hadn't] said가 와야 한다.

25 의미상 과거사실에 반대되는 상황을 나타내야 하므로 if절은 「주어+had+과거분사」의 형태가 되어야 한다. 따라서 ask를 had asked로 바꿔야 한다.

26 「as if+주어+과거형」은 '마치 ~인 것처럼'이라는 의미로 현재 사실에 반대되는 일을 나타내는 가정법이다. 따라서 is를 were로 바꿔야 한다.

27 의미상 가정법 과거완료의 형태인 「If+주어+had+과거분사 ~, 주어+조동사의 과거형+have+과거분사 ~」가 되어야 하므로 if절의 have를 had로 바꿔야 한다.

28 조건을 나타내는 부사절은 현재시제가 미래를 대신한다. 따라서 if절의 will을 생략하고, go를 goes로 바꾼다.

29 '내가 너라면 선생님께 곧장 말씀드리겠다.'라는 의미로, 실현 가능성이 없는 일을 가정하고 있으므로 가정법 과거 형태인 「If+주어+동사의 과거형 ~, 주어+조동사의 과거형+동사원형 ~」의 문장 구조가 되어야 한다. 따라서 빈칸에는 were, would가 적절하다.

30 '내 말을 들었으면 사고가 나지 않았을 텐데.'라는 의미로, 과거의 일에 대한 반대 상황을 나타낸다. 따라서 빈칸에는 가정법 과거완료로 had listened, would not[wouldn't] have happened가 적절하다.

31 '여권이 있다면 이 나라를 떠날 수 있을 텐데.'라는 의미로, 현재 상황과 반대되는 일에 대한 소망을 나타낸다. 따라서 빈칸에는 가정법 과거로 had, could leave가 적절하다.

32 '프로젝트를 끝내지 못했다면 휴가를 가질 수 없었을 것이다.'라는 의미로, 과거에 일어난 일에 대한 반대 상황을 나타낸다. 따라서 빈칸에는 가정법 과거완료로 had not[hadn't] completed, could not[couldn't] have had가 적절하다.

33 '네가 더 어른스럽다면 네 잘못을 인정할 텐데.'라는 의미로, 현재 사실에 반대되는 내용을 나타낸다. 따라서 빈칸에는 가정법 과거로 were, would admit이 적절하다.

보너스 유형별 문제

p.154

1 had been

2 If I were Fluffy, I wouldn't clean anything.

3 ⑤

[1-2] 고양이로 태어났으면 좋았을 텐데.

오늘은 비가 내린다. 나는 봄바람이 내 피부에 닿는 것을 즐기며 현관에 앉아 있다. 내 애완묘인 Fluffy는 내 옆에서 낮잠을 자고 있다. 갑자기 엄마가 나를 부르시는 소리가 들린다. 그리고 나는 오늘이 집 대청소 날이라는 걸 깨닫는다. 어젯밤 엄마는 나에게 집 구석구석과 각자의 방을 청소할 거라고 말씀하셨다. 그리고 엄마는 나에게 지하실을 청소해달라고 요청하셨다. 이제 나는 가서 내 방과 지하실을 청소해야 한다. 나는 Fluffy가 너무 부럽다. 만약 내가 Fluffy라면 어떤 것도 청소하지 않을 텐데. 엄마가 화내시기 전에 일을 시작해야겠다.

1 '~였다면[했다면] 좋았을 텐데'라는 의미로, 과거에 이루지 못한 일에 대한 유감을 나타낼 때 과거완료(had + p.p.)를 쓴다.

2 가정법 과거는 「If + 주어 + 동사의 과거형, 주어 + 조동사의 과거형 + 동사원형」의 형태로 쓴다.

3 외동은 부모가 그들이 원하는 건 무엇이든 주기 때문에 버릇이 없는 경향이 있다. 나도 외동이기는 하지만, 우리 부모님은 그렇지 않다. 두 분은 올바른 예절에 대해 매우 엄격하다. 하지만 많은 애정도 보여 주신다. 두 분은 나만 돌보면 되기 때문에 나와 함께 보내는 시간이 많다. 그래도 나는 원하는 것보다 더 많은 시간을 혼자 보내기 때문에 두 분이 아이를 더 갖기로 하신다면 난 괜찮다. 부모님이 일하러 가거나 친구들이 모두 바쁠 때는 남동생이 있었으면 좋겠다. 집에 이야기를 할 나와 비슷한 나이의 사람이 있다면 좋을 것 같다.

현재 이룰 수 없는 일에 대한 소망이나 유감을 나타내므로 「I wish+주어+동사의 과거형」을 써야 한다. 따라서 have를 had로 써야 적절하다.

Chapter 10

10-1 관계대명사와 선행사 p.156

Exercise 1

1 It
2 She
3 it
4 He
5 them
6 Her

Exercise 2

1 a girl
2 The TV
3 the guy
4 The girl
5 a book
6 The building

10-2 주격 관계대명사 p.157

Exercise 1

1 which, that
2 which, that
3 which, that
4 who, that
5 who, that
6 which, that
7 who, that
8 who, that
9 which, that
10 which, that
11 which, that
12 which, that
13 who, that

Exercise 2

1 was → were
2 go → goes
3 who → which [that]
4 which → who [that]
5 which → who [that]
6 don't → doesn't

Exercise 3

1 The accident that happened last night was horrible.
2 I work for a company that makes cell phones.
3 Have you met the new teacher who came from Los Angeles?
4 I loved the movie which was directed by James Cameron.

Exercise 4

1 An ostrich is a bird which[that] cannot fly.
2 Where is my lunchbox which[that] was in the refrigerator?
3 The thief who [that] stole my mom's jewelry chest has been arrested.
4 I have a smartwatch which [that] can last up to 30 days with a single recharge.
5 Do you know the gentleman who [that] is wearing a black hat?

10-3 목적격 관계대명사 p.159

Exercise 1

1 what
2 what
3 that, which
4 that, whom
5 that
6 whom
7 that, which
8 that, whom

Exercise 2

1 X
2 O
3 O
4 O
5 O
6 X

Exercise 3

1 of which → which [that]
2 of which → which [that]
3 is → are
4 whose → who(m) [that]
5 whom → which [that]
6 what → which [that]

Exercise 4

1 a game console which I recommended to him
2 what he meant to say
3 The boy that they were talking about
4 the language which my grandparents speak
5 the only person that I want to share my life with
6 the same purse that my dad bought me for my birthday

10-4 소유격 관계대명사 p.161

Exercise 1

1 whose
2 whose
3 whom
4 which
5 whose
6 whose
7 whose
8 whose

Exercise 2

1 The house whose roof is red
2 a man whose wife is a famous author
3 The tower whose height is over 50 meters
4 a friend whose brother is a well-known composer
5 the beautiful bird whose feathers are colorful and elegant

10-5 관계부사 p.162

Exercise 1

1 where
2 when
3 the way
4 why
5 in which

Exercise 2

1 why　　2 how
3 when　　4 where

Exercise 3

1 where, in, which　　2 how, the, way
3 why, for, which　　4 when, on, which

Exercise 4

1 a place where I can buy a used bike
2 the moment when I first held
3 the reason why Anne is loved by everyone
4 how the kids got into the locked classroom

Review Test p.164

01 ④	02 ①	03 ②	04 ⑤	05 ③	06 ③
07 ④	08 ①, ③	09 ②, ⑤	10 ①	11 ⑤	12 ⑤
13 ⑤	14 ④	15 ⑤	16 ①	17 ①	18 ⑤
19 ⑤	20 ⑤	21 ⑤	22 ③	23 ③	24 ③

25 whose
26 when [on which]
27 live → lives
28 whom → which[that]
29 Where, what
30 The bananas which[that] we bought from the market are rotten.
31 I know the reason why[for which] Gary was absent today.
32 The cowboy who is wearing the red shirt
33 the moment when I first saw him

01 빈칸 다음에 동사가 있는 것으로 보아 주격 관계대명사가 올 자리라는 것을 알 수 있다. 따라서 whose와 whom은 정답이 될 수 없으며, 선행사가 the bank이므로 사람을 선행사로 받는 관계대명사 who와 선행사를 포함하는 관계대명사 what은 정답이 될 수 없다. 따라서 빈칸에는 that이 적절하다.

02 빈칸 다음에 동사가 있는 것으로 보아 주격 관계대명사가 올 자리라는 것을 알 수 있으며, 선행사가 the girl이므로 빈칸에는 사람을 선행사로 받는 관계대명사 who가 적절하다.

03 선행사가 the day이므로 빈칸에는 관계부사 when이나 on which가 와야 한다.

04 remember의 목적어 역할을 하면서 선행사 없이 쓸 수 있는 관계대명사는 what이다.

05 관계대명사 who의 선행사가 복수(a lot of people)이므로 동사 needs는 need가 되어야 한다.

06 빈칸 다음에 동사가 있는 것으로 보아 주격 관계대명사가 올 자리라는 것을 알 수 있으며, 선행사가 a pair of boots이므로 관계대명사는 which나 that이 올 수 있다.

07 선행사가 the reason이므로 빈칸에는 관계부사 why나 for which가 와야 한다.

08 의미상 복사기를 고치는 방법을 가르쳐달라는 내용으로 where가 아닌 how나 the way가 와야 한다.

09 선행사가 a girl이므로 사람을 선행사로 받고 동사 introduce의 목적어 역할을 하는 관계대명사를 찾아야 한다. 따라서 선행사로 사람을 받는 목적격 관계대명사 whom과, 사람과 사물을 모두 선행사로 받을 수 있는 관계대명사 that이 올 수 있다.

10 빈칸 다음에 동사가 있는 것으로 보아 주격 관계대명사가 올 자리라는 것을 알 수 있으며, 선행사 the one은 the boy를 나타내므로 빈칸에는 who가 와야 한다.

11 넥타이를 쉽게 매는 방법을 가르쳐 준다는 내용이므로 빈칸에는 방법을 나타내는 관계부사 how가 적절하다.

12 동사 cooked의 목적어 역할을 하면서 선행사 없이 쓸 수 있는 관계대명사는 what이다.

13 ①, ②, ③, ④의 which, who, that, whom은 목적격 관계대명사로 생략할 수 있으나, ⑤의 who는 주격 관계대명사로 생략할 수 없다. 목적격 관계대명사로 whom 대신 who가 쓰이기도 한다.

14 • 빈칸 다음에 명사 tail이 온 것으로 보아 이를 수식하는 소유격 관계대명사가 와야 한다는 것을 알 수 있다.
• 선행사가 the reason으로 이유를 나타내는 관계부사 why가 적절하다.

15 • 선행사가 the house로 장소를 나타내는 관계부사 where가 적절하다.
• 선행사가 the day로 시간을 나타내는 관계부사 when이나 on which가 적절하다.

16 ① 문장의 주어는 the flowers로 복수이다. 따라서 관계대명사절 다음에 온 본동사는 is가 아닌 are가 되어야 한다.

17 ① '네가 좋아하는 활동은 무엇이니?'라는 의미로 의문사, ② '네 손에 있는 것을 나에게 줘.'라는 의미로 관계대명사, ③ '네가 정말 원하는 것을 말해 줘.'라는 의미로 관계대명사, ④ '내가 그에 대해 아는 것은 사실이다.'라는 의미로 관계대명사, ⑤ '그를 행복하게 하는 것은 그의 딸이다.'라는 의미로 관계대명사이다.

18 ⑤ 선행사가 장소를 나타내고 있으므로 in which 또는 where가 적절하다. in which 앞의 전치사 in은 문장 뒤로 이동할 수 있으나 생략할 수 없다. ④의 경우 관계부사 where는 이미 전치사를 포함하고 있으므로 전치사 in을 삭제하거나 where를 which로 바꾸면 올바른 문장이 된다.

19 ⑤ 내용상 방법을 나타내는 관계부사 how나 the way가 쓰인 문장이 적절하다. the way와 how는 함께 쓸 수 없다.

20 주어진 문장의 that은 목적격 관계대명사이다. ①, ③, ④의 that은 지시형용사이며 ②의 that은 접속사이다. ⑤의 that은 동사 lost의 목적어 역할을 하는 목적격 관계대명사이다.

21 ①, ②, ③, ④의 빈칸에는 관계대명사 what이, ⑤의 빈칸에는 목적격 관계대명사 which나 that이 와야 한다.

22 ①, ②, ④, ⑤의 빈칸에는 소유격 관계대명사 whose가, ③의 빈칸에는 전치사 in의 목적어 역할을 하는 목적격 관계대명사 which나 that이 와야 한다.

23 ③ 문장의 선행사가 장소를 나타내는 the town이므로, in which 또는 where가 와야 한다. 따라서 전치사 in을 삭제하거나, where를 which로 바꾸면 올바른 문장이 된다.

24 ③ 동사 took의 목적어 역할을 하는 목적격 관계대명사가 필요하다. 따라서 which 앞의 전치사 of를 삭제해야 한다.

25 명사 life를 수식하는 소유격 관계대명사가 필요하므로 whose가 적절하다.

26 선행사가 시간을 나타내는 the day이므로 빈칸에는 관계부사 when이나 on which가 올 수 있다.

27 관계대명사 who의 선행사는 3인칭 단수 the man이므로 동사 live를 lives로 고쳐야 한다.

28 선행사가 lots of things이므로 whom은 which나 that으로 고쳐야 한다.

29 '쇼핑센터에서 잃어버린 것 같습니다.'라는 답변에 알맞은 질문은 '어디에서 잃어버렸습니까?'가 되어야 하므로 첫 번째 빈칸에는 장소를 나타내는 의문부사 where가 와야 하고, 두 번째 빈칸에는 '이것이 당신이 찾고 있는 것입니까?'라는 의미로, 전치사 for의 목적어 역할을 하면서 선행사 없이 쓸 수 있는 관계대명사 what이 와야 한다.

30 선행사 the bananas를 수식할 수 있는 관계대명사는 which 또는 that이다.

31 이유를 나타내는 선행사 the reason을 수식하려면 관계부사 why나 for which가 와야 한다.

32 the cowboy가 문장의 주어이며 who가 이끄는 관계대명사절의 수식을 받는다.

33 the moment가 관계부사 when이 이끄는 절의 수식을 받아 동사 forget의 목적어가 된다.

보너스 유형별 문제 p.168

1 how

2 They eventually became the first people that flew an airplane.

3 ⑤

[1-2] 라이트 형제는 어렸을 때 사물이 날 수 있는 방식을 항상 이해하고 싶어 했다. 어느 날 그들의 아버지는 그들에게 헬리콥터 장난감을 주었다. 헬리콥터를 받은 뒤로 그들은 그것과 비슷한 것을 만들려고 계속 노력했다. 비록 그들은 여러 번 실패했지만 절대로 포기하지 않았다. 그들은 그들이 진정으로 만들고 싶어 하는 것이 무엇인지 정확히 알고 있었다. 그들은 마침내 최초로 비행기를 날린 사람들이 되었다. 그들의 훌륭한 발명품은 그들의 삶뿐만 아니라 우리의 삶도 바꾸어 놓았다.

1 선행사가 방법(way)을 나타낼 때 관계부사 how가 대신할 수 있다.

2 선행사가 서수가 포함된 the first people이므로 주격 관계대명사 that을 써서 수식한다.

3 평균적으로 예쁜 여자가 데이트 신청을 더 많이 받는 게 사실이지만 '매력적'이라는 것은 잘생긴 외모보다 다른 것들에 의해 좌우된다. 고등학교 남학생들에게 여학생들의 어떤 점을 좋아하고 싫어하는지 물었을 때, 이들은 열정이 미모보다 훨씬 더 중요하다는 점에 동의했다. 같이 있으면 즐겁고, 유머 감각이 있으며, 긍정적으로 생각하는 여학생들이 좋다고 했다. 선행사가 사람(girls)이고 뒤에 동사(are)가 나오므로 주격 관계대명사인 who나 that이 쓰여야 옳다.

Chapter 11

11-1 시간을 나타내는 전치사 p.170

Exercise 1

1 from
2 during
3 for
4 since
5 by

Exercise 2

1 since
2 during
3 by
4 until

11-2 장소·방향을 나타내는 전치사 p.171

Exercise 1

1 to
2 below
3 above
4 to
5 for

Exercise 2

1 for
2 below
3 to
4 above

11-3 기타 전치사 p.172

Exercise 1

1 like
2 through
3 in
4 with
5 of
6 with

Exercise 2

1 of
2 with
3 in
4 for
5 through

Exercise 3

1 for
2 by
3 in
4 as
5 of/from

Exercise 4

1 for
2 as
3 like
4 for
5 by
6 with

11-4 명사절을 이끄는 접속사 p.174

Exercise 1

1 보어　2 목적어
3 목적어　4 주어
5 보어　6 목적어

Exercise 2

1 whether　2 that
3 that　4 whether
5 whether　6 that

Exercise 3

1 I'm not sure whether the boy is Henry's cousin.
2 The problem is that he is always late for the meeting.
3 I was wondering whether you have a partner for the prom.
4 The most important thing is that we accomplished what we wanted.

Exercise 4

1 that Emma lost her mother at an early age
2 that you are transferring to another school
3 that you have to make your own decision
4 that my sister keeps using my stuff
5 whether he can swim or not
6 decide whether they punish the child or not [decide whether or not they punish the child]

11-5 간접의문문 p.176

Exercise 1

1 if she received
2 how old Amanda is
3 what your brother's job is
4 if my answer is
5 where I put
6 when she will come back
7 whether I called
8 why you were

Exercise 2

1 did like → liked
2 is she → she is
3 Do you think which → Which do you think
4 does he feel → he feels
5 did I study → I studied
6 that whether → whether

Exercise 3

1 who you like most
2 Melissa said to me
3 what he wants for his birthday gift
4 if [whether] she works for a law firm
5 if [whether] you can go to the amusement park

Exercise 4

1 We don't know what they want for dinner tonight.
2 I wonder whether she is a student or not.
3 Do you know when he arrives at the airport?
4 She asked me whether I attended the meeting yesterday.

11-6 시간을 나타내는 접속사 p.178

Exercise 1

1 until　2 as
3 While　4 before
5 since　6 grow up
7 after　8 are

Exercise 2

1 after　2 before
3 since　4 While

Exercise 3

1 until　2 When [As]
3 since　4 while
5 before

Exercise 4

1 since she was born
2 after you left the office
3 when [as] I opened the door
4 until summer comes
5 while we were in the middle of dinner

11-7 이유·양보를 나타내는 접속사 p.180

Exercise 1

1 because of　2 Even though
3 Though　4 since
5 Although

Exercise 2

1 Although I knew I couldn't win the race
2 because of your lack of responsibility
3 Even though we lost the game
4 even though I don't like him
5 because I coughed constantly

11-8 조건을 나타내는 접속사 p.181

Exercise 1

1 Unless
2 or
3 and
4 If

Exercise 2

1 will be → is
2 will come → comes
3 or → and
4 don't → don't 삭제 or Unless → If

Exercise 3

1 unless
2 unless
3 if
4 If
5 or
6 If
7 and
8 unless

Exercise 4

1 and
2 or
3 If, don't, or
4 or, If, don't

11-9 상관접속사 p.183

Exercise 1

1 but
2 Neither
3 are
4 am
5 or
6 not only

Exercise 2

1 both, and
2 either, or
3 Neither, nor
4 not, only, but, also

11-10 선택의문문 p.184

Exercise 1

1 Did, or
2 Who, or
3 Is, or
4 Where, or

Exercise 2

1 Is this your mother or your aunt?
2 Would you like to stay here or go home?
3 Does she study English or Spanish?
4 Do you want to be a doctor or an entertainer?

Exercise 3

1 She is cooking.
2 He lives in America.
3 I go to school by bus.
4 I like winter better.
5 My brother broke my computer.
6 The Empire State Building is taller.

Exercise 4

1 Was your car white or black?
2 Which is bigger, the earth or the sun?
3 Which would you like to have, beef or chicken?
4 Do you want a window seat or an aisle seat?

Review Test p.186

01 ④	02 ③	03 ⑤	04 ③	05 ③	06 ②
07 ④	08 ③	09 ⑤	10 ③	11 ②	12 ②
13 ③	14 ④	15 ②	16 ③	17 ④	18 ①
19 ②	20 ③	21 ④	22 ④	23 ④	24 ④
25 ①					

26 because of → because
27 for → since
28 does he like → he likes
29 Unless
30 as, well, as
31 why, she, left
32 Even, though
33 because [since/as]
34 What do you think will happen tomorrow?
35 Could you tell me what your favorite fruit is?

01 the winter break는 특정 기간이므로 '~ 동안'이라는 뜻을 나타낼 때 전치사 during과 함께 쓰인다. 전치사 for는 시간 및 기간을 나타내는 명사구와 함께 쓰인다.

02 '그는 자신을 경찰로 소개했다.'라는 의미로, 빈칸에는 역할이나 자격을 나타내는 전치사 as가 와야 한다.

03 'Ken이 오늘 올지 내일 올지 모르겠다.'라는 의미로, 빈칸에는 목적절을 이끄는 접속사가 와야 하며, 의미상 that보다는 '~인지 아닌지'라는 뜻의 if가 적절하다.

04 주절의 의미가 '시간 내에 역에 도착할 수 없을 것이다.'이므로 '서두르지 않으면'이라는 내용이 어울린다. 따라서 '~하지 않으면'이라는 부정의 의미를 내포하고 있는 접속사 unless가 적절하다.

05 '현금으로 지불하시겠습니까, 카드로 하시겠습니까?'라는 의미의 선택의문문으로 빈칸에는 접속사 or가 적절하다.

06 전치사 for는 leave, start 등의 동사와 함께 '~으로 향해'라는 의미로 방향을 나타내고, thank 등의 동사와 함께 '~ 때문에'라는 의미로 원인을 나타낸다.

07 첫 번째 빈칸에는 내용상 '~인지 아닌지'라는 뜻의 접속사가 필요하고, 두 번째 빈칸에는 조건을 나타내는 접속사가 필요하다. 따라서 공통으로 빈칸에 들어갈 접속사는 if이다.

08 '공공장소에서 큰 소리로 이야기하지 마라. 그렇지 않으면 사람들은 네가 예의가 없다고 생각할 것이다.'라는 의미로, 명령문 뒤에 쓰여 '그렇게 하지 않으면'이라는 뜻의 접속사 or이 적절하다. 명령문 뒤에 쓰이는 접속사 and는 '그렇게 하면'이라는 의미를 나타낸다.

09 간접의문문의 주절에 think, believe, imagine 등의 동사가 올 경우 의문사가 문장 앞으로 이동해 「의문사+주절+주어+동사 ~?」의 어순이 된다.

10 • 'Nick은 라디오를 듣는 중에 엄청난 굉음을 들었다.'라는 의미로, 때를 나타내는 접속사 while이 와야 한다.
• '이 지역에 이사 온 이후 지하철을 타는 데 어려움을 겪은 적이 없다.'라는 의미로, 주로 완료시제와 함께 쓰여 '~이후'라는 뜻을 나타내는 접속사 since가 와야 한다.

11 • '전부 분홍색으로 옷을 입은 여자아이들을 보아라.'라는 의미로, 전치사 in은 '~을 입고 있는'이라는 뜻을 나타낸다.
• '그 남자는 지난 화요일에 날치기로 체포되었다.'라는 의미로, 전치사 for는 이유를 나타내는 데 사용한다.

12 ② '월요일과 화요일 중 어느 날이 좋으냐?'라는 질문에 알맞은 대답을 찾는 문제로, '나는 어느 날이든 좋다.'라는 답변이 가장 적절하다. 대명사 either는 긍정문에서 '어느 쪽이든'이라는 뜻을 나타낸다.

13 '낮 동안 더워서 민소매 셔츠를 입고 있었다.'라는 의미로, since는 이유를 나타내어 '~ 때문에'라는 의미로 사용되었다. 따라서 접속사 because로 대체할 수 있다.

14 ④ 전치사 during과 for의 쓰임을 구분하는 문제로, 특정 기간 앞에는 during을, 시간이나 기간을 나타내는 명사구 앞에는 for를 사용한다.

15 ② '휴식을 취해라. 그렇지 않으면 몸이 좀 나아질 것이다.'라는 의미는 자연스럽지 못하므로 접속사 or은 '그렇게 하면'이라는 의미를 나타내는 and가 되어야 한다.

16 ①, ②, ④, ⑤의 that은 목적절을 이끄는 접속사로 생략 가능하며, ③의 that은 주어 역할을 하는 대명사로 생략 할 수 없다.

17 주어진 문장의 that은 목적절을 이끄는 접속사이며, ④의 that은 목적격 관계대명사이다.

18 'Robert는 멕시코뿐만 아니라 브라질에도 가본 적이 있다.'라는 의미이다. 「not only A but also B」는 'A뿐만 아니라 B도'라는 의미로 「B as well as A」로 바꿔 쓸 수 있다.

19 ② 간접의문문의 주절에 think, believe, imagine 등의 동사가 올 경우 의문사가 문두로 이동해 「의문사+주절+주어+동사 ~?」의 어순이 된다.

20 ③ 「neither A nor B」는 'A와 B 둘 다 아닌'이라는 의미이고, 「either A or B」는 'A와 B 둘 중 하나'라는 의미이다.

21 ④ 접속사 unless는 '~하지 않으면'이라는 뜻으로 이미 부정의 뜻을 내포하고 있기 때문에 부정어와 함께 쓰이지 않는다. 따라서 '집중을 하지 않으면'이라는 의미를 나타내려면 부정어를 삭제하여 'Unless you pay attention'이 되어야 한다.

22 ④ 주어진 문장은 '피곤했지만 잠을 전혀 잘 수가 없었다.'라는 의미로, 주절과 종속절이 역접의 관계인 문장을 찾아야 한다. 따라서 '비록 ~이지만'이라는 뜻을 나타내는 접속사 although가 쓰인 문장이 적절하다.

23 주어진 문장의 접속사 as는 때를 나타내어 '~할 때', '~하는 중에'라는 의미를 가지고 있다. ①, ③ '~로', '~로서'라는 의미로 자격이나 성질을 나타내는 전치사, ② 원급 비교 구문에 쓰인 부사, ④ '내가 TV를 볼 때'라는 의미로 때를 나타내는 접속사, ⑤ as well은 관용 표현으로 '게다가'라는 의미를 나타낸다.

24 ①, ②, ③, ⑤의 that은 명사절을 이끄는 접속사이고 ④의 that은 the monkeys를 수식하는 절을 이끄는 주격 관계대명사이다.

25 주어진 문장의 when은 접속사로 '~할 때'라는 의미를 나타낸다. ①의 when은 시간을 나타내는 선행사 the day를 수식하는 절을 이끄는 관계부사이다.

26 '비가 심하게 와서 우리는 소풍 가기로 한 계획을 취소했다.'라는 의미이다. 명사(구) 앞에 쓰이는 전치사 because of는 절을 이끌 수 없으므로 접속사 because로 바꾼다.

27 '그 공장은 1950년대 초반부터 우리 도시에 있었다.'라는 의미가 되어야 한다. 따라서 전치사 for는 '~이후'라는 의미로 완료시제 함께 쓰이는 since로 바꾼다.

28 접속사 whether를 이용한 의문사가 없는 간접의문문이며, 「접속사+주어+동사」의 어순이 되어야 하므로 does he like는 he likes로 바꾼다.

29 접속사 unless는 '~하지 않으면'이라는 의미로 if not과 같은 의미를 나타낼 수 있다.

30 「not only A but also B」는 'A뿐만 아니라 B도'라는 의미로 「B as well as A」로 바꿔 쓸 수 있다.

31 의문사가 있는 간접의문문으로 「의문사+주어+동사」의 어순으로 쓰여야 하며, 의미상 이유를 나타내는 의문사 why가 적절하다.

32 주절과 종속절의 관계가 역접인 것으로 보아 '~에도 불구하고', '~일지라도'라는 의미를 나타내는 접속사 even though가 적절하다.

33 의미상 늦게 일어난 이유를 나타내는 접속사가 필요하므로 because [since/as] 등의 접속사가 올 수 있다.

34 간접의문문의 주절에 think, believe, imagine 등의 동사가 올 경우 의문사가 문두로 이동해 「의문사+주절+주어+동사 ~?」의 어순이 된다.

35 의문사가 있는 간접의문문으로 「의문사+주어+동사」의 어순으로 쓰여야 한다. 따라서 what your favorite fruit is가 되어야 한다.

보너스 유형별 문제 p.190

1 Neither, nor, likes
2 Both, and, like
3 Not only, but also, enjoys
4 ①

1 Sebastian과 Zachary 둘 다 운동하는 것을 좋아하지 않는다.
「neither A nor B」에서 동사는 B에 일치시킨다.

2 Ezra와 Charlotte 둘 다 야외 활동을 좋아한다.
「both A and B」 뒤에 오는 동사는 복수이다.

3 Zachary뿐만 아니라 Rory도 독서를 즐긴다.
「not only A but also B」에서 동사는 B에 일치시킨다.

4 안녕, Anna! 오후에 있을 Amy의 발레 발표회 때문에 공항에서 너를 만날 수 없을 것 같아. 미안! 그냥 집으로 와. 집 열쇠가 어디에 있는지 알잖아. Michelle과 난 Amy를 우리 부모님 댁에 데려다주고 6시쯤 집에 도착할 것 같아. 그러고 나서 지난번에 전화로 이야기했던 식당에 데려갈게. 네가 로스앤젤레스행 연결 항공편 시간까지 4시간밖에 없다는 건 잘 알고 있으니 걱정하지 마. 저녁 식사 후에 곧바로 공항으로 데려다 줄게. 그 밖에 필요한 게 있다면 알려 줘!
뒤에 절이 아닌 구(Amy's ballet recital in the afternoon)가 오므로 because가 아닌 because of가 쓰여야 옳다.

Workbook

Chapter 1 p.194-196

A

1 worries, worry
2 do, does
3 plays, play
4 study, studies
5 love, loves
6 misses, miss
7 teach, teaches

B

1 mixes
2 winks
3 fries
4 catches
5 eat
6 hate

C

1 stopped
2 called
3 saw
4 spoke
5 watched
6 swam

D

1 respected
2 met
3 grew
4 saw
5 took

E

1 is driving
2 are, listening
3 is digging
4 are working
5 are swimming

F

1 were talking
2 were watching
3 weren't paying
4 was cleaning
5 wasn't studying

G

1 left
2 have
3 have never tried
4 has not spoken

H

1 has been sick
2 has gone to Paris
3 has lost her watch
4 has played the cello
5 have worn glasses

I

1 has come
2 haven't seen her
3 Have you had problems
4 has lost his backpack
5 have raised cattle
6 haven't received any messages

Chapter 2 p.197-199

A

1 Can[May]
2 rain
3 to repair
4 make
5 speak
6 be able to
7 Will/Can

B

1 May I ask several questions?
2 Should we keep quiet?
3 Must she log in to her account?
4 Can you download old songs for free?

C

1 must be
2 can't be
3 might get
4 may not understand

D

1 It may snow
2 Can[May] I help
3 will be able to walk
4 can write songs
5 May[Can] I sit

6 could run
7 Can you teach me

1 추가해야 해
2 똑똑한 것이 틀림없다
3 출근할 필요가 없다
4 도움을 요청하는 것이 좋겠다

F

1 May, take
2 may leave
3 can use
4 Can, watch

G

1 They have to follow the school rules.
2 Do I have to keep it a secret?
3 James has to put away his smartphone.

H

1 used to
2 would like to
3 used to
4 had better
5 had better

I

1 Did you use to skip classes
2 had better not hang out with them
3 What would you like to do
4 had better stay for another day
5 had better throw a birthday party for him
6 There used to be a bridge over the river

Chapter 3 p.200-202

A

1 sent
2 written
3 arrested
4 made
5 visited

B

1 were not folded up
2 to ride[riding]
3 Were
4 should be deleted
5 to

C

1 wasn't told by the student
2 aren't watered by him
3 should be made by us
4 Was, attacked by Russia

D

1 sold, was sold
2 invited, were invited
3 took, were taken
4 raised, was raised
5 broke, were broken

E

1 from
2 with
3 at
4 in
5 to
6 of
7 with
8 about

F

1 be seen
2 was made to keep
3 was cooked for me
4 must be handed in
5 was seen driving
6 is closed
7 was given to us

G

1 should be taken after each meal
2 Was the church destroyed
3 was asked to sit down
4 was not directed by me
5 was sent to the wrong person
6 was brought to me by a robot
7 was seen walking a dog

Chapter 4 p.203-205

A

1 not to be
2 to be
3 not to forget
4 to drink
5 to go
6 to order

B
1 목적어
2 보어
3 목적어
4 주어
5 보어
6 주어

C
1 a soda to drink
2 time to take your pills
3 someone to talk with
4 many things to do
5 some games to play

D
1 She is saving some money to buy a new smartwatch.
2 I was disappointed to see him leave.
3 James got up early to catch the train.
4 They were pleased to receive your message.

E
1 It, to charge my phone
2 It, to live without my parents
3 It, to learn how to edit videos
4 It, to bite your fingernails
5 It, to travel alone in Korea

F
1 of you
2 of him
3 of him
4 for them
5 of you
6 for her
7 for us
8 for me

G
1 so hard that we could pass
2 so strong that she could invade
3 are so busy that they can't go shopping
4 so sick that he couldn't come

H
1 too selfish to hang out with her friends
2 old enough to vote in elections
3 careless of him to skate on the thin ice
4 important for us to take vitamins every day
5 easy for me to get up early in the morning
6 too spicy for children to eat

I
1 in order to keep in shape
2 easy enough to solve
3 too hot to get a good night's sleep
4 lucky enough to make it to the finals

Chapter 5

p.206-208

A
1 talking about
2 working
3 Eating
4 flying
5 making

B
1 목적어
2 주어
3 보어
4 보어
5 주어
6 목적어

C
1 playing soccer with his friends
2 Talking to girls
3 Eating too much ice cream
4 writing computer programs
5 flying a KF-21
6 listening to K-pop

D
1 building
2 Meeting
3 breaking
4 not being
5 not getting
6 not telling

E
1 to buy
2 folding
3 keeping
4 working
5 to try
6 to ask

F
1 to pick up the $10 bill from the sidewalk
2 to take out the trash

3 seeing Matilda hanging out at the mall last Saturday
4 to return the books to the library by tomorrow
5 borrowing a pencil from Elliot

G

1 to become
2 to see
3 learning
4 to attract
5 reading
6 paying

H

1 trying to prove
2 tried putting on my sister's dress
3 agreed to postpone their meeting
4 loves pulling pranks
5 Quit watching YouTube videos.

I

1 I should finish writing my essay before dinner.
2 Don't avoid making eye contact with me.
3 Koreans like drinking and singing.
4 The student pretended to know the answer.
5 Rosie promised to be back by 9.
6 the girl started screaming at her classmates

Chapter 6 p.209-211

A

1 made
2 stealing
3 taken
4 interesting
5 sitting
6 falling

B

1 written in Spanish
2 talking on the phone
3 barking at the kids
4 built by the lake

C

1 Toby was so annoying
2 movies filmed in the 1990s
3 a man called "the Ice"
4 The structure shown in this picture
5 her stolen purse

D

1 is crying looking at the old photo
2 a pharmacist known to everyone
3 the boiling water
4 the seal performing with a ball
5 the kids swimming in the pool
6 the car parked at the bus stop
7 were amazed to see

E

1 Listening to the radio
2 Turning around the corner
3 Being tired
4 Working alone
5 Having a toothache
6 Taking a shower
7 Crying like a baby

F

1 When she heard about Dylan's accident
2 If you take the bus
3 as she yelled at us
4 After we won the race

G

1 Looking in the mirror
2 Being injured
3 Talking to her friends
4 Preparing dinner
5 Waving his hand

H

1 Smoking every day, your conditions will get worse.
2 Seeing the patrol car, the robber started to run away.
3 Doing his best, he still couldn't beat his opponent.
4 Working overtime, I heard someone screaming for help.
5 Being so shocked, the doctor turned pale.
6 Hearing the news, the soldiers dropped their rifles.

Chapter 7 p.212-214

A

1 herself
2 myself
3 ourselves
4 themselves
5 itself
6 himself
7 yourself

B

1 taught herself
2 help yourself
3 enjoyed ourselves
4 hurt himself
5 by herself
6 introduced themselves

C

1 It was impossible to understand his southern accent.
2 It is necessary to collect more data.
3 It is not hard to get an A in this course.
4 It was interesting to see their reactions.
5 It is dangerous to go jogging late at night.

D

1 It
2 it
3 one
4 ones
5 another
6 another

E

1 Some, Others
2 One, the other
3 One, another, the other
4 One, the others

F

1 some
2 some
3 some
4 any
5 any
6 any

G

1 Nothing
2 anything
3 somebody
4 No one
5 something
6 anyone

H

1 man
2 were
3 needs
4 One
5 It

I

1 is
2 feel
3 have
4 love

J

1 either French fries or chicken nuggets
2 both Dutch and German
3 Both (of) my parents and grandparents
4 neither cash nor credit cards

Chapter 8

p.215-217

A

1 The rich
2 the homeless
3 the unemployed

B

1 The actress has long blonde hair.
2 How much is that large crystal vase?
3 Maria is a smart girl.
4 The class is full of bright students.

C

1 surprisingly
2 fast
3 so bitter
4 high
5 well
6 carefully
7 hard
8 early

D

1 as[so] popular as
2 as[so] early as
3 as[so] lazy as
4 as effective as
5 as intelligent as
6 as well as

E

1 doesn't have as[so] much money as
2 is not as[so] heavy as
3 is as tall as
4 doesn't read as[so] many books as
5 runs as fast as

F
1 thick
2 as
3 more crowded
4 much worse
5 richest

G
1 looks taller than
2 is more important than
3 are more loyal than
4 three minutes earlier than
5 likes action movies more than
6 happen less frequently than

H
1 is larger than any other country in the world
(other) country in the world is larger than Russia
(other) country in the world is as large as Russia
2 is smarter than any other employee in the office
(other) employee in the office is smarter than Nora
(other) employee in the office is as smart as Nora

I
1 We bake the most delicious bread
2 Today is the most important day
3 What is the most expensive painting
4 Logan lives in the biggest house
5 He runs the most powerful company

Chapter 9

p.218-220

A
1 hadn't[had not] seen
2 be
3 go
4 had gotten
5 had tried
6 had
7 were

B
1 knew how to speak English
would live in Australia
2 had been rainy yesterday
would have just stayed at home
3 owned several buildings downtown
could stop working
4 had done his best
would have become the champion
5 weren't[were not] injured
could play in the finals
6 had hurried
could have watched the opera
7 had showed up on time
wouldn't have been so angry

C
1 had
2 were
3 ate
4 didn't
5 were
6 made

D
1 hadn't rained
would have gone
2 weren't
would have
3 had
wouldn't walk
4 had paid
wouldn't have fallen
5 had been
could have become

E
1 hadn't[had not] snowed
2 had stayed
3 didn't study
4 had been
5 had
6 were

F
1 had seen her in person before
2 didn't have lung cancer
3 had made an apology to her
4 had locked the doors
5 were as young as you
6 loved me unconditionally

G
1 as if he were
2 wish you could stay
3 as if there had been
4 wish they had practiced
5 as if he had understood
6 wish I had

H

1 as if he had saved the world
2 wish I lived in the suburbs
3 as if he had seen something scary
4 wish I hadn't said those stupid things
5 wish they had waited for me a little longer
6 wish I had known about his illness
7 as if he were a professional soccer player

Chapter 10 p.221-223

A

1 which
2 who
3 who
4 which
5 who(m)
6 whose
7 which

B

1 who(m)[that] I haven't seen in years
2 which[that] he sent to me
3 which[that] is her mother's
4 which[that] Kyle is wearing
5 who[that] studied at Harvard
6 whose father is a politician
7 who[that] solved the mystery

C

1 what
2 who
3 whom
4 which
5 that

D

1 X
2 X
3 X
4 O
5 O

E

1 which[that] I made
2 who(m)[that] you have
3 which[that] she is working
4 who(m)[that] we can trust
5 which[that] Mr. Brantley asked
6 which[that] the Russian missiles destroyed

F

1 which[that]
2 that
3 whose
4 whose
5 which[that]

G

1 whose voice is so deep and strong
2 whose first language is not English
3 whose body is made of stainless steel
4 whose hobbies are related to art
5 whose parents are also actors

H

1 why
2 when
3 where
4 how

I

1 Is this the right way (that) you print documents?
2 Do you know about the restaurant where your parents had dinner last night?
3 She will never forget the moment when[at which] she saw the car accident.
4 Nobody knows the reason why Jake quit his job.
5 I live close to the store where the police arrested the teenagers.

Chapter 11 p.224-226

A

1 in
2 on
3 at
4 on
5 on
6 at
7 in
8 in

B

1 by
2 for
3 until
4 during
5 during
6 during
7 by
8 for

C

1 in
2 on
3 at
4 for

D

1 Charlie repaired the table with a screwdriver.
2 Jacob works as a lifeguard in the summer.
3 Do many people die of skin cancer?
4 Mr. Clarkson walks like a penguin.
5 The woman in black looks suspicious.
6 Volunteers usually work for free.

E

1 whether
2 that
3 that
4 that
5 whether

F

1 where Emily was hiding
2 if[whether] you like Sophia
3 if[whether] those passengers are alive
4 when I can see my parents

G

1 If
2 when
3 because
4 before

H

1 although he was full
2 since she is an only child
3 until you apologize to me
4 after they watched a movie
5 as he passed the ball to me

I

1 Not only my friends but also my neighbors
My neighbors as well as my friends
2 Both Olga and Oksana
3 neither interesting nor boring
4 If you go down the street
5 Unless you take my bike
If you don't take my bike

MEMO

RAMMAR BRIDGE 2

The bridge that takes
your English to the next level

This 3-level grammar series for basic learners of English

- covers the middle school grammar curriculum
- provides complete and simple explanations
- helps learners to compose sentences properly
- includes a workbook section with extra exercises

초1	초2	초3	초4	초5	초6	중1	중2	중3	고1	고2	고3

Writing

- 공감 영문법+쓰기 1~2
- 도전만점 중등내신 서술형 1~4
- 영어일기 영작패턴 1-A, B · 2-A, B
- Smart Writing 1~2

Reading

- Reading 101 1~3
- Reading 공감 1~3
- This Is Reading Starter 1~3
- This Is Reading 전면 개정판 1~4
- 원서 술술 읽는 Smart Reading Basic 1~2
- 원서 술술 읽는 Smart Reading 1~2
- [특급 단기 특강] 구문독해 · 독해유형
- [앱솔루트 수능대비 영어독해 기출분석] 2019~2021학년도

Listening

- Listening 공감 1~3
- The Listening 1~4
- After School Listening 1~3
- 도전! 만점 중학 영어듣기 모의고사 1~3
- 만점 적중 수능 듣기 모의고사 20회 · 35회

TEPS

- NEW TEPS 입문편 실전 250+ 청해 · 문법 · 독해
- NEW TEPS 기본편 실전 300+ 청해 · 문법 · 독해
- NEW TEPS 실력편 실전 400+ 청해 · 문법 · 독해
- NEW TEPS 마스터편 실전 500+ 청해 · 문법 · 독해